RETHINKING MYCENAEAN
PALACES II

RETHINKING MYCENAEAN PALACES II

REVISED AND EXPANDED SECOND EDITION

MICHAEL L. GALATY
AND
WILLIAM A. PARKINSON, EDITORS

MONOGRAPH 60

THE COTSEN INSTITUTE OF ARCHAEOLOGY

UNIVERSITY OF CALIFORNIA, LOS ANGELES

This book is set in 10-point Janson Text, with titles in 32-point Fairfield LH Light.
Edited by Marjorie Pannell
Designed by William Morosi
Index by Robert Swanson

Cover image
Courtesy of the Department of Classics, University of Cincinnati
Watercolor by Piet de Jong
Digitally edited by Craig Mauzy

Library of Congress Cataloging-in-Publication Data
Rethinking Mycenaean palaces II : revised and expanded second edition / Michael L. Galaty and William A. Parkinson, editors. -- 2nd ed.
    p. cm. -- (Monograph ; 60)
  Includes bibliographical references and index.
  ISBN 978-1-931745-42-0 (pbk. : alk. paper) -- ISBN 978-1-931745-43-7 (cloth : alk. paper)
  1. Civilization, Mycenaean. 2. Palaces--Greece. 3. Greece--Economic conditions--To 146 B.C. 4. Greece--Politics and government--To 146 B.C. 5. Palace of Nestor (Pylos, Greece) 6. Inscriptions, Linear B--Greece--Pylos. I. Galaty, Michael L. II. Parkinson, William A. III. Title. IV. Series: Monograph (Cotsen Institute of Archaeology at UCLA) ; 60.

DF220.5.R47 2007
938'.01--dc22

                    2007036308

CONTENTS

PART II MYCENAEAN PALACES: THE 2007 CONTRIBUTIONS

ACKNOWLEDGMENTS

We would like to thank the Cotsen Institute of Archaeology at UCLA for asking us to publish a second edition of this book. We've enjoyed the opportunity to revisit the Mycenaean palaces. We would also like to thank the original contributors, all of whom remain our good friends and colleagues. The new authors deserve special thanks for their hard work and patience. Finally, we acknowledge the help of two Florida State University graduate students, Timothy Parsons and Hanneke Hoekman-Sites.

The first edition of *Rethinking Mycenaean Palaces* was dedicated to our wives, Tanya and Betsy. This one is dedicated to our kids, Liam, Josie, and Sadie, who make it all worthwhile.

LIST OF FIGURES

LIST OF TABLES

CHAPTER 1

2007 INTRODUCTION

MYCENAEAN PALACES RETHOUGHT

MICHAEL L. GALATY AND WILLIAM A. PARKINSON

MYCENAEAN ARCHAEOLOGY NEVER WILL experience another revolution as dramatic as that which occurred in the late 1950s, when Michael Ventris and John Chadwick discovered that Linear B was an ancient form of Greek. That discovery rewrote our understanding of what Mycenaean palaces were, and how they functioned within Mycenaean society. It is unreasonable to expect that another, similar event will so dramatically alter our perception of the Aegean Bronze Age. Indeed, ten years have passed since the "Rethinking Mycenaean Palaces" session was held at the 62nd Annual Meeting of the Society for American Archaeology in Nashville, Tennessee, and yet little has changed in the field of Aegean prehistory. There have been no major discoveries comparable to the decipherment that would have forced us to rethink completely our fundamental assumptions about Mycenaean society. Nor have there been any revolutionary paradigm shifts in theoretical perspective. But there has been progress—good, steady progress. In the past ten years new data have been collected and published, and old data and artifacts have been restudied and published again. In several instances, innovative, interdisciplinary approaches have offered fresh answers to outstanding questions about the Mycenaean world and its people.

This second, revised edition of *Rethinking Mycenaean Palaces* builds on the 1999 volume, reproducing in part I the original edition in its entirety.[1] Part II consists of five new chapters that address areas of interest not included in the first edition, the Corinthia, Thessaly, Mycenaean Crete, elite goods production, and interregional trade, by Daniel J. Pullen and Thomas F. Tartaron, Vassiliki Adrimi-Sismani, Jan Driessen and Charlotte Langohr, Robert Schon, and Eric H. Cline, respectively. These chapters were added to complement the studies included in the 1999 edition, which focused exclusively on the southern Greek mainland, and mostly on Messenia.

This introductory chapter describes developments in Mycenaean archaeology and Linear B studies since 1997. We pay particular attention to work that has advanced general theoretical understandings of Mycenaean state formation and organization. In this way we update our introduction to the first edition (titled "Putting Mycenaean Palaces in Their Place") as well as assess how well the original eight chapters have stood the test of time. We also respond to some of the concerns raised by John T. Killen and by John F. Cherry and Jack L. Davis in the first edition's concluding chapters, as well as those of various reviewers (e.g., Palaima 2000; Rutter 2001). Finally, we take the opportunity in this introduction to place each new chapter in the context of recent research on Mycenaean states generally.

Approximately one-third of our original introduction was devoted to discussions of the "Great

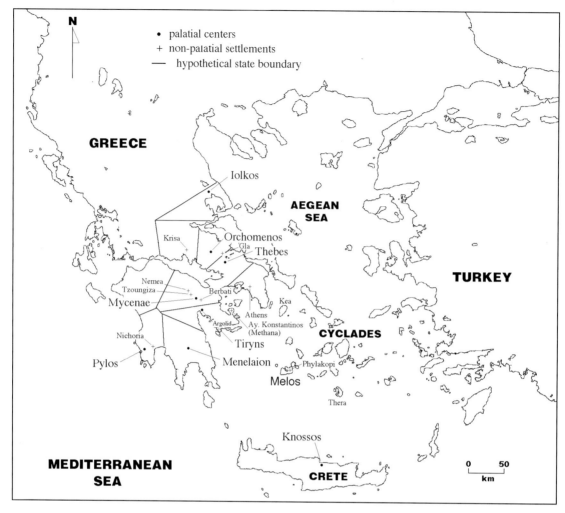

FIGURE 1.1 Map of the Aegean showing important sites and regions mentioned in the text. (Adapted from Bennet and Galaty 1997, figure 1.)

Divide" that separates classical from anthropological archaeology (Renfrew 1980; compare Renfrew 2003:317–318). We bemoaned the disciplinary rift between classically and anthropologically trained archaeologists and asserted that it was in the interest of both camps to repair it. Today, that rift seems much narrower and less permanent than it once did. In Britain, for example, no distinction is made between so-called classical and anthropological approaches to prehistory; rather, prehistoric archaeologists work together in departments of archaeology, and a "divide" does not exist (if it ever did). In the United States, however, classical and anthropological archaeologists, including prehistorians, continue to serve almost exclusively in departments of Classics and anthropology; rarely is there any crossover. This institutionalized segregation is the result of historical forces that are not easily overcome (see Davis 2001 and various papers in Cherry et al. 2005).

Regardless, classical and anthropological archaeologists who study Mycenaeans (of which there are many and few, respectively) continue to conduct fieldwork together on a regular basis, publish jointly and attend conferences together, work together in interdepartmental institutes of archaeology (such as the Cotsen Institute of Archaeology at UCLA), and more than ever share a common body of method and theory.

In terms of shared method and theory, the divide has been nearly closed. There is still, however, on the part of most Aegean prehistorians a surprising reluctance to practice cross-cultural comparison (which we lamented in our introduction to the first edition; see also Renfrew 2003:316–317; Whitley 2004:194). Similarly, anthropological archaeologists who work elsewhere in the world rarely consider Aegean states in general, comparative models of state formation and organization. There persists, therefore, an unfortunate lack of communication between Aegean prehistorians, on the one hand, and archaeologists who work in other times and other places, on the other (Blanton [2004] and Papadopoulos and Leventhal [2003] are notable exceptions). Regrettably, *Rethinking Mycenaean Palaces* has done little to close this last, lingering gap.

In our original introduction we also described several specific methodological and theoretical issues that we thought required attention if our understanding of Mycenaean palaces was to advance. First, we recommended that studies of Mycenaean states be theoretically grounded and based on general anthropological models. We suggested that building and testing models of Mycenaean political economies, ritual activities, such as feasting, and international trade relationships, for example, might shed light on strategies of palatial control. Second, we asserted that the Mycenaean states were very different from the earlier Minoan states, as well as most other states in the eastern Mediterranean. As a consequence of the contrasting developmental trajectories in these various places, general models, once engaged, might suggest very different patterns of Mycenaean state formation and organization compared with other eastern Mediterranean states. Finally, we argued that interdisciplinary field research should target specific questions (based on hypothetical expectations) regarding the formation and structure of Mycenaean states, those suggested by the modeling process. We urged our colleagues to employ both archaeological and Linear B data, not one or the other exclusively.

In 1999, when the first edition of *Rethinking Mycenaean Palaces* (hereafter RMPI) was published, all three of these theoretical and methodological issues were, more or less, already being addressed by some scholars, in some quarters. Although no major breakthroughs have occurred recently in our understanding of Mycenaean states, there have been a few surprises. Mostly, though, it has been steady, systematic archaeological and philological research, backed up by discussion and debate, that has led to gradual shifts in the ways Mycenaean states are perceived. In the remainder of this introduction, we first address recent models of Mycenaean economic production, exchange, and consumption and issues of palatial control. We then suggest the adoption of an integrated, comparative theoretical framework for approaching trajectories of change in the prehistoric Aegean. Finally, we describe various goal-oriented methodological approaches designed to collect sets of data necessary for answering specific questions about Mycenaean society.

MODELS OF MYCENAEAN STATES

Theoretical modeling is employed only rarely in the study of Mycenaean states. Voutsaki and Killen (2001:10) have warned that it is "not sufficient to transfer general models to Aegean archaeology"; rather, "[w]e need to pay attention to the specific historical and political conditions that prevailed in different periods and different regions of the Mycenaean world." We could not agree more; however, we contend that the main reason to use general theoretical models is that doing so encourages the production of hypotheses, research expectations that can be tested against specific archaeological data. The application of such approaches by Aegean prehistorians complements but does not replace the mostly inductive, particularistic, approaches that are more commonly used in the region. Theoretical modeling allows conclusions reached about developmental trajectories in one region to be compared meaningfully with those reached for other regions. Such cross-cultural and cross-regional comparisons, which are few and far between in Aegean prehistory, in turn serve to distinguish what is truly unique about a particular place and time. In this regard, questions surrounding the nature of economic production, consumption, and distribution, as well as those about the nature of political centralization, can be compared at intra- and interregional scales. When it comes to the prehistoric Aegean, we might ask, for instance, whether Mycenaean states were in fact highly centralized, controlling entities in comparison with other archaic states, as some have argued (e.g., Deger-Jalkotsky 1996). Did the Mycenaean palaces control people and resources in their vicinity, and if so, was centralization the primary means of gaining and exercising control?

Production and control

In the last ten years, Aegean archaeologists and Linear B specialists have grappled seriously with questions of Mycenaean state centralization and palatial control—of the economy in particular. In most publications, however, these terms are not defined clearly, nor are they used consistently. It is not always apparent what was supposedly centralized and controlled (labor? industry? power?) by the Mycenaean elite, or, more important, how centralization and control were accomplished (Voutsaki and Killen 2001:3). Sometimes the term centralization is used to imply nucleation of people and resources at a central place, a palace, without the recognition that decentralized (i.e., non-nucleated) strategies of control are equally possible (see Schon, chapter 13, this volume). Even in "primate" systems of settlement, in which one site in a region is abnormally large compared to all others, direct and efficient control of labor and resources by the state is not ensured. As David B. Small (1999:44–45) noted in RMPI, primacy is not always or often a strategy of control per se; rather, centralization (i.e., nucleation) of labor, industry, and power at a central place typically occurs in response to extraregional pressures (as at Monte Albán in Oaxaca) and results in centralization of certain state functions but not necessarily in regional, economic integration and control (as at Teotihuacán in the Basin of Mexico).

Perhaps the most developed discussion of centralization and control in Mycenaean states is to be found in Sjöberg's socioeconomic study of Asine's position in the larger region of the Argolid. Sjöberg (2004:4–5) notes that most Aegean prehistorians appear to equate centralization with a concentration of economic power in the hands of an upper class. So-called economic administrators are thought to have run a form of redistributive economy in which labor and resources were channeled to or through palaces. The geographic reach of the palace administrators and the amount and range of products administered, as indicated in the archaeological and documentary records, provide a proxy measure of control—that is, the ability of central authorities to recruit—using force, if necessary—individuals to participate in the system. This traditional, "substantive" approach to Myceanean economy has now generally been replaced (Sjöberg 2004:5–8), or augmented, by models of political economy that emphasize decentralized palatial control of economic activity, and private reciprocal and market transactions within a nonpalatial sector of the economy (see also Palmer 1998–1999; Shear 2004:22–32). The volume edited by Voutsaki and Killen (2001a) addresses these new models, without, however, reaching any firm conclusions about how centralized and controlling Mycenaean states really were. Another attractive new model that has not yet been systematically applied to Mycenaean states but has been applied to Minoan states (e.g., Schoep and Knappett 2004) is that of heterarchy, which we discuss shortly.

The topic of Mycenaean palatial control of labor and resources vis-à-vis centralization was pushed to the fore by Halstead, first in 1992, also in RMPI in 1999, and in a series of papers on palatial involvement in agriculture (see, e.g., 1998–1999, 1999b, 1999c, 2001,

2003). Building on his RMPI chapter on mobilization, Halstead (2003:260) recently argued that

> the picture emerging of palatial economy is not of a coherent and efficient system of resource mobilization. . . . Rather, resources were raised through a variety of methods, including "taxation" of local communities, share-cropping, and exchange, which might be understood in terms of the survival or transformation of a series of customary arrangements of varying antiquity.

Halstead's take on control is now almost universally accepted by Mycenaean specialists (but see Hope Simpson 2002:132–133 as an example of the opposite viewpoint), though admittedly the details have yet to be hammered out.

Despite sitting atop primate settlement systems (Small 1998, 1999), Mycenaean elite did not centrally control all aspects of the economic system (as we argued in our introduction to the first edition), though they clearly administered certain industries from the palace. Of these various industries, some, such as the perfume industry, were highly centralized (i.e., they were headquartered at the palace itself), and therefore the industrial process—production—was, it seems, carefully controlled, whereas others, such as bronze working, were decentralized (i.e., they occurred at sites other than the palace) and were perhaps not as readily controlled (Gillis 1997; Killen 2001; Nordquist 1997).

For some industries, such as woolen textile production, certain key steps in the manufacturing process were decentralized (e.g., weaving), whereas others were centralized and more highly controlled (e.g., fulling and finishing) (Killen 1999a:89, 2001; see also Nosch 2000). Robert Schon (chapter 13, this volume) suggests that chariot manufacture was also at least partially decentralized and that the Northeast Building at Pylos served as a kind of clearinghouse or assembly point, and so it was not really a workshop in the true sense of the word (similar to but not the same as Bendall's [2003] hypothesis that the Northeast Building was a "redistributive" center; see also Palaima [2003:182–187], who supports Schon's interpretation). Still other industries were of little interest to the palace except in certain mundane or highly specialized contexts (e.g., pottery and stone tool production; see Galaty 1999; Parkinson 1999). Moreover, different Mycenaean states administered entirely different industries (e.g., glass-paste production is attested at Mycenae but not elsewhere) or, more often, administered the same types of industries

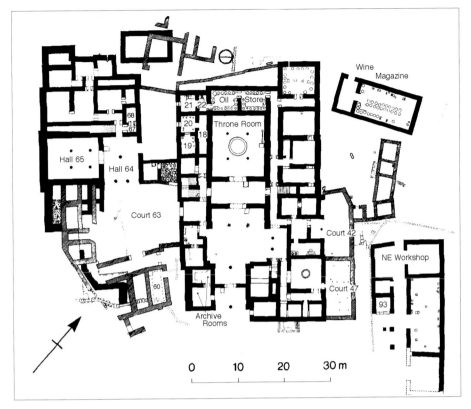

FIGURE 1.2 Plan of the palace at Pylos. Important rooms have been labeled. (After Blegen and Rawson 1966, figure 417. Courtesy of the Department of Classics, University of Cincinnati.)

differently (e.g., at Pylos, various steps in the production of cloth were centrally controlled and took place at the palace, whereas at Knossos, cloth production was completely decentralized, though still perhaps controlled by palace officials).

Likewise, direct management of regional agricultural resources by the palace seems to have been minimal. Foodstuffs, such as wheat and olives, were collected by the palace for allocation to state-supported administrators and workers, a small number of individuals relative to the entire population, or to temples and for feasts (Halstead 1999c; Killen 1998b; Palmer 2001). The Mycenaean palace economies were not redistributive in the anthropological sense of the term, which was formulated to describe chiefdoms (Cherry and Davis 1999:94): the palaces did not collect agricultural surpluses from all members of society and then reallocate them. Nor did they operate on the scale of Near Eastern states, which collected massive amounts of surplus food. Rather, the Mycenaean elite appear to have taken only as much as was necessary to run the palaces.

Linear B specialists have made great gains recently in determining which industries were, according to the tablets, centrally controlled in Mycenaean states

and which depended on decentralized production (see, e.g., the review by Killen 2001; various papers in Laffineur and Betancourt 1997; Michailidou 2001). Such work makes it possible to generate hypotheses about what types of artifacts we might expect to find in the archaeological record and where we might expect to find them. For example, the tablets from Pylos indicate that bronze was worked through the *ta-ra-si-ja* system by a large number of smiths living outside the center. We would expect, therefore, to find evidence for bronze working at small sites throughout the region. Evidence for small-scale bronze working has now been found at a small site called Katsimigas near Iklaina (Cosmopoulos 2006:221). Likewise, we might expect little evidence for large-scale perfumed oil production in nonpalatial contexts, and to the best of our knowledge none has been found. However, many of the herbs necessary to perfuming oil would have come to the palace through decentralized systems of exchange (Palmer 1999, 2003), so even the most centralized and controlled of Mycenaean industries would have depended at least in part on exchanges that were difficult to impossible to control fully. We also might expect to find a wide range of weaving implements—loom weights, spindle

TABLE 1.1 Greek chronology from earliest prehistory through historic periods.

	MAINLAND	CRETE	CYCLADES
		Whole Region	
ROMAN		31 BC–AD 337	
HELLENISTIC		323-31 BC	
CLASSICAL		480–323 BC	
ARCHAIC		700–480 BC	
DARK AGE		1100–700 BC	
BRONZE AGE	Helladic	Minoan	Cycladic
Late Bronze III*	1415–1100 BC	1405–1100 BC	1405–1100 BC
Late Bronze I–II	1680–1415 BC	1650–1405 BC	1600–1405 BC
Middle	2000–1680 BC	2000–1650 BC	1900–1600 BC
Early	3100–2000 BC	3100–2000 BC	3100–1900 BC
NEOLITHIC			
Final	4500–3200 BC	4000–3100 BC	4500–3100 BC
Late	5300–4500 BC	4500–3500 BC	—
Middle	5800–5300 BC	5000–4500 BC	—
Early	6500–5800 BC	6500–5000 BC	—
Aceramic	6800–6500 BC	7000–6500 BC	—
MESOLITHIC	9500–8000 BP	—	—
[Franchthi]	Hiatus?	—	—
PALAEOLITHIC	25,000–11,000 BP	—	—

*Late Helladic IIIB circa 1300 to 1200 BC

whorls, needles—on sites throughout the hinterlands of Mycenaean states, and a correlation between types and numbers of implements and site size and location might be found, but to the best of our knowledge, the necessary data have not been collected.

Since 1997, much has been written about Mycenaean pottery production, distribution, and consumption, some of it based on the collection of primary archaeological data. In RMPI, Galaty reported chemical analysis of a sample of coarse and finewares from sites in Messenia, including the palace (310 Late Helladic IIIB sherds from eighteen sites and eighteen regional clay samples). He argued that although the palace needed pots, and may even have sought to control the production of some ritually charged types, such as *kylikes* (see also Knappett 2001; Schon, chapter 13, this volume), pottery production generally was not centrally controlled, though pottery may have been made at or near the palace itself. A much longer report based on both chemical and petrographic data was published by Galaty (1999b) shortly after RMPI appeared. Results indicate that, in general, pots in Messenia were made using three different clay pastes: one based on common,

coarse, red illitic clays, variously tempered; one based on rare, fine kaolinites that required no preparation (such as levigation) before throwing and were never tempered (a similar clay was still used in 1995 by the traditional Vounaria potter); and one that mixed illites and marl. Vessels made from kaolinite were widely distributed yet may have come from a single source (indicating centralized production, perhaps at the palace; incidentally, the only site directly associated with a kaolinite source is the palace). Most finewares analyzed, including nearly all of the kylikes, were made from kaolinite. Vessels made from illites and "mixes" were probably produced in small workshops and were distributed less widely. These coarse vessels were likely produced and distributed outside the control of the palace and constitute good evidence for nonpalatial forms of private economic activity, though it is not clear what the mechanisms responsible for their distribution may have been (gifting, marketing, and so on).

Results of similar studies, in Pylos and elsewhere, have tended to confirm those of Galaty's (1999b) study. For example, Whitelaw (2001) and Knappett (2001) drew similar conclusions about the Pylian potting industry based on analyses of Linear B evidence and excavation data from the palace: the industry was relatively decentralized and uncontrollable (cf. Sherratt 1999; van Wijngaarden 1999a). The palace purchased or produced enough pottery to fill its own needs first, and excess pottery may have been given away, perhaps at ritual events such as feasts, and, more rarely, exported (e.g., to Canaan; see Gunneweg and Michel 1999). Whitelaw (2001:70, figure 2, 72), however, vastly overestimates the availability of good clay in Messenia and so also overestimates the numbers of facilities involved in pottery production. As he notes (2001:51), his conclusions are not at odds with those of Galaty (1999b), but the breadth of the pottery industry he reconstructs is.

New data from central Greece now confirm that decentralized, workshop production of pottery was perhaps the norm in Mycenaean states. Mommsen et al. (2001:346; see also Hein et al. 2002b) have identified more than eighty chemical groups, of which eight have been tied to specific production places. The so-called MB (Mycenae-Berbati) chemical group, for example, found at sites throughout the Argolid and beyond, can be associated with the kilns and workshops at Berbati (Buxeda et al. 2002; Hein et al. 2002:177; Mommsen and Maran 2000–2001; Mommsen et al. 2001:347, 2003). However, as is increasingly clear, this widespread chemical group may in fact include pots made from similar clays found throughout Greece (Mommsen et al. 2001:348).

Research into this problem is ongoing (Buxeda et al. 2002; Hein, Tsolakidou, and Mommsen 2002a), and we expect that eventually it will be resolved, perhaps by including clay samples in the analyses or by using other, complementary methods, such as petrography. Problems aside, it seems there were many, presumably independent (i.e., private, nonpalatial) workshops producing and distributing pottery throughout the Mycenaean world and abroad, as suggested, for example, by the large number of Argive and possibly southeastern Aegean pots at Pylona on Rhodes (Karantzali and Ponting 2000).

Consumption and exchange

What happened to the palace's finished products, how they were consumed, is also unclear (Sherratt 1999). Were the distribution and consumption of certain objects also controlled? Did the degree of control vary depending on the type of object produced? In RMPI we made a distinction between wealth (i.e., prestige) goods and staple goods and argued that the palace had good reason to control distribution of the former and less so the latter (Galaty and Parkinson 1999:7). In RMPI, Killen (1999a:89) suggested that there was little evidence in the Linear B records that finished prestige goods were redistributed back to those involved in their production, whether administrators or laborers. That being the case, what happened to all the loot? According to Cherry and Davis in RMPI (1999:94), "much of what goes up, stays up." This may be true, but only recently have Aegean archaeologists tried to test this proposition, mostly by looking more carefully at the range of items interred with the dead (e.g., Alden 2001; Bennet and Galanakis 2005; Boyd 2002; Branigan 1998; French and Shelton 2005; Gallou 2005; Karantzali 2001; Lewartowski 2000; Papadimitriou 2001; Sjöberg 2004).

In a series of important papers on Mycenaean state formation, Voutsaki (most recently, 2001) determined that prestige goods in the Argolid are found exclusively in elite burials and that the circulation of wealth becomes more restricted through time (cf. French and Shelton 2005:180; Shear 2004:6, 11, 18), culminating in the almost exclusive deposition of prestige goods in *tholoi* during the Late Helladic IIIB (Voutsaki 1998:48). She concluded that gift exchange among elite members of Mycenaean society accounted for this pattern (Voutsaki 2001:204; cf. Galaty and Parkinson 1999:7), which is duplicated in Messenia (Voutsaki 1998). In this model, prestige goods made by the palace (not necessarily at the palace) would have been exchanged among a small number of prominent individuals and then deposited in graves at the time of death. Given the very large volume of goods manufactured and moving through the palatial economy as recorded in Linear B, it is hard to believe that wealth items were allowed to circulate only among small numbers of palatial elite (with some obvious exceptions, such as chariots, the ultimate Bronze Age wealth item; see Schon, chapter 13, this volume). Perhaps some items were given away to nonelite (the graves of whom are more rarely found and excavated; Lewartowski 2000) at palace-sponsored feasts and festivals, and other items went to exchange partners overseas. Some prestige goods, such as textiles, were of course perishable and do not survive in the archaeological record. It may well be that once items had been manufactured, their subsequent disposition was not recorded in Linear B because it was the process of making wealth items that mattered to palace administrators (and drove the political economy), not how and to whom the items were then given (or sold?) (cf. Sherratt 2001:224). In any case, a significant amount of material appears to have exited the system somehow, going somewhere other than into chamber and *tholos* tombs (Sherratt 1999). Figuring out where elite goods went should be a top priority for Mycenaean archaeologists. As Schon (chapter 13, this volume; cf. Voutsaki 2001) demonstrates, the study of elite goods exchange is crucial to understanding the organization and intent of Mycenaean political economies.

One facet of the Mycenaean political economic system that is now very well understood is feasting. The attention devoted to this topic since 1997 is impressive and has drawn together Linear B scholars, archaeologists, and archaeozoologists in a truly interdisciplinary research effort. Much of the recent research on feasting has been collected in a volume edited by Wright (2004; see also Hamilakis 1998; Hamilakis and Konsolaki 2004; Tzedakis and Martlew 1999) and includes case studies from Pylos (see also Halstead and Isaakidou 2004; Isaakidou et al. 2002), Nemea, Crete, and Cyprus. As Wright (2004a:16, 2004d) describes, the very act of feasting, along with partaking in associated drinking, gifting, and religious activities, probably marked one as being Mycenaean or affiliated with Mycenaeans. Thus, the Mycenaean feast was a vehicle for Mycenaean identity creation (see also Davis and Bennet 1999). Robert Schon (chapter 13, this volume) makes a similar argument for elite activities that involved chariots, such as hunting and racing. Unlike chariot activities, however, feasting probably included a fairly wide segment of society and appears to have taken place both at palaces and at secondary centers (Bendall 2004), such as Tsoungiza (Dabney et al. 2004). Thus, feasting was one means whereby Mycenaean elite sought to build social cohesion and justify their social rank (Wright 2004a, 2004d). Another means to justify social position would have been through the acquisition and distribution of exotic, foreign objects and materials (Sherratt 1999). Obtaining and exchanging such items probably reinforced connections between elite in different Mycenaean states, and between Mycenaean and non-Mycenaean elite on an international scale. Displaying and gifting such items locally reinforced one's social, political, and, most probably, economic position.

Throughout the Late Bronze Age, and especially in the Late Helladic IIIB, Mycenaean material goods, pottery and bronze artifacts in particular, appeared in various non-Mycenaean territories, and vice versa (Cline, chapter 17, this volume; Cline and Harris-Cline 1998; Froussou 1999; Laffineur and Greco 2005; Stampolidis and Karageorghis 2003; van Wijngaarden 2002). Mycenaean items may have arrived in some places—Epirus, Albania, Italy—as a package that included vessels for serving and drinking, weapons and armor, and items associated with dress. In this way Mycenaean identity, a lifestyle, was exported as well.

It still is not clear how these goods were traded or who did the trading. The evidence from shipwrecks seems to indicate a variety of seaborne trade mechanisms, ranging from tramping in small vessels (such as the Point Iria wreck; Phelps et al. 1999) to large-scale trade missions that may have been state sponsored (such as the Ulu Burun wreck; e.g., Pulak 1997). In some cases Mycenaeans may have been physically present in foreign, non-Mycenaean territories, perhaps as colonists. For example, in a thorough review and reanalysis of the excavation evidence, and based on the collection of primary survey data, Tartaron (2004; also Tartaron 2001; Tartaron and Zachos 1999) argues that there may have been a Mycenaean colony (a "port of trade") at Glykys Limin in Epirus. The harbor and port there would have provided safe haven to traders sailing up the Adriatic coast (see also Galaty 2007; Tomas 2005). Additionally, Mycenaean colonists interacted with indigenous peoples, who received Myceanean-style pottery, weapons, and accoutrements in return for various local products, such as hides. Hitherto, past, Aegean prehistorians had conceived of such trade interactions in terms of core–periphery models and had sought to identify the boundary between the Mycenaean and outside worlds (Feuer 1999). Tartaron (2004:165–173; 2005), however, rightly refocuses the discussion by demonstrating that Mycenaean trade connections were dendritic; that trade partners were sought out in various places, at greater or lesser distance from the core, for different reasons, using different trade strategies and generating different patterns of consumption; and that the Mycenaean periphery was discontinuous and porous. Recent research reinforces this image, indicating that Mycenaean trade was nodal, including various different points and routes of more or less importance (see Sherratt 1999, 2001). It is no longer enough just to say that some territories were seemingly within the Mycenaean world and some were outside it. We need better models that more precisely articulate the nature of relationships between Mycenaeans and their neighbors.

One region that always seemed to be connected to the Mycenaean world but not a part of it is Thessaly. It now seems very clear, however, that the region of Iolkos, at least, was as Mycenaean as many regions typically included in the so-called Mycenaean core area, such as Achaia and Aetolia. Vassiliki Adrimi-Sismani (chapter 15, this volume) marshals a vast array of evidence to demonstrate this point, including evidence for Mycenaean megara at Dimini. There also is now very good evidence for a Mycenaean presence in Crete (Driessen and Langohr, chapter 16, this volume; Driessen and Farnoux 1994, 1997, 2000) and Italy (Borgna and Càssola Guida 2005; Buxeda et al. 2003; Jones et al. 2002; Sgouritsa 2005; Vagnetti 1998, 1999a, 1999b, 2000–2001), probably including colonies, as well as a Mycenaean presence or strong influence in Anatolia (Mountjoy 1998; Niemeier 1998, 1999), the Cyclades (Barber 1999; Deger-Jalkotsky 1998a; Schallin 1998), Cyprus (Swiny et al. 1997), Greek Macedonia (Buxeda et al. 2003; Jung 2003), Rhodes (Karantzali 2001), and in the Near East (e.g., Gunneweg and Michel 1999), at, for example, Ugarit (Matoïan 2003; van Wijngaarden 1999b) (for comparative regional approaches, see Darcque 2004; Sherratt 1999; van Wijngaarden 2001).

In the past ten years it has become increasingly clear that Cyprus was a key broker in the trade between Mycenaean and eastern Mediterranean peoples and that Mycenaean pots (and practices) were incorporated by Cypriot and some Near Eastern cultures (Steel 1998; Walz 1997). For example, the Point Iria, Cape Gelidonya, and Ulu Burun ships may have been based in or at least sailed via Cyprus. The Point Iria boat in particular almost certainly originated in Cyprus, given its cargo of Cypriot-style pottery, and may have stopped in Crete on its way to the Argolid (Day 1999; Vichos and Lolos 1997). In fact, it seems increasingly likely that the control of local trade routes, including roads (chapter 13, this volume; Hope Simpson 1998, 2002; Jansen 1997, 2002), and particular bodies of water may have been one source of regional, elite power in Mycenaean times. Pullen and Tartaron (chapter 14, this volume) make an excellent case for Mycenaean interest in the Saronic Gulf, based on evidence from newly discovered harbor towns along its western shores and from Kolonna on Aegina. To these we can also add the Mycenaean "palatial" site of Kanakia on Salamis (Lolos 2003).

Despite the evidence for long-term, sustained communication and trade between Mycenaean and other Mediterranean states, there are strong indications that trajectories of state formation and development in these various regions were different. Whereas we might still accept the idea of a Mycenaean *koine*, much comparative, theoretical work remains to be done before we really understand exactly how the Mycenaean states were similar to or different from other Mediterranean states, including those on Crete.

AN INTEGRATED, COMPARATIVE FRAMEWORK

In their discussion in the first edition of this book, John F. Cherry and Jack L. Davis rightly noted that whereas we editors urged taking a comparative approach to Mycenaean states, we did not actually do so, either in the introduction to the volume or in our individual chapters (on pottery and obsidian exchange, respectively). Likewise, they pointed out that there was little comparison elsewhere in the book, with the exception of Nick Kardulias's world systems approach and David Small's references to Mesoamerican states. In the end, they noted that "it does not help to project onto the Mycenaean archaeological record, willy-nilly, ill-grounded analogies jerked out of time and place. . . It is not enough to say merely 'this state looks like that state'" (98). We certainly agree with this assertion; thus our call for an integrated, systematic cross-cultural approach (Galaty and Parkinson 1999:3).

To demonstrate how such an integrated, comparative approach to Mycenaean states might work, we recently published a paper (Parkinson and Galaty 2007) that sought to explain Mycenaean state formation by drawing together various general theoretical models—traditional, neo-evolutionary approaches that emphasize notions of hierarchy (e.g., Flannery 1995), Marcus's (1993b, 1998b) dynamic model of state evolution (which takes a generational, developmental approach to state cycling), world systems theory (e.g., Kardulias 1999a, 1999b, 1999c, 2001; Stein 1999), and dual processual approaches that incorporate notions of heterarchy and factional competition (e.g., Blanton et al. 1996; Brumfiel 1994; Crumley 1995; Feinman 2000; Mills 2000). Our analysis indicates that Mycenaean states (1) were secondary, first-generation states that formed from earlier competing chiefdoms while in contact with the Minoan and other eastern Mediterranean states; (2) were for this reason very different from the Minoan states; (3) were "networked" as opposed to "corporate," and therefore are not amenable to heterarchical models of political organization; and (4) can be profitably compared with other such states in other parts of the world, such as the Lowland Classic Maya.

These factors, once identified and contextualized, can be shown to have affected not just the formation of Mycenaean states but their organization and subsequent collapse as well. Additionally, they help demonstrate why Minoan and Mycenaean states developed differently and were differently organized.

Aegean trajectories: Crete and the Greek mainland

Regional archaeological data from Prepalatial Crete indicate that beginning in the Neolithic, the island was divided into numerous, small "tribal" (i.e., segmented, lineage-based, relatively egalitarian) territories. This type of social organization is reflected in the cemetery remains, which vary in structure and content across the island but generally allowed communal, kin-based burial (Murphy 1998, n.d.). The members of these different "tribes" apparently sought access to Near Eastern and Egyptian trade goods, and the number of exotic, foreign items on Crete increased throughout the Prepalatial and into the Protopalatial period (Cline 1994, and chapter 17, this volume). Around 2000 BC, large palaces appeared in several places—Knossos, Mallia, Phaistos—having grown rapidly from Prepalatial roots. There does not seem to have been an intervening period of competitive chiefdom cycling during which social hierarchies and militarized systems of political control would have developed and hardened. Rather, the Minoan states evolved directly from tribal entities and continued to emphasize shared, "corporate" identities, reinforced through communal, ritual practices (see Blanton et al. 1996 for a definition of the corporate versus network distinction, and Galaty and Parkinson 1999:7–8, where this idea was first applied to Aegean states). For this reason, heterarchical models, which emphasize alternative, nonhierarchical forms of leadership and power sharing, have been successfully applied to Proto- and Neopalatial Minoan states (e.g., Schoep and Knappett 2004). The "secondary," "first-generation" Minoan states occupied a semiperipheral position vis-à-vis the peripheral Cycladic and mainland Greek societies to their north and the older, "primary" core states to their east (see Kardulias 1999a, 1999b for a world systems approach to Aegean prehistory). It is likely that the Minoan elite fostered and mediated trade connections between mainland Greece and Crete, on the one hand, and between the mainland and the eastern Mediterranean on the other.

The trajectories of Mycenaean state formation were very different from those on Crete, and this is demonstrably so when the two are compared in reference to the model outlined above (see Parkinson and Galaty 1997 for a detailed comparison). Mycenaean states appeared after their Minoan counterparts, following a period of chiefly competition. Pre- and early Mycenaean chiefs appear to have competed, sometimes violently, for access to and control of prestige goods, some of which were imported from a distance (Voutsaki 2001). The appearance and use of the shaft graves and early tholoi at Mycenae and elsewhere provide dramatic evidence of this process (Shear 2004).

Whereas Minoan states had their origins in corporate, "tribal" systems, and were therefore more heterarchical than hierarchical, Mycenaean states formed as elite ("chiefly") families fought to harness the various available sources of power (Wolpert 2004). If modern chiefdoms are any indication, managing factions and building alliances would have been one important aspect of this effort (Wright 2004b). For this reason, the Mycenaean states were "networked" states, in which lines of trade, marriage, and ideology loosely bound leaders within and between palatial centers. As a result, Mycenaean palaces were smaller than Minoan palaces, and functioned differently. For example, open spaces such as courtyards in Mycenaean palaces were designed to accommodate fewer people and were probably used for different purposes, for processions and feasting as opposed to public, communal rituals (Cavanagh 2001). This is because the different buildings served very different sociopolitical systems with very different needs. Like Minoan states, Mycenaean states were first generation and secondary. They evolved in close contact with Crete, and the Mycenaeans adopted some Minoan practices, but the Mycenaean state system did not simply duplicate the Minoan one. Eventually—by the start of Late Helladic IIIB—the Mycenaean states became semiperipheral, local cores in the eastern Mediterranean world system, usurping the Minoan trade networks. The result was a precipitous drop in trade between Crete and the eastern Mediterranean and a corresponding growth in trade between mainland Greece and the eastern Mediterranean (Cline 1994, and chapter 17, this volume). At the same time, the Mycenaeans recruited new trade partners to the west and north.

The history of the Mycenaean states and their relationship to the Minoan states is very similar to the history of the Lowland Maya states, in particular in their relationship to Teotihuacán (see Marcus 2004). The primary difference is that Teotihuacán was a first-generation, primary core state, whereas the Minoan states were secondary and semiperipheral to the older Near Eastern and Egyptian states. Both state systems appeared suddenly, perhaps from tribal roots. In terms of structure, the Minoan states were strikingly similar to Teotihuacán. Both employed corporate systems of organization (Blanton et al. 1996:9–10), maintained sprawling ceremonial centers, were led by "faceless" rulers who employed ritual and ideology at the expense of violence, and were heterarchical in terms of social organization. Both depended on and mediated regional trade. In the case of Teotihuacán (AD 200–700), trade goods, such as worked obsidian, flowed from the Basin of Mexico to Oaxaca, the Gulf Coast, and the territory of the Maya (Blanton et al.1981:141–142). Whereas the Preclassic Lowland Maya seem to have been organized into unstable chiefdoms (Blanton et al. 1981:189), and the Protoclassic Lowland Maya emphasized corporate strategies of archaic state organization (perhaps under the influence of Teotihuacán?), this changed abruptly and dramatically at the start of the Classic period (circa AD 300; see Blanton et al. 1996:11–12; Marcus 2003), when strongly networked, second-generation, secondary states formed. Named kings operating out of independent city-states competed, often militarily, for control of territory and resources, and social organization was very hierarchical. The scale of production and trade of prestige goods during this period is truly astounding, and it is not yet entirely clear how the economy was organized and whether or not it was controlled by the elite (Blanton et al. 1981:205). Both Teotihuacán and the Classic Maya states eventually collapsed, in AD 700 and 900, respectively.

Pylos in perspective: Messenian versus Argive settlement patterns

When an integrated, comparative framework such as that sketched in the preceding section is employed, many problematic details of Mycenaean state development, organization, and collapse can be explained. As was the case in 1999, in 2007 we still know the most about the Mycenaean state of Pylos. There are several reasons for this situation: (1) no less than three, large-scale survey projects have taken place there—the University of Minnesota Messenia Expedition (McDonald and Rapp 1972), the Pylos Regional Archaeological Project (Davis 1998), and the Iklaina Archaeological Project (Cosmopoulos 2006); (2) there is a large, well-studied corpus of Linear B tablets from the palace; and (3) several cemetery and settlement sites have been excavated,

including the center (at Ano Englianos) and a secondary site (Nichoria). The same type of archaeological evidence is not available for most of the other Mycenaean states, including Mycenae itself. Nevertheless, it is possible to draw some conclusions about developments in Mycenaean states other than Pylos.

Great strides were made in understanding the formation of the Pylian state as a result of the work of the Pylos Regional Archaeological Project. Through complete site-surface collection, PRAP was able to demonstrate that in the Middle Helladic period, during the period of chiefdom cycling, Pylos had several rivals (see Bennet 1999b; Bennet and Shelmerdine 2001). As Pylos expanded in the Late Helladic, the other settlements in the vicinity also grew in size, but only slightly, and they produced far fewer diagnostic artifacts as compared with earlier periods and as compared with Pylos (Bennet and Shelmerdine 2001:137). The only active Late Helladic IIIB tholos tombs were those at Pylos (Bennet 1999a, 1999b:15). Pylos also was associated with a coastal site, Romanou, which had been the largest site in Early Helladic Messenia (Bennet 1999b:17) and may have served as the state's port during the Late Helladic (Zangger et al. 1997; see also Parkinson 1999), perhaps in association with the very large, nearby Mycenaean town of Beylerbey (Shelmerdine 2001:123). It seems likely, therefore, that Mycenaean Pylos actively encouraged (or allowed) the growth of some settlements at the expense of others, depending on the needs of the state (Bennet and Shelmerdine 2001; Shelmerdine 2001), perhaps through "networked" management of various sources of secondary elite power, such as by controlling prestige goods and wife exchange. Some sites in the border zone between the Hither and Further provinces were abandoned entirely when the two were integrated, perhaps at the end of Late Helladic IIIA (Bennet 1999a; Shelmerdine 2001). In this way, manipulation of the regional settlement system, perhaps through manipulation of regional elite relationships, was one important source of elite power (Galaty 2005:314–315).

Despite the lack of good regional data from the northern Argolid (Wright 2004c:128), there do seem to be some interesting similarities when state formation there and in Messenia is compared. On the Argive Plain, just as in Pylos, state formation was preceded by a period of elite competition (in the late Middle Helladic and early Late Helladic). Different family groups appear to have sought access to foreign, exotic goods (from Crete and elsewhere in the eastern Mediterranean), which then were deposited in shaft, chamber, and tholos tombs at a number of similarly sized settlements, including Asine, Dendra, Kazarma, Kokla, Prosymna, Tiryns, and Mycenae (Sjöberg 2004:132–133; see Shear 2004 regarding Mycenae specifically). Prestige goods, particularly those brought in by sea, must have circulated within and between sites, perhaps through gift exchange, with no one site immediately outpacing the others.

However, as was the case with Pylos in Messenia, Mycenae eventually gathered the lion's share of goods. Already at the start of Late Helladic III, Mycenae served as the emerging center of what by Late Helladic IIIB would become a full-blown Argive state. But, according to Sjöberg (2004:144), Mycenae never completely dominated the region, through central control of the economy, for example. Most of Mycenae's former rivals, such as Midea, prospered during this period, managing to attract a fair number of exotic, imported items (Sjöberg 2004:135). Some sites, however, such as Argos and Berbati, though still occupied during Late Helladic III, appear to have been demoted by Late Helladic IIIA; there are no exotic prestige goods from either site (Sjöberg 2004:135), which is particularly interesting, given Berbati's thriving LH IIIA pottery industry.

Tiryns may have served as the port town for Mycenae (Shear 2004:62), as Romanou and Beylerbey apparently served Pylos. The palaces at Midea and Tiryns may have been occupied in Late Helladic III by leaders who once had competed with those at Mycenae but eventually intermarried with them. Intermarriage also may have bound the ruling family at Pylos to secondary elite at various regional centers (the capitals of the so-called tax collection districts). Evidence for intermarriage between relatively small numbers of elite families in Messenia, the Argolid (at Mycenae and Tiryns at least), Thebes, and Knossos has been found in the Linear B tablets. Killen (1995a; see also Olivier 2001; Rougemont 2001) argues that the "collectors" at the various palace centers shared a relatively small number of patronyms (i.e., family names), too few to be coincidence. Names and social positions, therefore, must have been controlled and exchanged by elite, as was wealth. Processes of Argive secondary-state formation thus produced strongly networked, hierarchically organized sociopolitical systems that were quite similar to those at Pylos.

Wright (2004c) analyzed what survey data there are from the Argolid and concluded (as did Sjöberg 2004) that Mycenae exercised variable amounts of control over settlements in its vicinity and in adjacent regions (see also Cherry and Davis 2001 for a very similar argument). According to Wright (2004c:127–128), there are three general types of settlement distribution apparent in the northeastern Peloponnesos, each more or less affected by Mycenae. Wright's Central Place Model, which works for the Argive Plain, expects that sites in the immediate vicinity of a state center will have been occupied continuously from the time of their founding, and that the overall number of sites will have increased steadily through time, peaking when the state center was at its most powerful. (As Wright notes [2004c:127], fully testing the foregoing will require intensive survey of the Argive Plain, which has yet to take place.) Wright's Dependency Model, which works for Berbati-Limnes, expects that overall site numbers in the immediate hinterland of a primate center, such as in adjacent, subsidiary valleys, will have increased when growth occurred at the center. There is evidence from Berbati-Limnes, for example, for increased population and agricultural intensification during LH IIIB, when surplus grain may have been directed to a growing Mycenae (Wright 2004c:123). Finally, Wright's Periphery Model, which works for the Nemea Valley and the southern Argolid, expects that site numbers in some regions will have experienced stepwise (as opposed to constant) growth, depending on when and the degree to which sites became integrated into the regional economy. Nemea, for example, was heavily populated in the Early Helladic, abandoned for most of the Middle Helladic, and experienced growth and centralization at Tsoungiza in the Late Helladic (Wright 2004c:125), when Mycenae was also expanding. There may have been direct economic and perhaps political links between elite at Tsoungiza and elite at Mycenae (Wright 2004c:125–126).

We would argue that Wright's models can be successfully applied to Pylos as well, and that the different settlement patterns he has identified are typical of first-generation secondary-state formation, leading to networked systems of state organization, in situations of semiperipherality where leaders at the center broker prestige goods (and other) exchanges between central and secondary elite, as well as with elite in other nearby and distant states. These patterns should hold equally for other Mycenaean states, and perhaps for similar states in other parts of the world.

In Messenia, the Central Place Model works well to explain the situation in the vicinity of the palace, where several sites grew steadily along with Pylos (e.g., Ano Englianos) through the early phases of the Late Helladic (Bennet 1999a, 1999b; Bennet and Shelmerdine 2001).

Some other nearby sites were abandoned, however, at the end of the Middle Helladic (Shelmerdine 2001:115). Interestingly, the largest Middle Helladic settlements after Pylos disappear abruptly in LH I (Shelmerdine 2001:118). Other Hither province settlements, such as Romanou, Ordines, and Beylerbey, which later may have been capitals of taxation districts, were promoted at the start of LH IIIA and would have had strong political and perhaps family ties to Pylos, as various Argive sites had to Mycenae.

These ties would have facilitated economic exchanges, as did the system of land tenure (Palmer 1998–1999). Most of the land granted by palatial officials, as recorded in Linear B, for example, is located in the immediate vicinity of the palace (Killen 1999a:89). Likewise, Killen (1998b) has argued that most grain collected by the palace, and recorded in Linear B, was grown on village (*damos*) as opposed to palatial land. Halstead (2001:40–41) argued for a share-cropping system whereby grain was sown, harvested, and sent to the palace, with little need for centralized palatial control of the process. This grain would have supported individuals living at the palace, but it would also have been redistributed to those working for the palace who manufactured prestige goods. This system of land tenure and surplus mobilization would have affected settlements in the vicinity of the center, but also may have affected settlements in the hinterlands of the palace, in particular those that provided needed raw materials, like flax for linen production. As Killen (1999a:89) noted, palatial officials took some interest in types of land far from the center, such as places well-suited to flax production (see also Halstead 2001:44–46).

Settlements and microregions that had something to offer the palace may have been integrated (or chose to integrate) into the regional economy (e.g., many of the settlements that provided flax, according to the *Na* series of tablets, were in the Further province), creating a system of partial dependency (as in Wright's Dependency Model). In addition, the fortunes of strategically important sites, such as Nichoria (Bennet 1999a) and Mouriatadha (Bennet 1998–1999), were, it seems, also strongly tied to the center. Most interestingly, the port town of Romanou, of obvious importance to the palace, is the only site in Messenia that was large in the Early Helladic, abandoned in the Middle Helladic, and resettled in the Late Helladic (Shelmerdine 2001:125).

Finally, some settlements in Messenia would have been only peripherally (as in Wright's Peripheral Model) affected by events at the center. For example, several sites along the boundary between the Hither and Further provinces were abandoned in Late Helladic III (Bennet 1999a; Shelmerdine 2001:118). Likewise, Peristeria, located in the north of Messenia, was once a large, thriving community but does not appear to have been occupied in Late Helladic IIIB (Bennet 1999a). Nevertheless, a new settlement, Mouriatadha, located very close to Peristeria, was founded in LH IIIB (Bennet 1998–1999). It is difficult not to associate this foundation with the influence and (perhaps direct) participation of Pylos (Bennet 1998–1999:24; Bennet 1999a).

When state organization in Pylos is thus compared to Mycenae, there is evidence for a similar range of regional integrative strategies, variously implemented. Some settlements and regions experienced (or allowed) considerable control by the palace, others less so. This is to be expected from highly networked states, wherein mobilization of materials and resources for prestige goods manufacture and distribution is the primary concern. Wright's models work equally well for the Classic Lowland Maya states, which were, as we have described above, also hierarchical and highly networked.

Aegean states in perspective: Mycenaean versus Mayan settlement patterns

Like the Mycenaean settlement patterns around primary centers, Lowland Maya settlement systems also were hierarchically organized and very centralized (Blanton et al. 1981:195–196; Marcus 2003). Settlement pattern studies indicate that house compounds were clumped (5–12 house ruins per clump) and that for every 50–100 houses, there existed a secondary center (Blanton et al. 1981:195). In every region there was at least one very large, complex site, a major center, with palaces, pyramids, and plazas (Blanton et al. 1981:195–196). According to Blanton et al. (1981:201), "[t]he landscape must have been organized in complex ways—both vertically, with hierarchies of dependent centers, and horizontally, with territorial divisions between centers of equivalent function."

Each of the settlement patterns Wright outlined in Aegean contexts can be identified in Mayan contexts, depending on the particular state under consideration (e.g., Tikal versus Calakmul; see Marcus 2004), its political affiliations with other nearby states, and the types of prestige goods being manufactured and exchanged. For example, secondary centers in some states apparently experienced shifting strategic importance depending on the changing patterns of social and military alliance that linked the elite leaders of the various states (see Marcus 1993b, 1998b), creating patterns that fit Wright's Dependency Model. The primary evidence for such shifting alliances is documentary and comes in the form of dedicatory stelae found at various centers (Blanton et al. 1981:202–203). Furthermore, foreign prestige goods, such as obsidian, are found almost exclusively in elite burials (which is very similar to the Mycenaean situation), and the density of deposition varies depending on the region. Some regions have produced very little exotica, even from elite graves (Blanton et al. 1981:195). This also is similar to the Mycenaean situation, and may fit the expectations of Wright's Peripheral Model.

Settlement patterns tend to differ within corporate and network states. In general, network states tend to exhibit clinal rank-size distributions that are indicative of well-integrated settlements of different sizes. Corporate settlement patterns, by contrast, tend to be either very "flat" (i.e., many similarly sized, poorly integrated sites, such as Late Bronze Age Corinthia; see Pullen and Tartaron, chapter 14, this volume) or extremely "primate" in rank-size terms (i.e., many small, secondary settlements surrounding one very large center, such as Teotihuacan, particularly in the Tzacualli and Middle Horizon periods, AD 1–700, Blanton et al. 1981:129–142, figures 3.6 and 3.8; see also Johnson 1980; Zipf 1949). Interestingly, during the Protopalatial and (to a lesser extent) Neopalatial periods, both settlement patterns are found in different parts of Crete (Driessen 2001b:59, 61). What is more, during Late Minoan IIIA, when Knossos was under Mycenaean influence or control (see, e.g., Driessen 1998–1999; Driessen and Farnoux 2000; Driessen and Macdonald 1997), the systems of settlement and administration shifted (but interestingly, ideological systems apparently stayed the same; Driessen and Langhor, chapter 16, this volume; Hägg 1997; Olsen 1998) and more closely resembled those associated with networked states (Driessen 2001b; see also Sherratt 2001:230–231). As Driessen (2001b:99) has argued, "[t]he Knossos kingdom was not so much a territorial state as an economic enterprise." In this way, Late Minoan IIIA Knossos was much like other Mycenaean states, albeit even less able to exercise centralized economic control than the Mainland states (Driessen 2001b:112). For this reason, Late Minoan IIIA settlement patterns in central Crete are best explained by Wright's Peripheral Model.

There may be two reasons for this: (1) the palatial administration at Knossos seems to have sought in particular to exercise decentralized control over wool production through interaction via secondary elite with independent shepherds (Halstead 2001:41–44), thereby having only a peripheral effect on outlying territories, never creating systems of dependency; and (2) the inhabitants of the hinterlands of Late Minoan IIIA Knossos were not Mycenaean and therefore had no ethnic, social, or political ties to the center. Many of the personal names in the Knossos Linear B tablets are non-Greek (59%), compared to only 21.2% non-Greek names, mostly female, recorded at Mycenae (Morpurgo Davies 1999; Varias 1998–1999:364). This is perhaps why there were so many more "collectors" needed in Knossos as compared to other Mycenaean states, such as Pylos (Olivier 2001; Rougemont 2001); networked systems of political economy, which depend on personal relationships, were not easily applied to territories once subject to systems of corporate political economy. Networked systems tend to be inherently unstable (Galaty and Parkinson 1999:8); even more so when they extend into potentially unfriendly territory. As a result, the Mycenaeans (or "Mycenaeanized" Minoans) on Crete appear to have worked hard to justify their political and economic claims on the island (Burke 2005; Driessen and Langohr, chapter 16, this volume).

Collapse

In the ten years since the RMP SAA session, there has been some discussion of Mycenaean state collapse, but we are not much closer today to identifying its cause(s). What has been clarified since 1997 is Late Helladic IIIC ceramic chronology (Deger-Jalkotsky 1998a, 1998b; Deger-Jalkotsky and Zavadil 2003; Jacob-Felsch 2000). Based on new readings of the evidence, it now seems that there was in fact a series of collapses that affected different Mycenaean states at different times (Mountjoy 1997), and that at many sites there was relatively substantial rebuilding in Late Helladic IIIC, in particular in the Argolid (Sjöberg 2004). Some sites, such as Tiryns, flourished in Late Helladic IIIC (French 1998:4; Maran 2001; Sherratt 2001:234–235). Pylos, on the other hand, which collapsed during a "Transitional LH IIIB2–LH IIIC Early" phase (Mountjoy 1997:110), became a backwater (Davis et al. 1999:181; Sherratt 2001:234).

It thus seems that the collapse was an even more variable, complex event (or process) than originally realized. Some archaeologists believe that the Mycenaean states fell as a result of a series of very strong earthquakes that occurred over the course of many decades and affected all of the Peloponnesos (Nur and Cline 2000;

Vanschoonwinkel 2002), a series of droughts (Moody 2005), or a large-scale, long-term plague (Walløe 1999). Each of these natural causes would explain the stepwise, pan-regional nature of the collapse.

We still argue, however, despite skepticism about economic causes (Cherry and Davis 1999:98), that the end of the Mycenaean states came at least in part as a result of shifting trade patterns that undercut the Mycenaean elite, rendering their primary sources of power, which revolved around control and manipulation of a wealth-financed economy, ineffective (Parkinson 1999; see also Deger-Jalkotsky 1996; Sherratt 1999). Sherratt (2001:235) has argued that the primary eastern Mediterranean trade routes shifted north sometime toward the end of LH IIIB, primarily owing to the growing influence of Cypriot traders, who sought new markets in the central Mediterranean and Adriatic. Without direct access to various imported raw materials, such as bronze, the Mycenaean elite could not long survive (Sherratt 1999). Settlements on either side of the Euboean gulfs, along the Corinthian gulf coast, and on Ionian islands prospered during Late Helladic IIIC, and most were occupied into the Dark Age (Sherratt 2001:235). The palaces, and the networked systems that supported them, disappeared. As de Fidio (2001) has argued, it was the villages—the *damoi*—that constituted the system; the palace and its administered economy were the *anti*-system. As a result, after the collapse some regions, such as Pylos, where the anti-system was very highly developed, were almost fully abandoned, whereas other regions returned to a small-village, tribal existence. Some Mycenaean elite may have fled to the east, perhaps as Sea People, but the verdict on this count is still out (see articles in Gitin et al. 1998).

TESTING MODELS: TARGETED, INTEGRATED RESEARCH

In RMPI we called for targeted research projects that would collect the right sets of data needed to test the expectations of general models of Mycenaean state formation, organization, and collapse. Despite a recent general slowdown in primary field research in Greece, several new projects have been launched to collect specific data related to specific questions about the past. Such goal-oriented research projects are now becoming the norm in Aegean prehistory.

A very good example of targeted research and general model testing is provided in this volume by Daniel J. Pullen and Thomas F. Tartaron. The Eastern Korinthia Archaeological Survey (EKAS) sought, among other things, to determine why there was no Mycenaean palace in the Corinthia (cf. Morgan 1999). Was it in fact the case that the Corinthia was territorially peripheral to the Argolid, and perhaps administered from Mycenae, and therefore without a palace? Or might there be geographic or developmental reasons why the Corinthian system was very differently organized?

EKAS deployed a very sophisticated intensive survey and Geographic Information Systems (GIS) approach to this problem and drew several interesting conclusions, namely (1) the Corinthia was a "political periphery" contested by Mycenae and Kolonna on Aegina; (2) the region was characterized by a kind of environmental and political stasis; and (3) unlike in other Bronze Age territories, such as the Argolid and Messenia, a more heterarchical system was maintained into and through the Mycenaean period (i.e., unlike other regions during the Bronze Age, the Corinthia did not experience secondary, networked state formation). Settlements in the Corinthia do not seem to have become economically dependent on or peripheral to Mycenae, as in the southern Argolid (Wright 2004c); Corinthian sites were all fairly large, evenly spaced along the edge of the coastal plain, continuously occupied from the Neolithic to the Late Bronze Age, and did not experience changes in their growth patterns that might be attributed to Mycenaean influence (Pullen and Tartaron, chapter 14, this volume).

The results of EKAS for the Corinthia and PRAP can be compared with the results of IKAP, which is investigating the region stretching from the secondary Mycenaean center at Iklaina to the Palace of Nestor (Cosmopoulos 2006). IKAP is another, recent example of a targeted research project that has asked and answered questions specific to Pylos but of general, comparative value. Iklaina was perhaps a Hither province district capital, that of a-pu_2 in the Linear B documents. Whereas the Palace of Nestor (*pu-ro*) and a Further province capital, Nichoria (*ti-mi-to a-ke-e*), have been excavated, and portions of the palatial hinterland surrounding several possible Hither province district capitals (e.g., Ordines [*pe-to-no*], Beylerbey [*a-ke-re-wa*]; Bennet and Shelmerdine 2001:138–139) have been intensively surveyed (by PRAP), until IKAP, a Hither province capital had not been placed into a regional context through survey and then excavated. Cosmopoulos (2006) reports on the results of survey and site-surface collection (Phase 1 of the project), which will be followed, it is hoped, by future excavations, at Iklaina and other sites in the district. The primary goal of IKAP's Phase 1 was to determine the nature of the settlement system that surrounded and connected Iklaina, and the *a-pu₂* district, to Pylos.

IKAP found evidence for a four-tiered site-settlement hierarchy in the *a-pu₂* district (Cosmopoulos 2006:222), as did PRAP in the areas it surveyed (Bennet and Shelmerdine 2001:136). Iklaina was a large, second-order site (12 ha in Late Helladic IIIA/B), somewhat smaller than the palace (circa 20 ha in Late Helladic IIIB) and seemingly much larger than other possible district capitals, such as Ordines (2.1 ha) and Beylerbey (3.52 ha) (Cosmopoulos 2006:220; Shelmerdine 2001:121–123). One difference, then, between the PRAP results and those of IKAP is that Iklaina is much larger than most of the other sites close to the palace. Perhaps it served a special purpose and therefore was "encouraged" to grow (to use Bennet and Shelmerdine's [2001:138] terminology), as a dependent adjunct to the palace (following Wright 2004c). Linear B texts indicate that there may have been a shrine at *a-pu₂* and that the site and district supported at least nine smiths (confirmed by discovery of the industrial site of Katsimigas; see above), some of whom received *ta-ra-si-ja* bronze from the palace (Cosmopoulos 2006:217). The differences in the *a-pu₂* district as compared to those areas investigated by PRAP, which, of course, probably cut across several districts, are evidence for the variable nature of settlement organization in the Pylos state, an artifact of the networked system of political economy on which the palace depended to meet its needs.

IKAP's high-resolution look at one district demonstrates the existence of a four-tier settlement system composed of the palace and a second-order town surrounded by small villages and agricultural installations, but with variation from district to district, and confirms the work of PRAP in a powerful way. Furthermore, the similarities between Messenia and other first-generation, networked, secondary Mycenaean states (e.g., Mycenae/Tiryns, Mycenaean Knossos) are likewise confirmed, as are the strong differences between them and polities that emphasized heterarchical or corporate forms of political economy, such as in the Eastern Corinthia and Minoan Crete.

CONCLUSIONS: THE STRUCTURE OF THIS VOLUME AND A LOOK TO THE FUTURE

As we have tried to demonstrate in this introduction, study of the Mycenaean palaces and the states they administered has advanced noticeably and, we believe, impressively in the last ten years. Advances have not come, however, through any major breakthrough akin to the identification of the Palace of Nestor by Carl Blegen or the decipherment of Linear B by Michael Ventris; rather, the field has advanced through the steady accumulation of numerous small discoveries, many the result of interdisciplinary and international cooperation and communication.

This new edition of *Rethinking Mycenaean Palaces* includes five new chapters that expand its scope and, we hope, further attest to the power of international and cross-disciplinary research. The first edition focused strongly on Pylos, for reasons outlined in the original introduction. This edition takes a much wider view, including additional discussions of the Argolid (in this introduction) and new chapters regarding the Corinthia, Crete, and Thessaly. Eric Cline's chapter situates the Mycenaean states within a much larger, eastern Mediterranean world. The original chapters were written entirely by American and British scholars; this edition includes papers by a Greek scholar, Vassiliki Adrimi-Sismani, and two Belgians, Jan Driessen and Charlotte Langohr. We trust that their Continental perspective has helped to balance the Anglo-American tilt to the first book.

In the introduction to RMPI, we attempted "to provide a skeletal frame of Mycenaean social structure upon which might be hung more complex models of Mycenaean state systems" (Galaty and Parkinson 1999:8). As is perhaps clear in this introduction, we feel that much more attention needs to be paid to building better models of Mycenaean political economy; thus the new chapter on industry and elite power at Pylos by Robert Schon in this volume. In particular, we need to define better the terms we use, such as *power*, *centralization*, *wealth*, and so on. Many of these terms have been well defined in the anthropological theoretical literature on state formation and organization, and we encourage our nonanthropological colleagues to continue to access this body of work. Doing so, however, will necessitate more, not less, cross-cultural comparison, since most of this literature addresses non-Aegean states. For this reason, we stand by our original call for more cross-cultural comparison.

The past decade has seen remarkable advances in our understanding of the Mycenaean states through the collection of new data and the gradual development of new models. We look forward to the next ten years, and can only imagine what Mycenaean palaces might look like in 2017.

NOTES

1. Changes were made to some of the original chapters to correct minor typographical errors and impose stylistic consistency with the new chapters, and they were reordered. The original bibliography was updated to reflect additional references in the six new chapters, and we have included an index. When the original volume was published we decided not to correct errors of interpretation that were identified by the discussants, John T. Killen, a Linear B specialist, and John F. Cherry and Jack L. Davis, archaeologists. For example, whereas Galaty (1999:51) thought Pylos tablet *Vn 130* might record the transaction of some type of specialized pot, Killen (1999:89) indicated that the vessels were most likely bronze, not clay. We believed that this kind of exchange, and others apparent in the book, demonstrated the type of give-and-take sharing of ideas and knowledge between classical and anthropological archaeologists and philologists that is needed in the study of Mycenaean states (cf. Palaima 2003:166).

PART I

MYCENAEAN PALACES:
THE 1999 TEXT

CHAPTER 2

1999 INTRODUCTION

PUTTING MYCENAEAN PALACES IN THEIR PLACE

MICHAEL L. GALATY AND WILLIAM A. PARKINSON

THE CHAPTERS WE HAVE brought together in the following pages were written by a diverse group of specialists, each of whom is, in his or her own way, trying to figure out what it was like to live in southern Greece about three thousand years ago. More generally, we are all interested in the evolution and variability associated with archaic states. We are curious why these strangely complex sociopolitical forms developed, both in Greece and elsewhere in the world. We want to understand how they worked, how they differed, and how they were, in several respects, quite similar. Despite the fact that some of the contributors to this volume call themselves anthropologists, others refer to themselves as Aegean prehistorians, and still others consider themselves classicists or historians or philologists, we all agree that it is through mutual cooperation that we are most likely to arrive at a more precise understanding of the various evolutionary and historical processes that produced the palaces and states that were central to the Mycenaean world during the Late Bronze Age.

It is in this spirit of collaboration that we offer this volume, which we hope will serve two modest goals. The first of these is to highlight some of the important research being conducted in the field of Mycenaean archaeology, and to bring to the attention of our anthropological colleagues working in other parts of the world the many advances that have been made recently in Aegean prehistory. Today more than ever before we are in a position to work together, to compare results, and to learn more precisely how the Mycenaean states fit within the larger context of archaic states known from other parts of the world. Meeting this first goal depends heavily on meeting the second: stimulating the formation of new, theory-based research philosophies within the arena of Greek archaeology and Aegean prehistory, that is, research designs capable of supporting common methodological ground and more easily occupied by the wide assortment of scholars now studying Mycenaean states. The various chapters included in this volume provide excellent examples of this newly emerging program and demonstrate the many benefits to be gained by assuming an integrated approach to understanding and explaining the past, one that combines multiple forms of data—both textual and material—and incorporates an explicitly comparative theoretical perspective that looks beyond the eastern Mediterranean for comparanda.

CLOSING THE "GREAT DIVIDE"

Over the years, several scholars have remarked on the schism—Renfrew's "Great Divide"—that appears to separate classical from anthropological archaeology

(Bennet and Galaty 1997; Donohue 1985; Dyson 1985, 1989, 1993; Morris 1994; Renfrew 1980; Snodgrass 1985, 1987). This perceived separation can be attributed to a variety of different historical and social factors (as described by Morris 1994). The unfortunate result is two different fields that rarely interact. For example, reports on archaeological fieldwork in the Aegean are most often placed in publications unfamiliar to (and therefore unread by) anthropologists (Bennet and Galaty 1997:100). Furthermore, anthropological archaeologists seldom attend annual meetings of the Archaeological Institute of America (AIA), where Aegean prehistorians tend to present their research, and papers on Aegean prehistory are rarely, if ever, given at annual meetings of the Society for American Archaeology (SAA). As a result, important research on the archaic states of the Aegean never reaches the majority of anthropological archaeologists, and the extremely well-studied and well-understood states of the Aegean Bronze Age are seldom included in anthropological graduate seminars or journal articles that compare archaic state systems (see, e.g., Stein 1998:1–2). Aegean prehistory is thus passed over, often going unnoticed and unconsidered in formulations of general archaeological method and theory—though there have been outstanding exceptions, notably, Renfrew's (1975) "early state module" and Renfrew and Cherry's (1986) "peer polity interaction." Conversely, very little of the immense body of sociocultural theory on the evolution and organization of complex societies has been incorporated into Mycenaean archaeology.

The great divide is therefore a loss to both anthropologists and Aegean prehistorians. If this gap between the fields is to be closed, we must each take an active role in closing it. The chapters included in this volume serve to demonstrate ongoing attempts to break down the classical versus anthropological dichotomy and reveal the gains to be made through their explicit combination in a cooperative methodology. Our purpose here is to delineate what we understand to be the history of the great divide and to propose ways to cross it. To achieve our goals, however, it is important to understand how this awkward situation came about and what we can do to rectify it.

Classical and anthropological archaeology did in fact evolve in different academic environments: classical archaeology in the context of ancient history and philology; anthropological archaeology in support of departments of ethnology. Just as Darwin's finches developed morphologically different beaks because of

their isolation, each discipline developed a distinct body of method and theory appropriate to its own needs. Aegean prehistory is still strongly associated with the so-called classical world and later historical periods, and it is standard practice for those studying Mycenaean states to be trained in Classics departments rather than in departments of anthropology. Thus, Aegean prehistorians are generally taught methods designed for dealing with questions of an art historical nature rather than of an anthropological nature. Consequently, research papers by Aegean prehistorians tend to be more descriptive in intent and rich in detail, sorting out complex artifact seriations or striving to link text with site. Those by anthropologists, on the other hand, tend to be (or try to be) more explanatory and are concerned with explaining cross-cultural variation and understanding evolutionary processes (for further descriptions of this distinction, see Binford 1968a, 1968b, 1982; Kelley and Hanen 1988; Trigger 1989). To a certain extent, therefore, Aegean prehistorians and anthropological archaeologists should communicate, and do have much to talk about, but they do not always speak the same language and are in fact trained to ask different questions.

One of the major problems in communication between the two disciplines stems from the basic philosophy of research design. Anthropological archaeologists are trained to formulate research projects that are guided by explicit theoretical frames of reference and are structured to test multiple and competing hypotheses (see Renfrew 1972). Since much of their funding comes from the National Science Foundation, this hypothetico-deductive approach is largely rote and simply assumed as the standard operating procedure for anthropological archaeologists. In general, this basic philosophy of research design does not characterize most of the research into Aegean prehistory. Correspondingly, the majority of research projects in the Aegean are funded by the National Endowment for the Humanities.

The Greek Late Bronze Age provides fertile ground for building explanatory models of state formation and economic organization (as demonstrated by Renfrew [1975] and Renfrew and Cherry [1986]). Such issues cannot at present be efficiently addressed, however, until specific, targeted research projects are operationalized and the right sets of data have been collected. Aegean prehistorians must construct new research philosophies, frameworks that will allow theoretical modeling to take place. For example, Costin (1991:2, 44) has called for the general cross-cultural investigation of the origins of craft specialization. Aegean prehistorians certainly have much to contribute to this effort. (In this regard, the recently held *TEXNH* conference represents a step in the right direction [Laffineur and Betancourt 1997].) Explanatory models of craft specialization cannot, however, be properly tested in Greece until Aegean prehistorians adopt a research philosophy that allows general questions to be raised and engaged. Some chapters in this volume (chapters 8 and 9, for instance) do take up problems of craft production and distribution (of ceramics and chipped stone), but the research questions those chapters seek to answer were constructed in concert with the operation of a large ongoing project, the Pylos Regional Archaeological Project (PRAP), which was itself motivated by theory-driven research goals (see chapter 4, this volume; Davis 1998; Davis et al. 1997; Zangger et al. 1997). We therefore encourage our Aegean colleagues to more often ask general questions when designing field projects, to actively cultivate cross-cultural comparison, and in this way to begin work on a bridge over the great divide.

Anthropological archaeologists interested in archaic states can also do their part to close the divide between disciplines by recognizing the tremendous opportunities of working in an area, like Greece, with a rich archaeological record supplemented by extensive textual information. The Aegean in particular provides an excellent testing ground for methods of combining complex documentary evidence with archaeological data and with anthropologically based socioeconomic theory. As such, the Aegean Late Bronze Age should be of immense interest to scholars working in other cultural contexts where it would be beneficial to link text and other archaeological data more systematically with theory, such as in Mesoamerica and in China (see Kepecs and Kolb 1997). Aegean archaeologists have access to a large corpus of administrative records, written in an archaic form of Greek and kept by Mycenaean bureaucrats (see Hooker 1980; Ventris and Chadwick 1973). The documents record state-wide transactions in a script called Linear B and were preserved at several primary centers (Mycenae, Pylos, Knossos, Chania, Tiryns, and Thebes). They provide an invaluable glimpse into the workings of Mycenaean states and have been the subject of very sophisticated investigation and intense debate (see, for example, Shelmerdine and Palaima 1984). Bennet (1988a) has developed a strategy for the profitable combination of both forms of data, textual and artifactual; his chapter

and several others show the strategy at work. As this volume illustrates, archaeological investigations in document-rich regions need not pit those who employ textual information against those who do not. Much more may be gained through systematic cooperation and combination.

TOWARD AN INTEGRATED COMPARATIVE APPROACH

Detailed descriptions of what are essentially static phenomena, such as Linear B tablets, provide the means whereby dynamic processes of past human behavior can be meaningfully investigated and eventually understood. If the primary goal of the social anthropologist, or in this case the anthropological archaeologist, is, to paraphrase Harris (1987:xv), the elucidation of the recurrent reasons for cultural similarities and differences, then the melding of classical and anthropological frameworks in the context of a cooperative methodological and theoretical paradigm provides a compelling vehicle for both description, as well as explanation of social process. A thoughtfully constructed comparison of Aegean cultural systems with those of other regions can only help to reveal the deep behavioral structures responsible for the operation and reproduction of state-level societies in general.

To this end, we suggest that it is necessary to assume an *integrated comparative theoretical approach* to Aegean prehistory—an approach that applies the explicit theoretical frameworks of anthropological archaeology to the document- and artifact-rich environment of the Aegean in an attempt to understand the variability associated with archaic states in their various cross-cultural forms. While there has been a general trend toward such an integrated comparative perspective in recent years, many of the concepts and interpretations commonly accepted and applied by Aegean prehistorians deserve some further attention.

The comparative method has of course been employed in Aegean prehistory, but rarely do the comparisons drawn by Aegean archaeologists extend beyond the confines of the eastern Mediterranean, and they almost never reach the shores of the New World. In this capacity, anthropologists can perhaps provide more and better analogues (both archaeological and ethnographic) to Mycenaean states than those that have been traditionally utilized (for a discussion of analogy in archaeology, see Wylie 1985). For instance, many Mesoamerican polities—especially post-Classic polities in the Basin of Mexico and conquest-period Mixtec polities circa 1500 AD (Marcus 1998b; see also Marcus 1989)—appear to be of similar geographic size and organizational scale to Mycenaean states and may have followed similar developmental trajectories (see chapter 5, this volume; Wright 1994). As such, these more geographically remote states, as well as others, provide better analogues to the small-scale states of Mycenaean Greece than do the much larger Near Eastern states, which often are treated not simply as analogues but as parallels.

The tendency to compare Mycenaean states almost exclusively to Near Eastern ones is in part the result of a historical tradition that encourages interpretation of ancient economies based entirely on documentary evidence (in this case, Linear B tablets and Near Eastern texts). All too often this occurs at the expense of the archaeological data, much of which argues against such comparisons. There is an immense difference in the geographic extent and organizational scale of Near Eastern and Mycenaean state systems. The Near Eastern states to which Aegean prehistorians frequently draw their parallels were much larger and more complex than the small-scale states of the Mycenaean mainland. During the Late Helladic IIIB phase (circa 1300–1200 BC; see table 1.1), for example, the state center of Pylos grew to a maximum size of 21 ha (Davis 1998; Davis et al. 1997; see also chapter 3, this volume). In contrast, by the beginning of the Dynastic period (circa 3100 BC), the Near Eastern center of Uruk covered 100 ha. By the end of the Early Dynastic period, the city encompassed 400 ha, with a possible population of 50,000 people. Nowhere is there any evidence that Mycenaean centers ever reached such sizes. Not only were contemporary Near Eastern state centers much larger than Mycenaean "palaces" and their associated towns, but the area they controlled was also much larger. For example, Postgate (1992:44) notes that the Akkad Dynasty state (circa 2350–2150 BC) covered more than 50,000 km^2 at its maximum territorial extent. The reaches of Hammurapi's empire reached a similar scale during the Babylonian period (circa 1800–1750 BC). This area is roughly equivalent to the entire Peloponnesos, in which Renfrew (1975) suggests there may have been as many as five different Mycenaean "early state modules" (ESMs) or independent states. If it is necessary to compare Mycenaean states to the ancient Near East, the best analogues seem to be in earlier periods (prior to 3200 BC) and in regions other than in the vicinity of Uruk. For example, state evolution and organization on the Susiana Plain—to which writing was relatively unimportant before the Late Uruk and just prior to systemic collapse (and where the state center, Susa, grew during the Late Uruk to a maximum extent of 28 ha; Johnson 1973)—reveals interesting similarities to Bronze Age developments in Greece, especially in Pylos.

In addition to being critically self-conscious of the comparisons being drawn between different archaic state systems, we must be extremely careful when comparing different entities within the same system. To this end, it is necessary to cease conflating data from individual Mycenaean states (see chapter 9, this volume) as though all functioned similarly. Each individual autonomous state (that is, early state module; figure 1.1) deserves to be investigated in its own context, and the possibility of parallel systemic organization needs to be treated as a hypothetical but as yet unproved construction. Furthermore, Linear B documents should be combined sparingly and only with caution with textual data collected at different Mycenaean centers, such as Pylos and Knossos (see chapter 7, this volume). There is good archaeological and textual evidence that regional economies in both of these state systems were structured very differently (Killen 1985; Olivier 1984). Presuming differences in environmental setting and evolutionary trajectory, especially on the part of Pylos and Knossos, this is not surprising. Nevertheless, the tendency of Aegean prehistorians to combine data from different Mycenaean states leads to inaccurate assumptions with regard to how each may have functioned as an autonomous entity.

Finally, it is necessary to focus on collecting excavated data from smaller sites—those toward the bottom of regional settlement hierarchies (Davis 1988). There are very few examples of excavated Mycenaean towns (one being Nichoria; McDonald and Wilkie 1992) and hamlets (one being Tsoungiza; Wright 1990), let alone farmsteads. As a result, models of Mycenaean state formation and evolution are usually built on data excavated at primary centers only, or at best from the primary center and one or two other settlements in the second tier of the hierarchy (as is the case in Messenia), a practice strongly called into question by the results of regional, intensive surface survey. Excavation bias therefore contributes to the pervasive tendency on the part of Aegean prehistorians to view Mycenaean states from the top down and from the center out (see also Bennet 1988b for a similar assertion). Rather, it is necessary to assume an integrated theoretical perspective that understands primary centers within the context of an active, and highly variable, regional landscape.

WHY SELECT THE TOPIC OF MYCENAEAN PALACES?

Given our interest in expanding archaeological and anthropological understanding of the organizational dynamics of Mycenaean states, the question of why we chose to focus on palaces—the most intensively studied of all Mycenaean sites—is perhaps inevitable. As we mentioned earlier, archaeological conceptions of Mycenaean centers strongly influence models of Mycenaean states, yet we do recognize the importance of excavating and understanding the evolution and operation of a state's primary center. Consequently, this volume and this introductory chapter seek to define more precisely what is meant by the word *palace*, and, more importantly, to describe the integration of the center into a wider, more diverse social and ecological landscape. The center—the palace—and those living at the center surely had wants and needs (as recorded in Linear B documents); however, these concerns only partially reflect those of the general populace. To understand the interplay of central and localized interests, it is necessary to view each Mycenaean polity in its entirety, as an interconnected and interdependent system, within which the center represents one large (albeit atypical) cog.

The word palace has been variously defined by Aegean archaeologists. Many, such as Shelmerdine (1997:558; see also Barber 1992), employ an architectural definition: "a large ashlar construction centered on a *megaron* unit: a rectangular room with four columns surrounding a hearth, its long walls extending to form a porch and a vestibule" (figure 1.2). Such a definition is perfectly acceptable but does not account for function or functions. The word palace usually refers to the residence of a king, and in fact, many Aegean prehistorians grant the Mycenaean head of state, the *wanax*, kingly powers (Dabney and Wright 1990; Kilian 1988a; Shelmerdine 1997; Thomas 1976; Walcot 1967; Wright 1995a). The palace apparently housed the Mycenaean ruler (king or not), his family, and retainers, but the building was certainly more than just a royal residence. It served other functions, and its architectural features were designed to support these various functions (Shelmerdine and Palaima 1984): sacred rites were held in ritual spaces (see

chapters 3, 4, and 6, this volume); craft activities were organized in workshop areas (see chapters 4 and 6, this volume; Laffineur and Betancourt 1997; Shelmerdine 1984, 1985), goods were stored in pantries and magazines (see chapters 8 and 9, this volume; Morris 1986), and records were kept in archives (Palaima 1988).

Although we prefer to use the more neutral term "center" to refer to the building (palace) and settlement that together dominated so many Greek Bronze Age landscapes, we must acknowledge that the word "palace" is here to stay. It is a term used out of convenience, and to attempt to replace it would doubtless prove futile. Aegean prehistorians need not, however, continue to describe in increasing detail the already well-documented palatial centers; Mycenaean centers and artifacts have been well described through both the archaeological and the textual records. To define more accurately what we mean by the term palace, it is necessary to fit the Mycenaean center—and the economy that supported it—more firmly into a regional archaeological framework and into theoretical models of political, economic, and social structure. Only in doing so can the palaces be more fully understood.

MODELING THE MYCENAEAN STATE

The theoretical models of state organization within which Aegean prehistorians operate are rarely explicitly stated. Nevertheless they do exist and have exerted tremendous influence over the archaeological interpretation of Mycenaean palaces and states. Unfortunately, the majority of these theoretical models are vestiges of the era in which Linear B was first deciphered. Based on their reading of the Linear B documents, Ventris and Chadwick (1973) conceived of the Mycenaean world as being similar in many respects to feudal Europe. In their translation the wanax, the paramount leader, was thus referred to as a king. The king's men, his *equeta*, are called knights. Finley (1957), on the other hand, compared Mycenaean to Near Eastern states. As a result of such inappropriate comparisons, scholars erroneously concluded that the main purpose of primary centers was the large-scale redistribution of goods.

Such text-driven models viewed a powerful central authority that held indisputable command over the regional economy and ensnared the countryside in a repressive tangle of bureaucracy. Totalitarian control was assumed. Even though the first models of Mycenaean states were created using inappropriate analogies (that is, medieval Europe) and outdated understandings of Near Eastern states (in particular, redistribution), this early and overarching framework continues to shape most current research on Mycenaean political economy. However, when the organizational dynamics of a Mycenaean state are approached from the bottom up, from the direction of the ceramic (chapter 8, this volume) or lithic (chapters 9 and 10, this volume) industries, for instance, there is much less certainty as to how the system functioned. As Stein (1994a:13) remarks, in reference to the Near East,

> instead of viewing states as all-powerful, homogeneous entities, it is probably more accurate to characterize them as organizations operating within a social environment that, for a variety of reasons, they only partially control.

Anthropologists (e.g., Blanton et al. 1993; Stein and Rothman 1994) often describe archaic states according to how their central bureaucracy was organized and controlled. In this volume there is a general consensus that Mycenaean centers probably employed several strategies to optimize their influence over regional territory (see also Shelmerdine 1997:570). For example, Halstead (chapter 7, this volume; 1992a) argues that Mycenaean administrators developed the means to mobilize the raw materials necessary for the production of high-value prestige items. It is likely that local and provincial leaders who negotiated the transfer of such materials expected the corresponding return of a portion of the finished goods manufactured by the state, known in Mycenaean literature as the *ta-ra-si-ja* system (Halstead 1992a; Killen 1984b). Such a system of financial transactions is often referred to as a wealth-financed system (chapter 7, this volume; D'Altroy and Earle 1985; Halstead 1992a). In a wealth-financed economic system, elites pay for state-sponsored activities with high-value, easily-transportable prestige goods. Whereas some empires, such as the Inca (D'Altroy and Earle 1985), were able to employ successfully a regional staple-financed economic system alongside their elaborate wealth-financed systems, the Mycenaean states most likely were not capable of such an extensive undertaking. Only in the vicinity of the centers themselves would it have been cost-effective for the state to underwrite the palatial economy by exchanging bulky staple products for finished goods and services (Halstead 1992a). Staple finance certainly occurred at the Mycenaean centers and in the area directly surrounding them, but there is no compelling evidence that staple finance operated at a regional level.

Within the Mycenaean system, prestige goods would most likely have circulated between regional elites in a system of reciprocal gift exchanges (Renfrew 1975), only later trickling down through the tiers of the political system, gaining more and more value as they reached lower levels of the social hierarchy (Halstead 1992a; Wright 1995a). Killen (1984b, 1985) has suggested that different qualities of cloth, both wool and linen, were finished at state centers (in particular, at Knossos and Pylos). These different cloths may have been granted to regional elite to serve as markers of rank, a system similar to that which appears to have operated in the Inca Empire (Halstead 1992a; Killen 1985; Morris 1986). The regional mobilization of prestige goods would have created a system of patronage that reinforced social inequality while at the same time driving the economy and reproducing political hierarchies.

Inherent in this brief sketch of Mycenaean economy are two important distinctions missing from most current models applied by Aegean prehistorians to Mycenaean economics: (1) localized versus palatial (that is, state) economic action and (2) restricted versus free circulation of wealth. Mycenaean state and local economies would have functioned with some degree of autonomy. Many forms of economic action would have occurred outside the direct control of the regional elite. Exchange could take the form of reciprocal (face-to-face) transactions, redistribution (transfer via an intermediary), or marketing (Polanyi 1968). Many models of Mycenaean economy focus on the redistributive role of the palace, ignoring the possible importance of both reciprocity and markets (Morris 1986). As a result, the exchange of manufactured items (mainly utilitarian goods) in Mycenaean states within the context of the local economy is ripe for serious archaeological investigation (chapters 8–10, this volume; for an excellent example, see Morris 1986). In addition, there is very little evidence that systems of statewide redistribution, such as those that may have functioned in the Near East (Postgate 1994), ever operated in Mycenaean states (see chapter 9, this volume). The concept of redistribution itself is in fact undergoing reanalysis and redefinition (see Earle 1977; Feinman and Neitzel 1984; Yoffee 1993). Many anthropologists now question the importance of large-scale regional redistribution to economic systems at any level of social complexity.

States may encourage the free circulation of prestige items or restrict such circulation, depending on elite strategies for political and economic control of regional territories (Brumfiel and Earle 1987:7). This distinction bears directly on the question of Mycenaean state organization. For example, H. J. Morris (1986) suggests that the Mycenaean state of Pylos was in the midst of structural transformation from a tribute state to that of a "prestige goods/dualistic state" (PGDS as defined by Friedman and Rowlands 1977) at the time of its collapse. In a PGDS, the paramount succeeds in transforming the nature of his relationship to regional elites, who, through shifts in marriage alliances, become members of the paramount lineage (also referred to as a "segmentary" state; Stein 1994b). At the same time the center attempts to increase its control of the economy. Indeed, both Linear B tablet information and the archaeological record indicate the centralization of industry at the palace as well as in the vicinity of subordinate centers (see Morris 1986; Shelmerdine and Palaima 1984). As this system evolves, nonelites are no longer granted access to wealth goods, and exotic or prestigious items are increasingly used by the state to mark status differences. In the new system, local (nonstate) leaders and common folk are cut off from traditional avenues to the advancement of economic power, and with it, from social and political prestige.

Blanton et al. (1996) describe similar processes in Mesoamerica, making a meaningful distinction between "network" and "corporate" political economies. In a network system, individuals maintain political economic power by excluding competitors' access to exchange relationships, whereby prestige goods are mobilized and symbolic knowledge is shared (Blanton et al. 1996:3). Blanton et al. state that "exclusionary power strategies were principally associated with comparatively small, autonomous polities linked by trade, war, and the strategic marriages of rulers" (1996:3). Networked systems theoretically linked the leaders of individual Mycenaean states (that is, peer polities).

Corporate systems, on the other hand, often are characterized by increases in regional scale and a corresponding shift from "patrimonial rhetoric, which emphasizes the controlling roles of particular individuals," to "cognitive restructuring," which "allows the incorporation of disparate ethnically defined subgroups" and "legitimates the appropriation of surpluses of primary production, especially agricultural goods." Whereas network strategies tend to be "volatile" and "laden with potential for conflict," the corporate strategy "emphasizes . . . solidarity of society as an integrated whole, based on a natural, fixed, and immutable interdependence between subgroups" (Blanton et al. 1996:4, 6). In this light, Blanton et al. (1996) compare the lowland Maya states to Teotihuacán.

Mycenaean states, such as Pylos, appear to have employed a networked system of political economy (emphasizing wealth finance and the increasingly restricted circulation of prestige goods), for the most part dismissing the corporate option. The transition from the tribute state to the PGDS thus marks the intensification of exclusionary power strategies.

The foregoing begs the following question: If a Mycenaean state, such as Pylos, only partially controlled the region it was seeking to manipulate, how was the transition to a more tightly integrated and efficient system to be realized? Given different degrees of regional control, how did the elite encourage the outlying populace to participate in a system from which they may not have gained much benefit? In fact, there are several methods whereby elite draw individuals into their political orbit, perhaps the most common of which is ritual activity, such as feasting (with regard to the possibility of Mycenaean feasts, see Killen 1994; Saflund 1980), including drinking ceremonies (see chapters 3 and 8, this volume; Wright 1994, 1995b).

In archaic states, such ritual activities often operated to placate disgruntled citizens and to integrate an otherwise unstable sociopolitical system. The manipulation of trade in foreign goods and the mediation of contact with the outside world offer another means to sociopolitical control (see chapter 10, this volume; Helms 1988, 1993; Wright 1995a). Indeed, Mycenaean states appear to have utilized both ritual activities and the manipulation of foreign trade to strategically incorporate regional hinterlands into the palace-sponsored economic system, thereby ignoring costly methods of forcible incorporation, such as those employed by archaic states elsewhere—the Aztec, Mixtec, Zapotec, and Maya are examples. In the end, however, these strategies failed, and the Mycenaean state systems faltered (circa 1200 BC; see chapter 9, this volume). The nature and timing of this collapse are open to interpretation and are poorly understood (see Drews 1993 for review of earlier theories and a conflict-based explanation for the end of the Bronze Age), but the causes of the collapse can surely be addressed by careful study of the pertinent archaeological data (see Shelmerdine 1997:580–584; on collapse generally, see Yoffee and Cowgill 1991).

THE STRUCTURE OF
THE VOLUME

The chapters that make up this volume (chapters 3–12) were written by members of Classics, archaeology, and anthropology departments. All authors have made an effort to integrate anthropological and classical approaches to archaeology and to incorporate textual as well as archaeological data. As a result, the scholarly work assembled in this volume represents an integrated approach to Mycenaean archaeology.

A postscript to the volume was kindly provided by Dr. Emmett L. Bennett, Jr., Emeritus Professor of Classics at the University of Wisconsin–Madison and one of the scholars responsible for the original transcription, decipherment, and interpretation of Linear B. We have worked with Professor Bennett in the field and have firsthand knowledge of his commitment to both Linear B studies and dirt archaeology, and to their profitable union. We are honored to be able to include him in this volume.

The first concluding chapter (11) was provided by an eminent Linear B philologist John Killen, Emeritus Professor of Mycenaean Greek at Cambridge University. The second response (chapter 12) was written by Professors John Cherry, Brown University, and Jack Davis, Blegen Professor of Greek Archaeology at the University of Cincinnati and currently Director of the American School of Classical Studies at Athens. Each scholar provides insights and critiques appropriate to his specialty, and all three demonstrate remarkable facility in aspects of both the textual and archaeological records.

We have attempted in this introduction to provide a skeletal frame of Mycenaean social structure upon which might be hung more complex models of Mycenaean state systems. In so doing, we have tried to inject Aegean prehistory with a dose of dynamic energy—a format in which individual actors were vital players and the palace functioned as a nexus for the systemic interplay of regional power relations—such as might have contributed to the evolution of more and more complex Mycenaean sociopolitical organizations.

Each chapter in its own way peels back a bit of the archaeological veil that shields Mycenaean behavioral patterns from anthropological eyes. In publishing this book, we hope to introduce the complex laboratory of past human activity that is the Mycenaean world to scholars working in other regions and in other periods of time.

CHAPTER 3

PYLOS

THE EXPANSION OF A MYCENAEAN PALATIAL CENTER

JOHN BENNET

THE PALACE OF NESTOR stands today atop the Englianos ridge, a powerful symbol to local residents and tourists alike of Greece's rich prehistoric past. The processes by which it became a modern cultural symbol are not the topic of this chapter (see, e.g., Davis 1998; Lolos 1994). Rather, my goal is to examine how the site came to dominate its environment immediately before its destruction, about 1200 BC, as the paramount center in the southwestern Peloponnese, a symbol of political, economic, and ritual power in the Navarino Bay region of southwestern Messenia. To this end, I employ new data generated by the Pylos Regional Archaeological Project (PRAP) to chart the growth of the site of Bronze Age Pylos from about 2000 BC until its destruction. I then place this new, more refined picture of the expansion of Pylos in the wider context of settlement in its broader region, again using data generated by PRAP that clarify the relative sizes of settlements in this area in the Middle and Late Bronze Ages (circa 2000–1200 BC). Instead of relying solely on relative site sizes to determine sociopolitical hierarchies, I also include analysis of strategies of elite display and emulation as exemplified in burials in the region. Using these different strands of evidence, I suggest a more precise time scale on which Pylos came to dominate its region and outline some of the strategies the Pylian elite may have used to develop and secure that dominance.

BACKGROUND: THE PALACE OF NESTOR

The destruction of the palace in circa 1200 BC preserved not only a rich and complex archaeological site but also a large archive of documents inscribed in the Linear B script that recorded an early form of the Greek language (Chadwick 1987). A combination of these archaeological and documentary data sets has allowed us to reconstruct in extraordinary detail the operation of this palatial center (Shelmerdine and Palaima 1984) in the years immediately before its destruction, at the end of the phase known as Late Helladic IIIB, and the extent of the polity over which the site exerted some form of political control (Bennet 1995).

The excavations by Carl Blegen of the University of Cincinnati (Blegen and Rawson 1966; Blegen et al. 1973; Lang 1969) revealed a complex of structures centered around a monumental room with a prominent central hearth ringed by wooden columns, a megaron, in which, it seems, the ruler (called in Mycenaean Greek the wanax) met with the elite and carried out rituals. Around this central monumental room were storerooms for agricultural products, chiefly olive oil and wine. These were not all staples; many were exchange items. Perfumed oil was exported from Pylos to other sites within (and beyond) the Mycenaean world (Shelmerdine 1985). The wine was apparently used in rituals throughout the polity, as evidenced partly in administrative documents (Palmer 1994) and partly in the presence of drinking cups—kylikes, in Mycenaean ceramic terminology—at all sites, including the palace, where thousands were kept in storerooms adjacent to the megaron. Workshops and manufacturing facilities were also in the immediate vicinity of the megaron (Shelmerdine 1985, 1987:563–564).

From this central place, approximately 2000 km² of territory was controlled (figure 3.1), extending east from Pylos to the foothills of the Taygetos mountain ranges and north at least as far as Kyparissia (Wilson 1977:74, n. 32). The University of Minnesota Messenia Expedition surveyed the whole region extensively in the 1960s (McDonald and Rapp 1972), and their data have been used as the basis for reconstruction of the eco-

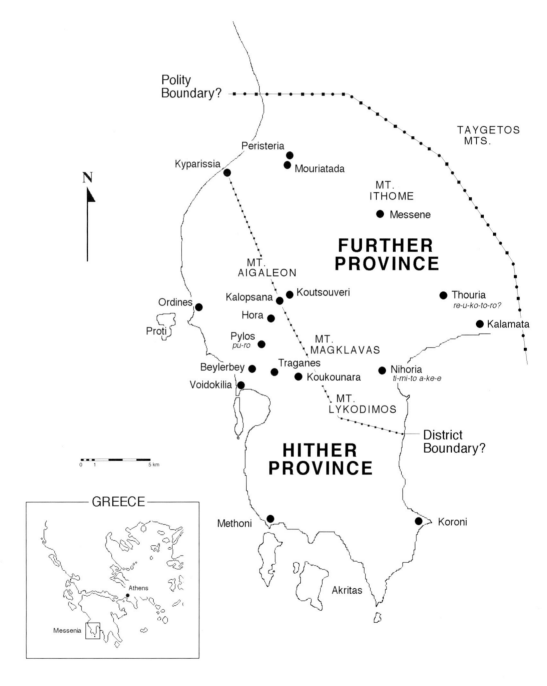

FIGURE 3.1 Map of the southwest Peloponnese, Greece, showing hypothetical boundary of the Pylian kingdom, its division into "Hither" and "Further" provinces, and significant sites. (Map drawn by J. Bennet and M. Galaty.)

nomic and sociopolitical organization of the polity in the period of the Linear B documents (e.g., Carothers 1992; Morris 1986). Once again, textual and archaeological evidence combine to demonstrate the existence of two major districts within the polity in its final phase, and topographic evidence suggests that the boundary between the two districts was a prominent mountain range, the Aigaleon. The Linear B terminology for the two districts—"this-side-of-Aigaleon" and "beyond-Aigaleon"—strongly suggests that the palatial center at Englianos had expanded its political control from its own region in the west—"this-side-of"—to the Messenian valley in the east—"beyond" (the Hither and Further provinces, respectively) (Bennet 1995, 1999a).

This much is well known about the political structure, and it is relatively widely accepted among Aegean prehistorians. These data formed the background to PRAP's recent fieldwork in a 250 km² area centered on the palatial structures on the Englianos ridge (figure 3.2, site B7) (Davis 1998; Davis et al. 1997; Zangger et al. 1997). The survey project aimed at complete diachronic coverage, but our prehistoric research is in a unique position to answer these questions:

How did the community immediately surrounding the palatial structures—often referred to as the "Lower Town"—expand and change through time?

How did the Englianos settlement come to dominate its broader region?

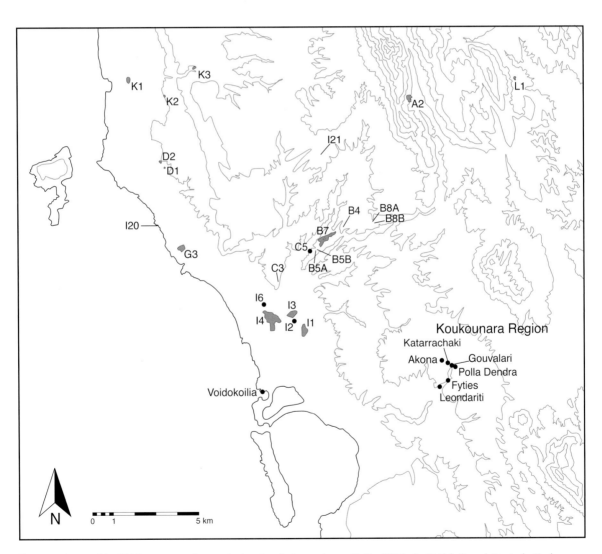

FIGURE 3.2 Map of the PRAP survey area showing the location of relevant sites studied by PRAP, plus Voidokoilia and sites in the Koukounara region. The palace is site B7. (Map drawn by J. Bennet.)

THE EXPANSION OF BRONZE AGE PYLOS

As a first stage in determining the extent of settlement around the excavated palace structures, survey teams walked the entire Englianos ridge, enabling us to define those areas with the highest density of artifactual material. From this phase of our research, the vicinity of the palace stands out quite clearly as a "hot spot" of artifactual density on the ridge. Our second stage was total collection of artifacts on a 20 m grid defined by areas in which pedestrian survey observed the highest density of material. Artifacts were collected from 468 grid squares, and these collections formed the basis for the graphics summarizing densities presented in figure 3.3. Approximately 5500 lines of data were generated in the course of study of this material, many representing more than one ceramic object. A total of 35,700 ceramic artifacts were studied and dated in this manner.

Settlement prior to 2000 BC, the end of the Early Helladic phase, appears to have been minimal. The Englianos settlement seems to have expanded first within the Middle Helladic phase, circa 2000–1700 BC (see figure 3.3); our research suggests a maximum extent of 5.48 ha. Excavation adds little of significance to this picture other than a few structures revealed beneath the later palatial structures and in tests beyond their limits (Blegen et al. 1973:32–40). At the end of the Middle Helladic phase, roughly contemporary with the well-known Shaft Graves at Mycenae, our study suggests an increase in both the extent and the density of material. In the following periods, known as Late Helladic I and Late Helladic II (circa 1700–1500 BC), the settlement had extended to about 7.08 ha, with a noticeable expansion along the ridge to the northeast.

This period is marked in the excavated record at Pylos by the construction of elaborate funerary structures, tholos or "beehive" tombs (figure 3.4). The first of these,

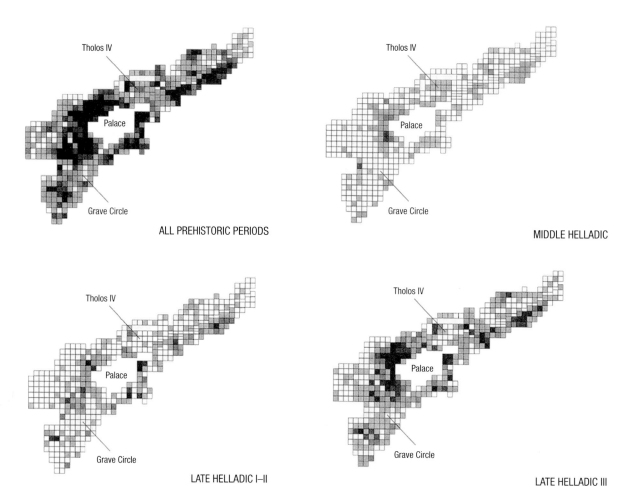

FIGURE 3.3 Palace of Nestor Lower Town (PRAP B7) showing relative densities of material for: all prehistoric periods; Middle Helladic (circa 2000–1700 BC); Late Helladic I–II (circa 1700–1400 BC); Late Helladic III (1400–1200 BC). 20 m grid. The four levels of shading correspond to sherd densities (1–375, 375–750, 750–1500, and 1500+ per ha). (Illustration by J. Bennet. Reprinted from Davis et al. 1997:429, figure 12.)

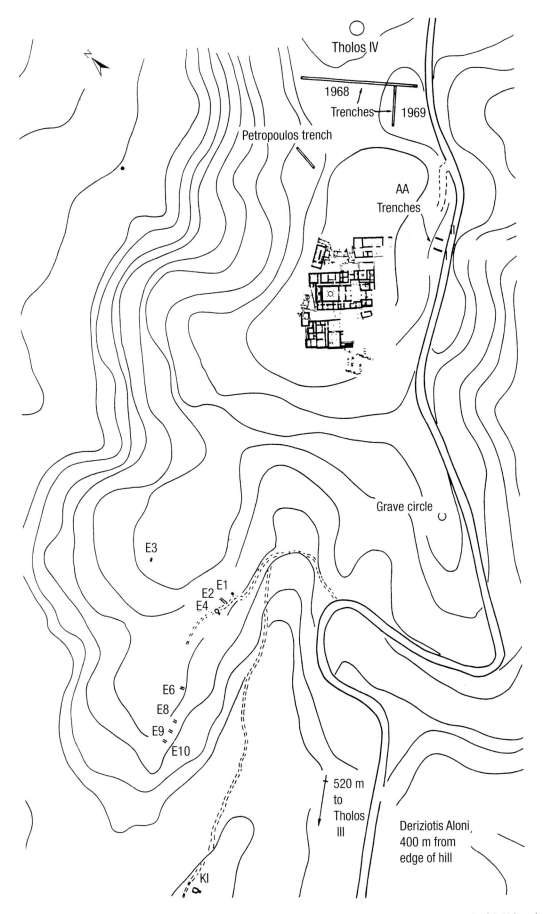

FIGURE 3.4 The Englianos ridge, showing the location of the Palace of Nestor and burial sites (Tholos IV; Grave Circle). (Adapted from Blegen et al. 1973: Fig. 301. Used with the permission of the Department of Classics, University of Cincinnati.)

called the Grave Circle (diameter approximately 5.5 m), was built in the late Middle Helladic to the southwest of the later palace (Blegen et al. 1973:134–176). Then, in LH I, perhaps two generations later, Tholos IV (diameter approximately 9.35 m) was built to its northeast (Blegen et al. 1973:95–134). It is also in this phase, the late Middle Helladic to early Late Helladic, that a fortification wall was built around the highest point of the settlement, defining the area later to be occupied by the palatial structures (Blegen et al. 1973:4–18). Although there is little evidence for structures of this phase beneath the later palatial remains, it is significant that the northeastern sector of this circuit has an elaborate entranceway aligned directly toward Tholos IV. By LH II there were further changes in the funerary structures associated with the settlement: a new structure, Tholos III (diameter 7.66–7.71 m), was built about 900 m southwest of the palace on the ridge top (Blegen et al. 1973:73–95). The construction of this tomb may reflect an extension of habitation in the immediate vicinity of the palace, leaving no more room for funerary structures. The fact that a new location was chosen may, however, also suggest a social reason: was this structure perhaps the tomb of a newly preeminent elite group?

The next phase, LH IIIA (circa 1400–1300 BC), saw the first excavated remains of substantial structures on the palace site, plausibly interpreted as a functional predecessor to the final palace (Kilian 1987:209, figure 5; Blegen et al. 1973:32–40). It is also probable that the earliest administrative documents (a few fragmentary Linear B tablets) belong to this phase of the settlement (Palaima 1983). These criteria strongly suggest that the site was fulfilling centralized administrative functions by this date. Our surface collections suggest a maximal extent of settlement in LH IIIA of circa 2.36 ha. It should be noted, however, that diagnostic artifacts of specifically LH IIIA, as opposed to generically LH IIIA–B, are relatively difficult to isolate. We should therefore regard this size estimate very much as a minimum. A better indication of size is probably afforded by considering all LH III material, giving a total extent of 12.4 ha, twice that in the preceding LH I–II phase.

By the end of the first part of LH IIIA, the Grave Circle to the southwest of the palace had gone out of use (Blegen et al. 1973:155), and PRAP's artifact collections in the vicinity suggest that this area was overrun by settlement. Tholos IV seems not to have been used for burials after the end of LH IIIA (Blegen et al. 1973:108; Lolos 1987:188), at the time the latest palace structures were constructed. It is possible that Tholos

IV, although no longer in use as a funerary structure, remained as a prominent marker, dominating the broad plaza that lay northeast of the palace citadel. Blegen's excavations here revealed no architecture (Blegen et al. 1973:64–68), perhaps confirming that the area lay open, dominated on the southwest by the palatial structures themselves and on the northeast by the prominent dome of the tomb.

At the beginning of LH IIIB (circa 1300 BC), the final palatial structures were constructed. It is in the final phase of this palace, after a number of modifications to the structures that increased workshop space in its immediate vicinity, added additional storage capacity, and restricted access (Shelmerdine 1987; Wright 1984), that the administrative documents in Linear B belong. Strictly LH IIIB material from surface collection covered 4.6 ha in this phase, twice the area of strictly LH IIIA material. Again, we need to be aware of the probability that much of the generic LH III ceramic material could belong to this later phase, and we should regard the extent of the settlement as 12.4 ha at a minimum, excluding the central buildings, which take up a further 2 ha. The total area of the site at this period would have been in excess of 14–15 ha.

By LH IIIB, the fortification wall ringing the citadel had gone out of use (Blegen et al. 1973:18). Geophysical investigations carried out as part of PRAP's overall research have turned up a number of subsurface anomalies to the west of the palatial structures, most prominent among which is a 60-m-long linear anomaly (see Zangger et al. 1997:606–613). This anomaly seems to reflect a broad structure (circa 2–2.5 m thick), perhaps a retaining wall or fortification. Though it is impossible to date the structure from the geophysical data, it may represent a continuation of the late Middle Helladic/early Late Helladic fortification circuit, suggesting that the wall had demarcated a larger fortified area than previously thought. Surface densities appear to drop off beyond the anomaly, which may support the conclusion that it bounded the settlement in this direction. Until the structure can be examined by excavation, however, the possibilities remain that it represents either a retaining wall for construction or a fortification wall belonging to a later phase of the palace. Nevertheless, we should not rush to the conclusion that Late Bronze Age Pylos was encircled by massive fortification walls like those at Mycenae and Tiryns.

The beginning of the LH IIIB period saw the continuity of only one funerary structure in the immediate vicinity of the palace: Tholos III, nearly 1 km distant

down the ridge. Assuming it was used by the ruling palatial elite for burials, we can imagine extensive funeral
processions along the ridge as part of the public ritual
of burial there. It is also in this phase that the center at
Pylos is likely to have incorporated the area of eastern
Messenia into the 2000 km² polity (Bennet 1995). In
the case of Nichoria, a site just over the boundary
into the Further Province, its incorporation may have
been marked by the construction of a new tholos tomb
for the Pylos-sponsored elite (Bennet 1995:598–599;
McDonald and Wilkie 1992:766–767; Shelmerdine
1981). The case of Nichoria has implications for the
process of expansion that Pylos must already have carried out within its more immediate region.

STRATEGIES FOR EXPANSION

In the wider region of Pylos, PRAP carried out similarly
detailed collection on a number of other Late Helladic
sites. On the basis of these collections, we can determine that only two sites appear to have come close to
rivaling the palace in size and complexity: these are
sites I1 (in our system), known as Beylerbey, and K1,
known as Ordines. Both were collected on a 20 m grid,
like the palace. Beylerbey (figure 3.5) has extensive prehistoric material, extending over 6.7 ha. Its size before
Middle Helladic was minimal, but it reached perhaps
1.64 ha in that period, as opposed to 5.48 ha at Pylos.
It grew in LH I–II (perhaps to 3.32 ha) and reached a
maximum size in LH III, only slightly larger at 3.52 ha.
Although the site is significant in the Middle Helladic,
it was quickly outstripped by the palace in size. Another
important feature of Beylerbey is that it lay close to
an early tholos—I2 on the map (see figure 3.2), usually referred to as the Osmanaga tholos (diameter
approximately 6 m)—whose construction date is indistinguishable archaeologically from that of the earliest
funerary structure at the palace, the so-called Grave
Circle (Lolos 1989). Assuming the tomb is associated
with Beylerbey—and there seem to be no rival sites
occupied at the same time as the tomb's construction—
then it is possible that, at the end of the Middle Helladic
period, the palace and Beylerbey were potential rival
centers in the region, each of considerable size and
each with its own elaborate burial structure. By the
end of LH I, however, the Osmanaga tholos had gone
out of use, the palace had far outstripped Beylerbey,
and a second, larger tholos tomb, Tholos IV, had been
constructed.

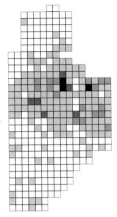

ALL PREHISTORIC
PERIODS

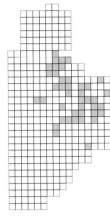

MIDDLE HELLADIC

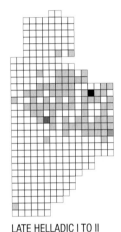

LATE HELLADIC I TO II

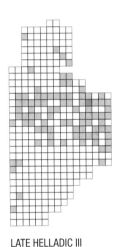

LATE HELLADIC III

FIGURE 3.5 Site of Beylerbey (PRAP I1), showing relative densities of
material for: all prehistoric periods; Middle Helladic (circa 2000–1700
BC); Late Helladic I–II (circa 1700–1400 BC); Late Helladic III (circa
1400–1200 BC). 20 m grid. Levels of shading correspond to sherd
densities (1–375, 375–750, 750–1500, and 1500+ per ha). (Illustration by
J. Bennet.)

The Osmanaga and palace tombs were not the only
ones constructed in this region, which is well known
for tholos tombs (figure 3.6; see Pelon 1976:392–403;
Hope Simpson and Dickinson 1979). The second phase
of tholos construction, however, took place during LH
I. Tholos IV was constructed at the palace, and tholos
tombs were built at Voidokoilia (diameter 4.93–5.03
m; Hope Simpson and Dickinson 1979:131–132, their
site D8; Lolos 1987:179–181), and two at Routsi (1
and 2: diameter approximately 5.0 m; Hope Simpson
and Dickinson 1979:145–146, their site D54; Lolos
1987:208–210). The third phase of tholos construction in
the palace region, in LH II, included Tholos III near the
palace and the two tombs at Tragana (1: diameter 9.2–9.3
m; 2: diameter 7.1–7.2 m; Hope Simpson and Dickinson
1979:132–133, their site D11; Lolos 1987:182–183).

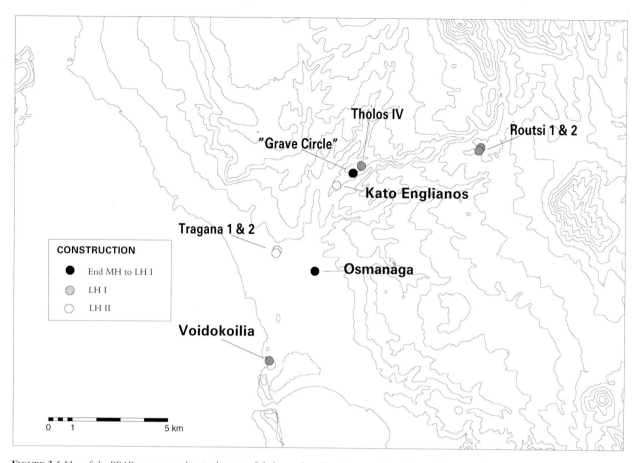

FIGURE 3.6 Map of the PRAP survey area showing location of tholos tombs within the area of the Palace of Nestor and their sequence of construction. The three periods correspond to circa 1700 BC (end of MH–LH I), circa 1600 BC (LH I), and circa 1500 BC (LH II). (Illustration by J. Bennet.)

We might consider the construction of these tombs as marking the landscape under palatial sponsorship and perhaps reflecting the consolidation of palatial control over the whole region by the end of LH II. It is interesting to note that no settlement can clearly be associated with the Voidokoilia tomb that lies on a small headland. It is tempting to imagine that it is a funerary marker sponsored by the palace, marking its effective control of the coastline here. The situation of the tomb is particularly striking: it was constructed in the center of an earlier tumulus belonging to the Middle Helladic period and itself situated over an earlier habitation site (Korres 1990:5–8), enhancing its symbolic significance by laying claim to this earlier marker in the landscape.

It is possible, therefore, to link the construction of tholos tombs as elite funerary structures to the emergence of centers at the Middle Helladic/Late Helladic boundary, but then to see their function changing through time to serve as indicators of integration within the ambit of Pylos. The new LH IIIA2 tholos at Nichoria (McDonald and Wilkie 1992:231–344) in the Further Province would be another example at a

later stage of expansion by Pylos in the wider scale, beyond its immediate region. Almost all tholos tombs in the region of the palace had gone out of use by the beginning of LH IIIB, except for the Kato Englianos tholos—Tholos III—the tomb closest to the palace itself, and perhaps that at Voidokoilia, where LH IIIB material is attested (Lolos 1987:181)—further evidence for the special status of the Voidokoilia tholos.

It seems, however, that the nature of investment in these funerary structures changed with time. Initially, tholos tombs were not only demanding of resources for construction, they also tended to contain objects of great intrinsic and cultural value. They served, in other words, as focal points for elite display to a wider community, perhaps display in support of claims to rule by those members of the elite (Wright 1995a; compare Voutsaki 1995a for a parallel process in the northeast Peloponnese). By the time most tholos tombs had gone out of use in Messenia, those that continued in use had less valuable offerings, perhaps suggesting that they were now more intimately linked to the ruling elite and were not symbols of display to a wider community.

Their value may have lain more in their particular association with the ruling elite, and as affirmation that this association had deep historical roots. Tholos III near the palace, for example, may have been in use for over 200 years by the time of the final palace. The function of elite display at the community level in the later phases, perhaps not before LH IIIB, appears to have been taken over by public festivals involving the consumption of wine and foodstuffs acquired through palatial mobilization (Killen 1984a; Piteros et al. 1990), as evidenced both in ceramic remains from the palace and in iconographic representations in wall paintings within the megaron (McCallum 1987).

Roughly comparable in size to Beylerbey is the site of Ordines (figure 3.7), in the north of the survey region. It is striking that Ordines reaches significant size only in LH III, when our collections suggest an area of 2.1 ha, over half that of Beylerbey in the same period. In earlier periods, however, the site was much smaller—just over half a hectare (0.6 ha) in the Middle Helladic and almost a hectare (0.92 ha) in LH I–II. In this instance, a site appears to have grown within the period of operation of the palace, not a potential rival in the late Middle Helladic that the palace had overtaken. It is probably significant, therefore, that no tholos has been identified in the vicinity of Ordines. Nevertheless, it does stand out as one of the larger sites in the region at the time of the Pylos polity's maximum extent, perhaps the next large site as one traveled north from the palace. Its situation, too, may be significant, because it lies immediately south of a prominent river valley in an otherwise predominantly flat coastal plain. It may have been ideally situated to deal with minor settlements in the coastal lowlands northwest of the palace site.

As a final comparison, I also include information from site I4, Romanou, one of the largest sites defined by PRAP in the region as having a prehistoric component, although its prominence was in the post-prehistoric phases. Because of its size—its total extent was defined at circa 38 ha—we used subdivisions of the original tracts walked as the units of collection, not a standardized grid. Site size estimates are therefore somewhat less precise than those already discussed, and this is reflected in the diagrams, where numbers of artifacts belonging to each particular period rather than densities are noted. Nevertheless, our collections convincingly demonstrate the presence of a number of smaller but significant prehistoric components. Prehistoric material congregates in the west-central area of the site, and the Early Helladic component

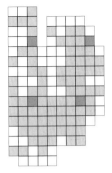 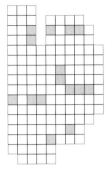

ALL PREHISTORIC PERIODS

MIDDLE HELLADIC

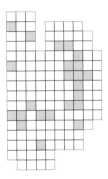 

LATE HELLADIC I TO II

LATE HELLADIC III

FIGURE 3.7 Site of Ordines (PRAP K1) showing relative densities of material for: all prehistoric periods; Middle Helladic (circa 2000–1700 BC); Late Helladic I–II (circa 1700–1400 BC); Late Helladic III (circa 1400–1200 BC). 20 m grid. Levels of shading correspond to sherd densities (1–375, 375–750, 750–1500, and 1500+ per ha). (Illustration by J. Bennet.)

was quite large, perhaps extending over 2.23 ha (figure 3.8). If the size of the settlement was in fact anything like this order of magnitude, it would have been a significant Early Helladic site, larger than any known to date in the area, while its location close to the coast would match those of known Early Helladic sites, such as that on the Voidokoilia headland and PRAP site I20, Nozaina (Davis et al. 1997:417–419). In LH III (figure 3.9), its extent might again have been as large as 2.5 ha, still smaller than its near neighbor Beylerbey, while in Middle Helladic and in LH I–II it was considerably smaller: 0.3 ha and 0.5 ha, respectively.

CONCLUSION

The data presented here represent work in progress in understanding the prehistoric phases of the region PRAP has studied. If we concentrate on the palace and its vicinity, we can demonstrate that the site on the Englianos ridge had reached a considerable size

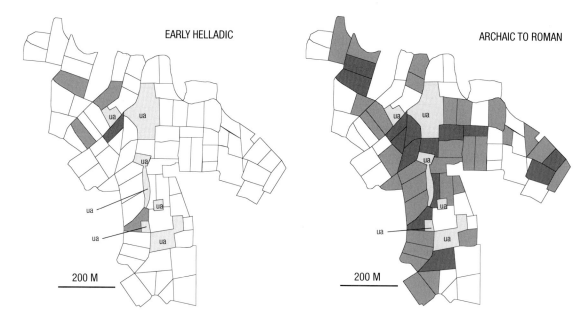

EARLY HELLADIC

ARCHAIC TO ROMAN

200 M

200 M

FIGURE 3.8 The site of Romanou (PRAP I4) showing relative densities of material for: Early Helladic (circa 2500–2000 BC) and Archaic to Roman (circa 700 BC–AD 400). The two levels of shading correspond to artifact counts of 1–10 and 11+ per unit. Areas marked "ua" were not available for investigation. (Illustration by J. Bennet.)

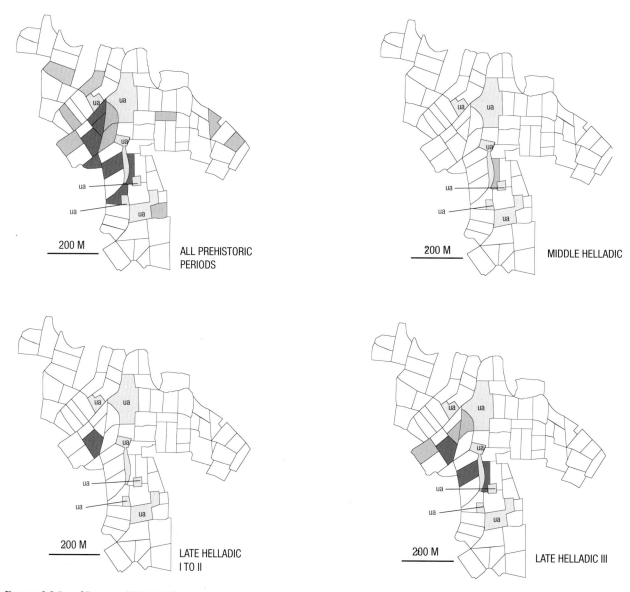

200 M

ALL PREHISTORIC PERIODS

200 M

MIDDLE HELLADIC

200 M

LATE HELLADIC I TO II

200 M

LATE HELLADIC III

FIGURE 3.9 Site of Romanou (PRAP I4) showing relative densities of material for: all prehistoric periods; Middle Helladic (circa 2000–1700 BC); Late Helladic I–II (circa 1700–1400 BC); Late Helladic III (circa 1400–1200 BC). The two levels of shading correspond to artifact counts of 1–10 and 11+ per unit. Areas marked "ua" were not available for investigation. (Illustration by J. Bennet.)

by the end of the Middle Helladic period, rivaled only by Beylerbey to the south. It is surely significant that Beylerbey lay in a zone regarded early in the twentieth century as distinct from that in which the palace lay, namely, the Navarino region or low-lying land around the Bay of Navarino, as opposed to the Kampos, the tableland extending from the Aigaleon ridge, of which the Englianos ridge forms a fingerlike extension running from northeast to southwest. Up to a certain point, therefore, one could imagine the two sites emerging as independent centers. Other sites in the area were, on the basis of size, of minor relevance in the late Middle Helladic period.

By the end of LH II, circa 1500 BC, the palace had probably extended its control over much of its immediate area, as indicated by tholos tombs and strongly suggested by its relative size. We can assume that Beylerbey had become a subordinate site, although probably one of some importance, to judge by its size. Some two hundred to three hundred years later, by the end of LH IIIB, Beylerbey retained its importance and other sites, such as Ordines, had come to prominence (perhaps through direct involvement in palatial economic strategies). Sites like Beylerbey and Ordines are likely to have been the regional centers mentioned in the Linear B documents, sites that participated in and contributed to the Pylian elite's periodic displays of ritual consumption. The process of expansion documented here at the microlevel for the area immediately around the palace site continued both in time (into LH III) and in space (to the north and east), as Pylos rose from a local paramount center to the dominant center in this region of the southwestern Peloponnese. That, however, is another story already told on another occasion (Bennet 1995, 1999a).

Acknowledgments. I would like to thank members of the Minnesota Archaeological Researches in the Western Peloponnese (MARWP) team, directed by Frederick Cooper and Mike Nelson, for assistance in surveying the grids for collections at the Palace of Nestor (B7) and Beylerbey (I1). Completion of the Palace of Nestor grid and surveying grids at other sites were carried out by PRAP personnel, to whom I am also grateful, particularly Sebastian Heath and David Stone. Major funding for PRAP's fieldwork and publication was provided by the National Endowment for the Humanities (grant no. RO-22441-92; RK-20170-95), the National Geographic Society (grant no. 4798-92; 5004-93; 5227-94), and the Institute for Aegean Prehistory. Additional support came from the Universities of Cincinnati, Illinois at Chicago, Michigan, Wisconsin–Madison, and Texas at Austin, as well as from private donors.

For comments and discussion on and relating to this contribution, I am grateful to Jack Davis, Paul Halstead, and Cynthia Shelmerdine. For study of the material on which many of the conclusions are based, I am grateful to PRAP's prehistoric ceramics team: Cynthia Shelmerdine, Sharon R. Stocker, and Yannos Lolos. Needless to say, none of the above can be held responsible for the use to which I have put their advice.

CHAPTER 4

ADMINISTRATION IN THE MYCENAEAN PALACES

WHERE'S THE CHIEF?

⌐⌐⌐⌐⌐⌐⌐

CYNTHIA W. SHELMERDINE

IN THE THIRTEENTH CENTURY BC, the king of Pylos controlled most of the modern province of Messenia, some 2000 km² (see figure 3.1). A simple and probably true statement, but what does it mean? What kind and degree of authority did a Mycenaean king have? What were his duties and responsibilities? In what sense did territorial control rest in his hands, and what was the nature of that control? These questions are the starting point of this chapter, and I must admit at the outset that Mycenaean scholars have no complete and universally accepted answers to any of them.

From the Linear B tablets at palatial centers, especially the large archive at Pylos, we know that the king was the highest ranking member of a ranked society in each kingdom. This is particularly clear from Pylian landholding documents, where he holds a plot three times as big (or productive) as that of other officials. The occupational term for this supreme political official is wanax. In later Greek, including Homeric epic, this word means lord or master. The easy assumption that Mycenaean kings were, however, just like Homeric kings, so attractive to the generation of Heinrich Schliemann, is now seen to be as inadequate as the old Indo-European model of kingship. There is another potential external source of information: references to the Mycenaeans in contemporary documents of other cultures with whom they were in contact. For example,

a Hittite king wrote to the king of Ahhijawa as an equal, and some believe that "Ahhijawa" refers to a Mycenaean state. The identification is not proven, however, and I will not attempt to cover this complicated issue here. Instead, I will stick to our most direct and reliable sources of information: the Linear B tablets, however elliptical their references, and archaeological data, from which occasional help can be extracted.

Each major Mycenaean center contains a monumental building organized around a standard central core, the megaron (see figure 1.2). The large megaron itself, with its central hearth and columns supporting a second-story balcony (figure 4.1; see also figure 1.2) seems to be a formal audience hall. A cutting in the floor, half-way along the right-hand wall as one enters, is preserved at Pylos and Tiryns. The chair that occupied this spot is the focal point of painted decoration on both the floor and, at least at Pylos, where preservation is better, the wall. Flanking lions and griffins make an appropriate setting for a king's throne (figure 4.1).

The seat may not, however, have been intended for a king but for a high religious official. For example, Rehak (1995:109–112) argues from iconographic associations of seated figures and griffins that the "throne" was in fact the seat of a priestess or queen, not a king. There is sufficient evidence, however, to suggest that the king was himself a high religious official. This

FIGURE 4.1 Reconstructed view of the throne room at Pylos. The throne is flanked by lions and griffins. (Drawing by Piet de Jong Courtesy of the Department of Classics, University of Cincinnati.)

evidence is not artistic; one of the great anomalies of the second millennium BC is that this Mediterranean culture has no ruler iconography whatsoever. Rather, we must turn to the written records of the Mycenaean palatial centers, the Linear B tablets.

The scope of these documents is limited to economic administration.[1] This means we never see the king functioning as a military leader, a lawgiver, or an international statesman. Even within the administrative sphere, references to the wanax are extremely limited. The noun and its related adjective appear just thirty-two times in the whole Linear B corpus of about five thousand tablets, and only two texts show the king actually doing anything. Pylos tablet (PY) *Ta 711.1* refers to an occasion "when the king appointed Augewas to the position of *damokoro*," probably a provincial official, perhaps a governor (Carlier 1984:98-99). PY *Un 2* is one of several texts now recognized as lists of supplies for a ceremonial banquet, including barley, cyperus, honey, figs, olives, animals of several kinds, wine, and cloth. The heading reveals the kind of occasion that would prompt such a feast. It refers to a special ceremony at *pa-ki-ja-na*, an important Pylian

sanctuary. The king either undergoes or presides over this ceremony; the most plausible translation is "upon the initiation of the king" (Aura Jorro 1985:80–81 s.v. *a-pi-e-ke*, 459–460 s.v. *mu-jo-me-no*; Carlier 1984:91–94; Killen 1994:72; Ventris and Chadwick 1973:440–441, 562). In addition, a tablet fragment recently found by Fred Cooper in Blegen's excavation dump at Pylos joins with another existing, yet fragmentary, *Un* tablet. These joined tablet fragments form another such banquet list. The Pylos textual evidence for feasts thus links them both to the king and to religion.

Archaeological evidence suggestive of communal feasts also comes from religious contexts. It may be only a question of terminology whether one views animal bones in ash layers and kylikes (stemmed, handled wine cups) in cult settings, as evidence for sacrifice and libations or for ritual meals (Bergquist 1988). Two instances in particular suggest the latter. One example comes from LH IIIC levels of the Tiryns Lower Citadel, where animal bones were found in the courtyard outside the cult building (see Kilian 1981), characterized by Kilian (1988b:148) as "bone waste from meals" (see also Albers 1994:106–110, 132–134). Another is an early LH IIIA2 deposit of figurines, kylikes, bowls, and animal bones at Tsoungiza: here the discard pattern of the bones is consistent with feasting (Wright 1994:69).

An illustration of just such a ceremonial feast appears on the northeast wall of the Pylos megaron, behind the throne (figure 4.2). It is the culmination of a procession of men and women with a bull in Vestibule 5 (Lang 1969:38–40,192–193, see reconstruction plate 119). At the right end of the megaron wall the famous bard with a lyre entertains at least two pairs of men seated at tables, while nearer the throne is a bull either standing or, in a more recent reconstruction, recumbent and actually trussed for sacrifice (McCallum 1987:68–141; see figure 4.2), though only the bull's shoulder actually survives (Lang 1969:109–110, no. 19 C 6, plates 53, 125). That the fresco decorated the megaron is no guarantee that the ceremony took place in this room. The cumulative testimony of this painting, the miniature kylikes and an offering table near the hearth, and a libation channel beside the throne cutting, however, strongly supports the view that the megaron was a locus of ritual activity (see chapter 8, this volume; Hägg

1995:389–390; Hiller 1981:117–119; Kilian 1992:17). The archaeological picture thus reinforces the textual evidence, which suggests that the king himself presided over this kind of event.

It seems clear, then, that the king had a paramount role in religious affairs and that ceremonial banquets may have been one way for him to display and reinforce his authority. We cannot tell, however, whether his subjects regarded him as a priest, an intercessor between them and their gods, or as a divine king. The last possibility is the least likely, and as far as I know has no champions among Mycenaean scholars. Some Pylos texts do show the wanax receiving offerings, and a few also list the goddess Potnia as a recipient. These have not led to the assumption that the king himself is divine, but they have been used to argue that the word wanax may refer to a divine being as well as to a human lord. Opinion is divided, and since such tablets include both clearly human and clearly divine recipients, the evidence is ambiguous at best.

In the secular sphere, evidence for the king's role in administration is more indirect. It is clear from the

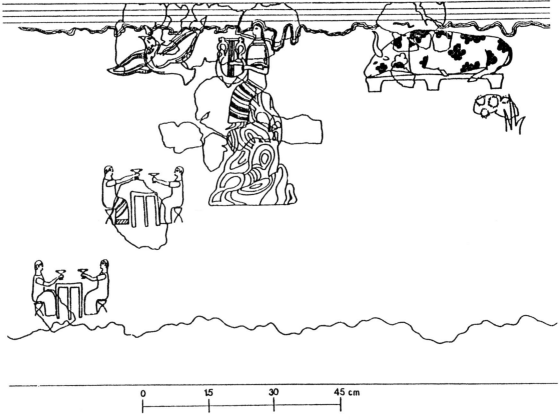

0   15   30   45 cm

FIGURE 4.2 Iconographic representation of ritualized drinking (so-called toasting ceremony) with kylikes, as reconstructed by McCallum (1987:68–141). From a fresco recovered in the throne room at the palace at Ano Englianos. Note also the trussed sacrificial bull and the lyre-playing bard. The toasting with kylikes in this fresco was entirely restored by McCallum based on other known parallels. Drawing by L. McCallum.

Pylos records that the palace collected taxes in the form of six different commodities from the districts of the kingdom. Palace officials oversaw land tenure and personnel management and organized at least some agricultural and industrial production. Debate is ongoing about the degree to which control of agriculture and industries in the Mycenaean world was centralized. A persuasive case can be made that not all operations within a state were directed by officials at the center (see chapters 1 and 2, this volume). One difficulty with our sources is that the Linear B tablets are exclusively concerned with topics of interest to the central bureaucracy, and so references to activities outside this official sphere are rare and incidental. This is a likely reason why pottery production receives no attention, though a potter does figure in the records (see below; see also chapter 8, this volume). Nevertheless, the archaeological record, as well as some indirect textual evidence, allows us to talk about nonpalatial as well as palatial economy.

As Halstead (1992b) has observed, the archaeological record reveals a much wider range of crops than the barley and one type of wheat that figure in the tablets. Thus the center did not control all agricultural production, though it took a direct interest in certain foodstuffs, such as wine, olives, and some wheat (Halstead 1992a:esp. 60–61, 64, 1992b). Similarly, the tablets differentiate between homespun cloth (designated by ideogram *146) and fine linen cloth. The former is of interest in that it is one of the commodities contributed as taxes by the sixteen districts of the Pylian state, whereas the manufacture of fine linen is a palatial industry controlled, staffed, and monitored by the central administration.

A related question is where the activities that *were* centrally organized took place. The textile industry illustrates well the various possible arrangements. In Mycenaean Crete this industry is pretty well decentralized: that is, the records were kept at Knossos, but they referred to activity at workshops, some of them quite large (for example, a minimum of seventy-four adults worked at the important subordinate center of Setoija), in a number of other places in central and western Crete (Killen 1984b:54). Even "finishers," those in charge of the final decoration of woven cloth, were located away from the center.

At Pylos textile manufacture is much more centralized, again in terms of the location of workers. It is clear from the *Aa*, *Ab*, and *Ad* personnel records that Pylian linen workers were concentrated in several groups. The largest of these were at Pylos, and at Leuktron, the putative capital of the Further province (see chapter 3, this volume). As Killen notes (1984b:55–59), the more specialized aspects of the industry in particular tended to be concentrated at the center. Even so, other groups of linen workers were stationed at subordinate centers; the two at Rouso were exceptionally large, and one of them was quite specialized. Furthermore, all these workers, whether physically at Pylos or not, were fully dependent on the palace for their support: the *Ab* series records the allocation to all the groups of monthly rations for them and their children. Even though industrial activity was centralized at the time of the tablets, such centralization may not have been the norm throughout LH IIIB. The large Northeast Workshop at Pylos, for example, dates to the latest stage of the Mycenaean settlement (see figure 1.2). This raises the possibility that late in LH IIIB, some activities were moved closer to the center than they had been before.

Evidence from Mycenae and Thebes also indicates that some industrial activity directed by these centers was actually conducted elsewhere. At each site a building has been found which served as a clearing house for a textile industry. The building where the Theban wool tablets were found was identified by its excavator, Theodore Spyropoulos, as a workshop where wool was stored, weighed, and spun. No spindle whorls were, however, recovered from the building, apart from one doubtful example. On the contrary, the *Of* tablets found here record amounts of wool being disbursed to workers elsewhere, once specifically to a spinner. The places mentioned include an Amarynthos (*Of 25*), which may be the site of that name on Euboea. This possibility is strengthened by the appearance of another Euboean toponym and the recurrence of this one on the Thebes sealings *Wu 55.β* (the toponym Karystos) and *Wu 58.γ* (the toponym Amarynthos). Thus the building seems to have served as a clearing house for wool sent in to the center and subsequently disbursed to workers elsewhere. At Mycenae, the House of the Oil Merchant seems to have had a similar function. Again, the records of disbursements are preserved, as are records allocating oil to the workers.

The textile industry is just one example of how the palace organized and monitored its dependent craftsmen. Pylian bronzesmiths, too, were located at a number of different sites throughout the state, while at the center records were kept of bronze allocated to them for working and rations for their support. The raw materials doled out to craftsmen—notably textile workers, smiths, and perfumers—are referred to as *talasia* (that is, an amount weighed out and allocated for processing; see chapter 2, this volume, regarding the *talasia* system). In Classical Greek, *talasia* is used only in connection with wool working, but in Mycenaean times it seems to have been the standard system within which palatial industries operated, though there are hints of some craftsmen working more independently, with the palace as a client.

As with agricultural goods, some industrial production likely existed in Mycenaean Greece that was not controlled, or not completely controlled, by the center (as argued in several chapters in this volume). It is not the location of the work that tells us this but the absence of that work from the records kept by the central administration. Even when no mention is made in the extant tablets of a particular activity, such as obsidian working, the nature of our sample could be misleading (see chapters 9 and 10, this volume). Tablets from a single year, not all of those preserved, perhaps favoring one or another season, are not a complete checklist of all the interests a palace may have had.

There are a number of references to craftsmen in fields for which we lack tablets concerned with the actual work of the industry. Where is the allocation of blue glass paste to the *kuanoworgoi* (blue glass paste workers) at Mycenae? This lacuna could be blamed on the sparse preservation of tablets from that site, but what of the leathermen, the bakers, or the mysterious *etoworgoi* at Pylos, who receive rations? Gold is requisitioned on tablet *Jo 438*, and gold workers are stationed at the site of *anuwa*, though no records of gold working survive. A famous example of a lacuna is the craft of pottery manufacture. The ground floor of the palace at Pylos is largely given over to storage in late LH IIIB; pantries are littered with the remains of crockery, 2853 kylikes in room 19 alone (Blegen and Rawson 1966:125; see chapter 8, this volume). Yet the tablets ignore pottery production, except for the mention of two potters in nonoccupational contexts. One of these is described as *wanakteros* (royal). This designation allows me to bring together the two threads of this chapter, the king and the administration, and to finish by considering what role the former played in the latter.

The adjective "wanakteros" in the extant records is applied to some textiles at Knossos (such as textiles "of the king" on PY *La 622*), and it describes a limited number of personnel at several sites. Knossian workers who specialize in royal textiles are mentioned on tablet *Le 654.4*, and a reference to royal purple dyers on Knossos tablet (KN) *X 976* [+] *V 961* may also be textile related. Likewise at Thebes a textile finisher or finishers (*asketriai*) may be called royal: on tablet *Of 36.1* the phrase *a-ke-ti-ra₂, wa-na-ka[-te-ra* is restored (Spyropoulos and Chadwick 1975:106).

As a description of goods and those who make them, "royal" is parallel to several others. Perfumed oil at Pylos and some textiles at Knossos are called *ksenwia/o* (for guests): the reference is either to the specific destination of the cloth or, more probably, to a type or quality suitable for guests. Other textiles (at Knossos) and wheels (at Pylos) are *eqesijo, heqwesian* (for or suitable for the elite functionaries known as *heqwetai* [followers, as in followers of the king]). At Pylos a wheelwright (tablet *Ea 421, 809*) and a group called *maratewe* (tablet *Na 245*) are associated with the *lawagetas* (the second-ranking state official); so are men named *Kuro₂, Rukoro*, and perhaps *Eumenes* (in the *Ea* series of tablets). The latter two names recur as craftsmen: *Eumenes* is a bronzesmith (tablet *Jn 725*) and *Rukoro* is assigned to the Northeast Workshop (tablet *An 1281*). In fact, of ten other men associated with him on *An 1281*, five are bronzesmiths.

Even more interesting is the association of other workers with divinities. For instance, along with the probable royal finisher(s) on Thebes tablet *Of 36* there appears another (or others) assigned to the house of the goddess Potnia. At Pylos, a perfumer and several bronzesmiths are described as Potnian, as is a man named Werajo (tablets *Eb 364/Ep 613*). The role of the religious sphere in craft activities is an interesting problem now being investigated by Susan Lupack (see chapter 6, this volume). For our purposes, it is enough to note that workers can be characterized by their association either with certain divinities or with state officials.

All the references just mentioned are in occupational contexts; they distinguish one group of workers from others. Thus Potnian smiths at Pylos appear alongside "regular" groups of smiths, while at Thebes a royal and a Potnian worker (or worker group) are distinguished. What do such designations mean, and specifically, why are some few individuals and textiles singled out as royal? On the analogy of other such designations, they made commodities either for the king or of a high quality or type somehow associated with him. This means that these workers served the king's personal requirements (Carlier 1984:72; Palaima 1997) or, more plausibly, that their duties were directly connected with his (Palaima 1997). That they were a privileged minority, at least at Pylos, is clear from a further three examples not so far mentioned.

Only three royal workers are specified at Pylos, none in an occupational context. Atuko the *etedomo* (armorer?), Pekita the fuller, and Brithawon the potter figure among the privileged holders of *kitimena* (private) land plots at the sanctuary of Pakijana; the other holders are religious personnel (contra Carlier [1984:68–69], it is unlikely that Atuko is the same man as Atuko the *ktoinokhos* on tablet *Ep 301.5*). In the case of the fuller and potter, it has been specifically argued that they supply garments and vessels that the king would use or distribute on ceremonial or ritual occasions (see chapter 8, this volume). Garments and vessels are both said to figure in the ritual iconography of the Pylos megaron frescoes (Palaima 1995:132–134, plate 41), and the numerous kylikes found in the pantries could have been for ritual banquets at which the king presided (see again chapter 8, this volume). The frescoes do not, on the other hand, seem to me to provide much support for the ritual prominence of textiles, though there are in fact arguments to support this. One is the notation on PY *Fr 1225* of perfumed (or otherwise treated) oil going to the goddess *upojo* Potnia "as ointment for cloths." Another is *lekhestroterion* (a month-name) on PY *Fr 343*. In addition, cloth designated by the ideogram **146* is included among the banquet supplies on tablet *Un 2*, but this textile, identified by Killen (1984b:62) as a plain, homespun cloth, comes into the palace as taxes, and is not made by the state-controlled industry.

Nor do I think the duties of a royal craftsman were necessarily confined to the ritual functions of the king. The royal armorer Atuko does not fit easily into this context. But he may support the notion that "royal" signifies a link to the particular concerns of the king, just as "lawagesian" may have been associated with the concerns of the *lawagetas* and Potnian ones with the concerns of religious establishments. The name Atuko is found on three bronze tablets (PY *Jn 658/725* and *927*). And a recently published sealing from Pylos, *Wr 1480*, carries the notation "javelin handles" along with the syllable "wa," conventionally an abbreviation for wanax. So one can argue that the king had a particular interest in certain arms and armor, as well as certain textiles (compare Knossos tablets *Vc 73*, *Vd 136*?; see Palaima 1997). The designation "royal" does not accompany Atuko on the bronze tablets, though, or on tablet PY *Ep 301* where he holds a plot of *kekemena* (publicly held) land from the *damos* (community). The adjective only occurs with this name on the *En/Eo*

landholding documents, the (only) context where the other two royal craftsmen also appear. The adjective there must thus be part of their credentials, as it were, to justify their inclusion in a rather exclusive company of religious personnel. Presumably they held their plots of land by virtue of their royal service. Even though the adjective is not relevant outside this context, however, royal workers may not be such a rarity as it appears at first. The reference to textiles "of the king" on PY *La 622*, and the analogy of other designations and royal workers at other sites, suggest that at Pylos, too, there were very likely other craftsmen who worked on the king's business, however narrowly or broadly defined.

Throughout, one gets no sense that the king was intimately involved in the details of this business, in contrast to the Hittite or Old Babylonian rulers. The royal work and workers are monitored in the ordinary way, along with everyone else. Why then use the distinction at all? The association is not only with the royal interest in the products of these workers but, in the landholding texts, with the privilege that royal authority can guarantee. The king, furthermore, seems to be just one of three sources of authority and administrative control in the Mycenaean state, along with the religious sphere and the *damos*. This word *damos* continues in use in Classical Greece and refers to the land held by a community or its body politic as a governmental entity.

There are crucial problems concerning which authority outranked which in Mycenaean times, and how much overlap there was among the three. Here I simply want to articulate their existence, and to stress that the palace is not synonymous with the king in administrative matters. We have already seen the pairing of the royal and the religious spheres in the opposition of divine and royal craftsmen. The king is also paired with or contrasted to deities as a recipient of offerings, for example of perfumed oil. This has led some to suppose that the term wanax could refer to a god as well as to the human king. I have never seen any need for this inference. Though most of the perfume allocations are religious, some also go to servants as well as to the king, just as there are lawagesian as well as royal and divine workers.

The third body with administrative authority is the damos, generally interpreted as a community authority that has land and the power to grant it (Pylos tablets *Ea*, *Eb/Ep*). Its level is usually deemed to be subordinate to that of the state, but there are signs that it is no minor village body. As already noted, the king of Pylos appoints a *damokoro* (mayor) on tablet *Ta 711*.

Carlier (1984: 98–99) has argued that this is the chief official of one of the two provinces into which the state is divided. His view is reasonably based on tablet PY *On 300*, where the title appears after a list of Hither province governors and before a Further province list. Was the damos then a political entity left over from a time before the center ruled Messenia so completely? On PY *Un 718* this body is a donor of offerings to Poseidon, along with three others: the lawagetas, an individual who may be equated with the king, and a lesser group. The authority of the damos is most visible, though, in the PY *Ep* records, where it allocates plots of land. Indeed, it is a dispute between the damos and the religious sphere that gives us our longest extant sentence in Mycenaean Greek (see also chapter 6, this volume). The dispute on tablet *Ep 704* concerns a priestess called Eritha (lines .3, .5–.6). She has one small land share in line .3. That in lines .5–.6 is much larger; she claims it has a special status because it is "for the god," but the damos, unimpressed, says it is a perfectly ordinary holding. The reason this matters is clear from the entry in line .7. In return for the benefits they derive from this land, the shareholders are obligated to work it for the damos. The damos complains in line .7 that Karpathia the "key-bearer" (perhaps a religious title) has such a share and, being obligated to work it, she does not do so. The authority of the damos here is at least equal to that of the priestess, and indeed it may have the power to rule against her. She is said to "claim" (*euketo*) the special status of her land, while the verb *pasi* (assert) is used of the damos. Either way, the damos and the religious sphere are here opposed, just as the king and the religious sphere are elsewhere. To complete the circle, the royal armorer holds some land by virtue of that position, and some more from the damos. Each of

the three types of authority has therefore some autonomous power.

To sum up, then, we are left with a king whose ceremonial/ritual role is clearer than his administrative one. People assigned to his work are distinguished from other categories of craftsmen, and three of them—potter, fuller, and armorer—are specially rewarded with land. Yet the king is not the only person with the power to have workers, grant land, or even receive offerings. In each area he has human as well as divine colleagues. The best argument for his supreme status is his title; with the word wanax we can begin to answer the question, where's the chief? We still do not know very much about *who* he is or *what* he does.

NOTES

1. Editors' note: Excerpts from Linear B tablets are often prefixed by an abbreviation indicating origin: PY = Pylos, KN = Knossos, MY = Mycenae, TH = Thebes. Linear B specialists group tablets primarily by topic, and each series is designated by a letter or letters indicating topic and form of tablet. For example, the *Jn* series of tablets pertain to bronze working. Individual tablets have unique numbers within each site. Linear B scribes also employed logograms standing for individual commodities, which are given either a three-letter Latin abbreviation (*VIN* = vinum = wine) or (where their reference is as yet undetermined) a number; they are prefixed by an asterisk, thus: *OLE, or *146. Linear B documents record an archaic form of Greek, and the writing system is syllabic. Individual Linear B signs thus denote the various syllables that compose Mycenaean Greek. For example, the three signs *wa-na-ka* indicate Greek wanax. See Hooker (1980) or Ventris and Chadwick (1973) for an introduction to Linear B.

CHAPTER 5

MYCENAEAN POLITIES

STATES OR ESTATES?

𐆊𐆊𐆊𐆊𐆊𐆊𐆊

DAVID B. SMALL

I CONSIDER MYSELF TO BE a specialist not in Late
Bronze Age Greek civilizations but in the evolution and structure of archaic polities, a definition
that fits well the mainland Mycenaean systems. My
contribution to this volume, therefore, stems from
the application of observations I have made of small
states in other times and cultures. Specifically, I want
to discuss how results from rank-size analysis of the
Pylian settlement system and comparative research
into regional collapse affect our understanding of the
Mycenaean state. These two approaches have yet to
be applied fully to the Mycenaean case. The results
of their application cogently indicate that we need to
rethink some of the underlying assumptions that have
for many years governed investigations into mainland
Mycenaean polities.

I should note at the outset that I have decided to
remove from consideration the Mycenaean presence
at Knossos (see figure 1.1). Although I do not doubt
that mainland Greeks occupied the political center of
Knossos during Mycenaean times, Crete has a long history of prior political development that makes analysis of
Mycenaean control very complex (see chapters 1 and 16,
this volume). The mainland situation is much more easily
investigated, given that the Mycenaean palaces were the
first polities of their kind to appear in the region.

Our understanding of the Mycenaean polities has
improved since the initial days, when Pylos and other

Late Bronze Age Greek centers were simply equated,
à la Finley (1957), with those of archaic Near Eastern
states—an equation that had more to do with the
discovery of tablets at sites from both cultures than
with concrete structural similarities (but see Killen
1985). Our concept of the economic underpinning of
Mycenaean polities, while still sketchy, is probably the
most developed. In my view, the best is that of Halstead,
who recreates a system with two distinct economic
spheres, one under direct control of the palace and one,
a nonpalatial sector, outside the confines of the palace's
lands (1992a; see also chapter 7, this volume). In piecing
together both the documentary and archaeological data
and incorporating cross-cultural analogies, Halstead
argues that the palatial sector of the economy had direct
control over the production of wool, wheat, olives, figs,
and grapes from estate lands. These estate-produced
staples were used as rations to support people working
within *ta-ra-si-ja* workshops, which produced specialized craft goods that were exported to parts of the polity
itself as well as to different parts of the Mediterranean.
The nonpalatial sector of the Mycenaean polity was tied
to the palatial sector in that it would, at times, receive
subsistence relief in the form of staple items produced
on estate lands and allocations of land in return for
services provided to the palace. Perhaps the most
important tie between the palace and the nonpalatial

sector was the system of assessment or taxation of nonstaple items such as wood, olive oil, honey, spices, and so on, which were used to supply the *ta-ra-si-ja* workshops.

This system of taxation, which appears in different forms on the Linear B documents, has supplied the primary foundation for reconstructing the political and administrative contexts of the Mycenaean state. Not only have scholars focused on requisitioned materials, they have also attempted to reconstruct the administrative and evolutionary character of the Mycenaean polity by analyzing the documentation of this extension of the palace into the nonpalatial sector of the polity. More notable examples of these reconstructions have been Wyatt's (1962) and Chadwick's (1972) recreation of the provincial districts of the Pylian polity, Shelmerdine's (1973) and Carothers's (1992) reconstruction of taxation districts, Morris's (1986) tribute/prestige goods state, Cherry's (1977) and Kilian's (1988a) attempts to reconstruct an administrative hierarchy, and Bennet's (1995) modeling of the evolutionary development of the Pylian state.

These attempts represent the best of scholarship on Mycenaean political structure, but I would argue that they are problematic in that they carry a false assumption, namely, that the Mycenaean polity resembled other archaic states in the degree of control and oversight of its territory. Rather than a polity with a developed administrative structure that became articulated with the secondary administrative centers in its territories (as seen in numerous examples of archaic state formation— that of the Inca, Aztec, and later Zapotec [Oaxaca], to name just a few), territorial control of the Mycenaean polities remained centralized, barely moving beyond the palatial centers. I argue that in reconstructing the Mycenaean polities—at least at Pylos, where we do have the greatest documentation—it would be best to begin with a more minimalist concept of the polity as an exploded estate, an estate that, because it had become part of larger economic network, was extending its influence beyond lands under its direct control. The nature of this extension was basically limited to supplying necessary goods to attached workshops.

RANK-SIZE CONSIDERATIONS

One of the most important pieces of my argument comes from settlement analysis (for Messenia, see Carothers 1992; Carothers and McDonald 1979;

McDonald and Rapp 1972). The approach I employ here is that of rank-size analysis, which has been applied only once, by Ian Hodder (1977), to the Pylian material. Hodder's analysis, however, was surprisingly shallow. Having run the data through a rank-size filter, he attempted to show that there were different identifiable steps in the rank-size curve and that these steps would correspond to different levels of administrative control. In truth, his steps are clusters of settlements that are so small that one wonders whether or not they could have functioned as administrative centers.

Rank-size analysis measures the degree to which a region has become economically integrated by graphing the distribution of differentially sized settlements. Zipf (1941, 1949; also Johnson 1980, 1981) first noticed that in a well-integrated region, the rank of a settlement with relation to its size, when multiplied, produces a constant equal to the size of the chief settlement in the region. Regional economic integration is the product of formalized institutional mechanisms. These may be institutionalized markets as well as political and economic administrative systems incorporating primary and secondary regional centers. Two major deviations from a normal log falloff are *convex* and *primate*. Convex distributions indicate a very low degree of hierarchical integration between sites. This type of distribution has been charted in colonial North America, where the different colonies stood as independent polities, and early Aztec-period Mexico, when the Basin of Mexico was occupied by several competing city-states. Primate distributions are somewhat different from convex; in a primate distribution, the leading settlement is much larger than the other sites in its territory. Reasons for this distribution vary (Blanton 1976; Kowalewski 1982), but center around two causes, examined in detail below.

When I took both the information from the earlier Messenia project (the University of Minnesota Messenia Expedition; see McDonald and Rapp 1972) and the results from the latest work of the Pylos Regional Archaeological Project (PRAP; see chapter 3, this volume; Davis 1998; Davis et al. 1997; Zangger et al. 1997), and analyzed them according to rank-size scaling, the result was a definite primate distribution. At approximately 21 ha the community of Pylos itself stands in relative isolation from all other settlements in its territory (figure 5.1).

What is going on? Comparative examples may help to understand the combination of factors working at Pylos. A first example from Oaxaca indicates that a

Rank-size relationship

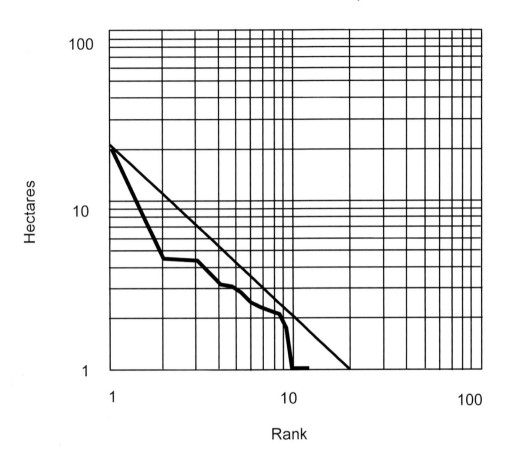

FIGURE 5.1 Rank-size analysis of southwestern Messenia during the Late Bronze Age.

settlement will become much larger than others in its territory (primate) because it is responding to forces operating on a larger regional scale. Monte Albán, founded around 500 BC, was the result of a synoikism of several communities in the Valley of Oaxaca (Blanton et al. 1993; Flannery and Marcus 1996). In comparison with other early settlements in the valley, Monte Albán was very large. As argued by archaeologists working in the Valley of Oaxaca, one of the primary purposes for which a new capital might be established was the promotion and protection of the larger Valley of Oaxaca in response to outside threats. To some degree, then, Monte Albán was much larger because it was responding to demands on a larger, pan-Mexican scale rather than to more local needs.

Although I do not think a case can be made for Mycenaean polities being the result of synoikism, as with Monte Albán in the Valley of Oaxaca, they were actively operating on a much larger scale. Mycenaean

centers, such as Pylos, were actively engaged in the economic and political dimensions of the larger Mediterranean world, including Crete, Asia Minor, the Near East, and parts of the western Mediterranean (Wright 1995a). Thus their size in relation to that of other settlements is probably due in some measure to their participation in affairs outside Greece proper.

Our second example again comes from Oaxaca, for the presence of a primate center can be the result of several factors. The issue here is simply time lag: the foundation of the center of Monte Albán was not followed by any immediate move toward economic and administrative integration of the valley. Indeed, until Monte Albán IIIA (AD 300–500), when the rank-size distributional pattern was reaching a log normal falloff, there was little evidence for administrative activity in the settlements outside Monte Albán, and even less evidence for any type of economic integration, even though the center must have been extracting some regional resources. During this time, Monte Albán's oversight of its territory was based on a centralization of functions rather than on regional dispersal and integration. A classic example of this relationship again comes from Mesoamerica: Teotihuacán in its Tzacualli phase (AD 1–100), a giant of a city in comparison with its outlying communities (Blanton et al. 1993). In the case of Teotihuacán, the city itself captured most of the region's political and economic systems, as well as what was probably a major share of the region's population. Unlike in previous phases of occupation in the Basin of Mexico, the region during the Tzacualli phase was populated by small settlements, with very little indication that any were administrative subcenters, and little or no evidence for specialized production. These features—administration and specialization—had been adsorbed by the capital itself, with its monumental political and religious architecture, a massive market, and economically specialized house compounds. This second factor, centralization of regional functions, was also operating at Pylos, as may be demonstrated by an examination of the collapse of the Mycenaean polities.

A LOOK AT COLLAPSE

The study of the collapse of past civilizations has been directed mainly toward an understanding of the why of the collapse (e.g., Renfrew 1978; Tainter 1988; Yoffee and Cowgill 1988) rather than a reading of the archaeological record to determine the structure of the economic and administrative systems at the time of the fall (but see Marcus 1989). Although little work has been done to determine the nature of certain cultural systems at the time of their collapse, it appears safe to make some general observations. When polities with administrative systems that have achieved an established measure of regional, distributed integration in secondary and lower regional centers collapse, the structure of their regional administrative system survives the fall, at least to some extent. Such was the case with the administrative structure of the Roman Empire. After the collapse of the central authority at Rome, provincial administrative systems in the western provinces continued to operate, although now headed by non-Roman peoples. Examples more applicable to the Mycenaean case can again be provided by a consideration of archaic state collapse in Mesoamerica, as in the Valley of Oaxaca and the Basin of Mexico. I do not here consider the collapse of lowland and southern

highland Maya polities, because these polities managed little regional administrative integration. A hallmark of even the most expansive of these centers, such as Tikal, is their lack of a formalized system of administration, relying instead, I would argue, on direct control of defeated ruling elites (see Freidel 1981).

In Mesoamerica, as with the Roman Empire, the civic (as seen in the repetition of public architecture) and administrative (as seen in settlement hierarchies) institutions of Monte Albán were perpetuated during Monte Albán IV, the period following its collapse, and used in various ways by the several competing small states that occupied the valley (see Blanton 1978; Blanton et al. 1982; Winter 1989). The same scenario is evident at Teotihuacán in the Basin of Mexico following collapse, where state-level institutions, perhaps even the characteristic form of militarism developed at Teotihuacán, continued in use at the various city-states that now occupied the territory (Hirth 1989; Nagao 1989). Marcus (1989) has presented a very interesting and relevant argument with regard to the continuation of institutions of the Classic period into the epi-Classic. She suggests that many of the institutions of the small city-states that represent the epi-Classic might well have been embedded in the secondary centers of the Classic.

I should point out that study of the so-called collapse of large centers in Mesoamerica, such as Monte Albán and especially Teotihuacán, is much more problematic than I have indicated here. There are difficulties, for example, in cross-dating sites and interpreting the decline of Teotihuacán (see Diehl and Berlo 1989).

What was left of the Mycenaean polities after their fall? Very little. Archaeological investigation has shown that in Messenia, at least, and probably elsewhere, there was a significant collapse, with cessation of monumental construction, a drastic reduction in settlements, and a possible migration of population to a few isolated centers, such as Athens. Written documentation supplies additional matching information. Writing disappeared after the collapse of the palaces and was not introduced again into Greece until the eighth century BC. Even given this lacuna, we can, however, compare the written documents from the Mycenaean period (the Linear B tablets) with the Homeric epics to determine what, if any, of the administrative system of the Mycenaean polities continued into later-period Greece.

The oral epics—those attributed in written form to Homer—supply us with descriptions of society in the eighth century and perhaps a little earlier. What information do these documents supply that can help us to determine the extent to which institutions in the Greek Late Bronze Age continued into later periods? One approach is to match titles in the epics to those that appear as administrative titles in the Linear B texts. The Linear B texts give us several titles that appear to have had some sort of administrative connection (see chapter 4, this volume):

> *wa-na-ka*, or chief official;
> *ra-wa-ke-ta*, perhaps second in command;
> *e-qe-ta*, of which thirteen are mentioned at Pylos, possible representatives of the center out in the territories;
> *da-mo-ko-ro*, some kind of provincial functionary;
> *du-ma-te*, who was perhaps similar in function to the *da-mo-ko-ro*;
> *po-ro-du-ma-te*, again perhaps the same in function;
> *mo-ro-qa*, another possible provincial functionary;
> *qa-si-re-u*, possible provincial supervisors;
> *ko-re-te-re*, some type of official; and
> *po-ro-ko-re-te*, also some type of official.

These last two titles are connected with palace assessment units, and the *ko-re-te-re* and *po-ro-ko-re-te* probably collected nonstaple goods from areas outside the palatial lands.

When we pick up the documentary thread again in the Homeric epics, most of these terms have disappeared from Greek (Palaima 1995). Only *wa-na-ka*, the Homeric wanax (lord, master), *ra-wa-ke-ta*, which might be the *lawagetas* (second in command), "leader of the host" of Homeric composition, *e-qe-ta*, which might be the Homeric *epetas* (followers), and *qa-si-re-u*, probably basileus (prince), survived. Except for the *qa-si-re-u*, these titles represent officials who were closely connected with oversight of palace-centered affairs. Almost all the officials with duties outside the palace lands have been lost. Their positions and functions in the Mycenaean polities were not formalized enough for transmission to the eighth century. The one exception to this is the *qa-si-re-u*, who, in the Linear B documents, appears to have been located out in the territories. Etymological analysis (Palaima 1995) can perhaps explain this retention. *Qa-si-re-u* is a non-Indo-European title and most likely represented local leaders, those who held power before the rise of the Mycenaeans. Their power base must have been locally entrenched, and it makes perfect sense that when the palace centers collapsed, only they weathered the catastrophe.

The collapse of the Mycenaean system caused the significant truncation of central influence beyond palatial lands, and, as I have argued elsewhere (Small 1998), the main element that connects the Late Bronze Age with later Greece is the continuation of the aristocratic *oikos*, an elite household dating to the age of Homer, the core feature of Late Bronze Age Greek polities.

CENTRALIZATION VERSUS REGIONAL INTEGRATION

Rank-size analysis of the Pylian polity leads to the conclusion that the center's control of its territory was based not on the evolution of secondary administrative or economic centers but on a centralized mode of oversight. This was probably the result of a lag between the center, Pylos, which was growing in response to its own position within a larger economic sphere, and its hinterland, which was trailing behind. Corroborating support for this model comes from the Linear B tablets, which describe a centralized control mechanism linking different communities to Pylos without employing any secondary administrative centers. In her analysis of the strength of the connectivity of different places mentioned in the Linear B documents from Pylos, Carothers (1992:276–277) identifies a group of twelve villages that are connected to the palace just as strongly as are possibly larger settlements. In fact, she concludes that the palace's interest in these villages existed "irrespective of province, taxation unit or major town." Rather than working through an intermediary, second-level administrative post, the palace oversaw small villages directly. This fact makes suspect any modern identification and interpretation of communities as possible secondary administrative centers with relation to the palace.

Carothers (1992:276–277) goes on to argue that the palace was interested in at least five of these villages because they appear to have provided rowers, thereby reflecting the palace's interest in defense shortly before its destruction. This could very well be the case, but I hesitate to affirm this scenario. The state of military emergency postulated for Pylos was proposed by Ventris and Chadwick (1973:184), but our knowledge of naval warfare or coastal defense in the Late Bronze Age is almost nonexistent.

Further support for the argument that Pylos's oversight of its territory was more centralized than regionally integrated again comes from a consideration of the collapse. Although I have yet to see such an argument formally presented (but see Marcus 1989), my work with small, archaic states now leads me to conclude that the almost complete disappearance of a polity's regional settlement system results when the majority of settlements are directly connected to a significant Achilles heel—the central site itself. In such cases, the collapse of the center has a tremendous effect on smaller settlements, much more so than would have been the case had the settlements been regionally integrated, able to fall back on regional administrative systems that replicated those extending from the center, as existed in Oaxaca and the Basin of Mexico.

RETHINKING THE MYCENAEAN STATE

How does this conclusion affect present interpretations of Pylos? First, I am forced to question the current administrative model, based on the early work of Chadwick (1972). He rightly pointed out that Linear B place-names appear to be grouped: nine place-names are associated with one, apparently distinct, place-name referring to the "hither," and seven other place-names are associated with the term for "thither" or "further" (see chapter 3, this volume). In light of my analyses, however, I would question the interpretation of these two terms. How justified are we in calling each of these two category place-names provinces—implying very complex, administrative, state-level organization—if we do not yet have an identifiable settlement pattern that may be equated with current and accepted provincial models of control, models that always include hierarchically ordered regional centers? These terms could equally have been no more than scribal categories used at the palace. I am highly suspicious, therefore, of attempts to identify centers and different levels of administrative subcenters for mainland Mycenaean polities, as recently attempted by scholars such as Shelmerdine (1973), Lejeune (1979), Kilian (1988a), Wright (1995a), and Bennet (1995, 1999a). I do, however, make an exception for Bennet's work with administrative systems at Knossos (1985, 1988a). Since Cretan polities were in existence for around five hundred years before the coming of mainland Greeks, it is most likely that the Cretan Linear B records reflect an administrative system with a true element of regional integration.

TOWARD AN ESTATE MODEL

Attempts to reconstruct the Mycenaean polities have typically borrowed from those models, both static and dynamic, already well established in general cultural-evolutionary studies (Bennet 1995; Kilian 1988a; Wright 1995a). While such applications have been useful for charting the dynamics of social stratification, they miss the more essential characteristics of Mycenaean polities. In truth, the case of Pylos, on which most reconstructions are based, presents a ripe opportunity for exploration of the noticeable lack of correspondence between assumed concepts of state evolution, such as stepped administrative hierarchy and centrality, and the results of rank-size analyses. We desperately need to know what the economic and political structure of the entire region of Messenia was like before, during, and immediately after the appearance of the palaces. Survey has taken us just so far here. A sophisticated, integrated project of excavation of rural sites in Pylos's territory presents the only real hope of taking us any farther in addressing this question.

It would be better if we were to take a minimalist approach to reconstruction and return to the economic core, as established by Halstead (1992a, chapter 7, this volume). Extensions beyond the immediate palace lands appear to have existed more to supply palace workshops than to provide a wider economic power base, as seen in classic examples such as the Inca and Mesopotamian city-states. As mentioned, goods that Pylos was collecting beyond the borders of its own estate lands were not staple items but nonstaples, and specifically nonstaples that were used in its workshops. The most curious and probably the most important feature of the tax system are the ratios that exist between the goods being taxed (see also chapter 7, this volume). The evidence from Pylos shows that palace assessments of six important goods were in a consistent ratio, 7:7:2:3:1.5:150. While the assessment might vary according to the size of different taxed units, the ratio remained the same. The fact that this assessment is nonstaple and that there is a definite consistently applied ratio between the goods being taxed indicates strongly that the assessment is tied to the productive demands of the palace workshops. This conclusion demonstrates that the structure of the Pylian polity was probably closer to our concept of an estate that was reaching out beyond its borders to supply goods for its workshops, which were producing goods for distribution on a scale larger than the polity itself. I would thus argue that Pylos at least, and probably the other mainland Late Bronze Age polities, were actually expanding estates rather than small early states, as they are commonly conceived. Such a reconstruction would put the Mycenaean polity closer to the estate-based kingdoms of early Medieval Europe and several of the Classic Maya polities, which, under the guise of lineage compounds, were also estate-based (Freter 1994; Kurjack 1974; Sanders 1989).

What Pylos gives us is an important example of a Late Bronze Age estate, energized by the larger Bronze Age world—an estate that had begun to tap resources beyond its close confines not to support some political structure but, in a very narrow sense, to supply goods for its own workshops. The mainland Mycenaean polities, then, were estates with pituitary problems—even inventing their own writing systems—but estates just the same. They flashed onto the scene for an all-too-brief period before burning out in the widespread conflagration that marked the end of the Mediterranean Bronze Age.

Acknowledgment. Special thanks to John Bennet, who graciously gave me information from the Pylos Regional Archaeological Project in advance of publication.

CHAPTER 6

PALACES, SANCTUARIES, AND WORKSHOPS

THE ROLE OF THE RELIGIOUS SECTOR IN MYCENAEAN ECONOMICS

𝕫𝕫𝕫𝕫𝕫𝕫𝕫

SUSAN LUPACK

VENTRIS AND CHADWICK NOTED in the first edition of *Documents in Mycenaean Greek* (1956) that some personnel at Mycenaean workshops were picked out as special and distinct from the others by being recorded as *po-ti-ni-ja-we-jo*, or "Potnian." They translated this designation as "of or belonging to [the Mycenaean goddess] Potnia" and cautiously surmised that the workers might somehow have been associated with the religious sector. They left it to other scholars, however, to speculate as to what that might mean for our understanding of the role of religion in Mycenaean economics. Leonard Palmer (1963) picked up this line of investigation, and through his careful work with the Linear B tablets he was able to detail the involvement of the religious sphere in the management of Mycenaean workshops. Most scholars today, however, would agree that to characterize the Mycenaean economic system as a "temple economy," as Palmer did, ignores much evidence that speaks for the dominant position of the palace in the administration of economic matters. More recently, Hiller (1981) considered the question of the role of religious personnel in the workshop, but no one has attempted to analyze exactly how this connection affects our understanding of Mycenaean economics.

A connection between the two spheres has also been noted archaeologically. Often on Cyprus, Crete, and the mainland and islands of Greece, shrines and workshops are found in close association with one another. Tegyey

(1984) in particular has discussed the connection as it is manifested in the Northeast Workshop at Pylos (see figure 1.2), and Hägg (1992) has looked briefly at its widespread existence in the Bronze Age Aegean. This relationship has not been thoroughly analyzed except on Cyprus, where Knapp (1986) and more recently Kassianidou (1995) explored the full economic implications of the involvement of shrines in the bronze-working industry.

In this chapter, both bodies of evidence, the textual and the archaeological, are drawn on in an attempt to see how, when used together, they can illuminate the role of religious institutions in Mycenaean economics. The scope of the chapter is limited to the Mycenaean material (despite the interesting archaeological evidence that is found in Cypriot and Minoan contexts) because of the increased relevance the Linear B evidence takes on when interpreted in conjunction with contemporaneous sites.

LINEAR B EVIDENCE

The Linear B tablets provide us with a great deal of evidence detailing the integral part sanctuaries played in the economics of the palatial systems of both Crete and mainland Greece. One example is found in the offering tablets. Usually these tablets are consulted for the information they provide concerning Mycenaean religion, but they are helpful for this type of study as well, because they demonstrate the large economic commitment the palaces made with regard to the sanctuaries. The offerings that the palace made to the various gods and goddesses were quite substantial, and apparently there were many different sanctuaries that had to be considered (for example, Pakijane and the Posidaion at Pylos on *Tn 316*, and the Dictaion and the Daidaleion at Knossos on *Fp 1*). It is also important to recognize the economic import of how those offerings were used. The honey, cheeses, cattle, grain, spices (some of which were imported), perfumed oil, and so on, were all useful and sometimes quite valuable commodities. When they were not allocated to a specific ritual feast, they were probably intended to be used for the daily maintenance of the sanctuaries' personnel. Interestingly, the offerings were most often made in the names of the different deities, indicating that this support was given to religious personnel in tacit recognition of the religious services they performed for the society, as well as the prestige they accrued thereby. Certainly, this would have been an important source of support for the sanctuaries. Other tablets indicate, however, that they also had a more active role in procuring their livelihood.

The Pylos land tenure tablets, for instance, indicate both the high status of quite a few religious personnel and the fact that their economic interests were intertwined with those of the palace. Bennett (1956) first discussed the preponderance of religious personnel found on these sets of tablets. Many "servants of the gods" (as they are called on the tablets), and one who is specifically described with the adjectival form of Potnia (PY *Ep 613.14*), hold plots of palace-administered land. Other religious functionaries, such as Karpathia, "the key bearer" (*Ep 704.7*), and Eritha, "the priestess of Pakijane" (*Ep 704.3*), hold special plots of land. Furthermore, most of this land is specified as being located in the area called Pakijane, which has long been recognized as a sanctuary site near Pylos whose main deity was Potnia (Chadwick 1957). Interestingly, Eritha is mentioned again (*Ep 704.5*) as being involved in a dispute with the *damos* (community) over the status of her land (see chapter 4, this volume). Deger-Jalkotzy (1983) has proposed that the key reason for the dispute was that Eritha expected her land to be tax- or burden-free because of her religious status, and apparently the damos did not agree. This indicates clearly what we might otherwise have assumed anyway, that the palace, and in some cases also the damos, expected some return from the land. But the religious personnel must also have benefited from these land holdings, and it seems that Eritha might have been trying to maximize her return.

While it is possible that Eritha may have stood to gain personally from her landholding, most of the land recorded for the sanctuary site of Pakijane was probably allocated for the support of Potnia's sanctuary. This would have been particularly likely for the land of the servants of the gods, who hold most of the land in this particular series. If the sanctuary did have control over the produce of its land, then it is possible that the sanctuary of Potnia at Pakijane, and perhaps other sanctuary sites like it, presided over their own economic systems of collection and redistribution that paralleled the palace's, although they probably operated on a smaller scale. Their primary purpose would have been to provide sustenance for their religious functionaries and support staff. But we can take this a step further to propose that by acquiring economic assets and perhaps even a certain amount of wealth, the sanctuaries might also have gained some prestige and influence within the community that was not based solely on their role as intermediaries between heaven and earth. In other words, such a system could have resulted in some economic independence for the religious sphere.

Another example of the religious sector's involvement in economic pursuits is found in the Knossian *D*, *Dl*, and *Dp* series of tablets. On tablet *D 411*, Hermes is recorded as the "collector," meaning that the personnel working in his name were effectively the owners, or at least the managers, of the flock of sheep listed against his name. Furthermore, on a full eight of the *Dl* tablets, the adjectival form of Potnia stands in the position of the collector. In addition, two tablets in the *Dp* series record the fleeces that were ascribed to Potnia. As Ilievski (1992) points out, when a scribe used the adjectival form of a deity's name, it was probably understood that the deity's sanctuary had possession of whatever commodity or person was being described in this way. Thus the sanctuary of Potnia was the collector of the sizable flocks of female sheep listed on these tablets.

Although it is clear that the palace kept track of these flocks, expecting to receive its share of the wool and fleeces, nonetheless, it is reasonable to suppose that these flocks and their produce were also used for the daily maintenance of Potnia's personnel. In addition, as Carlier (1992) has discussed, the keeping of sheep could have constituted quite a profitable business for the collector. It is interesting to speculate on how the surplus goods were handled. Of course, the palace administrators could have been instructed to gather in any surplus, but this does not seem to be how the palace operated. The tax documents and wool production tablets show that the palace administration set targets for the amounts that the palace expected to receive, and the scribes recorded whether those targets had been met or if a deficit had been incurred. Never do we have any indication that extra goods were sought or accepted by the palace. It seems more likely, therefore, that the sanctuary itself, like the other collectors, would have retained possession of the surplus and would have been able to exploit the extra goods for its own ends.

This evidence supports the idea that the religious sector operated something of a redistributive system of its own, in parallel with but separate from the palace. Sanctuary sites could have acted as economic centers just as the palace sites did, although on a much reduced scale. It is interesting to note in this context that on five of the Potnian *Dl* tablets (*Dl 930, 933, 946, 950,* and *7503*), the flocks are located at one place, Sijaduwe. This could indicate that Sijaduwe was itself a rural sanctuary that acted as an economic center whose main source of support was animal husbandry.

It seems from this evidence that various sanctuary sites existed in the Late Bronze Age and that the personnel of these sanctuaries engaged in economic activities, such as agriculture and sheepherding, that were meant to provide for their daily sustenance and that probably also provided the sanctuary with some disposable surplus and economic influence. It is not surprising, then, to find that the Linear B tablets indicate that the religious sector was involved in forms of industrial production as well.

There is an interesting set of references to workers who are designated as Potnian but who were apparently working in palatial workshops. For example, Knossos tablet (KN) *G 820* lists rations allotted to female workers who are recorded as Potnian. We may surmise that they were working for the palace, since they were supported by palatial resources, but some connection with the religious sphere is implied by their being designated as Potnian. PY *Un 249* lists amounts of spices being delivered to an unguent boiler named Philaios, who is also described as Potnian. Furthermore, in the PY *Jn* series, nineteen of the extant bronzesmiths are described as Potnian. The bronzesmiths in particular are marked out as special by the scribes: although they appear on tablets with secular workers (on *Jn 431* and *310*), they are distinguished from the secular workers by being set off in their own paragraphs. Indeed, one tablet, *Jn 431*, was deliberately cut so that the Potnian group would have stood on its own within the file. Thus, these Potnian workers were considered to be distinct from the other workers in their respective industries. Nonetheless, it is apparent that the Potnian bronzesmiths,

like Philaios on *Un 249*, were working for the palace, since it is the palace that supplied them with their raw materials and kept track of their production. Thus, these Potnian workers must have had an established working relationship with the palace, and yet it was still important to the scribe, and therefore also to the palace, that their connection with the religious sector be recorded.

The question is, what did that religious connection signify within the secular sphere? It is interesting to wonder whether these workers were religious personages themselves, some sort of monk-craftsmen. However, it is difficult, if not impossible, to determine the religious status of the workers themselves. It is more profitable to speculate on the economic significance of the workers. Three scenarios seem possible here. The first is that the workers were called Potnian simply because they were producing goods that the palace intended to send to Potnia's sanctuary. In this case the palace would most likely have had administrative control over the goods and the power to decide how much of the goods would go to the shrine. While this arrangement is certainly feasible, it is also conceivable that the Potnian workers were sent to the secular workshops by the sanctuary, perhaps because the sanctuaries did not have such facilities of their own. In this case the sanctuary would have had jurisdiction over the majority of the goods the Potnian workers produced, after the palace had taken its cut as usual. This scenario would parallel the role of the religious sphere in agriculture and animal husbandry. Just as the sanctuaries' religious personnel were active players with regard to their landholdings and flocks of sheep, so the religious sector could have had some control over their workers' finished products. If this is the case, not only could these goods have been used in the sanctuary, they may also have been traded, and the sanctuary could have gained by the profits of such trade. Finally, it is also possible that the Potnian workers' time and goods were given over to the palace in exchange for something that the palace had given (or gave on a regular basis) to the sanctuaries. This third scenario could actually have operated in tandem with the second, and indeed it also posits the shrine as an economic entity of its own.

The idea that the shrine was in control of its economic assets is made more plausible by further textual evidence demonstrating that the personnel in Potnia's service managed their own workshops, apart from the palace. PY *An 1281*, for instance, provides such evidence. On *An 1281* Potnia appears twice, and each time she is described differently: in line 1 she is Potnia Hippeia, and in line 9 she is the Potnia of Potijakee. These two references to

Potnia set up a two-paragraph structure for the tablet. According to Palmer (1963:226), each Potnia should be seen as allocating workers to foremen. Ventris and Chadwick (1973:483), however, believed the goddess was receiving workers as the head of a workshop instead of allocating them. In either case, the religious personnel working in Potnia's name are shown to have had administrative control of workshop activities.

Interestingly, the second line of *An 1281* specifies that Potnia is at her seat or shrine. Since *An 1281* was found within the Northeast Workshop at Pylos, it is possible that the specific area referred to was, in fact, the Northeast Workshop itself. It is interesting to note in this context that *An 1281's* Potnia Hippeia, or "Mistress of the Horses," would be, as Blegen and Lang (1958:171) pointed out when the tablet was first found, quite an appropriate patron deity for the Northeast Workshop, the chief occupation of which was the repair and production of chariots (see chapter 13, this volume). The word describing the second Potnia on *An 1281* has no such fortuitous connections to the workings of the Northeast Workshop, but, since it is considered to be a place name, it does indicate that there might have been a second workshop over which Potnia presided, and in which, therefore, religious personnel had administrative control.

The religious nature of the Northeast Workshop is also supported by other tablets found within it. For instance, *Qa 1299* records an allocation of what may be a kind of cloth (Ventris and Chadwick 1973:485) to a man named Kaeseu, who is designated as being Potnian. Although Potnia herself is not mentioned again in the *Qa* series, five other *Qa* tablets (*1289, 1290, 1296, 1300,* and probably *1303*) also appear to have cultic associations in that they record allocations of that special type of cloth to priests and priestesses. These textual connections (in addition to others, which would require a lengthier discussion than can be undertaken here) all build a case for religious personnel operating within the Northeast Workshop, probably under the auspices of Potnia, as well as at some other religious workshop.

The possibility that religious personnel did in fact preside over cultic workshops is also supported by the *Of* tablets from Thebes. On *Of 36*, Potnia is seen to receive wool for her finishers of cloth, indicating that personnel working in the name of Potnia managed a textile workshop. The *Of* tablets also give possible evidence that the Mycenaeans saw religious workshops as somehow different from the palatial ones in that they distinguished the two types linguistically. This is seen in the interesting opposition set up between the words *do* and *wo-ko*, discussed by

Spyropoulos and Chadwick (1975). *Do* is seen in four cases in the *Of* series, and these occurrences are all associated with men's names in the genitive. The translation would thus be "to the house of *x*." In contrast, on *Of 36* we see Potnia receiving wool at her *woikos*, not her *do*. Thus we see the two forms of the word "house" used in clearly distinct contexts, one secular and the other religious.

Another possible example of the religious sphere's involvement in the textile industry may be found in PY *Cc 665* and its associated tablets. A flock of sheep is ascribed to Potnia on *Cc 665*, along with a herd of pigs. Interestingly, they are recorded as being kept at a place called Newopeo, the same location at which female textile workers (and their children) are recorded to have been on tablets *Aa 786, Ab 554,* and *Ad 688*. As has been clearly set out in table form by Bennet (1992:94), many collectors' names can be traced in other series that deal with the textile industry. This could indicate that, as Carlier (1992:163) has proposed, "it is even possible that certain collectors have concentrated in their hands the complete chain of production, from sheep to the woolen cloth" (my translation). Perhaps we could, therefore, infer from the combination of *Cc 665* and the *A* tablets that religious personnel not only kept flocks at Newopeo but were also managing a textile workshop there. An analogous situation could be proposed for the sanctuary site Sijaduwe that I mentioned earlier, although it is true that we do not have the textual evidence that would confirm it was involved in manufacturing textiles.

Thus, from the Linear B evidence, it seems that religious personnel were involved in agriculture, animal husbandry, metalworking, the perfumed oil industry, and textile manufacture. They both managed their own workshops and had craftsmen working, in the name of Potnia, within palatial workshops. The goods produced were probably used for the general support of the sanctuaries and their personnel, but in their role as economic organizers and providers, the religious functionaries could also have accrued some economic influence, which could have strengthened their position within the society.

ARCHAEOLOGICAL EVIDENCE OF THE MYCENAEAN PERIOD

Archaeological evidence from Pylos and Mycenae appears to confirm that there was a connection between the religious sector and industrial production. The only place at Pylos (other than possibly the megaron)

that is considered to have had a religious function is the shrine, which was, in fact, an integral part of the Northeast Workshop, the site in which *An 1281* was found (see figure 1.2). It has to be said that little of a clearly cultic nature was found within the shrine: there were no cult figures or any sign of a bench on which cult figures might have been placed. It would be easy to endorse Blegen's statement that the floor of the shrine must have "vanished altogether" as explanation for the lack of a bench and other cultic finds. Many of the other facts of the site indicate, however, that Blegen could have been mistaken when he proposed that the floor of room 93 (see figure 1.2) had vanished. The poros blocks framing the door were neatly dressed and meant to be seen; in other words, they were not undressed foundation blocks that would be expected at a basement level. Furthermore, the threshold blocks seem to be at the same level as the floor to which they give entrance.

Here, perhaps, is the clue to why Blegen asserted that there was no floor. Blegen proposed that two or three more steps should be reconstructed on top of the extant threshold blocks. Following the suggestion of Joe Shaw (personal communication, 1997), however, I propose that room 93 is too small to accommodate these two or three extra steps and that Blegen, with Classical models in mind, may have been misled by his own conception of what a shrine should look like when he reconstructed the shrine's entrance in this way. In fact, in Blegen's account of the room, the two issues are immediately juxtaposed:

> Between the two anta bases . . . is a row of four flat poros blocks which *evidently* formed the bottom step of two or three that rose to the level of the floor inside the shrine. The upper steps and the floor itself have vanished altogether since they *must have* reached a level higher than that of the modern ground. (Blegen and Rawson 1966:304; my emphasis)

If we remove the postulated steps, then the floor level does not have to be, and in fact should not be, higher than the threshold blocks. Blegen's description of the floor of room 93—"Only the clayey broken-up stereo that supported them was left"—might have presented problems to this proposal, but only if the rest of the rooms in the Northeast Workshop had possessed clear floors (Blegen and Rawson 1966:304). In fact, the floors were evidently somewhat difficult to distinguish and are variously described: "The floor [in corridor 95] was made of a clayey earth and could hardly be recognized"; "the clay floor [of room 96], which rested on a fill of greenish stereo-like earth"; "the floor [of room 97] itself

was of earth." Finally, of room 99, "The best indication of [the floor level] seemed to be a stratigraphic change from the fallen reddish disintegrated crude brick to the greenish-white stratum resembling stereo." It could very well have been that what Blegen accepted as floor levels in other rooms did not impress him as constituting a floor in room 93 because he had already decided that the floor must have vanished.

If indeed what we have is the actual floor level, then we must attempt to explain the finds in that light. Actually, the room was not devoid of finds. Fragments of thirty-two normal-sized kylikes (wine cups) were found, as well as one miniature votive kylix. In addition, there was a fineware dipper, along with other vessels used for the pouring and storage of liquids. Very often items of this type are found in ritual contexts and are thought to be used in ritual drinking and the pouring of libations (see chapter 8, this volume). I suggest that this was their function in room 93. Another interesting point concerning the nature of the finds in room 93 is the distinct lack of any kind of workshop materials. Since such materials were found in abundance in the other rooms of the building, it is unlikely that they had been scavenged or cleaned out of room 93. The fact that room 93 is without those materials leads us to believe that the room served some purpose different from that of the other rooms. In other words, it was not used for industrial purposes.

The special nature of room 93 is further indicated by its architectural details. Two large poros blocks framed the room's wide door, and in the upper surfaces of these blocks were dowel holes into which additional blocks or wooden beams may have been fitted. Blegen was correct in calling the poros blocks "decorative antae" (Blegen and Rawson 1966:304). In addition, the room's threshold was marked by four stone slabs (not the three pictured in figure 1.2), a feature not found anywhere else in this otherwise utilitarian building. Hence we can conclude from the architectural details that the people who built this room were trying to set it off from the others in the building. The religious nature of room 93 is confirmed by the altar that stands in front of the shrine's doorway (figure 6.1). Like the altars found at Mycenae, this one was plastered on all four sides and across its top. It surpasses them, though, in its decoration: at least four layers of painted plaster were found, and the same design seems to have been used each time, which speaks of a long-standing tradition such as one might expect in a religious setting. This archaeological evidence, combined with the many tablets that were found in the Northeast Workshop demonstrating a religious connection for workshop per-

FIGURE 6.1 Altar with painted decoration at Pylos. (Reprinted from Blegen and Rawson 1966, figure 228. Courtesy of the Department of Classics, University of Cincinnati.) Scale is 1m.

sonnel, leads me to conclude that room 93 was a shrine whose personnel were directly involved in the industrial activities that were performed in the workshop.

Fred Cooper (1994) has confirmed that the Northeast Workshop complex was the last building project that the Pylians accomplished before the palace was destroyed. Shelmerdine (1987) has proposed that it was deemed necessary, at a time when there was unrest in the area, to bring the production of special goods, such as perfumed oil and bronze weaponry, close into the palace. This idea is consistent with the theory put forth by Wright (1984) to explain the modifications made in the palace toward the end of its existence. The changes made to the palace, such as adding courts 42 and 47 for industrial purposes to what was originally a rather impressive façade (see figure 1.2), make it clear that the Pylians refurbished the palace so that it would be a more utilitarian complex. It seems they were aware that their strategic position was not as secure as it had been when the palace was first built (see chapter 9, this volume). Hence their desire to have the industries that were vital to them close by, even though

these changes detracted from the impressive nature of the building's original architecture. It is conceivable that wherever the original workshop that preceded the Northeast Workshop was located, the shrine may have had a more dominant position. Furthermore, it is possible that this workshop and its activities were connected with one of the sanctuaries mentioned on the tablets (such as Pakijane), but we have no archaeological confirmation on this point. Another possibility is suggested by the second designation applied to Potnia on tablet *An 1281*. If indeed we can see a reference to a second workshop in the phrase "Potnia of Potijakee," then perhaps this was the original location of the chariot industry (see chapter 13, this volume). In this case, production clearly had not entirely ceased there but continued in conjunction with the Northeast Workshop. In either case, even though the palace clearly had a high degree of interest in the Northeast Workshop, the shrine's religious personnel seem to have had some administrative control over its activities.

At Mycenae there is evidence for a connection between the religious sector and industrial production (French

1981; Taylour 1969, 1970). Many finds of an industrial nature have been found within the Cult Center itself (figure 6.2), although their exact nature has recently been the subject of renewed discussion. It was noticed that different types of workshop materials were appearing in several areas of this complex, and it was thought that the main industrial activity of the area was ivory working because of the large number of partially worked ivory pieces found. Two storeroom areas were proposed (French 1981), and after a full reexamination of the evidence, French (n.d.) has not changed her interpretation of these rooms (see Moore and Taylour n.d.; Krzyszkowska [1997] is more cautious, but deals only with the ivory material). Ivory inlays, beads, and boars' tusks were all found in basement II of the building in the Cult Center called the Megaron. Too small and ill-lit to be a workshop, this room was thought to be a storeroom for workshop materials.

Significantly, the second storeroom was room 32, whose dual nature is very interesting. A block of raw ivory from which several layers had already been taken was found in this small room, along with several other pieces of worked ivory. At first Taylour (1969) called this room an ivory workshop, but when the remainder of the Main Balk was removed, it was discovered that it had a cultic nature as well. Against the southwestern corner of the room was a platform on which a female figurine with upraised arms was found. Here in one small room, religion and workshop activities were combined. French (1981; Moore and Taylour n.d.) has proposed that the ivory was stored here so as to be under the guardianship of the deity worshipped in that room.

The actual workshop space was thought to be area 36, and it is consequently labeled "workshop" in figure 6.2. Indeed, several factors recommended that it be classified as such. It was not roofed, and therefore there would have been plenty of light to work by. Also, the finds of the two storerooms were very similar to those in area 36, further substantiating a connection between the three rooms. Those finds consisted of, but were not limited to, several bronze and bone tools, mortars, pounders, a pestle, five antler tools, and lead sheeting. An unfinished ivory (bone?) box, two definite and three possible partly worked ivory pieces, and one ivory attachment help connect this area with the shrine room of the Room of the Fresco complex. A richly worked steatite mold was also found that still had some glass clinging to its surface, indicating that it had been used for the manufacture of glass plaques. The finding of gold fragments also suggested that the manufacture of luxury items was one of the main focuses of the workshop.

French and others have, however, recently noted that despite the varied types of workshop materials found in area 36, there is no debitage (French, personal communication, 1997; Krzyszkowska 1992, 1997; Moore and Taylour n.d.}; Tournavitou 1992b). In other words, there is no evidence for the actual working of the partially worked pieces that were found, particularly the ivory ones. French does not deny the fact that many of the objects found within the area indicate that several different types of manufacturing processes could have been conducted in the vicinity of the shrines. For instance, Mossman has suggested (in French n.d.) that the lead sheeting found in area 36 could have been used either as a raw material or for the beating of gold foil in a way that would not mark the gold. Also, the antler tools could have been used for pressing the gold leaf into molds. Hence, along with the fragments of gold, we therefore have possible evidence for the manufacture of gold jewelry. Nonetheless, the lack of clear debitage has caused French (personal communication, 1997, and n.d.) to say adamantly that area 36 is not a workshop but instead more like a storeroom of sorts. This leaves us wondering where the workshop proper was located. Thinking that it should be close to the storerooms for ease of access to the materials, I have proposed that the area between the Room of the Fresco complex and Tsountas's House may have served as at least one of the workshop areas for the site. It is spacious and open to the sky and in a very central location, convenient to all three areas that had workshop materials. Unfortunately this area has not been fully published; therefore, no evidence for or against this proposition is available.

The second possibility is that the workshop may have been located on the terrace immediately above the Cult Center. This proposal is based primarily on an interesting set of tablets called the *Oi* series, which discusses the allocation of an as yet unidentified liquid (*190) to various types of workers. The tablets from this series must have fallen from this upper terrace to their findspot within the Cult Center (room 4) during the LH IIIB destruction (Chadwick 1963). The area from which these tablets came has not been excavated, but it is possible that the workers listed on the tablets may have done their jobs near the findspot of the tablets, as may have been the case for the tablets found in the Northeast Workshop and for those from other areas of Mycenae. The connection of these workers with the religious sphere can be inferred from the fact that Potnia is mentioned several times in the series alongside the craftsmen. One of these

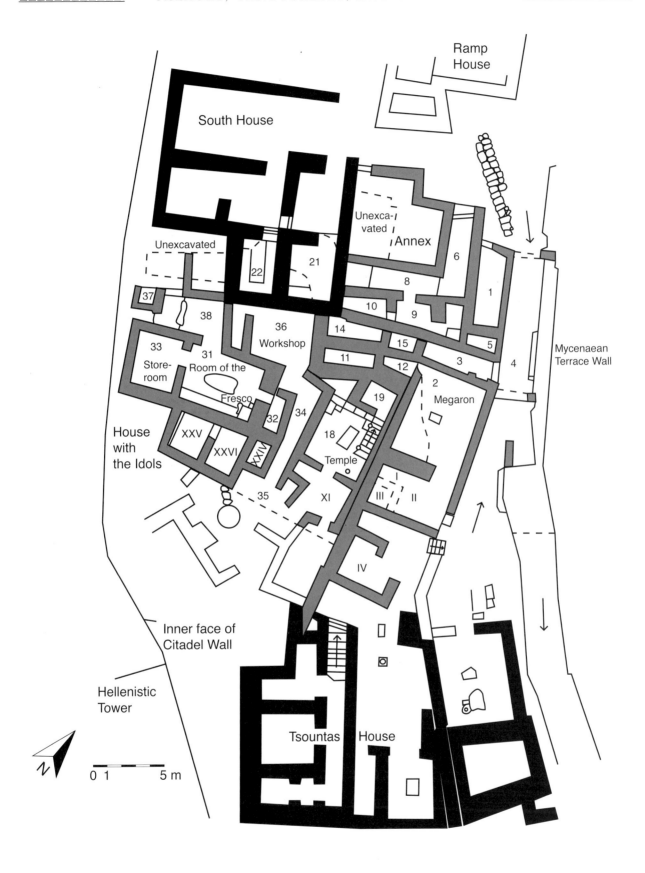

FIGURE 6.2 Plan of the Cult Center at Mycenae. (Reprinted from Palaima and Shelmerdine 1984:115, figure 7. Courtesy of E. French.)

references, to a "Mistress of the Grain" (*si-to-po-ti-ni-ja*), could provide us with a link for these tablets to the goddess depicted carrying a sheaf of grain in each hand in the Room of the Fresco (Chadwick 1963). At least one major piece of evidence for industrial activity occurring in the area, the elaborately worked steatite mold, is also thought to have been brought to area 36 from the place in which it was originally used (Evely and Runnels 1992). It may very well have come from the terrace above.

Interestingly, again the tablets and the archaeological evidence support one another: blue-glass workers (*ku-wa-no-wo-ko-i*), who could have used such a mold, are frequently mentioned in the *Oi* series. Furthermore, a quadruple ivy glass plaque, found in area 36, was most likely made from the same mold (although not the one we have preserved) as two other pieces that were found in rooms 2 and II of the megaron. Significantly, the latter of these two pieces was warped, as were several other glass pieces found in room 11. These finds, which actually constitute debitage, suggest that there was a glassmaking shop in the vicinity (French n.d.).

In sum, we do not have clear evidence at Mycenae for an actual workshop in close proximity to the shrine complexes. There are indications, however, that one—or several, for that matter—did exist. The shrines of the Cult Center, and the religious personnel working within it, did have control over raw materials. This situation is similar to the one found at Pylos in the Northeast Workshop. Here, as at Pylos, it is likely that the religious personnel in control of these goods may have been accorded high status within the community. Furthermore, they probably gained materially from the management of manufacturing processes, as was proposed on the basis of the textual evidence.

Both the Linear B tablets and the archaeological materials thus provide evidence that religious personnel had some involvement in industrial activities. And the religious personnel and the sanctuaries to which they belonged probably derived a part of their livelihood, and perhaps a profit, from the goods produced in these workshops. Yet the palace, whose interest is demonstrated by the Linear B tablets, must also have gained in some fashion from the religious workers' goods. It seems, then, that the palatial and religious spheres cooperated with each other in a situation that could have been beneficial to them both, even if one sphere did have the upper hand. The question then becomes, how did this mutually beneficial situation come into being? How did it come about that religious personnel were able to share in the economic aspect of the production of goods in a system that seems dominated by the palace?

One explanation for this situation could be that a relationship between religion and industry may have existed prior to the growth of the palaces, and that this relationship was incorporated into the palatial system as it grew in size and power. If this thesis is correct, then we would expect to find such a relationship in sites geographically apart from the palaces and chronologically prior to them. Interestingly, we do have such evidence.

For instance, there is the recently excavated LH III site of Methana (Konsolaki 1991, 1995; see map, figure 1.1). No plan of the site has been published thus far, although good photographs of the rooms can be seen in Shelmerdine (1997). (The information presented in her published reports has been generously supplemented by the excavator herself, Eleni Konsolaki, through personal communication, 1997.) The site has produced a very interesting shrine complex that consists of five rooms arranged around a courtyard. The main shrine room contained a stepped bench shrine, a pig's head *rhyton* (vessel for pouring liquids), and a multitude of figurines, including a large number of group figurines.

Significantly, just south of this main shrine was a room (called room delta) that did not contain any finds of a religious character. Instead, its contents indicated that it was used for industrial purposes. In addition to some stone tools, the excavators found bits of corroded metal, a few lead blobs, and a crucible. A whitish substance that has not yet been analyzed was also found. On the basis of these finds, it is safe to say at least that Methana constitutes a nonpalatial example of a shrine engaged in manufacturing processes.

Phylakopi on Melos provides us with another such example (figure 6.3; see also figure 1.1). The West and East Shrine complex at Phylakopi had three main phases of use, which Renfrew (1985) outlines as follows: In the first phase, which corresponds to the LH IIIA period, the West Shrine was built. The East Shrine was built in the second phase, which corresponds to the IIIB1 period. At the end of the IIIB period Phylakopi suffered major damage, whether from an earthquake or from purposeful destruction is uncertain. The shrine continued to be used after this destruction but in a more limited way. It is at this time that the Blocking Wall was built, closing off half the West Shrine. Numerous figurines and bench shrines were found in both the West and the East Shrines in every period that the buildings were in use. The Lady of Phylakopi, who was found in a corner of room A in the West Shrine, was perhaps the finest of them all. Renfrew (1985) has proposed that she made epiphany appearances through the niche that communicated with the main room of the West Shrine.

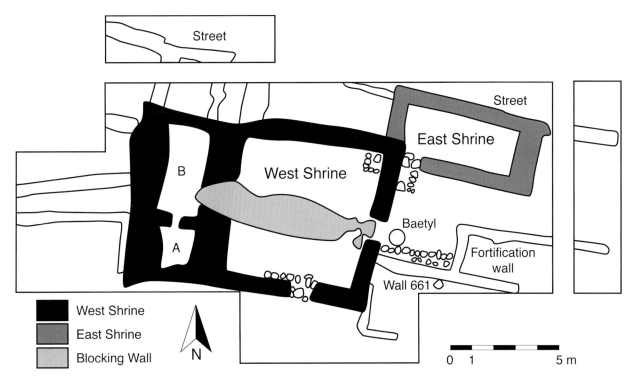

FIGURE 6.3 Plan of Phylakopi, the Shrine Complex, post-IIIB destruction phase (Reprinted from Renfrew 1981b:68, figure 1. Courtesy of C. Renfrew.)

Within the shrines, interesting metal objects were also found, including twelve pieces that were considerably corroded and unrecognizable, seven pieces of slag, and several lumps of bronze, one of which looks like a puddle ingot. A terra-cotta mold that was probably used in the manufacture of metal objects was also found. Although these pieces could represent the raw materials and by-products of metal working, there was no indication of a furnace in the area. For this reason it has been proposed that these metal objects were brought to the shrine as votives (Renfrew 1985; see also Schallin 1997b). This in itself provides us with an interesting connection between cult and industry, but we also have evidence that the shrine was involved in another manufacturing activity, the production of obsidian blades (see chapter 9, this volume).

A large number (2724) of obsidian artifacts were found within the shrine (Torrence 1985), including finished blades, cores, chips, and flakes. No doubt, blade manufacturing was conducted within the confines of the shrine. The large number of obsidian fragments is doubly significant when compared with finds in other domestic areas of Phylakopi where blade manufacture also occurred. In the other areas the magnitude of production was much smaller; most likely those blades were made for immediate household use. The shrine's scale of production, in contrast, certainly surpassed the immediate needs of the shrine's personnel. Since the households within Phylakopi made their own blades, it seems possible that the shrine's obsidian tools were destined for external trade. It is difficult to determine whether the governing power of Phylakopi was in charge of the trade or whether the shrine's personnel handled it. It is likely that the shrine not only provided for its personnel's maintenance through this industry but also accrued a certain amount of prestige and influence because of it.

Interestingly, but not surprisingly, the findspots for much of the obsidian may indicate that the shrine's personnel considered the obsidian precious. During the IIIB period, the obsidian was concentrated in room B, while room A had the next highest concentration. These rooms probably functioned as basic storage rooms for the shrine, but, in the case of room A in particular, where the Lady of Phylakopi was found, they might also have been considered to be special inner rooms sacred to the goddess who resided therein. It is interesting to compare this situation with the Shrine of Mycenae (room 32), where the majority of the ivory in the Cult Center was stored, and where, as I mentioned, a goddess figurine was found in situ on her platform. Perhaps it was thought that at Phylakopi, as at Mycenae, the goddess would keep watch over the costly materials whose successful manufacture was her responsibility.

Also, it is not surprising that there would be a religious connection with obsidian on Melos, considering the importance that must have been attached to the control and manufacture of this unique substance. (This situation can be compared with that of Cyprus and its copper-producing industry.)

With the Methana and Phylakopi material we have established that there was a religious connection with industry that existed apart from the palaces. This implies that the phenomenon was indeed a part of Mycenaean society in general. In Berbati we find evidence that the relationship between the two spheres existed much earlier, in the LH II period, at a time when the Mycenaean palaces' elaborate economic system was probably just beginning to take on the form that we see reflected in the tablets.

We can tell from the abundant wasters that a pottery workshop was in operation at Berbati from the late Middle Helladic period until the end of LH IIIB (Åkerström 1968, 1987; Schallin 1997a; figure 6.4; see also figure 1.1). The only actual kiln that has been found dates to the LH II period, which is contemporaneous with the first indications of cult activity on the site. Figure 6.4 indicates the location (A) of a bench made of unworked stone. Pieces of two female figurines were found lying on and around this bench, indicating its religious nature. In situ on this bench was also found a spoon, whose special nature was indicated by the fact that its interior was also decorated, and thus it was not used for everyday purposes. This spoon, along with the other vessels around the bench, could indicate that some sort of libation ritual was conducted in this area.

Later in LH II, both the kiln and the bench were built over. Although another kiln has not been found in the immediate area, the large amounts of pottery and wasters confirm that the next phase of the building was also used to produce pottery. Two more cultic installations were also found in the building, probably built to replace the first one. One (figure 6.4) consisted of a channel of stones (B) that terminated on the left in the earth. On the right the channel was blocked off by more stones, and in these stones the base of a *kylix* was fixed. It looks as if this installation, like the bench shrine that preceded it, was used for some libation ritual. This theme is continued in the third installation (figure 6.4), which was constructed after the channel with the kylix, although the two seem to have been in use contemporaneously. It consisted of a large amphora (C), whose bottom had been deliberately pierced and then buried in the ground.

Berbati is different from the other sites discussed thus far in that it does not consist of a shrine with an industrial component. Rather, it is a workshop with a religious aspect. Therefore, it can not be said to constitute an example of religious personnel managing the production of an important commodity. Nonetheless, Berbati does demonstrate a link between the two realms of religion and industry. It is possible that the potters at Berbati were worshipping a deity whose responsibility it was to oversee and ensure the positive outcome of what was a delicate manufacturing process, as I have suggested that the goddesses at Mycenae and Phylakopi were expected to do. This patronage of a certain deity could have translated into power and prestige for the religious personnel who performed the rites and rituals for that deity. Perhaps eventually it was deemed beneficial for the religious personnel to be given control of the industry's practical aspects in addition to its religious ones, or perhaps the shrines, as their sanctuaries grew, may have set up their own workshops, in order to support their personnel.

Whatever the mechanism by which the shrines gained administrative control of certain workshops, Berbati demonstrates that the relationship between religion and industries was a longstanding one that existed before the palace had come into its own as an economic force within the community. If this was the case, then it is possible that the palaces, as their administrative systems took shape and their economic interests expanded, had to deal with the already existing economic power wielded by the sanctuaries (just as they probably had to work with other preexisting elements of the culture from which they emerged, such as the damos; see chapter 7, this volume).

Apparently the palatial administrations and their rulers found it to their advantage to incorporate the sanctuaries and their industries into their developing economic system. The wanax certainly benefited from his relationship with the religious sphere in ways that were not only economic: his position as head of the community most likely had to be sanctioned by the deity, and this could only occur through rituals conducted by the religious sphere (Palaima 1995; chapter 4, this volume). Certain sanctuaries, in their turn, probably benefited from the patronage of the ruler. The result was that the two realms operated in a system of economic cooperation that presumably was to their mutual benefit in both economic and more ephemeral terms. The palace received from the sanctuaries both its percentage of the religious sphere's profits and the divine sanction necessary to buttress its claim to power, while the sanctuaries were able not only to support themselves but also to wield some economic influence of their own.

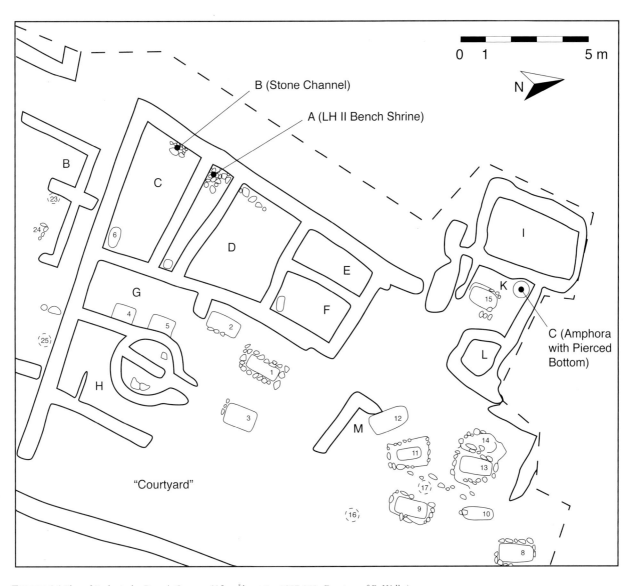

FIGURE 6.4 Plan of Berbati, the Potter's Quarter. (After Åkerström 1987:141. Courtesy of B. Wells.)

CHAPTER 7

TOWARD A MODEL OF MYCENAEAN PALATIAL MOBILIZATION

PAUL HALSTEAD

AEGEAN PREHISTORIANS HAVE LONG wrestled with the problem of how the Mycenaean palatial systems were financed. As with other early complex societies, emphasis has gradually shifted from the question "How did a grateful populace manage to produce the agricultural surplus necessary to support a managerial elite?" (Renfrew 1972) to "How did a self-serving elite dupe, bully, or cajole this surplus out of its exploited subjects?" (Gamble 1982; Gilman 1981; Renfrew 1982b). In practice, however, participants in this debate have primarily been concerned with rival models of the origins of Aegean palatial society. Advocates of ecological specialization (Renfrew 1972), capital intensification (Gilman 1981), risk buffering (Branigan 1988; Halstead and O'Shea 1982), or feasting (Hamilakis 1996; Moody 1987) have supported their case by more or less selective appeals to textual or archaeological evidence for particular forms of palatial mobilization. Several valuable surveys of the relevant textual evidence have appeared (e.g., Bennet 1988b; de Fidio 1982, 1987, 1992; Godart 1977; Killen 1985), but, with the notable exception of Morris (1986), there have been few serious attempts to define the character of Mycenaean palatial mobilization drawing on both textual and archaeological evidence.

This chapter attempts an essentially inductive synthesis of the available evidence for Mycenaean palatial mobilization, broadly following the integrated textual and archaeological approach advocated by Bennet (1988a) and exemplified by Shelmerdine (1985), Palaima and Wright (1985), Palmer (1994) and Bennet (1995). The chapter is divided into five sections: a brief critical review of the basic sources of information used, a summary of the principal flows of resources that can be inferred, a consideration of the forms of integration (Polanyi 1957) through which these flows were channeled, an attempt at quantitative evaluation of the different forms of palatial mobilization recognized, and a consideration of some implications of this provisional model for understanding both the function and the origins of Mycenaean palatial mobilization.

SOURCES OF INFORMATION

The information deployed here is drawn from three basic sources—texts, material remains, and analogy—each with its attendant strengths and weaknesses.

Texts

Linear B texts record goods and services paid to or due to the palace and, less commonly, disbursements of goods from the palace. The great strength of these texts is the detail recorded on the context of transactions, such as the identity of the persons or places contributing and the basis of assessment, including exemptions and deficits carried forward. Much of the meaning of the texts is implicit rather than explicit. Most notably, the texts fail to specify the extent of palatial bureaucratic control over economic activity, even whether this was total or partial (Finley 1957). The texts were also working records, not intended to be filed for posterity; as a result, surviving texts were short-term documents, mostly covering only the last few months of each palace (although different palaces were destroyed at different dates).

Material remains

Artifacts and ecofacts provide additional information on the range of goods (and, less so, of services) consumed by the palaces and, in the case of exotic materials or styles, information on their source. The principal weakness of such material evidence is the lack of contextual detail on transactions, which is exacerbated by the traditional failure of Aegean prehistorians to pay as much attention to the spatial as to the temporal context of artifacts and ecofacts. The great strength of the material evidence is in demonstrating that the palaces consumed commodities that do not appear in the texts and so were not, in all probability, produced under palatial control. The material record also has great potential—as yet largely unrealized, thanks to the bias toward excavation of palaces and rich tombs—to illuminate nonelite sites and contexts. Finally, the material record is less discontinuous in time than the ephemeral texts (Bennet 1988b).

Analogy

Analogy with the present, particularly with present-day farming practice or the ecology of domestic plants and animals, points to lacunae in the textual and material records. For example, records of grain harvests and wether (that is, a male sheep, castrated before maturity) flocks imply the existence of wholly or largely unrecorded reaping gangs and breeding sheep, respectively; archaeobotanical finds of cereal and pulse grains imply recurrent risks of crop failure and a range of probable buffering measures. This approach can significantly expand the range and scale of inferences concerning agricultural production and produce, which in all probability occupied and sustained the overwhelming majority of the population of Mycenaean Greece.

FLOWS OF RESOURCES

A simplified model has been presented elsewhere (Halstead 1992a) of the flows of goods and services into and out of the palaces that can be inferred from a combination of texts, material remains, and analogy. For the sake of brevity, this model is merely summarized here, with some emendations in the light of subsequent publications. Three principal categories of resource flow may be distinguished—taxation, direct production, and unrecorded transactions.

Taxation

"Taxes" are levied, variously from subcenters or their constituent local communities or local officials. The commodities so levied are primarily raw materials for palatial workshops (flax, bronze, wax, hides, honey, spices) but also include modest numbers of personnel (probably for military service; see Killen 1983). The central bureaucracy was not concerned with the production or collection of these commodities but contented itself with monitoring the tax assessments, exemptions, payments, and deficits of each subcenter or local community. Obligations to contribute at least some categories of tax (flax, bronze, military service) are bound up with grants of land (or land use) to certain officials and master craftsmen, while exemptions from tax seem to be granted in respect of services rendered by such persons to the palace (see, e.g., Foster 1981; Killen 1985:244–250, 258–259, 1993a; see also chapters 4 and 5, this volume). Different communities paid different absolute amounts of tax, presumably based on a factor such as population size or wealth, and on the same basis the palace distributed wine to local communities, probably for use in festivals (Palmer 1994:75–78).

Direct production

Direct production under palatial control is implied for wheat (cf. Palmer 1992; Halstead 1995a), olives, figs, grapes, and sheep (kept for wool) by textual references to plow teams, harvests of wheat and olives, nurseries of figs and vines, and central monitoring and replenishment of sheep flocks (see also de Fidio 1992:183). Unlike resources acquired through taxation, crop harvests are not set against production targets and presumably represent the entire yield (or a standard proportion thereof, as in recent sharecropping and tithe-collecting arrangements) from particular blocks of land. The suggestion of large-scale grain production on palatial estates (Halstead 1992a, 1992b) must be revised in the light of Killen's recent demonstration that palace oxen were assigned to *damos* (community) land (Killen 2001). Bureaucratic recording of the assignment, however, suggests that this land, whatever its nominal status, was effectively under palatial control, and Killen's reconstruction leaves open the possibility of sharecropping, with the palace providing plough oxen and the *damos* human labor. Wool and lambs were set against expected yields per head of stock, presumably because of the difficulty of auditing the productivity of mobile flocks. Commodities acquired through direct production included raw materials for use in palatial workshops and also staple foodstuffs, which presumably supported the associated workers. Both the issuing of rations and raw materials and the receipt of finished craft goods were again subject to bureaucratic control in writing.

Unrecorded transactions

Unrecorded flows of goods, both into and out of the palace on both an intra- and interregional scale, are attested archaeologically or can be inferred by analogy.

Intraregional to the palace. Pottery (see chapter 8, this volume) and a wide range of cereal and pulse grains, found archaeologically on palatial sites, and young male sheep, needed to restock palatial wool flocks (Halstead 1993a), were presumably produced within their territories.

Intraregional from the palace. Palatial craft products (jewelry, perfumed oil) are found widely in the hinterlands of the palaces, and elderly wool sheep, of which thousands must have been discarded annually, were presumably not eaten solely by the elite.

Interregional to the palace. Exotic raw materials (ivory, semiprecious stones) are attested archaeologically both in waste products from palace workshops and in finished articles.

Interregional from the palace. Palatial craft products (notably, containers of perfumed oil) are found "abroad," especially in the eastern Mediterranean.

FORMS OF INTEGRATION

Linear B evidence affords valuable clues to the institutional basis of textually documented flows of resources; taxation represents the classic redistributive flow of resources between palace and hinterland on the basis of established rights and obligations. Direct production of food and raw materials on palace land or from palatial flocks and the subsequent distribution of these resources to palatial staff and workshops essentially represents the internal administration of an elite household economy (Earle 1977:215; see chapter 5, this volume). The collection of taxes was evidently left to local communities or community leaders. For example, in recognition of craft service by particular individuals, local communities in the Pylian state were granted tax exemptions on unrelated commodities, implying that tax was a communal burden (Foster 1981). In addition, the assessments of different commodities for some communities are not divisible by any common denominator, thus precluding equal payment by all eligible tax payers (Lejeune 1979). Conversely, palace officials actively interfered in the composition of palatial wool flocks, while the lack of yield assessments for crops from palatial agriculture implies that officials must have measured actual yields during harvest or, as in recent times, on the threshing floor (see Killen 1995b:331). The distinction between these two forms of mobilization is somewhat blurred, however, by the close and complex relationship among tax assessments/exemptions, landholding, and service to the palace, such that taxation and direct production should perhaps be seen as representing the decentralized and centralized extremes, respectively, of a continuum of bureaucratically administered resource flows (see also Killen 2001).

The basis on which unrecorded flows of resources took place is less clear. Written records were apparently made of taxation and associated land grants and of direct production and associated craft activity in order to monitor the fulfillment of obligatory transactions or deliveries of predictable size or timing (Killen 1984a). Unrecorded transactions, by contrast, were presumably nonobligatory or unpredictable; for this reason, their fulfillment was not monitored in writing. Given that the palace was both donor and recipient in unrecorded flows, it is tempting to relate the disbursement of palatial craft goods outside the palaces and outside the southern Aegean to the complementary acquisition by the palaces of local pottery and pulses and of exotic raw materials, respectively.

There are hints that some interregional transactions took the form of gift exchange. These hints occur in the form of textual references to *xenwia* ("guest gift," perhaps) textiles and perfumed oil (Killen 1985:263–264; Shelmerdine 1985:79), archaeological finds in Aegean palaces of oriental seals and pharaonic cartouches (Peltenberg 1991), and artistic representations in Egypt of apparently Aegean bearers of "tribute" (Cline 1995a:273). Early Near Eastern diplomatic texts, however, show that, just as in the provision of modern Western aid to Third World countries, the language of gift giving could be a vehicle for very businesslike exchanges (Postgate 1994:210; Zaccagnini 1987:61). Killen (1995a) has recently argued that one important individual in the Pylos records may have served as a middleman in such transactions.

On an intraregional scale, rare *o-no* (purchase) texts clearly record the acquisition of one commodity in exchange for specified quantities of others (Killen 1988, 1995a; Palmer 1994:91–94). Moreover, the rarity of these purchase texts must be evaluated against a consideration of their function and duration. Although all surviving Mycenaean texts were intended to be short-lived administrative records, those relating to taxation, land grants, and direct agricultural or craft production served to monitor the fulfillment of recurrent and predictable transactions. Such transactions were likely to be represented more or less permanently—for example, by an assessment record, by a record of payments and of any deficits, by an assessment record for the following year, and so on (Killen 1984a:184). Indeed, sometimes accounts of the same obligation recur in surviving documents relating to successive stages in the administrative process (e.g., detailed records and totaling records; Killen 1996; Olivier 1967), to successive seasons (e.g., flock composition and shearing records from Knossos; Killen 1964:10), or even to different years (flock replenishment and reallocation records from Pylos; Killen 1993b). Purchase records, on the other hand, were probably internal memos from one department that had purchased alum or linen textiles to another department, authorizing the issuance of a specified quantity of wine, wheat, or bronze in payment (Palmer 1994:93). An hour after being written, such a text might have been carried along the corridor to another department, acted upon, and discarded into a basket to await pulping. In other words, surviving purchase texts might represent transactions that took place literally in the final hours before the destruction of a palace and so might well be underrepresented, relative to texts covering recurrent obligatory transactions, by a factor of several hundred or even several thousand. The few surviving purchase texts may therefore represent a major sphere of economic activity. Even if the unrecorded transactions inferred from material evidence and from analogy were never

the subject of such short-term purchase texts, there is no a priori reason why these complementary flows into and out of the palaces should not have taken place on the basis of the exchange of commodities and services one for another. For the sake of brevity, rather than to foreclose debate, these unrecorded flows of resources are referred to below under the term "exchange."

QUANTITATIVE EVALUATION OF PALATIAL MOBILIZATION

The contributions of taxation, direct production and exchange to palatial mobilization cannot be compared directly because of differences both in the types of commodity or service delivered and in the problems of preservation or inference involved. Nonetheless, a crude relative quantitative assessment may be informative.

Taxation procured a number of commodities, including some of more or less uncertain identity sometimes measured in unknown units. Flax targets at Pylos may have taken account, inter alia, of regional differences in the capacity to produce this crop (Chadwick 1976; Foster 1981). Assessments in the main *Ma* and *Mc* taxation records at Pylos and Knossos respectively were, however, based on a fixed ratio between commodities, and so made no allowance for the local ecology of each contributing subcenter or community, implying that taxes were collected in readily attainable quantities (Shelmerdine 1973:263). (An alternative but much less parsimonious interpretation is that taxes were high and that communities met their assessments by exchanging surpluses of local specialties with other communities.) Moreover, it has been argued (most recently by Killen [1996]) that local tax assessments were derived from the sharing out between contributing communities of a round-number total assessment, ignoring exemptions; this hypothesis implies that the volume of each commodity collected by taxation was determined by historical convention, moderated by unrelated and probably variable exemptions and not by calculation of the palace's requirements. Some taxable resources are of known identity, were measured in known units, and included basic raw materials, such as flax and small amounts of bronze for palace workshops or several hundred men apparently mustered for military service (Chadwick 1976:77).

On the other hand, raw wool was collected in large quantities from palace-run flocks (thirty to fifty tons annually at Knossos; Killen 1984b:50). Both Knossos

and Pylos also supported several hundred fully dependent women textile workers (Chadwick 1988; Killen
1984b), and rations for these workers probably came
from palace-administered agriculture. At Pylos, two-
thirds of palatial workers were supported by land grants
(assigned here to taxation) and only one-third by rations
(derived, it is suggested, from direct production), but
those supported by land grants apparently owed only
part-time service (Killen 1979a), while many of those
drawing rations were full-time dependents (Chadwick
1988; Hiller 1988). In other words, taxation was
apparently secondary to direct production in palatial
mobilization of raw materials (possibly), personnel
(probably), and staple foods (almost certainly).

The scale of some direct production was clearly
considerable, most notably in the case of the Knossos
records of wheat harvests (one record of perhaps 800
tons; Chadwick 1976:118) and sheep flocks (80,000 or
more head; Olivier 1988). The palatial specialization in
wheat and sheep farming, implied by the texts, contrasts
sharply with the diversity of available bioarchaeological
evidence (Halstead 1992b). Late Bronze Age sites, both
palatial and nonpalatial, have yielded a wide variety of
cereal and pulse crops, and consideration of their very
different densities and processing requirements effectively precludes the possibility that the single textual
category "wheat" covers the range of grains attested to
archaeobotanically (Halstead 1995a). Likewise, Late
Bronze Age faunal assemblages suggest a more balanced mixture of domestic species and a wider range
of ages than the textual emphasis on adult male sheep
might indicate (Halstead 1996). This contrast suggests
that textually attested palatial farming represents only
a part of overall regional farming and that nonpalatial
farmers supplied the palaces with crops that are absent
from and animals that are rare in the texts. It further
suggests that the latter, unrecorded mobilization of
crops and livestock was on a sufficiently large scale
that the bioarchaeological evidence from palatial sites
(which must derive from both documented and unrecorded production) affords no hint of specialization in
wheat or sheep.

In sum, palatial mobilization, particularly of staple
food resources, was arguably dominated by unrecorded
transactions involving some form(s) of exchange.
A major role was also played by direct agricultural
production, but taxation, the most obvious and intensively studied form of resource mobilization, played a
relatively minor direct role. The mobilization through
taxation, however, of nonstaple raw materials and of

skilled master craftsmen was of vital indirect importance
to the palatial economy, if palatial craft goods played a
major role in unrecorded exchange transactions.

WIDER IMPLICATIONS OF THE MODEL

To place this synthesis in a wider context, Mycenaean
palatial mobilization was based on a combination of
staple and wealth finance (Brumfiel and Earle 1987;
Polanyi 1957; see also chapter 2, this volume) and there
are several further indications that the form of mobilization was related to distance (Killen 1985:246–247,
256–257), as predicted by Brumfiel and Earle (1987).
Bulky staple grains were directly produced in the
vicinity of the palatial centers and major administrative subcenters (Bennet 1985:246), and in the case of
Pylos, fully dependent textile workers were similarly
concentrated (Killen 1984b). Raw materials for craft
production were widely collected by taxation and
exchange both within and beyond the dependent territory of each palace, while finished craft goods such as
perfumed oil and jewelry were distributed by exchange
on a similar scale. Moreover, in the case of textile
production, wool was gathered from wether flocks
run in the inner provinces, while replacement wool
sheep were drafted in from breeding flocks in the outer
provinces (Bennet 1992; Godart 1971, 1977, 1992;
Halstead 1993a). In the case of the Mycenaean palaces,
wealth finance served to mobilize a much wider range
of resources over much greater distances and probably
in much greater quantities than staple finance, but the
production of staples in the vicinity of the palaces and
major subcenters financed the craftswomen who made
the "currency" needed for such wealth finance.

On what basis were resources mobilized by the
palaces? As Killen (1985) has stressed, control of land
played a key role. Grants of land to high-ranking
personnel secured a variety of administrative, craft,
and military services and also carried obligations to
provide certain raw materials to the center. Other
raw materials (oil, wine) were produced under central
control on palace land. Palatial control of large areas of
land close to the major centers and of smaller plots in
other communities might be a historical legacy of the
assimilation of local elites and their land in the process
of agglomerative state-building plausibly outlined for
Pylos by Bennet (1995; chapter 3, this volume). Much
land, however, was not controlled by the palace (de

Fidio 1992), and it is possible that the rations to feed low-ranking workers were produced on damos land, with the palace contributing plow oxen (Killen 1993c). Plow oxen, being costly to feed, were often restricted in the recent past to a minority of farmers who cultivated on a scale sufficient to justify their maintenance (Halstead 1995b).

Menial workers receiving rations were in many cases accompanied by children, suggesting full-time dependence on the palace, while references to training and the apparent recurrence of the same women in successive censuses imply long-term dependence (Chadwick 1988). In the Near East, such dependent workers seem to have been drawn both from foreign captives and from destitute members of the local population. Ethnic labels attached to some groups of female workers in Linear B hint at a similarly mixed origin (Chadwick 1988; Killen 1979b). There are many possible causes of such destitution, including the economic failure of households in the face of periodic crop failure. In Mycenaean Greece, many common domestic strategies for coping with agricultural risk were undermined by palatial control of much land; by palatial extraction from nonpalatial farmers of surplus grain, labor, and livestock; and by palatial monopoly of specialized craft production. In these circumstances, failing households may frequently have needed external subsistence relief, which could have been provided either from palatial grain stores or from the hundreds of palatial wool sheep that must have been pensioned off each year (Halstead 1993b). Enforced recourse to such subsistence relief may account for the existence of groups of fully dependent female workers, although textual hints of a link between these women and men fulfilling military service (de Fidio 1987:138) may indicate that female obligations of service are also bound up with grants of land.

Palatial mobilization clearly financed central defensive and ritual services. Military personnel and bronze to produce javelin points were raised through the taxation system (Foster 1981), and palace workshops built and maintained chariots. Land, flocks, and workshops attributed to various deities (though administered by the central bureaucracy) imply that a proportion of palatial direct production was devoted to the upkeep of sanctuaries or performance of rituals (de Fidio 1977; Killen 1987a). Administrators at both Knossos and Pylos recorded the issuing of a range of offerings, including perfumed oil manufactured in palatial workshops (Foster 1977; Shelmerdine 1985). Whether or not military personnel were also used internally to back up mobilization with coercion, the performance of ritual doubtless helped to legitimize palatial authority.

There is also textual evidence for other state-sponsored ceremonies, including major banquets at Thebes, Knossos, and Pylos, the last of which may well have been held to celebrate the accession of a new king (Killen 1994). In the case of the Thebes and Knossos banquets, animals for slaughter and other foodstuffs were contributed by a range of communities or persons, in a manner reminiscent of the taxation system. Texts at Pylos record the disbursement, on the same basis, of substantial quantities of wine, suggesting central sponsorship of feasting in local communities (Killen 1994; Palmer 1994). In the palace of Pylos, an elite banquet is depicted on a fresco in the megaron (central portion of palace) and the contents of the nearby pantries suggest provision for entertaining large numbers of guests of more modest status (Wright 1995b; chapter 4, this volume), while a deposit full of figurines, cups and bowls, and animal bones at Nemea-Tsoungiza seems to represent feasting at a small rural shrine (Wright 1994:69). Such acts of conspicuous consumption and apparent generosity may have played an important role in rewarding and reaffirming obligations of service (Hamilakis 1996).

Finally, it is striking that the commodities disbursed by the palaces through wealth finance tend to be not only valuable, in the sense of embodying scarce raw materials or specialist craftsmanship, but also socially significant. Clothing is a common vehicle for marking status, and one of the most important palatial industries was the production of ornate textiles. Some types of cloth were even named after a particular social rank (Killen 1985:288, n. 47) and textiles may have been distributed at ceremonial feasts (Killen 1994). Wine was distributed in quantity by palatial administrators (Palmer 1994), and it is clear from iconography that the etiquette and equipment for pouring and drinking wine were important markers of status (Wright 1995b). The palaces also manufactured jewelry that, whether attached to clothing or worn separately, advertised and affirmed status. Such jewelry is mainly found (though it need not have been mainly used) in graves, and it is clear that both perfumed oil, another major product of palatial workshops, and wine played important roles in funerary ritual (Cavanagh 1998; Shelmerdine 1985:125–128). Grave goods of possibly palatial origin are widespread even in the simpler Mycenaean burials (e.g., Lewartowski 1995), and clear distinctions of rank (as opposed to gradations of wealth) are not readily apparent in the mortuary record (Cavanagh and Mee 1990), suggesting some potential for negotiation of status in death through displays of wealth or, more strictly, access to prestige goods.

The most elaborate prestige goods from palatial workshops were probably used in gift exchanges with visiting dignitaries or high-ranking palace officials, while more modest examples may have rewarded local leaders for their role in collecting taxes and mobilizing corvée labor (also Morris 1986). Palatial craft goods were also apparently distributed to individuals of only modest rank, either directly from the center or through local community leaders; in return, it is suggested, whether under the guise of gift exchange or as explicit *o-no* transactions, the palace acquired the many commodities that do not appear in records of taxation or direct production. Thus the basis of Mycenaean wealth finance was palatial disbursement of craft goods that were not merely valued objects but also included prestige goods playing an active role in the affirmation and negotiation of status.

Mycenaean palatial mobilization was effected by a combination of taxation, direct production, and exchange, and was variously enforced, rewarded, or legitimized through control of land, provision of rations, manipulation of status differentiation, conspicuous consumption, and the provision of ritual and defensive services. A fruitful agenda for future research into palatial origins would be a diachronic exploration of these different forms of and bases for mobilization. For example, to what extent can the three forms of mobilization distinguished in this chapter be detected in the earlier Minoan palaces of Crete? The Minoan Linear A texts are far fewer in number, less consistently formatted, and undeciphered, but some commodities, quantities, and structural principles can be identified (Palmer 1995). Very large volumes of staple grains and figs, especially at Hagia Triadha, suggest the possibility of large-scale direct production, while large groupings of personnel, in some cases associated with commodities in quantities that might represent rations, may represent centrally controlled work groups, perhaps for craft production. In addition to small numbers of livestock, perhaps intended for consumption or sacrifice, some larger sheep flocks at Zakro suggest the possibility of centrally directed animal husbandry (Palmer 1995). Repetitive texts suggesting taxation, however, at least on the fixed-ratio pattern of Linear B, appear to be lacking (Palmer 1995:146), although evident differences between Linear A and Linear B in contexts and systems of recordkeeping (Olivier 1990; Palaima 1987a) indicate

the need for caution. The small corpus of hieroglyphic records must be approached with even greater circumspection, but Olivier has argued persuasively that large numbers, unqualified by any indication of what is being counted, are records of personnel (Olivier 1990). Such records, suggestive of the large-scale mobilization of corvée labor, again seem more compatible with centralized direct production than with decentralized taxation or exchange. Some of the social strategies that underpinned Mycenaean palatial mobilization may be traced archaeologically back to the first palaces on Crete and even into the Early Bronze Age or Neolithic: conspicuous hospitality (Halstead 1995c; Hamilakis 1996; Vitelli 1993; Wright 1995b), the production and consumption of fine craft goods (Branigan 1987; Day et al. 1997; Nakou 1995; Perlès 1992; Whitelaw et al. 1997), communal ritual activity (Branigan 1995; Peatfield 1992), and perhaps the use of oxen to facilitate agricultural overproduction (Pullen 1992). At what point do these various strategies become subject to centralized control and manipulation?

CONCLUSIONS

This brief treatment of a complex subject oversimplifies many problems and ignores many potential avenues; the subtitle, "Toward a Model of Mycenaean Palatial Mobilization," was chosen advisedly. Critics will variously wish to correct or reject this model, but two conclusions of a positive nature do seem justified. First, although serious investigation of Mycenaean mobilization has hitherto been dominated by text-based scholars, it is becoming increasingly clear that most economic activity within the territories of the Mycenaean palaces took place outside the scrutiny of the Linear B bureaucracy. The same is very probably true even of transactions involving the palaces themselves. Indeed, the Linear B records seem to offer not only a very incomplete account of the resource flows that financed the palaces but also a very biased picture of the forms of integration through which these flows were channeled. The responsibility now clearly lies with archaeologists to make imaginative but rigorous use of the material record to explore those spheres of Mycenaean economy and palatial mobilization that are invisible in the textual record.

Second, there is evident potential in a diachronic analysis of different forms of mobilization and of the various "carrots and sticks" (Renfrew 1982b) that underpinned them. Such attention to changing social strategies would offer a valuable complement to the more usual emphasis on the material manifestations of changing social structure—the settlement hierarchies, grand architectural complexes, and rich burials financed by elite mobilization.

Acknowledgments. Thanks are due to Mike Galaty and Bill Parkinson for inviting me to the SAA meetings in the appropriately labyrinthine environment of Opryland in Nashville. My participation was made possible by the generosity of the Department of Classical and Near Eastern Archaeology at Bryn Mawr College, the Museum of Anthropology and Department of Classical Studies at the University of Michigan, and the Department of Classics at the University of Cincinnati. Many thanks are owed to Jim Wright, John O'Shea, John Cherry, and Jack Davis for mobilizing these resources. I am grateful to John Killen and Chris Mee for advice during the writing of this chapter, to participants in the Nashville session for many perceptive comments on an early version, to John Bennet and Glynis Jones for deservedly critical observations on the penultimate written draft, to Bill Cavanagh and John Killen for access to work in press, and to Keith Branigan for bibliographic help.

CHAPTER 8

WEALTH CERAMICS, STAPLE CERAMICS

POTS AND THE MYCENAEAN PALACES

卐卐卐卐卐卐卐

MICHAEL L. GALATY

ARCHAEOLOGISTS WORKING IN SEVERAL regions of the world have found ancient ceramic industries to be fertile sources of information concerning the socioeconomic structure of state-level societies (e.g., D'Altroy and Bishop 1990; Feinman 1985; Johnson 1973; Knapp and Cherry 1994; Peacock 1982; Rice 1987a; Stein and Blackman 1993; Whitbread 1995). In this chapter, chemical analysis of pottery from the Mycenaean state of Pylos is presented, with results significant to the study of Late Bronze Age Greek economic systems. Finewares such as kylikes (wine cups; see figure 8.1) apparently were produced at a single, nucleated workshop, whereas coarse, utilitarian wares appear to have been manufactured at several dispersed workshops. Nucleated production of fineware ceramics may have been the ultimate result of increased opportunities for commercialization in response to the functioning of a regional palatial economy, one that valued and circulated wealth items (see chapters 1, 2, and 13, this volume), and certain classes of fineware pottery, such as kylikes, may be broadly defined as wealth items. As such, palatial elite may have had reason to extend increasing control over a nucleated workshop, only selectively interacting with dispersed, regional systems of staple (utilitarian or subsistence) ceramic manufacture and distribution. If indeed individuals gained political might and social standing by directing the wealth economy, then comparison of the production and distribution of kylikes to that of utilitarian wares may help to establish how they did so.

KYLIKES

Greek ceramic industries represent networks of social, political, and economic concerns: pots were placed in burials; inscribed and painted with meaningful symbols; and used for cooking, serving, storage, and the transport of valuable commodities such as perfume, wine, and oil. Kylikes (figure 8.1) are stemmed and handled cups that appear to have functioned in a wide variety of ritual contexts (Hägg 1990, 1995; Saflund 1980; Wright 1994, 1995b). Therefore, as politically charged commodities (Brumfiel and Earle 1987:5; Stein 1994a:14), the patterns of their production, distribution, and consumption can be expected to differ from those of utilitarian wares, such as cookpots and storage jars.

Pots serve as both tools (Braun 1983) and symbols (Kenoyer 1995). As a result, their production and distribution are influenced by economic as well as sociopolitical and religious factors (Hodder 1981). Mycenaean pottery has typically been categorized by probable function (Furumark 1941; Mountjoy 1986; Tournavitou 1992a), sometimes determined by analogy to the known uses of pottery in Classical times

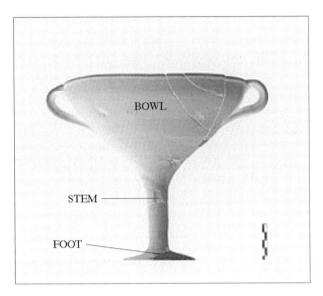

FIGURE 8.1 Kylix morphology. (All illustrations by M. Galaty.)

(Weinberg 1965). In addition, Bronze Age pots have been described according to their role in ritual, for example, in processions (Mantzourani 1995) and burials (Weinberg 1965; Zerner 1988).

In recent years, Aegean prehistorians have made great strides in identifying the material correlates to ritual action, including pottery (see Morris 1986; Shelmerdine 1997; Warren 1986; Wright 1994, 1995c; various articles in French and Wardle 1988; Hägg and Marinatos 1981; Hägg and Nordquist 1990). For example, the so-called throne room in the palace at Pylos can now be interpreted as a ritual space (chapter 4, this volume; Wright 1994) in which sacrifices may have been offered (McCallum 1987) and libations poured (Hägg 1990) (see figure 1.2, a plan of the palace, and figure 4.2, an iconographic depiction of Mycenaean ritual, including a toasting ceremony). It is also quite likely that such activity took place in conjunction with feasts (Killen 1994; Saflund 1980; Wright 1994), and that these feasts were held in the large courtyard (room 63) and the halls of state (rooms 64 and 65) located to the west of the palace (Blegen et al. 1973:426; Morris 1986).

Nearly 1100 kylix fragments were recovered from the floors of rooms 64 and 65 (Morris 1986:130). According to Morris (1986:138), 90.6 m² of palace space (out of an approximate total of 2000 m²) was devoted to the storage of pottery, and the total number of pots found in storage may have exceeded 8000. Of these 8000 pots, nearly 50% were kylikes (Morris 1986:141), with 2853 from room 19 alone (Saflund 1980:238). The other 50% of the pots were primarily bowls, cups, and

dippers (Morris 1986:141–142). Given such evidence, it becomes impossible to avoid the conclusion that palatial elites were hosting feasts in combination with massive amounts of drinking, mostly of wine (Wright 1995b; see also, chapters 1–4, 6, and 13, this volume, as to the importance of feasts), and that pottery, specifically kylikes, marks the location of this activity.

To a certain extent, kylikes tend to survive in, on, and around archaeological sites because of their form. The well-built stem and foot especially withstand decomposition. Furthermore, kylix fragments are easily recognized by surveyors and excavators and may for this reason be selectively found, saved, and catalogued. The biased collection of kylix fragments is not, however, simply a function of differential survival and identification. Their dominance in LH IIIB pottery assemblages, especially at those sites that appear to have been primary and secondary centers, may be due to their more intensive storage and use relative to all other pottery types, as at the palace. If kylikes can indeed be associated with the drinking of wine in such ritual contexts (Wright 1995b) as feasts (Saflund 1980), then feasts may have taken place not only at palaces but in other settlements as well. There are very good archaeological parallels for this kind of decentralized political activity, such as is evidenced in Inca regional subcenters (see Costin and Earle 1989). Preliminary analysis of the faunal assemblage from a small shrine at Tsoungiza, a settlement associated with the palatial center of Mycenae, appears to indicate remains consistent with feasting (Wright 1994:69).

Several Aegean pottery specialists have argued that kylikes constitute everyday tableware used by Mycenaean elites and commoners for the drinking of wine and water (Shear 1987; Tournavitou 1992). They do not dispute the possible use of kylikes in ritual activity, and yet do not attach overt symbolic importance to kylikes themselves. Tournavitou (1992:205) describes the place-setting of Mycenaean domestic tableware, including kylikes, based on the pottery excavated at so-called houses located in Mycenae's Lower Town: the House of Shields, the House of the Oil Merchant, the House of the Sphinxes, and the West House. It can be argued, however, that these houses—from which Linear B tablet fragments, foreign trade goods, and fresco fragments were also recovered (in short, artifacts suggesting the elite character of these structures)—do not represent average domestic contexts. In fact, there have been very few excavations of small Mycenaean settlements (see Davis 1988), and where such sites have been excavated (such as at Nichoria; McDonald and Wilkie 1992), house floors have rarely been preserved in situ because of deep plowing. Thus, pottery excavated at these sites cannot with certainty be termed domestic either.

Even if kylikes were commonly used in domestic contexts, this does not exclude them from symbolic attachments. Material objects often used for seemingly mundane purposes may still have deep ideological and ritual significance. As Kenoyer (1995:12) observes, with regard to Pakistan's Harrapan period pottery:

> The fact that red slipped and black painted ceramics become the diagnostic form of painted pottery during the Indus state would indicate that anyone desiring to emulate, affiliate or integrate to this social-ritual-political system would acquire and visibly display such ceramics. Such ceramics were not used only in the domestic context but are found set along the public road in front of houses.

Every Mycenaean household may have possessed a kylix or two, or more. As Renfrew (1994:47) notes, however, cult activity is often inextricably embedded within the other activities of daily life. In addition to functioning as tableware, kylikes may have also symbolized elite power in that they recalled the ritualized drinking of wine (see figure 4.2) and, therefore, processions, sacrifices, feasting, and the dispensation of wealth, as well (see Wright 1994, 1995b, 1995c). Furthermore, they are frequently found in locations of suspected cult activity, as in House G at Asine, where a kylix and an upended receptacle vessel, probably once used for ritual libations, were excavated (Wright 1994:65). In fact, Hägg (1990) identifies the kylix, as well as miniature kylikes (see Wright 1995b:16), as the vessel most commonly used in both public and private Mycenaean libation ceremonies. Religious figurines, found in both civic and domestic ritual contexts, are often depicted raising a goblet or kylix (Wright 1994:65). In addition, it is possible that kylikes "marked the attainment of status" and were given to young Mycenaean men "as part of an initiation into manhood" (Wright 1995b:12). As Wright contends, "[it] may well be [that] the remnants of Mycenaean belief [are] manifested in the most accessible, humble and traditional forms of symbol and action" (1994:72).

It is of course possible that iconographic representations of Mycenaean (see figure 4.2) and Minoan drinking rituals (such as portrayed on the "Chieftain" cup and the "Camp Stool" fresco) depict "toasting" not with clay but with metal vessels. The use of metal kylikes at ceremonial gatherings, such as those associated with the palace, does not detract from the foregoing argument. In fact, the possibility that ceramic kylikes were used by secondary elites and commoners in imitation of those who could afford precious metals might help to explain their wide distribution. If anything, processes of emulation would have enhanced the symbolic importance of ceramic kylikes, making their commercialized production and controlled regional exchange that much more meaningful and potentially profitable.

Perhaps as a result of their ritual importance, kylikes, as opposed to most other forms of pottery, may have been of special interest to state bureaucrats in the economic climate of the LH IIIB. If indeed the state was tightening control of prestige goods and ritual was being used more frequently and more intensively to integrate different segments of society (see chapters 1–3, this volume), then kylikes may have been a logical target for palatial administration. In their production and distribution, as revealed in the chemical data, kylikes appear to differ from the other Mycenaean wares studied.

UTILITARIAN WARES

Although kylikes were of interest to the palace because of their political and symbolic significance, other wares were of interest for their more general value as much-needed equipment. Evidence for the palatial acquisition of utilitarian pottery is provided by Linear B tablet PY *Vn 130*, which consists of thirteen lines (see Morris 1986:102; compare chapters 1 and 11, this volume). Lines 1 and 2 of this tablet read:

.1   o-ze-to , ke-sa-do-ro , *34-to-pi ,
.2a   pa-ro
.2b   a-ke-a2

As with most Linear B inscriptions, it is far from clear exactly what is meant by lines 1 and 2, but the most plausible translation is "And so Kessandros took [or received] containers with strainers." Lines 2 through 13 go on to list the people from whom he took vessels, "from *e-ru-si-jo* (person) at *a-pi-no-e-wi-jo* (place)," and so on. Each designation is followed by a number, perhaps a unit of measurement, but more likely the number of vessels taken or received. Line 12 refers to *ro-u-so*, a major town located to the south of the palace. It contributes twenty-four vessels, much more than any other place, and no personal name is associated with it. Most towns or individuals provide between three and nine pots. Many provide only one.

Several questions can be raised with regard to this tablet. First, what kind of vessel is changing hands? The Mycenaean word a-ke-a₂ is translated into Classical Greek as *aggos* (pl. *aggea*). Aggos is used in different ways in Classical literature to refer to many types of pottery. In modern Greek, it is a general term meaning container. As a result, there is little certainty as to what specific vessel type a-ke-a₂ refers. The word *34-to-pi* appears to refer to some sort of strainer, probably made of fired clay and fitted over the mouth of the a-ke-a₂. *34-to-pi* may also refer to the type of a-ke-a₂ needed, a vessel that was itself a strainer.

Shelmerdine (1985) describes such tools in the context of perfume production. If indeed the vessels referred to in *Vn 130* were used in the making of perfume, they were likely vital to the operation of the industry, which had been centralized at the palace. Based on the Homeric use of the word *aggos*, Morris (1986:102) suggests that Kessandros was collecting cooking pots. If the vessels were used for making perfume, they would have been the functional equivalent of cooking pots in terms of fabric and shape.

Second, why would some people contribute only one vessel while others contributed many? Morris (1986:102) implies that this tablet records the collection of pottery from regional heads of potting workshops, some of which, such as ro-u-so, were larger than others and thus responsible for providing more pots. Given the structure and vocabulary of the document, it is not clear whether the pots collected compose a "tithe" or "operating permit," in the sense of an obligatory pottery payment, or represent the fulfillment of contracts negotiated for the palace on the part of Kessandros. If the pots were tithed, then the palace filled its need for a special type of pottery, at the same time exercising some control over regional pottery workshops. If, on the other hand, the palace was buying the pots outright, and collection was not an exercise in economic control, why did Kessandros spread the purchases over such a wide territory? Why not buy from one workshop, that located closest to the palace? It may be that Kessandros did not travel to these places to collect the pots but that they were delivered to him. He may have "taken" or "received" them while sitting on the front steps of the palace. Either way, the system seems quite inefficient. Surely ro-u-so, which already provided twenty-four of fifty-six *aggea*, could have come up with an additional

thirty-two pots, or the palace could have moved production of *aggea* to the center.

To Halstead (1992a), such tablets record very irregular economic transactions. Consequently, tablet *Vn 130* represents a temporary, soon-to-be-disposed-of note which was intended to remind an administrator (perhaps Kessandros himself) that the palace perfumery needed pots and that they had been ordered and/or collected. Such transactions, because they occurred so rarely, appear to be handled inefficiently, especially when compared to the streamlined collection of regional taxes (as in the *Ma* tablets) or the regular allocation of raw materials in the ta-ra-si-ja system (as in the *Jn* bronze tablets). The palace bureaucrats somehow announced, perhaps through secondary regional elites, the center's need for *aggea*, which were either sent or collected. In this way, the palace transferred the expense of transporting pots and the responsibility for their delivery to regional subcenters or to individual merchants.

As indicated in the Linear B texts, the palace apparently collected utilitarian wares from many different regional pottery workshops. Unlike kylikes, which appear to have been made in a relatively few workshops, perhaps even one, utilitarian wares show much more regional variation in elemental chemical content. Thus, as described in more detail later in the chapter, archaeological data agree with the documentary references to utilitarian pottery.

METHODOLOGY: FIELDWORK

The foundations for this research were laid in three seasons of work with the Pylos Regional Archaeological Project (PRAP), under the direction of Jack Davis (see chapter 3, this volume; Davis 1998; Davis et al. 1997; Zangger et al. 1997). Selected for chemical analysis were 310 ceramic samples (table 8.1) from eighteen LH IIIB Messenian sites located in the vicinity of the palace at Ano Englianos (figure 8.2), with the help of Cynthia Shelmerdine and Joan Carothers in collection and analysis. (Carothers [1992] analyzed a sample of 198 sherds, included in table 8.1, as part of her doctoral dissertation research.) Of these, 114 fragments are without doubt from kylikes. For the most part, all sampled kylikes appear to have been of the unpainted variety, plain and apparently mass-produced. Sherds were analyzed for elemental chemical composition by weak acid extraction followed by inductively coupled plasma (ICP) spectroscopy (see Burton and Simon 1993, 1996)

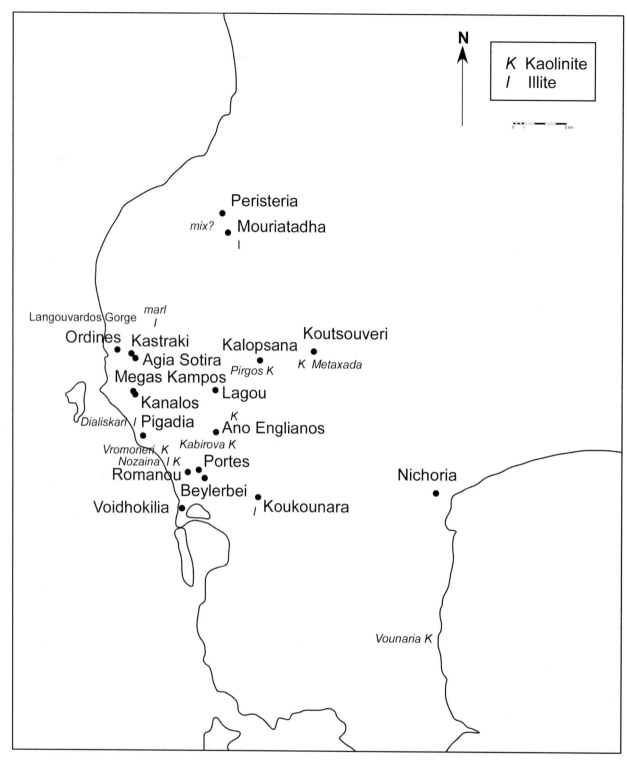

FIGURE 8.2 Map of Messenia, with LH IIIB sites and clay beds sampled.

TABLE 8.1 Late Helladic IIIB sites from which ceramic material was analyzed.

SITE	ID NO.	PRAP SHERDS	CAROTHERS'S SHERDS	EST. SIZE (HA)[4,5]	LBA PLACE NAME
Romanou	I4	6		3.4	
Megas Kampos	D2	4		1.6	
Pigadia	G3	1		1	
Beylerbei	I1	16		12	*a-ke-re-wa*[1]
Kalopsana	A2	1		6.9	
Koutsouveri	L1	1		1.5	
Ordines	K1	20		4.6	*pe-to-no*[1]
Portes	I3	16		0.1	
Lagou	I21	2		1	
Kastraki	K3	4		2.1	
Agia Sotira	K2	1		0.8	
Kanalos	D1	1		0.5	
Epano Englianos	B7	39	45	21	*pu-ro*[2]
Nichoria	100		33	5–6	*ti-mi-to a-ke-e*[1,3]
Voidhokilia	8		25	?	
Koukounara	35		59	.8 min	*ro-u-so*[6]
Peristeria	200		21	?	
Mouriatadha	201		25	?	
Total		112	198		
Grand Total: 310					

Sources:
1. Davis et al. 1997:426.
2. Chadwick 1972:101.
3. Shelmerdine 1981.
4. PRAP Internet Edition (http://classics.uc.edu/PRAP/).
5. McDonald and Rapp 1972.
6. Bennet 1999.

in the Laboratory for Archaeological Chemistry at the University of Wisconsin–Madison, with the help of T. Douglas Price and James Burton.

In preparing this project, PRAP's computer data and survey logs were searched, with very little success, for evidence of on- and off-site ceramic production, including any references to ceramic wasters, slag, other kiln debris, pottery anvils, molds, and lenses of ash (Feinman 1985; Nicklin 1979; Pool 1992; Stark 1985). In addition, every PRAP site that had produced LH IIIB pottery was revisited and checked for evidence of pottery manufacture, again with no success. Each site was also evaluated in terms of its ceramic resources, such as the availability of water, fuel, clay, and temper. Resurvey was combined with intensive and systematic clay and temper collection in the vicinity of each site (Neff et al. 1992; Talbott 1984). This procedure allowed for a more complete definition of the region's ceramic capabilities.

Traditional Messenian potters were also helpful in defining the study region's ceramic ecology (see Day 1988, 1989; Helmsley 1991). Two traditional potters were interviewed: one from Vounaria, located to the southeast, quite a distance outside the PRAP study region; and one from Skala, near Kalamata, again in Messenia but far outside the study region. They both agreed that workable clay exists in the study region, mostly in river valleys. Local villagers confirmed this obnservation, directing me to several regional clay sources.

Frederick Matson begins his contribution to *The Minnesota Messenia Expedition* with the statement, "Availability of clay has never been a problem in this region" (1972:200). On the contrary, even with the help of potters and villagers, workable clay was very difficult to locate. Most Bronze Age sites are surrounded either by well-developed red soils, *terra rossa* alfisols, or, where these have eroded, silty, unstable soils derived from the region's marl C-horizon (Zangger et al. 1997). These poorly developed, marly soils are produced primarily by the plowing activities of modern farmers. If marls were used during the Bronze Age as a source of potting or tempering material, they must have been mined. The intact red soils are fairly high in clay content, as much as 20% to 30%, whereas marl soils, having scarcely undergone pedogenesis, contain substantially less clay. The red beds formed from marine terrace sediments, as well as from colluvium from similar material eroded at higher elevations (Zangger et al. 1997:628). X-ray diffraction analysis, undertaken in the Department of Geology at the University of Wisconsin–Madison (with the help of James Burton), indicates that this soil's primary clay mineral constituent is illite. Illites were likely included in colluvial or alluvial deposits eroded to lower elevations from bedrock sources in the uplands.

Illitic clay was separated from red soil by levigation (the mixing of clay or soil with water to allow coarser particles to wash and settle out of the suspension [Rice 1987b:118]), and was subjected to various experimental procedures (following Rice 1987b; Vitelli 1984) to test plasticity, shrinkage, strength, and workability, and was found to be less than ideal for the general production of pottery. Marls were found to be nearly unusable.

The region's gray and yellow marine clays, however, required no levigation or tempering and were easily worked. They compared very well to a control clay sample provided by the Vounaria potter, who still mined all his own clay from a local deposit. Several of these clays, including the sample from Vounaria, were also subjected to X-ray diffraction analysis and were found to be kaolinites. The relatively rare Messenian kaolinite beds are primary clay mineral deposits formed in a low-energy, probably marine, environment. Of note, these marine clays occur rarely in outcrops, and in only a few instances are they associated with sites, such as at Englianos. Thus, good potting clay represents a "patchy" regional resource. Given the results of experimental work and regional ceramic ecology, it is probable that some Late Bronze Age sites were in a better position to mass-produce pottery than were others. It may be that pots were, for the most part, produced at sites having access to workable clay.

In all, sixteen Messenian clay samples were collected, some from primary kaolinite beds and some (illites) from red beds (see figures 8.2 and 8.3). Five of these samples were collected from red illitic soils. One sample is from marl. Another sample, from Peristeria, is a possible natural mix of clay minerals and soils. The other nine are kaolinites, including the control sample provided by the Vounaria potter. The clays themselves would have placed certain identifiable restraints on Bronze Age potting, and responses on the part of Pylian potters, such as clay mixing, to the technical limits of their craft must also be considered in interpreting the results of chemical analysis.

In the end, little or no direct archaeological evidence could be found in the study region for Mycenaean pottery production. No Late Bronze Age pottery

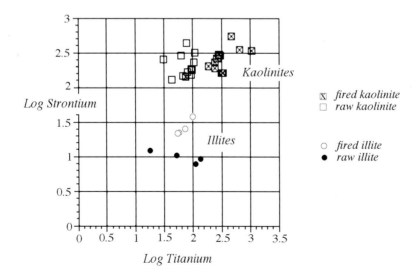

FIGURE 8.3 Scatterplot of log strontium versus log titanium for all clay samples. Note the strong compositional differences between kaolinites and illites.

workshops have been discovered and excavated. The landscape itself records no trace, toponymic or architectural, of a regional ceramic industry. Traditional Messenian potters, such as those visited at Vounaria and Skala, are a dying breed. Inferences as to the organization of the Pylian LH IIIB ceramic industry must therefore be made indirectly, by arguing from the artifacts themselves (Costin 1991).

METHODOLOGY: CHEMICAL ANALYSIS

The chemical analysis of ceramics has strongly influenced Aegean archaeology, perhaps more intensely than any other region in the world (Day 1989:139). Seminal research was conducted by Catling et al. (1963; see also Catling et al. 1980), who employed optical emission spectroscopy (OES) to analyze a large sample of Linear B inscribed stirrup jars (used to transport perfumed oil), demonstrating the west Cretan origin of these wares. This early work sought to reconstruct patterns of interregional long-distance trade through discovery of clay provenance. Since then and up to the present, chemical work in the Aegean, including neutron activation analysis (NAA), has for the most part combined two important goals: determining provenance (preferably exact provenance) and revealing international trade connections. More rarely, methods of chemical analysis have been applied to questions of ceramic technology, intraregional exchange, and the organization of ceramic production (Day 1989).

To a certain extent, archaeologists have avoided programs of intraregional investigation because elemental provenance studies tend to be somewhat confounded in restricted geographic areas (Day 1989). This problem, applicable to other regions of the world as well, results in part from the implicit desire on the part of archaeometrists to analytically equate ceramics with geological samples. As Burton and Simon (1996) have emphatically responded to this equation, however, "A pot is not a rock!" Geological samples, especially minerals, can usually be assigned an exact source, especially when the scale of analysis and comparison is very large (that is, Crete or Cyprus versus the Peloponnese). Potsherds are, however, not simply analogous to sedimentary—perhaps, more precisely, low-grade metamorphic—rocks. Pots encode significant behavioral information, whereas minerals do not. For precisely this reason, pots are of interest to archaeologists.

Potters do not simply dig clay out of the ground, make a pot, and fire it. They almost always employ elaborate recipes, combining different kinds of clay and soil, sometimes organic material, often exotic liquids such as seawater (even milk), and innumerable mineral tempers (see Barlow and Idziak 1989; Day 1988, 1989; Helmsley 1991; Maniatis and Tite 1978; Rice 1987b). Purification of clays (that is, sieving, washing, and so on) and the act of firing, often at variable temperatures in uncontrolled kiln atmospheres, further complicate matters (Kilikoglou et al. 1988). Chemical noise caused by the actions and behavior of potters may be smoothed out in the comparison of ceramics manufactured in very different geological regimes. This seemingly random noise, however, makes identifying the provenance of chemically similar, locally produced wares very difficult to impossible.

In applying chemical analysis to Pylian LBA ceramic samples, my goal is not the establishment of exact provenance. In fact, I have not been able to attach with certainty any ceramic sample to an identified regional clay source. Rather, this research has more in common with programs of stylistic and formal analysis. Chemistry reveals variations in the standardized manufacture of pottery, variations created by the aforementioned propensity on the part of different potters to use not only different clays but also different pottery recipes. Patterned variations in ceramic chemistry, taken in isolation, can be very difficult to interpret. By measuring standardization, however, chemistry does provide an important baseline for the reconstruction of ceramic industries and for the middle-range connection of theoretical models of ceramic production and distribution to raw archaeological data.

When considered together with textual (Linear B), ethnographic, ethnoarchaeological, and ecological information, chemically identified paste groups can be attached to hypothetical production types, functioning at different economic scales. To provide a very simple example, all 310 LH IIIB pots analyzed might hypothetically have had the same chemical signature (they did not). This might be caused by the use of one homogenous regional clay source by all Bronze Age potters (disproved in actuality by collection and analysis of regional clays). Such a pattern in the chemical data might also indicate centralized production and intraregional distribution of all pottery by one large potting facility (as it turns out, this is highly unlikely). In reality, the chemical data collected in this research do not absolutely disprove a completely centralized ceramic industry, owing to the effects of equifinality (Costin 1991; Rice 1987b), but they do make imagining such a system difficult. It can thus be said with a high degree of probability, based on ceramic chemistry considered in combination with other lines of evidence, that the Pylian LH IIIB ceramic industry was not centrally located and controlled. More important, establishing exact clay provenance is not crucial to this argument.

The specific type of chemical analysis employed in this research is weak acid extraction (WAE), followed by ICP spectroscopy (see Burton and Simon 1993, 1996). A portion of each sherd was cleaned of encrustations, slip, and paint, then ground with an agate mortar and pestle. Next, 2000 mg of fine powder from each sherd was dissolved in 1% molar dilute hydrochloric acid over a period of two weeks. After two weeks, the acid was poured into disposable test tubes and subjected to ICP spectroscopic analysis. Spectroscopy measured the amounts of twelve elements—aluminum, barium, calcium, iron, manganese, magnesium, phosphorous, potassium, sodium, strontium, titanium, and zinc—present in each sherd. Fired (800 degrees C.) and unfired clay samples were also analyzed following the same procedures.

Recently, WAE has been attacked, primarily by those doing NAA. Neff et al. (1996; see also Triadan et al. 1997) claim that WAE is, for example, overly sensitive to the effects of firing, and thus patterns in chemical data are obscured to the point of being uninterpretable. These problems with WAE do in fact exist. The method is somewhat susceptible to the effects of variable firing temperatures; however, the debate over the accuracy of WAE stems directly from the aforementioned disagreement as to what should comprise the appropriate goals of ceramic chemical analysis. Whereas archaeologists using NAA typically aspire to exact provenance, those applying WAE have primarily used chemical analysis as a starting point for more complex investigations of regional ceramic industries based on interpretation of relative provenance. Burton and Simon (1996) make the point forcefully that although firing temperature may complicate attempts at provenience, it is a variable that is potentially crucial to the understanding of regional differences in pottery manufacture and thus not "noise," as Neff et al. (1996; Triadan et al. 1997) contend.

RESULTS

Laboratory work with regional Pylian clays and a small sample of utilitarian wares was first reported (in papers co-authored with William Parkinson) at annual meetings of the Society for American Archaeology (in 1995) and the Archaeological Institute of American (in 1996). In a preliminary project, forty-one coarse potsherds from six LH IIIB Messenian sites (Ano Englianos, Koukounara, Nichoria, Voidhokilia, Peristeria, and Mouriatadha; see figure 8.2) were analyzed chemically and petrographically. This initial work supported the utility of both methods by demonstrating that Pylian clays/soils (see figure 8.3) did indeed differ in elemental and mineral content, as did pottery. Several different ceramic pastes were identified, with substantial mixing of all compositional groups at the various sites (that is, no single paste was particular to a single site), thereby suggesting the exchange of pots. These results were used, in conjunction with Parkinson's obsidian data (see Parkinson 1997, and chapter 9, this volume), to argue for the local production and distribution of certain items—which we broadly equated with staple (utilitarian) as opposed to wealth goods—manufactured and exchanged outside the direct control and interest of palatial authorities.

This chapter presents results of the chemical analysis of the remaining 269 ceramic samples. Generally speaking, these new data support original impressions as to the organization of the Pylian utilitarian ceramic industry and reveal, in comparison, a marked difference in the production, distribution, and consumption of finewares, especially kylikes. Kylikes are represented by far fewer paste groups and by a much higher degree of elemental homogeneity than utilitarian wares.

Ceramic chemical data are especially interesting when combined with chemical data produced by the analysis of regional Messenian clays (figure 8.4). In short, many pots appear to have been manufactured from kaolinite, whereas a subset was manufactured from illite, most probably obtained from red beds. These illitic samples—several kylikes and a substantial number of utilitarian pots—are characterized by a dark red fabric (the result of low-temperature firing) and are coarsely tempered with numerous mudstone and grit inclusions (Carothers 1992). These data thus accord well with the results of work done by Maniatis and Tite (1978) in which two broad ceramic traditions were identified for the Aegean, one based on the use of *calcareous* clays, the other on the use of *noncalcareous* clays.

It is very likely that these coarse pots (both utilitarian wares and a small number of kylikes) were manufactured locally by potters devoted to the production of ceramics from inferior, though very abundant, sources of clay.

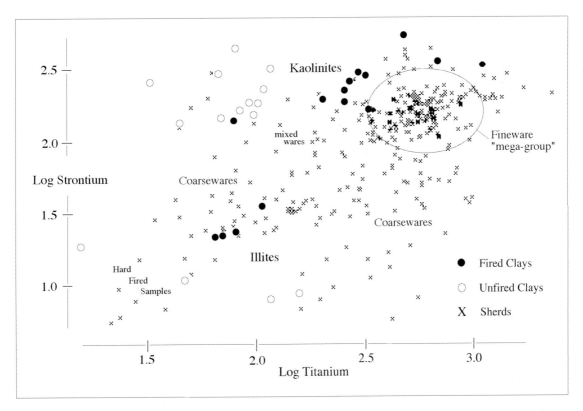

FIGURE 8.4 Scatterplot of ceramic and clay samples for log strontium versus log titanium. Many Pylian pots appear to have been manufactured from kaolinite. A significant number were also manufactured from illite, or perhaps in some cases from a mixture of kaolinite and illite.

The small scale of these hypothesized establishments accounts for the limits to their regional distribution. Furthermore, the time invested in the manufacture of pottery from illites would have been great. Pottery, such as the majority of kylikes, made from the naturally clean kaolinites could be mass-produced using fast wheels. Illite, given its coarseness, would not have been amenable to fast-wheel production.

Kylikes can be roughly divided into two groups (figure 8.5): a megagroup, composed of fineware kylikes made from kaolinites and chemically very homogenous; and a small compositional group made up of kylikes manufactured from illites. It is quite possible that these coarse kylikes were made in imitation of fineware kylikes. Compared to kylikes, utilitarian wares are much more chemically diverse (figure 8.6). As indicated in the pilot work, utilitarian wares represent more potential compositional groups, perhaps as many as three or more. One or more of these groups, perhaps as many as half the utilitarian wares, are composed of pots that were made from illites or perhaps a mixture of kaolinite and illite (very different clay/soil types are commonly mixed by modern-day Cypriot potters [Helmsley 1991]). The other utilitarian pots appear to be made from kaolin-

ites, and in fact can be classified as finewares. They are similar chemically to fineware kylikes.

The paste groups composed of pots made from illites, both kylikes and utilitarian wares, have somewhat restricted regional distributions. Utilitarian wares made from kaolinites and mixed clays account for several different paste groups with somewhat wider distributions. Kylikes that make up the so-called megagroup are found at all LH IIIB sites sampled. The data therefore provide evidence for two scales of production operating at different levels of intensity in Late Bronze Age Messenia: one local and small-scale, perhaps involving dispersed workshopping; the other producing for a larger regional market, likely nucleated workshopping (see Costin 1991; Peacock 1982).

The majority of kylikes (and many fine utilitarian wares) appear to have been mass-produced using fast wheels from the naturally clean kaolinites at one large pottery workshop. This industrialized concern might have potentially supplied all of the palace's kylikes, as well as the bulk of the kylikes distributed in the state. It is in this kind of operation that might have interested the palace bureaucrats. Surely, the palace routinely did business with such an operation. Linear B documents

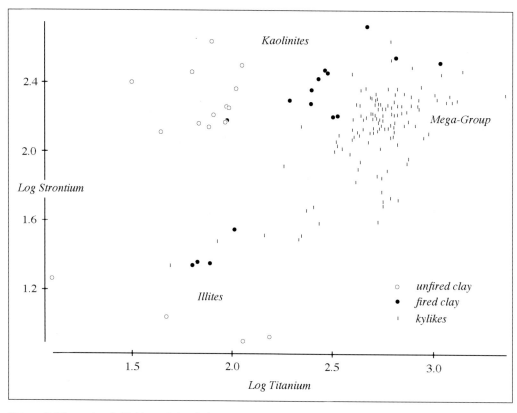

FIGURE 8.5 Scatterplot of all kylikes and clays for log strontium versus log titanium. A number of the kylikes appear to have been manufactured from illites.

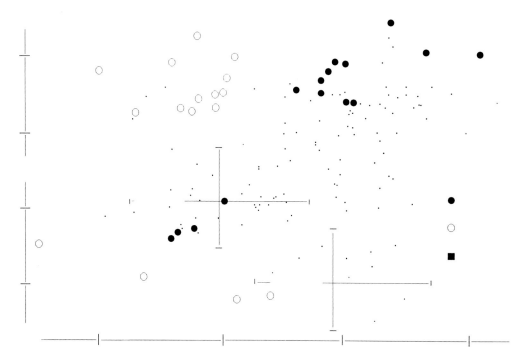

FIGURE 8.6 Scatterplot of utilitarian wares and clays for log strontium versus log titanium.

indicate that at least one potter—Brithawon, the "royal" potter—had been incorporated into the palace's workshop system (perhaps as an independent entrepreneur [Killen 1995a]), receiving land in return for his service (see chapter 4, this volume). Industries appear to have been pulled into the palace's workshopping system when the item produced was of prestige or ritual value or regularly used in great amounts by central elites. Of all pottery classes, kylikes best fit these expectations.

Utilitarian wares, as opposed to kylikes, display a much greater degree of variability in chemical content and regional distribution. Paste recipes are much less standardized. These data thus accord well with the Linear B documents, which, for example, indicate the highly decentralized collection of *aggea*. The transaction described in tablet *Vn 130* was informal and irregular, and the workshops that produced utilitarian pottery had been drawn only superficially into the palace's bureaucratized economic system.

DISCUSSION

In other polities, such as in the Inca Empire (D'Altroy and Bishop 1990), and in several Near Eastern states (Johnson 1973; Stein 1994a), local industries were eventually co-opted by the regional state administration and integrated into the state-level economy. As Gil Stein (1994a, 14) describes:

> centralized institutions attempted to extend administrative, political, and economic control over villages in the surrounding countryside in order to gain access to the surplus labor, agricultural goods, and pastoral products which were critical for the survival and social reproduction of Mesopotamian elites. . . . Uruk elites at Susa centralized ceramic production as a way to break the economic autonomy of villages on the Susiana plain, thereby drawing the latter into urban-based exchange networks.

According to administrative documents, the regional Late Bronze Age Messenian economy was primarily a wealth-financed economy (see D'Altroy and Earle 1985; chapters 1, 2, and 9, this volume). The state focused its economic power on the creation and control of easily transported products with pronounced ritual, aesthetic, or commercial value. As a result, the state depended for the acquisition of staple/utilitarian goods (that is, those goods necessary to daily life in Mycenaean Greece, but without the concentrated value of wealth items) on the

local systems of exchange that operated independently of the state economy itself. These local economic systems—with origins in earlier Neolithic times—are only rarely referred to in the Linear B palace documents (Halstead 1992a).

It cannot yet be established whether Pylos's leaders centralized ceramic production of pottery at the palace. Given the ceramic data thus far obtained, it appears that they did not. The most simple means of proving centralized production is to find an attached workshop (see, e.g., Sinopoli 1991; Stein and Blackman 1993; Tournavitou 1988; Whitbread 1995). However, unlike in other regions of Greece (such as Berbati in the Argolid [Åkerstrom 1968] and Myrtos in Crete [Warren 1972a]), no certain Bronze Age pottery workshop, let alone an attached one, has yet been located or excavated in Messenia. Blegen (Blegen et al. 1973:19–20) uncovered a small updraft kiln (around 2 m in diameter) at the northeastern end of the Pylos acropolis, to which he attached an unconfirmed date of Early Mycenaean. He asserts that although he found no evidence for LH IIIB pottery production at the palace itself, workshops must have been located nearby to supply the buildings large pantries:

> Variations from pantry to pantry in material, character, and types of wares definitely imply that two or three, if not more, potteries were at work in the era of the palace. (Blegen et al. 1973:20)

Blegen's impression receives partial confirmation in Wright's (1984) study of the pottery stored in rooms 18–20, 60, 67, and 68 of the palace. According to Wright, a systematic variation in ware types, vessel shapes and method of manufacture (such as handle attachment) from room to room is evident, suggesting that the products of at least two different workshops were stored in separate parts of the palace. For example, pots found in the pantries (rooms 18–20), which open to court 63 via court 88, are very different from those found in room 60, which opens both to the palace's exterior and to court 63 (see figure 1.2). According to Blegen and Rawson (1966:352), pots from room 60 are characterized by a fabric that is coarser and darker than that found in the pantries (see also Wright 1984:23). Room 60, as compared to the pantries, also held much less specialized pottery. Thus, storage of pottery in the palace appears to differentiate two broad ware types (see Wright 1984:23), which accords well with the results of chemical analysis. Furthermore, different wares appear to have been stored at the palace in similar proportions to those identified chemically.

In addition, Linear B tablet *Tn 996* recovered in room 20 may represent an inventory of some of the vessels found there. Wright (1984:23) argues that this tablet demonstrates that "individual potters' shops which contribute to the palatial economy are controlled by the palace bureaucracy." Given current anthropological understanding of the operation of ceramic industries in state-level societies, *Tn 996* might, however, as easily represent a purchase order or delivery receipt as it does bureaucratic control of potters. The tablet records the acquisition, or intended acquisition, of only twelve very specialized ceramic forms, among them "three drainable tubs for bathwater" (Ventris and Chadwick 1973:338), and thus would hardly appear to constitute evidence for palatial control of the ceramic industry.

Instead of directly controlling the regional ceramic system, palatial bureaucrats may have contributed to the ongoing commercialization of pottery production by acquiring kylikes from one manufacturer, the "royal" potter, at the expense of others, subsequently storing these pots in the large royal pantries. Furthermore, given their pronounced interest in wealth goods, palatial administrators may have had a greater desire to control the production of kylikes (and perhaps other finewares, such as pictorial vases) than utilitarian wares. Either way, the results of this research, while admittedly provisional, appear to support the existence of an independent and parallel local economy that only superficially intersected with the palace economy. Over time, this local economy may have been slowly driven out of existence or integrated into the state's economy. Given the evolutionary trajectory established for other states, such as those in the Near East and Mesoamerica, the palace may have eventually tried to attach the two or more largest potting villages to the palace, thereby increasing their control of the regional economy, curtailing the economic independence of smaller settlements, and lowering costs.

Peacock (1982) provides a good example from Roman times of attached pottery production. According to Peacock, many self-contained Roman estates operated slave-based pottery workshops to avoid the expense of purchasing and transporting pots (1982:10). In some instances, Roman estate production of pottery assumed a commercial role. Rice (1996) describes a similar situation at postcolonial Peruvian wine and brandy hacienda (that is, estate) sites (called *bodegas*) where many storage pots were manufactured, again in order to avoid purchase and transport costs. Small (chapter 5, this volume) compares the operation of the palace at Pylos to that of a very large estate. In light of this comparison, the palace may have determined, as did many large Roman estates and the Peruvian bodegas, that in the long term it was more cost-effective to manufacture utilitarian goods, such as pottery, than to purchase them. Working during the LH IIIB to cement its control of the production and distribution of wealth items, the palace may have also turned its attention to more direct involvement in the manufacture of utilitarian products.

IN CONCLUSION: A WORD OF CAUTION

Data generated by chemical analysis provide only a starting point for the investigation and reconstruction of ceramic industries. The conclusions drawn in this chapter are provisional and await further testing. Patterns in the chemical data have been examined in light of Linear B references to pottery manufacture. Likewise, ecological constraints on the pottery industry have been considered. Once thin-sectioned, all 310 ceramic samples are to be analyzed petrographically, following the methods of Stoltman (1989, 1991) and Whitbread (1995). It may be, for example, that the kylix megagroup is composed of several smaller, chemically indistinguishable paste groups, as opposed to one. Petrography may expose (for instance, through analysis of ground mass differences) more variation in the megagroup than was initially identified. The eventual integration of textual, ecological, and chemical data with petrographic data is expected to reveal more thoroughly the organization of ceramic production, distribution, and consumption in Mycenaean Messenia.

CHAPTER 9

CHIPPING AWAY AT A MYCENAEAN ECONOMY

OBSIDIAN EXCHANGE, LINEAR B, AND "PALATIAL CONTROL" IN LATE BRONZE AGE MESSENIA

WILLIAM A. PARKINSON

FOR A LONG TIME, anthropological archaeologists have been interested in the organization of economic and political systems in ancient state-level societies (e.g, Dalton 1961; D'Altroy and Earle 1985; Finley 1973; LeClair 1962; Polanyi 1969). This chapter seeks to contribute to the literature that has addressed this subject by combining regional archaeological data with textual evidence to infer sociopolitical and socioeconomic levels of integration and centralization in a Late Bronze Age Aegean state.

The research focuses on the Mycenaean state that was centered at the Palace of Nestor near modern Pylos, in southwestern Messenia, Greece (see figures 1.1, 1.2, and description in chapter 3, this volume). By analyzing how chipped-stone blades made on obsidian from the Cycladic island of Melos (see figure 1.1) were produced and exchanged within this region during the later Bronze Age, it is possible to begin to delineate accurately the bounds of palatial control over the regional economy during the Mycenaean period (see table 1.1 and chapter 10, this volume). The evidence from the regional exchange of obsidian suggests that the production and distribution of obsidian blades in southwestern Messenia operated beyond the scope of the central authority (Parkinson 1997). In addition, recent ceramic analyses (see chapter 8, this volume) suggest that Mycenaean ceramics were

similarly produced and exchanged independently of the central authority.

When the textual evidence from the Palace of Nestor is reviewed in light of these archaeological findings, it is clear that the internal organization of the Mycenaean state at Pylos was centered almost exclusively on the mobilization of resources for producing and acquiring prestige goods (see chapter 7, this volume). Within this system the palace functioned not as a redistributive center (see chapters 1–2, this volume), as traditionally interpreted, but rather as a center of elite competition, one that was organized almost exclusively around the production of prestige goods. In turn, the regional system as a whole was dependent on the successful functioning of autonomous systems of production and exchange that operated independently of the central authorities. Since the palatial economic system essentially grew up around these autonomous regional systems, which had been in place since at least the Middle Bronze Age, it never sought to consolidate them under its control. The functioning of this essentially wealth-financed economy (D'Altroy and Earle 1985; see also chapters 2 and 7, this volume) in the absence of a sufficient staple-financed support network created an inherently unstable system and may provide a plausible systemic explanation for the so-called collapse of this particular Mycenaean system at the end of the Bronze Age.

MYCENAEAN ECONOMY, POLITICS, AND LINEAR B

Scholars concerned with the economic and political operations of Mycenaean society have traditionally depended on the information contained in the Linear B tablets, which document the movement of several types of goods into and out of each of the palaces and functioned essentially as temporary economic records of in-house transactions. As such, the tablets contain a wealth of information that should certainly not be overlooked. In fact, the Mycenaean example is exceptional in that the Linear B tablets were used exclusively for keeping track of palatial records (Killen 1985), and they therefore do not suffer from the interpretative problems of having been used as propaganda, as was common in Near Eastern (Postgate 1994) and Mesoamerican states (Marcus 1974, 1993a). Overdependence on written evidence has, however, led to an overgeneralizing view of the Mycenaean economy that masks differences between the ways in which each palace functioned.

Overgeneralization and Linear B

To a large extent, the tendency to overgeneralize about the Mycenaean economy is a result of the nature of the information. The Linear B tablets themselves are very fragmentary, and they offer information relevant only to certain aspects of the economy (Finley 1957; Killen 1985; Ventris and Chadwick 1973). The fragmentary nature of the written evidence results in an overwhelming temptation to generalize about the Mycenaean economy as a whole. Most of the reconstructions of Mycenaean economy that have been proposed in the forty years since their decipherment have tended to use information from all of the available archives, an approach that implicitly assumes that each of the palaces functioned not just similarly but identically, both in their economy and in their use of Linear B records (compare Halstead 1992a). While such an assumption would be appropriate if all of the palaces were indeed integrated into one large state system, it is methodologically not acceptable if each palace functioned as an autonomous state, as certainly appears to have been the case (compare Renfrew 1975).

That each of the palaces functioned largely independently of one another must be acknowledged in the methodologies archaeologists employ in reconstructing the Mycenaean economic and political systems. Failure to do so results in masking differences between each of the palaces and in the reconstruction of a fictional system only marginally applicable to the entire area, and not applicable at all to each of the individual palaces. Aegean prehistorians must begin thinking about Mycenaean state economies in the plural. Only once it has been determined how each of the palaces functioned independently will it be possible to approach the question of how the palaces interacted with one another, and thus to reconstruct the Mycenaean economy as a whole.

Redistribution and Linear B

One of the most pervasive concepts associated with the Mycenaean economy is the idea that the palaces functioned very much like Near Eastern temples, as redistributive centers. Ventris and Chadwick (1973) were among the first to make this argument in their initial publication of the Linear B texts in the early 1950s. In 1957, Moses Finley noted that the Linear B tablets revealed "a far reaching and elaborately organized palace economy of a broad type well attested and heavily documented all over the ancient Near East." He further argued that the tablets "reveal a massive redistributive operation, in which all personnel and all activities, all movement of both persons and goods . . . were administratively fixed" (Finley 1957:135). More recently, John Killen (1985:241) remarked, "It has long been clear that the closest parallels for the type of economy which is revealed by the Linear B tablets are to be found . . . in the contemporary and earlier ancient Near East."

This view of Near Eastern temples as functioning as redistributive centers has recently come under attack. As Postgate notes,

> Until the 1950s the government of the early [Near Eastern] city was almost universally characterized as a "theocracy", and cuneiform scholars wrote of the "temple-city". Claims were even made that at Lagas the temple owned all the land and employed the entire population. . . . This extreme view is now discredited. We cannot any longer maintain that because the temple collected commodities and distributed them to its dependents the entire economy operated through "redistribution", or that the priests controlled all agricultural and commercial activity. (1994:109)

Hence, it is misleading to characterize even ancient Near Eastern economies as being based on the ill-defined concept of "redistribution," and even more misleading to base the interpretation of Mycenaean economics on their possible similarities to these much larger, and structurally different institutions. If each

Mycenaean palace was an autonomous entity, as seems to have been the case, then the type of large-scale redistribution that is perhaps, but not certainly, documented in various Near Eastern texts would bear only the faintest resemblance to redistribution in these much smaller states.

Despite the foregoing criticisms, it is clear from the Linear B data that all the palaces practiced some form of redistribution of goods. But only recently have archaeologists and philologists begun to explicitly define what they mean by the term "redistribution" in a Mycenaean context. Killen (1985:253) first argued for the palaces functioning as redistributive centers in his comparison of the Mycenaean economy to the Near Eastern temple system: "for there can be little question that the palaces in Mycenaean kingdoms, like the central palaces and temples in the ancient Near East, are functioning as redistributive centers." He proceeded to point out that the Mycenaean palace buildings contain two of the "key diagnostics of a major redistributive center—viz. administrative records and elaborate storage facilities (such as the western magazines at Knossos)" (Killen 1985:254). This comparison to ancient Near Eastern redistributive systems led Killen to assert that

> given even the limited amount which it is possible to say for certain about the range and, in some cases also, the depth of the involvement of the palaces in the life of the kingdoms, it is surely difficult (to borrow Finley's comment on the "private" sector in the Near Eastern economies) to elevate any such non-palace, local or private, activity to the prevailing pattern of economy. (1985:258)

Thus, in Killen's view, "the role which the palaces played in the economy of Mycenaean states was not merely significant, but central and dominant" (Killen 1985:255).

Killen was certainly correct in his assertion that there was a considerable degree of division of labor in Mycenaean society, and that this degree of specialization could not have developed in a nonmarket, nonmoney economy without the intervention of a central redistributive agency. As he noted, "Without the existence of such a redistributive system, there would have been no means in a world which lacked markets for a highly specialized worker to obtain his livelihood" (Killen 1985:253). It is necessary, therefore, to explicitly delineate the extent to which the individual palatial economies interacted with the regional economic systems in which they were embedded.

In the following section I attempt to model the internal economic organization of one Mycenaean palatial society by analyzing both the evidence contained in the Linear B tablets and the regional archaeological data that provide access to those aspects of the economy that are not documented in the texts—in particular, the production and distribution of obsidian blades.

THE INTERNAL ORGANIZATION OF A MYCENAEAN POLITY: THE CASE OF PYLOS

When one of these small-scale Mycenaean states—in this case, Pylos—is analyzed as an autonomous entity, using both archival and regional archaeological data that are directly relevant to it, it becomes clear that the palatial economy of this particular polity, at least, is best understood as a wealth-financed economy, concerned primarily, if not exclusively, with the production of elite goods. The Linear B archives from the Palace of Nestor indicate that several specialized industries were carried out under the direction of the central administration—in particular, bronze working, perfumed oil production, textile production, weapons production, and perhaps chariot production (Killen 1985). These various types of industrial production were carried out under the *ta-ra-si-ja* system, which entailed an allocation of raw materials by the central authority to dependent or semidependent workers who received rations (possibly of wheat) and sometimes plots of land adjacent to the palace. It is important to note that, with the exception of metalworking and some of the less specialized steps involved in textile production, all of these specialized industries occurred at the palace proper (Palaima and Shelmerdine 1984). This reflects the tendency of the palatial administrators to centralize those aspects of the economy in which they were most interested at the palace proper.

Although the information contained in the tablets is very useful for informing us about those aspects of the economy in which the palatial administrators were interested, the tablets are next to useless for telling us about those aspects of the economy that occurred beyond the control of the palatial authorities (Bennet 1988a). The common assumption in this regard is that the palaces controlled all "industrial" production that involved craft specialization (Killen 1985:253). While Killen noted the possibility that there was some private bartering of surplus allocations at the local, village level in the kingdoms, he argued that such activity does not constitute economy (1985:17). Halstead, on the other hand, argues that a comparison of the archival and archaeological evidence suggests that "a wide range of agricultural and craft production took place outside palatial control and that a range of commodities entered or left the palaces without being recorded by the Linear B bureaucracy" (Halstead 1992a:65, see also chapter 7, this volume).

To assess accurately the extent of palatial control over the regional economy, it is necessary to consult regional archaeological data and begin reconstructing the economy from the bottom up. By identifying goods produced, manufactured, and distributed independently of the central administrators, we can begin to delineate more precisely the bounds of the palatial control over different aspects of the regional economy.

Obsidian exchange in Late Bronze Age Messenia

One aspect of the Pylian economy that was not centralized at the palace and is not mentioned in the tablets is the production and distribution of obsidian blades (Parkinson 1997). Obsidian production and exchange are well-known topics in Aegean prehistory (see chapter 10, this volume), and exploitation of the large obsidian deposits on the island of Melos extends as far back as the latest Upper Paleolithic, as evidenced at Franchthi (Perlès 1987a). Studies of obsidian production and exchange in the Aegean have concentrated for the most part on the Neolithic and earlier Bronze Age periods (see, e.g., Blitzer 1991, 1992; Kardulias and Runnels 1985; Perlès 1990a, 1990c, 1992; Runnels 1985a; Torrence 1986). Although the study of obsidian exchange has proved quite fruitful in understanding state-level economic systems in other parts of the world (e.g., Clark's [1986] extensive work in Mesoamerica), the role of obsidian exchange has, for some reason, been conspicuously absent from discussions of Late Bronze Age economy in the Aegean. Although the extensive use of metals, particularly tin-alloyed bronze, placed less of a dependency on Melian obsidian as a source of raw material for tools throughout the earlier Bronze Age, the use of obsidian persisted, if in lesser quantities and fewer types, throughout the Late Bronze Age and even into the Classical period (Runnels 1982).

Aegean Bronze Age chipped stone assemblages are generally characterized by thin, parallel-sided obsidian blades (or bladelets) that were produced by pressure flaking or by applying indirect percussion to preshaped cores (van Horne 1976). Alongside this obsidian blade industry there is often a corresponding obsidian flake assemblage that would have required significantly less skill to produce. Throughout the Aegean Bronze Age, local sources of chert were also exploited for the production of flakes and, less commonly, blades (see chapter 10, this volume).

As Runnels (1985a) has suggested for Lerna, it is misleading to label Bronze Age collections as blade industries. As Kardulias and Runnels have suggested for the obsidian industry in the Argolid:

> The production of blades was clearly important, but it was not the sole focus of stone knappers . . . the knappers went to considerable trouble to produce blades. . . . Since most of the blades appear at sites without cores, perhaps many of these unretouched blades were intended for export to other settlements in the region. It was, perhaps, as an exchange commodity that obsidian acquired its greatest economic significance. (1995:241)

On the basis of a low coefficient of variation in the obsidian blade assemblage at the Early and Middle Helladic site of Lerna, Runnels (1985a) has convincingly argued that a certain degree of skill would have been necessary for the production of these blades. Although a high level of skill is assumed, no conclusion about the degree of specialization of the craftsmen (e.g., full- or part-time; compare Clarke and Parry 1990) can be made. Although several authors have argued for the existence of full-time obsidian workshops at the Bronze Age sites of Agios Kosmas (Mylonas 1959:144), Phylakopi (Mackenzie 1898:24; Bosanquet 1904:218), Mallia (van Effenterre and van Effenterre 1969), and Knossos (Warren 1972b:393), Runnels (1985a) and Torrence (1979, 1986:162) have recently suggested that part-time specialists or even domestic production could account for the production of blades at these sites.

Recent data collected by the Pylos Regional Archaeological Project (PRAP) during intensive survey in a sample of the 250 km^2 area around the Palace of Nestor (PRAP B7; see figure 3.2) provides insight into how obsidian was circulated throughout this region during the Bronze Age.

PRAP located twenty-eight sites with an identifiable Bronze Age component in the study area. All these sites were covered during intensive tract walking, and all observed lithics were collected. Twenty-five of the sites were collected intensively using either a total pickup strategy or, in the case of some of the larger sites, a stratified sample (see chapter 3, this volume). Given that all observed lithics were collected during tract walking and grab sampling, it seems likely that our data are representative of the entire assemblage.

Of the twenty-eight Bronze Age sites investigated by PRAP, twenty contain lithics. Five of these twenty sites (I23, I28, L5, L6, and M1) are restricted to the Early Helladic period or earlier. These earlier sites have been omitted from this discussion. This leaves fifteen sites with lithics dating to the Middle or Late Bronze Age. Most sites tended to have much more chert than obsidian, usually by a factor of 3 to 1 (figure 9.1). The single exception is site I4 (Romanou), located near the coast at the base of the Englianos ridge, where twice as much obsidian as chert was found. The fact that Romanou was one of the sites that was only sampled, rather than totally collected, suggests that these numbers would be even more striking if the site had been totally collected as had several of the other sites shown on the graph, including the area around the Palace of Nestor (B7), and Ordines (K1).

I4 is a large site (circa 38 ha) that has a small, spatially discrete LH IIIB component, as well as a later component. The lithic distribution at Romanou is confined to that part of the site where most of the prehistoric pottery was collected. The reduction sequence from the Romanou assemblage suggests that obsidian blade production occurred on the site. Primary, secondary, and tertiary flakes, all part of the obsidian reduction sequence, occured in very high frequencies in the surface assemblage (figure 9.2). Evidence for on-site blade production is further supported by the presence of five blade cores and two crested blades. Although this certainly does not constitute a level of intensive industrial production, it is curious that from the three excavated Middle and Late Bronze Age sites in the region (the Palace of Nestor, Malthi, and Nichoria), only two blade cores in total were found. The presence of five blade cores in the sampled surface assemblage at Romanou, therefore, appears quite significant in relation to the frequency of obsidian cores at other Bronze Age sites in the area.

The reduction sequence at Romanou suggests that the obsidian arrived there from the island of Melos in the form of roughed-out nodules, and that both core preparation and blade production occurred at the site. This is indicated by the high frequency of primary and secondary flakes in the Romanou assemblage compared with other Middle Helladic–Late Helladic sites in the region (figure 9.3). Interestingly, of the sites PRAP identified, Romanou is the only one that appears to have produced obsidian blades in any number during the later Bronze Age.

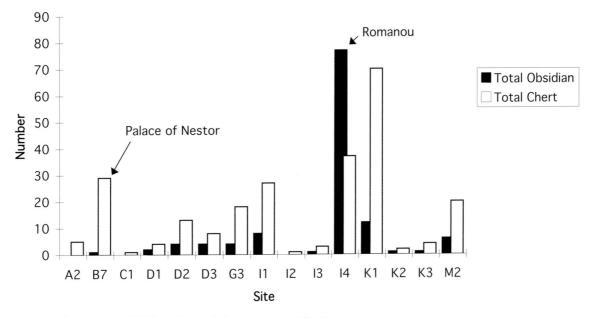

FIGURE 9.1 Obsidian and chert at Middle and Late Helladic sites investigated by PRAP.

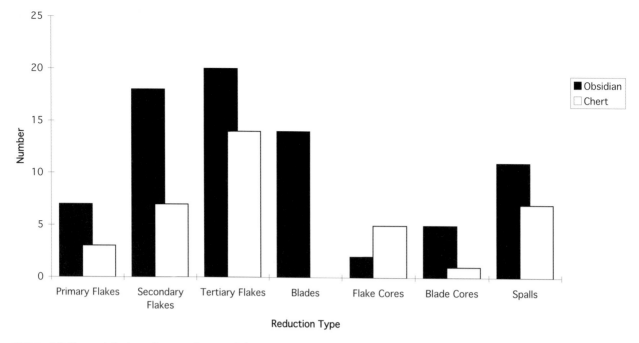

FIGURE 9.2 Chert and obsidian reduction at Romanou (I4).

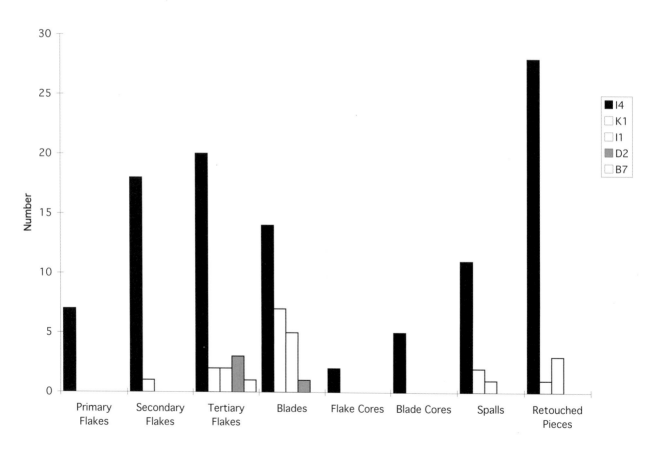

FIGURE 9.3 Obsidian reduction at larger Middle and Late Helladic sites investigated by PRAP.

The obsidian reduction sequence from the other later Bronze Age sites in the study area suggests that all of the other sites were acquiring premanufactured obsidian blades in their finished form, probably from Romanou or from some other blade-producing sites in areas that PRAP did not sample. With the exception of a single secondary flake at K1 (Ordines), there is no evidence of on-site obsidian reduction having occurred anywhere else in the region. Although there is evidence that the production of chert blades occurred at K1, as indicated by the three chert blade cores from this site, the production of obsidian blades during the Later Bronze Age seems to have been restricted within the study area to the site of Romanou. Given that obsidian blades normally constitute from 60% to 100% of the entire obsidian assemblage at these other sites, this pattern becomes even more convincing, despite the small sample size (figure 9.4)

Three sites have produced excavated obsidian assemblages that further enhance this pattern. Two of these sites, Nichoria and Malthi, are located outside the PRAP study area but were most likely incorporated into the Pylian Mycenaean state system. The third site is the Palace of Nestor itself.

Nichoria is located east of the PRAP study area, about 20 km east of the Palace of Nestor. Blitzer's (1992) preliminary analysis of the chipped stone from the site reports 202 obsidian artifacts recovered from Middle and Late Helladic deposits throughout the site. Although Blitzer does not describe each artifact in her catalogue and does not distinguish between primary and secondary flakes, it is nevertheless possible to briefly outline her findings (figure 9.5).

Of the 202 obsidian artifacts excavated at Nichoria that can be generally dated to the later (Middle and Late) Helladic period, Blitzer (1992:712) reports 93 blades, 76 flakes (primary, secondary, and tertiary), 18 "chips" or spalls, 11 points, 2 denticulates, 1 "chunk" (flake core?), and 1 blade core (very reduced). It is significant that obsidian blades constitute 46% of the total recovered obsidian assemblage. This figure approaches the 60%–100% figure that is common in the PRAP surface assemblages at other sites. The single tabular obsidian blade core is quite small (about 2 cm × cm) and very reduced. It was recovered from a mixed deposit (L23, Wc, level 4, lot 4038/3) with Middle Helladic, LH I–II, and DA II ceramics. Other than this one blade core, the only evidence of obsidian blade production

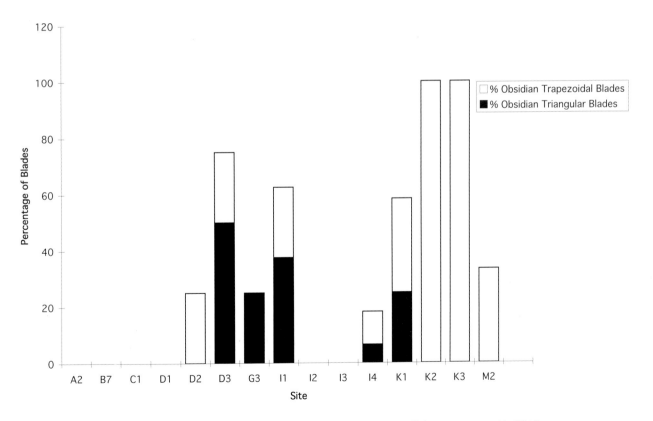

FIGURE 9.4 Percentage of obsidian blades of total obsidian assemblage at Middle Helladic/Late Helladic sites investigated by PRAP.

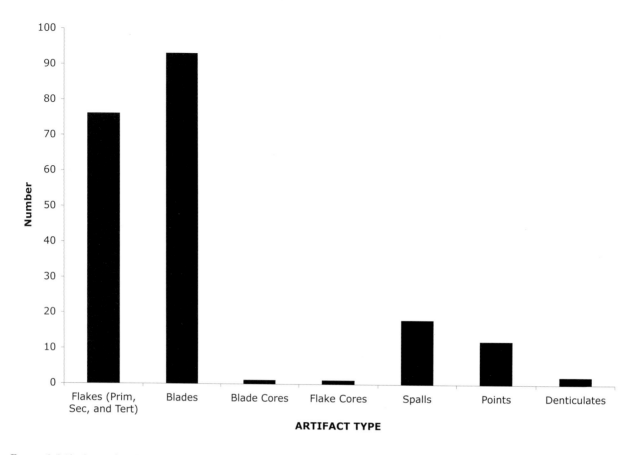

FIGURE 9.5 Obsidian artifacts by type from Nichoria. (Data from Blitzer 1992.)

having occurred on the site is a single crested blade. The absence of evidence for extensive blade production suggests that Nichoria, like the other sites within the PRAP study area, was receiving blades from another site, such as Romanou.

The site of Malthi is located outside the PRAP study area, roughly 25 km northeast of the Palace of Nestor. Blitzer (1991) reports that of the 161 preserved chipped stone artifacts, 59 are made on obsidian (figure 9.6). Since none of these can be assigned to their original excavated context, the entire assemblage must be viewed as originating from general Middle and Late Helladic deposits. Blitzer's catalogue lists the following quantities: 1 flake core, 1 blade core, 5 cortical flakes (that is, primary or secondary flakes), 11 noncortical flakes (i.e., tertiary flakes), 38 blades, and 3 points. Blades constitute 64% of the preserved obsidian assemblage. This figure is directly in line with the 60%–100% reported from the majority of sites within the PRAP study area other than Romanou. Other than the presence of the single blade core in the Malthi assemblage, there is little evidence to suggest that on-site blade production occurred

there in any significant amount. The high frequency of blades in the assemblage suggests that Malthi, like Nichoria, was acquiring blades from other sites, such as Romanou, where there is significant evidence for blade production even in the sampled surface assemblage.

The third site that has produced an excavated Late Bronze Age obsidian assemblage is the Palace of Nestor. Although Blitzer (1991) has studied the chipped stone from the palace, these data have yet to be published. Blegen and Rawson (1966) provide a room-by-room summary of the artifacts that were discovered during the initial excavation of the palace and the area immediately surrounding it. Unfortunately, until these lithics are published or reanalyzed, it is difficult to discern whether blade production occurred in any of the areas excavated by Blegen. Nevertheless, it is possible to summarize the lithic information that has been published (figure 9.7).

Although Blegen and Rawson (1966; Blegen et al. 1973) identify quantities of obsidian artifacts from in and around the palace, including the graves, from the photographs provided there do not appear to be any pri-

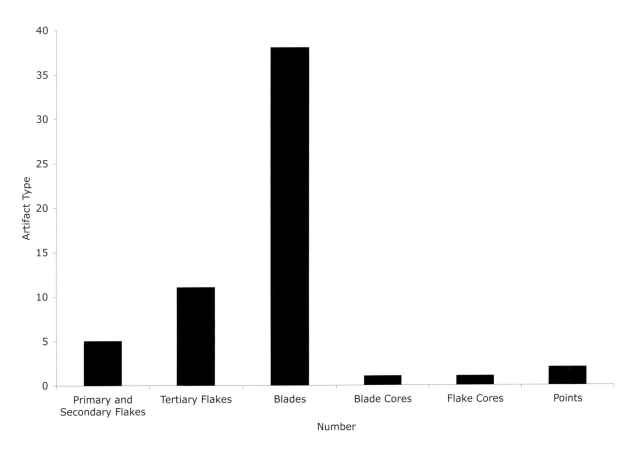

FIGURE 9.6 Obsidian artifacts from Malthi. (Data from Blitzer 1991.)

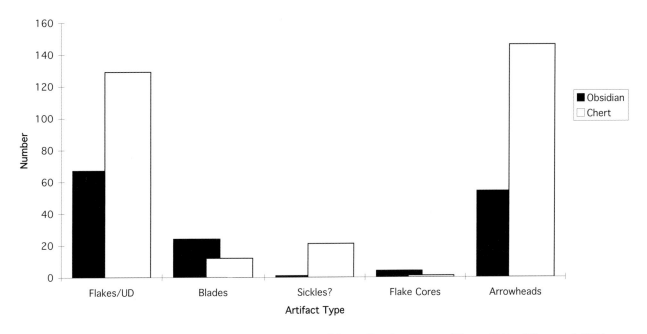

FIGURE 9.7 Obsidian artifacts from the Palace of Nestor, the Lower Town, and Graves. (Data from Blegen and Rawson 1966 and Blegen et al. 1973.)

mary or secondary flakes in the assemblage. In addition, there are no blade cores, although there are a few small flake cores. By far the most common obsidian artifacts from the palace and its surroundings are arrowheads and denticulates (possibly sickles). These types also occur in high frequencies in chert. Although there are a few obsidian blades in the palace assemblage, it seems that the blades arrived here, as at other settlements, in finished form. While it is possible that some of the final steps associated with the production of the arrowheads occurred at the palace, and possibly at Malthi and Nichoria, it seems quite unlikely, from this initial analysis of the palace assemblage, that blades were produced at any of these locations in any quantity. Hence, it appears the palace was acquiring the obsidian blades used to produce the arrowheads, and other implements, from some other source, possibly Romanou.

The centralized production of obsidian blades seems to be a common pattern throughout the Bronze Age in southern Greece. Several authors have inferred relatively unimpeded access to the obsidian sources on Melos (chapter 10, this volume; Kardulias and Runnels 1995; Torrence 1979, 1986) throughout the later Neolithic and Bronze Age. But despite this easy access to the sources, obsidian blades were frequently produced at centralized locations, usually near the coast, and subsequently traded to sites further inland, and possibly even further afield.

At the Early and Middle Helladic site of Lerna in the Argolid, Runnels (1985a) has argued that obsidian blades may have been produced at the site in exchange for chert blades that were imported in finished form from some distant source. This pattern is repeated in the southern Argolid during the Bronze Age (see chapter 10, this volume).

The PRAP data suggest that this pattern was also repeated in Messenia, where only one site identified within the study area seems to have produced obsidian blades throughout the later Bronze Age. All the other sites in the study area seem to have received these blades in their final form.

The repetition of this pattern of centralized blade production throughout various regions in southern Greece suggests, as Kardulias and Runnels (1995) assert, that this may have been a distinctive southern Greek craft activity. Furthermore, the fact that this pattern occurs during the Early Bronze Age in the Argolid suggests that it was also most likely in place since the Early Helladic period in Messenia. If this is the case, then this centralized system of obsidian blade

production at sites like Romanou would have already been in place in Messenia prior to the formative stages of palatial evolution in LH I–II.

During the formative stages of palatial evolution in Messenia, the emerging elite would have been faced with the decision of whether to incorporate this previously existing system of production and exchange into the realm of palatial control or to allow it to function essentially autonomously and independently of the palatial economy.

Given the tendency, evidenced in the Linear B tablets, of the palatial administrators to relocate specialist industries to the palace proper, and given the near total lack of evidence for obsidian blade production having occurred in or around the palace, the decentralized nature of the obsidian blade industry suggests that it most likely operated independently of palatial control. Furthermore, the fact that obsidian is never even mentioned in the Linear B tablets suggests that obsidian blades were not highly valued by the palatial elite. Although some industries do seem to have occurred at locations other than the palace—in particular, metalworking and some of the less specialized steps involved in textile and flax production—these items are all well documented in the tablets. That obsidian blade production was both not centralized at the palace proper and not mentioned in the tablets suggests that the elite probably did not seek to control or regulate its operation.

Obsidian blade production is not the only aspect of the economy that seems to have operated beyond the scope of palatial control. Recent chemical and petrographic analyses conducted on LH IIIB coarseware ceramics from several sites throughout the region suggest that the production and exchange of ceramics may also have occurred independently of the palace and was not centralized at the palace (chapter 8, this volume). It is most likely the case either that this industry was not highly valued by the central bureaucracy, or that the administrators chose not to control its independent functioning within the regional economy. Although these results remain preliminary, and certainly need to be augmented by further analyses in both cases, they suggest that we reassess our understanding of the Mycenaean palatial economy, at least in the case of Late Bronze Age Messenia.

Palatial control in LBA Messenia: Another look at the Linear B evidence

Since it appears that the palace was not directly controlling the production and exchange of coarseware ceramics or obsidian blades, what, as revealed in the Linear B archives, was the palace controlling? When viewed in light of the obsidian and ceramic data, which demonstrate that the palace took no interest in at least some other forms of specialized economic activity, the activities defined in the Linear B tablets can be best understood if they are incorporated into a model in which the palace functioned exclusively for the production of elite goods.

The Linear B tablets from the Palace of Nestor document palatial control over three aspects of the economy:

* Specialized industries at the palace, organized under the *ta-ra-si-ja* system
* Land adjacent to the palace
* Collection of tribute and ritual offerings

The archival records show that the palace centrally controlled the production and distribution of textiles, perfumed oil, bronze weaponry and vessels, and chariots, among other types of specialized products, such as furniture. All these would have served as elite-status goods that would have been exchanged with secondary and lower-level elites to secure alliances and legitimize the positions of those in power. In addition to being exchanged among elites within the regional economic and political system, such luxury items may also have been used in interpalatial exchanges (i.e., between the elites of primary centers) as well as in international exchanges (Killen 1985).

Under the *ta-ra-si-ja* system, the land that the palace controlled was allocated to holders in return for services to the center and under the condition that the landholders would continue to provide the palaces with those services, together with some of the produce (Killen 1985). Killen (1985) suggests that the palace tightly controlled land in the vicinity of the palace, and he envisions a much more decentralized regime in more remote areas. Halstead (1992b) has convincingly argued that the palace used these tracts of land to specialize in the production of wheat and olives and the keeping of sheep. He suggests that the palace redistributed much of these specialized products as rations and raw materials to the specialized craftsmen working in the *ta-ra-si-ja* system. Any remaining surplus, he argues, could have

been redistributed to provide subsistence relief to the population during shortage (Halstead 1992b:116). In other words, the land that the palace controlled served primarily to support the specialized craftsmen who were producing the elite goods, as well as to provision the palace proper (see chapter 7, this volume).

Finally, the palace collected proportional tribute from various secondary centers that were dispersed throughout the region. This tribute would have served mainly to support the dependent craftsmen of the *ta-ra-si-ja* system, but it was also redirected back to different villages, along with some of the wheat and lamb from the palatial tracts of land, to serve as ritual offerings to different divinities. These ritual offerings would have taken the form of village feasts funded by the central authority (see Killen 1994; Wright 1995b) and would have served to demonstrate the power of the local elites to the commoners, as well as to remind the commoners of the benefits they received from the state.

Analyzing the economy in this way suggests an essentially wealth-financed (D'Altroy and Earle 1985) economy—with a central authority that mobilized resources for the production of elite goods—rather than a redistributive economy in the Near Eastern sense, in which large amounts of produce and goods were pooled and redistributed to the general population for subsistence, despite the relationship of the recipient to the center as a laborer. This Mycenaean pattern of a status good–producing economy is what would be expected, given a political system in which several small-scale states competed directly with other similar states (Renfrew and Cherry 1986). Such a wealth-financed palatial economy would have been dependent on autonomous systems of regional exchange and production (such as obsidian blades, ceramic coarsewares, and perhaps long-distance trade networks) that were in place prior to the formation of the palatial system and operated independently of the palace itself.

Interestingly, this prestige-based model of the Pylian economy is quite similar to that developed by Halstead (1992a, 1992b; see also chapter 7, this volume), even though the latter was based on textual information from all of the palaces, ethnographic analogies, and paleobotanical remains from Bronze Age and Neolithic contexts. With regard to the scope of palatial control over the regional Mycenaean economy, Halstead writes:

The palaces exercised only partial control over economic activity within their territories: the palaces directly controlled only a small fraction of the total labour force, palatial crop production was concentrated in the vicinity of major centres and sub-centres, and several commodities were only produced in the non-palatial sector. (1992a:72–73)

In the case of Late Bronze Age Messenia, it would seem that obsidian blades and coarseware ceramics constituted two of the commodities that were produced in the nonpalatial sector. Correspondingly, Halstead (1992a:74) argues that

> [p]alatial economic activity was to a large extent directed to the manufacture of fine craft goods and these in turn were used to acquire exotic raw materials (for further craft production) and to draw in staple resources from the local non-palatial sector of the economy. . . . This upwards mobilisation of resources financed the palatial elite.

The main difference between the two models is that Halstead's model retains the concept of redistribution, in the form of subsistence relief, as a critical component in the system (see chapter 7, this volume). The model proposed here, on the other hand, suggests that almost all of the subsistence goods documented in the Pylian texts would have been used for supporting specialists and generally to mobilize goods and labor that eventually resulted in the production of elite goods. As such, the model proposed here is more similar to that generated by H. J. Morris (1986).

In her work on the Pylian economy, Morris (1986) suggests, in contrast to Halstead, that redistribution, in the form of subsistence relief to individuals who did not directly participate in a working relationship with the center, seldom occurred. According to Morris (1986:109), "almost 70% of the disbursement tablets show transfers of rations and raw materials to palace workers." She further notes:

> It is interesting that the relative proportion of collection and disbursement tablets is quite close, but that only 15% of the disbursement records show actual physical transfers of goods back to the regions. Of these, 7 are perfumed oil offerings to gods... This leaves only two tablets (Vn 20 and On 300)—about 0.1% of the total tablets—designating disbursements to the major town and not workshops or shrines. One records wine and the other hides. (Morris 1986:110)

Thus, viewing the Pylian system in vacuo leads to significantly different conclusions than if evidence is combined from each of the different palaces. There is no Linear B or archaeological evidence that the Palace of Nestor in Late Bronze Age Messenia regularly redistributed staple goods to anyone who was not directly associated with the palatial center either as an attached craftsman or as a secular or religious official. Furthermore, other than the inferred evidence for occasional feasts occurring at the primary and secondary centers, there is little evidence to support the contention that the palatial center regularly provided subsistence relief in times of shortage to anyone who was not directly participating in a working relationship with the central authority, as Halstead (1992a) has suggested.

Even the architectural organization of the Palace of Nestor itself suggests that it never assumed a significant role as a redistributive center. Morris (1986) estimates that only 17.5% of the area on the acropolis was used to store olive oil, which was used principally for the production of perfumed oils (Shelmerdine 1984); wine; and pottery. Certainly, if the palace had functioned as a redistributive center, even if only to regularly provide the local population with subsistence relief, more centralized space would have been devoted to the storage of staple products, as may have been the case at Late Bronze Age Knossos. Furthermore, the types of pottery located in the storage areas consisted not of storage vessels (for example, *pithoi* and amphorae) but of open-shaped vessels (mostly kylikes, but also bowls, cups, and dippers), which were possibly used in local feasting activities (chapter 8, this volume; Killen 1994; Wright 1995b) but certainly were not used to store and transport subsistence products.

While the possibility remains, as Halstead (1992a, 1992b, chapter 7, this volume) has suggested, that the palace stored significant quantities of meat "on the hoof" in the form of several flocks of sheep and goats that were owned (or regulated) by the palatial authorities, it is interesting that the Pylian texts record far smaller quantities of sheep than the eighty thousand or more documented at Knossos (Killen 1984a). Although this discrepancy results, at least in part, from differential preservation of the tablets at the two different locations, it is certainly significant that at Pylos, there is little direct evidence of the sheep being distributed back into the region in the form of meat, which could be interpreted as subsistence relief. Rather, the majority of the sheep that were controlled by the palace seem to have been used almost exclusively for the production of wool for textiles (Killen 1984a).

Finally, there is no reason to assume that it would have been necessary for the palace to fill a significant redistributive role within the regional system. As Halstead (chapter 7, this volume) notes, "it is becoming increasingly clear that most economic activity within the territories of the Mycenaean palaces took place outside the scrutiny of the Linear B bureaucracy." The fact that the Pylian system of taxation was based on the principle of "proportional tribute" (Killen 1984a), in which tribute was exacted from different centers (of different size and in environmentally different areas) in identical proportions, suggests that the burden of taxation would not have been significant enough to require palatial intervention in bad years of economic hardship. If the required tribute from each of these different centers had been such that it would have substantially drained local reserves that could be exploited in particularly bad years, the palatial administrators surely would have taken into account in their taxation scheme the effects of differential production at different centers. The fact that the palatial elite did not take differential production into account suggests that the taxes levied on different secondary centers were not significant enough to require redistribution of subsistence goods from the palace center in times of hardship.

The operation of a system almost exclusively through the mobilization of resources for the production of prestige goods would have depended on the efficient operation of several independent and autonomous systems of production and exchange, such as, among many potential others, obsidian blade manufacture and exchange, the production and distribution of coarseware ceramics, a long-distance trade network, and locally self-sufficient subsistence agriculture. These autonomous systems were most likely in place prior to the initial stages of palatial formation in the region. As the palace began to extend its control over the region, it appears to have left these previously existing systems in situ as it essentially grew up around them. For one reason or another, the palace seems never to have attempted to consolidate these systems under its authority.

Wealth finance and staple finance in the Pylian economy

The picture that emerges from this analysis is that of a palace organized almost exclusively around the production of elite goods. While the palace did, indeed, redistribute goods to its dependent craftsmen and laborers, there is little or no evidence to suggest that it regularly redistributed staple products to the general population in the form of subsistence relief, except for the occasional feast that may have occurred in the primary and secondary centers. In D'Altroy and Earle's (1985) terms, this constitutes a wealth-financed economic system in which special products are manufactured and used as a means of payment. D'Altroy and Earle argue that

the requirements of gross production and the constraints of security and of management costs will lead the state to develop a finance system based on production and circulation of both staple and wealth goods. (1985:196)

They proceed to argue that the mixture of staple and wealth finance allowed the Incas flexibility in regional and interregional finance, and that

A mixed strategy of labor taxation, control of staple goods, and production and circulation of wealth goods permitted the Inka state to meet its disparate economic requirements. (1985:196)

They suggest that this mixture of staple and wealth finance would be necessary in the successful functioning of any archaic state society.

If this is the case, what happened at Pylos? Although there is ample evidence for the centrally controlled production and circulation of wealth goods, there is little or no evidence for the controlled production and circulation of staple products to anyone other than the dependent craftsmen, laborers, and officials, all of whom directly or indirectly participated in some sort of working relationship with the palace itself. According to D'Altroy and Earle (1985), it is necessary for the state to articulate both the wealth-financed and staple-financed aspects of the economic system. That being the case, Late Bronze Age Messenia would have constituted an inherently unstable situation.

Since the palatial economy in Late Bronze Age Messenia had essentially grown up around a set of pre-existing systems of production and exchange, it never sought to incorporate these essentially autonomous systems under its control. Rather, the palatial system seems to have been dependent on the successful functioning of these regional systems, which operated independently of, but in a complementary fashion to, the essentially wealth-financed palatial system. This resulted in a dualistic economic system in which there was:

- Palatial control over the production of luxury goods within the essentially wealth-financed, palatial sector of the economy, on the one hand, and on the other:

- Autonomous systems of regional production and exchange (such as obsidian blade production and exchange, the production and exchange of coarseware ceramics, and locally self-sufficient agriculture) that would have operated independently of palatial control within the essentially staple-financed, nonpalatial sector of the economy.

The successful operation of the economy of Late Bronze Age Messenia was, therefore, dependent on the independent functioning of these two components within the regional system.

Although this complementary relationship appears to have functioned successfully for a short period of time, there are archaeological indications of instability within the system before the end of LH IIIB. During this time, there are indications that the palatial elite were attempting to increase their role as producers of luxury goods. This is indicated by the construction of additional workshop facilities on the acropolis later in LH IIIB

Morris (1986) has analyzed the sequence of building phases that occurred during the LH IIIB period at the Palace of Nestor (see Blegen and Rawson 1966; Wright 1984). Her functional breakdown of the additions that postdate the main building indicate that 59% of these later additions provided workshop space, and only 29% provided storage space (Morris 1986:145). This storage space, again, was utilized not for storing staple products, such as grain, but for oil, wine, and pottery. Certainly, if the state had been attempting to increase its role in regulating the circulation of staple goods within the regional system by redistributing them from the palace itself, these percentages would be reversed. Clearly, the Mycenaean center at Pylos was attempting to increase its role not as a redistributor of staple goods but as a producer of prestige goods. Unlike the Incas, who successfully articulated the wealth-financed and staple-financed aspects of their economy by centrally controlling the circulation of staple goods, the rulers of Mycenaean Pylos chose not to extend their control into the staple-financed, nonpalatial sector of the economy, but rather to increase centralized production of wealth goods in LH IIIB.

This example offers intriguing insight into some of the decisions that were made by the Late Bronze Age rulers of Messenia. At some point during LH IIIB, the rulers of the Mycenaean state found it necessary to alter the role of the palace within the regional economic system. They could choose either to increase the role of the palace within the regional economic system as a producer of elite goods by adding additional workshop facilities to the palatial center or to increase the authority of the center as a controller of staple goods by attempting to wield control over some of the autonomous systems of production and exchange that had previously functioned independently of palatial control. This control could have been accomplished, in part, by centralizing the storage of staples at the palace itself, as seems to have occurred at Knossos. The elite's seeming decision, to increase the production of wealth goods, resulted in the continued functioning of the staple-financed sector of the economy beyond the control of the palatial elite. By choosing not to attempt to control the essentially staple-financed aspects of the regional economy, the palatial elite would have been unable to control the circulation of staple goods if the need arose.

CONCLUSION

To begin to reconstruct the intricate functioning of the Mycenaean economic and political system accurately, we must begin by approaching each palatial system individually, using only the archival and archaeological data that are directly relevant to each independent system. I have attempted such a reconstruction by analyzing how obsidian blades were produced and circulated throughout the Mycenaean state of Pylos in Messenia. This analysis in turn led to a reanalysis of the information contained in the Linear B tablets and to some interesting conclusions about the nature of Aegean Bronze Age economic systems.

The Mycenaean state at Pylos was but one of several small state systems ("early state modules") on the Late Bronze Age Greek mainland (Renfrew 1975). As such, the rulers of Mycenaean Messenia were probably in constant competition with the rulers of other small states, such as Mycenae and Tiryns, for the allegiance of local elites at secondary and tertiary centers (Renfrew and Cherry 1986). This competition most likely took the form of gift exchanges between elites at various centers within a single state system. The administrators at Pylos may have exploited local kinship structures and extant networks of social inequality to encourage regional centers to interact in the mobilizing economy. Chiefs of outlying territories would have been recruited to supply the goods and services the palace used to underwrite its economic activities. This system of elite recruitment and competition in turn dictated the role that the palace had to assume within the regional economic system as the primary producer of the luxury goods necessary to retain alliances with elites at secondary and tertiary centers.

Though the palatial bureaucracy essentially grew up around a set of autonomous systems of regional production and exchange that had been in place within the region prior to the establishment of the "palatial economy," it never successfully integrated these systems under its control. This lack resulted in an inherently unstable system, one in which the Mycenaean elite were unable to develop a successful system of finance based on the production and circulation of both staple and wealth goods. This unstable economic situation in LH IIIB Messenia appears to have given way by the beginning of LH IIIC, when the palace was destroyed by fire and the majority of Mycenaean period settlements were abandoned. Within a span of time as short as a hundred years, the Pylian state developed, reigned, and disappeared, possibly because it had never successfully articulated all of the disparate economic requirements of the regional system in which it had developed. Unlike the Inca, who were able to articulate both the wealth-financed and staple-financed aspects of their system, the administrators at Pylos locked themselves into an inflexible, unstable system, one dependent on several autonomous systems of production and exchange.

Much like the Soviet Union of the twentieth century, whose economy ostensibly collapsed because of an inability to control the production and distribution of staple goods at the expense of producing weaponry—a kind of twentieth-century prestige good—so too did the economy of the Mycenaean state at Pylos collapse. However, the competition in Late Bronze Age Greece occurred not between two world powers but among several small-scale archaic states that were located at the edges of contact with the far more complex states of Mesopotamia and Egypt.

CHAPTER 10

FLAKED STONE AND THE ROLE OF THE PALACES IN THE MYCENAEAN WORLD SYSTEM

𝄢𝄢𝄢𝄢𝄢𝄢𝄢

P. NICK KARDULIAS

A MAJOR FOCUS FOR AEGEAN prehistorians has been the attempt to reconstruct the nature of cultural and economic contacts at different periods in the region. Such work is regularly directed at piecing together the often scanty or ambiguous evidence for trade among various localities. The presence of imported materials at a site may be indicative of direct long-distance trading expeditions or of exchange through a series of intermediate agents. Such commercial activity is significant not only for the transfer of valued commodities but also for the information that accompanies the movement of artifacts (Runnels 1983). The communication aspect of trade has been viewed as an important stimulus to the development of complex societies in the Aegean and elsewhere. The key problem here, as in most archaeological reconstructions, is developing a cogent, viable, dynamic model from a static data set.

WORLD SYSTEMS THEORY

Among the various approaches that archaeologists have utilized in this effort to understand Bronze Age (including Mycenaean) society is world systems theory (WST). While the original aim of WST was to explain the rise of capitalism in the early modern era (Wallerstein 1974), various scholars have utilized and modified the basic concepts to explain better the interlocking nature of ancient societies. Of particular interest to the present chapter are two publications that address the problem in terms easily transferable to the topic of this volume. In the first, A. G. Frank (1993) claims that a world system existed during the Bronze Age and experienced cyclical perturbations that affected both the major and minor players. Andrew Sherratt (1993) asks, "What would a Bronze-age world system look like?" and pursues that question in terms of the interaction between temperate Europe and the Mediterranean; he supplies archaeological substance to Frank's more general model. I propose to examine some of the propositions suggested by these and other WST theorists in light of the Mycenaean evidence, and particularly the role of stone tools in the Bronze Age Aegean.

World systems theory developed as a generalized approach to the study of intersocietal contact (Chase-Dunn 1989, 1992, 1995; Chase-Dunn and Hall 1991, 1997; Hall 1994, 1996a, 1996b; Hall and Chase-Dunn 1994; Shannon 1996) and originated with the work of Immanuel Wallerstein (1974), who studied the emergence of modern capitalism. More recently, Philip Kohl (1989) has modified Wallerstein's initial conception of WST to fit ancient conditions. In a careful critique of the primitivist views of M. I. Finley (1973) and others, Kohl cites many examples of price fixing, inflation, and market mentality that demonstrate the complexity of ancient economies. He builds a strong argument for the existence of an intricate multicentered world system during the Bronze Age in Southwest Asia. Unlike many modern technologies, ancient ones were often portable and could be moved easily from core to periphery. This fact, along with the lack of major colonization, made it possible for peripheries to retain their autonomy and precluded the exploitation and underdevelopment characteristic of the modern world system.

Kohl (1992) explores the core–periphery relationship specifically as it concerns the Transcaucasus and provides concepts useful for an examination of the Aegean Bronze Age. He borrows Chernykh's notion of "metallurgical provinces," defined by "their shared utilization of typologically similar metal ornaments, tools, and weapons; by a common technology of metallurgical production; and by the availability of or access to the same metallurgical sources" (Kohl 1992:134). What he says about the Transcaucasus is applicable to the Aegean area: if tin was not obtained locally, the very profusion of tin-bronzes in Transcaucasia from Late Bronze times onward suggests an interregional linkage with real economic dependencies (or, better, interdependencies). The barbarian "peripheries or northern frontiers of Transcaucasia and Central Asia, like their Aegean counterpart far to the west, did not palely reflect the light of civilization emanating from the ancient Near East; rather, they stimulated the latter civilized areas and profoundly affected their courses of development" (Kohl 1992:134–135).

Frank (1993) argues that areas on the margins of the Near East, while important as regions of economic interaction, were subject to the influences of the superpowers of the time: Egypt, Assyria, the Hittites, and other states in Mesopotamia. Frank argues that an Afro-Eurasian world system has existed for five thousand years, since the origins of the state in Mesopotamia and Egypt. In this chapter I argue that the Aegean Bronze Age trade network was an interdependent part of this larger Near Eastern world system. Although the trade in metals was central to this system, the exchange of stone tools was not; lithics did, however, play a role in intraregional exchange and can provide insight into the layered nature of the economy.

Of special relevance to the prehistoric Aegean is the distinction between two kinds of core–periphery relationships recently made by Chase-Dunn and Hall (1993:863):

The first is called "core/periphery differentiation," in which societies at different levels of complexity and population density are in interaction with each other within the same world-system as defined above. The second aspect is a "core/periphery hierarchy," in which political, economic or ideological domination exists among different societies within the same world-system. . . . We distinguish between differentiation and hierarchy because we think it is mistaken to assume that all relations among "more developed" and "less developed" societies involve exploitation and/or processes of the development of underdevelopment.

The exploitation of stone tools in the Late Bronze Age Aegean involved differentiation *within* Mycenaean society, so I believe we need to emend this schema to include intra- as well as intersocietal relationships. Later I discuss this aspect as the internal level of the Aegean world system.

Sherratt (1993) has used the term "margin" to refer to a zone that does not interact directly with a core but does provide materials that are critical to the operation of a world system. He points to the role of amber from the Baltic region and various metals from Central Europe in the Mediterranean trade system. The urban core of the Near East and the Aegean in the Bronze Age stimulated the exchange of many commodities through multiple links without members from either geographic extreme ever coming into direct contact. Parts of this system existed in the Neolithic and continued down into historic times, but not without alterations. The trade in metals, especially bronze, was particularly significant; the liquidity provided by bronze made possible the integration of "regional exchange cycles." Sherratt (1993) implies that the Bronze Age is aptly named, not simply because of the artifacts but because this metal alloy fueled the economic expansion on which many early states depended.

Sherratt (1993:44–45) provides useful definitions for this system. Of particular importance is his concept of the margin "as the area of 'escaped' technologies and long-distance contacts based on directional exchange-cycles." He describes the Aegean as one of several linked maritime exchange cycles in the Mediterranean that in the Bronze Age witnessed the shift from "'luxuries' to 'commodities' in the context of the emergence of palatial organization." The relatively rapid development of production centers and the concomitant supporting organizational structures moved the peoples of the Aegean from the status of periphery to "more equal participation in inter-regional trade." This process fostered the growth of trade in bulk materials.

THE AEGEAN WORLD SYSTEM

I have suggested elsewhere that the Aegean had a tripartite exchange system in the Bronze Age, with internal, intermediate, and long-distance components (Kardulias 1995). In general, bulk goods circulated in the first two cycles and prestige goods in the last; bronze and copper ingots held a special place in this system and require other considerations (Knapp and Cherry 1994). The study of stone tools in the Aegean may shed light on the nature of the first two levels.

Since flaked stone artifacts of chert and obsidian often assume both utilitarian and symbolic roles, such items tend to hold an unusual position in world systems exchange networks. In some prehistoric trade systems, such as among the Ohio Hopewell—where obsidian from Yellowstone often occurs in mound burials (Prufer 1964; Yerkes 1988)—flaked stone artifacts clearly traveled long distances. In other areas, flaked stone artifacts tended to move in incremental steps, by down-the-line exchange. This was the case in the eastern highlands of Papua New Guinea, where most of the obsidian tools originated in the region of Talasea on New Britain, 450 km distant as the crow flies. These tools were used primarily for medical bloodletting (Watson 1986:5–6), and moved by interisland, coastal, and interior trade routes (Harding, in Watson 1986:6).

To address the world systems aspects of the lithics tradition in the Aegean Bronze Age, I would like to suggest emendation of the system described by Chase-Dunn and Hall (1993). Whereas they see societies at different levels of sociopolitical integration interacting in such a system, I suggest there are instances in which the groups involved are at the same level of complexity, that is, peer polities (see Renfrew and Cherry 1986). While Frank (1993) is certainly correct in stating that one cannot fully understand the local developments in various regions without reference to the major powers (e.g., Egypt), he does not allow nearly enough play to local developments. If we are to answer Sherratt's (1993) query concerning the nature of a Bronze Age world system, it is probably best to begin at the local level and build our way up to the interregional level. In this effort, I will focus on the local and intermediate levels of the Aegean system.

Local/Internal System

Local or internal networks operated within a narrowly defined region in which land transport or short coastal hops sufficed for the transfer of goods. The local systems on Crete, Cyprus, and the Argolid peninsula would be of this type. In each area there existed a group of relatively small states, described as early state modules (ESMs) by Renfrew (1984). Within each polity were a number of settlements that exchanged a variety of commodities. I do not mean to suggest that the exchange was egalitarian. Some individuals and settlements certainly acted as key nodes in the system and siphoned off a significant share of the goods. I would argue, however, that there was a rough parity in the economic structure within each of the polities, and that most of the ESMs were on an equal footing. Involved in such exchanges would be a range of goods either native to each region or easily obtained by each. In addition, materials native to each region could form a significant part of the local economy. In terms of stone tools, this would mean exploitation of local material. This is the case in Lakonia, the southern Argolid, and on Crete. For example, at Kommos, Blizter (1995) identified three local chert sources that were used by the Minoan residents to produce tools.

Another source that provides considerable detail on other facets of the internal economic system are the Linear B tablets from palace archives, especially those of Pylos and Knossos (see chapters 3–6, this volume). The image that emerges from the texts is of a centralized system in which land tenure depended on one's relation to the palace (see chapter 7, this volume). Whether one looks at Pylos, Knossos, or Mycenae, the systems exhibit a considerable degree of homogeneity. Agricultural products found their way into the central storehouses, then lesser quantities went back out through the various channels. An important question is whether these palace economies constituted market systems. There is no evidence of markets in the Linear B texts, but these documents deal only with the flow of goods into and out of the palaces. There is reference, however, to private property (Chadwick 1976:117), and there is a stress on profit, whether from crops or secondary animal products, especially wool. In addition, it is hard to imagine that the residents of the villages and hamlets did not periodically gather to exchange what surplus remained after the palace "taxes" were paid. Chadwick (1976:158) suggests that some markets existed, but he questions the existence of a regular merchant class. The tablets, however, are silent on the matter of stone tool production and distribution (see also chapter 9, this volume).

Intermediate system

The interchange of material from island to island (and island to mainland) in the Aegean best represents this level of the Aegean world system. Through this system, products peculiar to specific parts of the Aegean found their way to all corners of the archipelago. In addition, the more productive areas, such as Crete, found outlets for their surplus. The much-debated question of a Minoan thalassocracy (Knapp 1993) in essence asks whether the Cyclades, Dodekanese, and the Greek mainland were peripheries under the core domination of Crete. Although not phrased in WST terms, Evans (1921) provided an early expression of this perspective. He believed not only that Mycenaean civilization received its generative stimulus from Crete but also that the mainland was under the political, economic, and artistic sway of the Minoans. When Wace (1949) and others demonstrated the independence of Mycenae, the way was opened to a more interactive model of Aegean Bronze Age economy. The archaeological record indicates a symmetrical economic relationship among many of the settlements, but there is also evidence that Crete's "pull" created some imbalances.

In the second millennium BC, Cycladic culture was a rich fabric of large settlements, unique expressive art, and material prosperity. Much of that prosperity probably derived from the fact that the various islands served as way stations for the commerce between Crete, the Greek mainland, and areas to the east. The Western String exchange system proposed by Cherry and Davis (1982) tied Kea, Melos, and Thera into a trading relationship with Attika and Crete. From Laurion in southeastern Attika came lead, used for rivets, plugs, and waterproof linings for storage bins, and silver, an important medium of exchange in the entire region (Wiener 1990). In the other direction went Minoan pottery, various manufactured status goods, and probably woolen textiles (Finley 1981:37–38). As the system of trade became increasingly important to Crete, evidence for Minoan infiltration of the Aegean increases. There is a Minoanization of pottery, town-planning, and artistic expression in various important sites, such as Akrotiri on Thera and Trianda on Rhodes (Wiener 1984). From such evidence, Wiener argues for the presence of many Minoans or their descendants in the Cyclades and Dodekanese, but the nature of the contacts

"may include casual, unofficial, small-scale migration involving merchants . . . or an expanding Minoan elite seeking to carve out baronies, or a Cretan nobility exercising loose diplomatic control" (1990:153). The Aegean intermediate or regional world system benefited many local communities and engendered, at most, a loose confederation within which Crete was unable to exercise hegemony even though her dynamic economy and elites generated much of the demand for goods that raised production levels and stimulated trade. While certain individuals may have desired to control the system, they could not fully exploit it because of the number of middlemen, and because of their relative isolation on so many islands.

FLAKED STONE IN THE AEGEAN WORLD SYSTEM

Distribution of material

A number of archaeological finds attest to the existence of a fairly extensive exchange system in the prehistoric Aegean. The distribution of nonlocal goods began in the Upper Palaeolithic, continued in the Mesolithic, gathered momentum in the Neolithic, and culminated in the extensive system of the Bronze Age. For the earlier periods, obsidian is a good indicator of the extent of the system. Sourcing studies by Renfrew and his colleagues (Cann and Renfrew 1964; Dixon and Renfrew 1973; Renfrew et al. 1965) indicate that obsidian from the island of Melos was widespread throughout the Aegean, beginning in the Upper Palaeolithic. For the Neolithic, obsidian has been found at Argissa Magoula, Sesklo (Theocharis 1981:37), Rakhmani, Dhimini, Tsangli, and other sites in Thessaly (Wace and Thompson 1912:43, 84, 122). Macedonian Neolithic sites with obsidian include Servia (Ridley and Wardle 1979:229; Watson 1983:123), Nea Nikomedia (Dixon et al. 1968:41), Soufli, and Sitagroi (Runnels 1983:417). In southern Greece, Neolithic sites with obsidian include Tsoungiza/Nemea (Blegen 1975: 272), Baroutospilia (McDonald and Hope Simpson 1969:158), and Lerna I (Caskey 1968:313). Island contexts include Kephala on Kea (Caskey 1971:391), Knossos on Crete (J. Evans 1964:162), Saliagos on Antiparos (Renfrew et al. 1965:238), and the Aspripetra Cave on Kos (Leekley and Noyes 1975:29).

During the Bronze Age, the number of sites with obsidian increased, as did the quantities of the material present. On the Greek mainland, such sites include

Mycenae (Mylonas 1966:102; Wace 1949:112), Tiryns (Shelford et al. 1982:190), Lerna (Runnels 1985a), Prosymna (Blegen 1937:342), Nichoria (Blitzer 1992), and many spots located by systematic surveys in Messenia (McDonald and Hope Simpson 1969; McDonald 1975:120; chapter 9, this volume), the southern Argolid (Kardulias and Runnels 1995), Lakonia, the Nemea Valley, and other regions. Among the key island sites are Agia Irini on Kea (Davis 1977:110–116 passim; see also Torrence 1991), Debla (Warren and Tzedhakis 1974:332), Myrtos, Knossos, and Mochlos (Warren 1972a:328) on Crete, Phylakopi on Melos (Renfrew 1982a:223; Torrence 1986), Akrotiri on Thera (Shelford et al. 1982:190), Kastri on Kythera (Huxley 1972:217), and several locations in the Dodekanese (Leekley and Noyes 1975:28, 31). By no means exhaustive, this list gives some sense of the geographic spread of the material. Although the use of chert and obsidian dropped off considerably after the Late Bronze Age, chipped stone has also been found on historic sites (Runnels 1982; Sackett et al. 1966:49). The distribution of millstones made of andesite, the sources of which Runnels (1981) identified in the Aegean, also demonstrates the existence of significant trade in the Neolithic and Bronze Age Aegean (Runnels 1983, 1985b, 1988).

A key point about obsidian procurement is that visitors to Melos seem to have had direct, unimpeded access to this resource (Renfrew 1982a:223–224; Torrence 1986). It seems that travelers roughed out conical cores, which they carried back to home sites for final tool production. The distribution of obsidian suggests that people in the Cyclades, Crete, and the Greek mainland all had the opportunity and knowledge to acquire and process the material (Renfrew 1972:443). What we find is that, apart from one or two gateway communities, the distribution of obsidian is relatively uniform throughout the individual regions. In addition, the pattern appears to be the same between regions and suggests that the ESMs attained a certain internal consistency. For example, Bennet (1990:199–200) argues that the palaces of Crete were indigenous developments and that, despite strong ties among them, no one center held hegemony over the others.

Lithics and the Aegean Bronze Age economy

The Sherratts (1991:371), along with others, contend that by the Late Bronze Age (1400–1200 BC), the palaces of the Greek mainland were the basis of the Aegean economy. At the broadest level, the Aegean acted as a semiperiphery for the Eurasian world-system. Cline (1995b) argues for a system of trade partnerships that tied rulers of the great Near Eastern empires to the Aegean elite; a system of reciprocal gift exchanges defined the various leaders as fictive kin. From their powerful neighbors, Aegean elites probably received alabaster bowls, ebony furniture, metal vessels, jewelry, and other luxury items. In return, Mycenaean elites could have provided elaborate pottery, perfumed oil, textiles, and other finished articles. Skilled artisans may have also formed part of such exchanges, along with a host of mundane objects and foodstuffs (Cline 1995b:147–150). The role of metal was certainly critical in this international trade. Its relative scarcity fueled competitive efforts to acquire more of the material, leading both to efforts to control access to sources and the intense regulation of ingots and finished products by the palace elites. Cyprus was a major source of copper for bronze. Recent analyses by Stos-Gale et al. (1997) indicate that many ox-hide ingots dating to the fourteenth century BC in Crete, Greece, Sardinia, Turkey, and Bulgaria derive from a single region in northern Cyprus. While the elites competed to accumulate metals, stone for the production of common tools held a significantly lower status (see also chapter 9, this volume).

In the Aegean, the only high-grade obsidian amenable to flaking is found on the island of Melos. There are two major outcrops on the island, at Sta Nychia near Adamas on the north coast and at Demenegaki on the east side (Torrence 1986). In her examination of how these two quarries were exploited during prehistoric times, Torrence (1982, 1986) considered two contrasting hypotheses in terms of the material correlates that should be evident in the archaeological record. The first conjecture rested on the notion that the prosperity of Bronze Age Phylakopi depended on the demand for obsidian in a competitive market economy. If this were the case, one would expect to find evidence of centralized control in the form of structures on the sites to guard access to the material, port facilities nearby to regulate the flow of obsidian, special artifacts used in extracting the stone, and definable activity areas where necessary tasks were conducted. The second hypothesis, suggested by Renfrew (1982a), envisioned a system of direct access by anyone who required a supply of the stone. In this case there would have been no centralized control, with obsidian transported throughout the Aegean by a series of interlocked reciprocal exchanges.

Torrence's (1982, 1986) examination of the Melian quarries revealed no evidence for boundary lines, structures, or port facilities. Although a great deal of work was carried out at the quarries throughout prehistory, it was undertaken with little investment in technical skill and labor, with material used in an unsystematic, expedient fashion. In general, the quarrying activities seem to have been conducted in an opportunistic and unorganized fashion (Torrence 1982:197, 204–207, 211–213). Ships from the mainland would have had ready access to the material, but the activity was probably on a small scale, with subsequent exchange taking place from a variety of mainland coastal sites to the interior (Runnels 1983:419). Torrence suggests that the exploitation of the Melos quarries was expedient, unorganized, required only a simple technology, and occurred in brief episodes (Torrence 1984:62).

It is important to note that Perlès (1990a, b) has argued, in direct contradiction to Torrence, that mainland lithic specialists regulated the acquisition of Melian obsidian in the Early and Middle Neolithic. While Perlès agrees that direct access was a probability for sites, such as those in the southern Argolid, close to Melos, she contends that the quantity and regularity of worked obsidian at inland sites in Thessaly and Macedonia were the result of indirect trade controlled by specialists at critical nodes. In addition, Perlès asserts that obsidian procurement was the primary goal of expeditions to the island. On the first point, Torrence's model of uncontrolled access and Perlès's model of controlled procurement are more complementary than contradictory. Coastal sites in the eastern Peloponnese, and perhaps as far north as Thessaly, could have obtained obsidian from Melos without the use of an intermediary, but it is highly doubtful that inland sites in the south or north would have had unimpeded access. On the second point, it is hard to imagine that Neolithic or, for that matter, Bronze Age people would have traveled from northern Thessaly to Melos, a distance of 500 km, solely to acquire obsidian. For various reasons, I believe obsidian procurement was embedded in other activities even for residents of the southern Argolid (Kardulias 1992).

By the Early Bronze Age, extensive population movements and exploration in the Aegean resulted in the initial habitation of islands with a wide range of ecological conditions (Cherry 1981:52; see also Cherry 1990 for earlier periods). Such diversity could have stimulated trade, with the products of different niches exchanged to compensate for local deficiencies.

Others have argued for conspicuous consumption as a motivating factor. The Sherratts suggest that various commodities "formed part of a cultural and ideological package as well as a subsistence one . . .[which] required investment and the mobilisation of manpower and capital" (Sherratt and Sherratt 1991:355). Whatever the specific motivation may have been, the wide and intensive distribution of obsidian in the third and second millennia in the Aegean involved procurement systems not very different from what existed in the Neolithic. Phylakopi was a growing community, but there is no evidence that it regulated the trade in obsidian. Evidently, visitors had direct, unimpeded access to this resource, even into the Late Bronze Age (Renfrew 1982a:223–225). The distribution of obsidian suggests that many people in the Cyclades, Crete, and on the Greek mainland had the opportunity and knowledge to prepare rough cores, which were then transported to various locations for final tool production (Renfrew 1972:443).

If any regulation of the obsidian trade did occur, it is more likely that such control started at the coastal sites where the rough cores arrived. Sites closest to Melos have the majority of the cores; as distance from the source increases, the number of cores drops while blades persist in the archaeological record. Van Horn (1980) records the relative abundance of blade cores in the Argolid and the accompanying abundance of blades. This contrasts to the situation at Servia in Macedonia, where blades seem to have been imported already made, since no cores were retrieved during the excavation (Watson 1983:122). A similar condition seems to have existed on Crete, with cores and blades at Mochlos, but only blades at Debla and Myrtos (Warren and Tzedhakis 1974:332; Warren 1972a:326–328). This pattern corresponds to what Renfrew (1972:465–471) terms down-the-line exchange. Wace and Thompson (1912:226) posited something akin to this model when they suggested that obsidian arrived in prehistoric Thessaly by way of an overland route after reaching outposts such as Orchomenos. Cherry and Davis's Western String exchange system (1982) is a somewhat more patterned version of the same phenomenon. This model envisions the western Cyclades as isolated from islands in the central and eastern Aegean. The presumably Melian obsidian in Messenia (McDonald and Hope Simpson 1972:131) may owe its presence there to a comparable system that skirted the southern coast of the Peloponnese. Since intermediate sites have not been identified (with the possible exception of Kastri on

Kythera), one cannot rule out the possibility of a more direct, controlled route.

The importation of Gialian obsidian into Crete in Middle and Late Minoan times indicates another aspect of the trade as societal and commercial complexity increased. This speckled obsidian did not lend itself well to blade production, but it was well suited to the manufacture of vases. This variety of obsidian was brought to Crete as early as Middle Minoan I. Lumps of the material were found in a stoneworker's atelier at Mallia dated to this period (Warren 1967:199). It has been retrieved from Middle Minoan II–III contexts at Knossos, and from Late Minoan associations at Knossos, Tylissos, and Palaikastro. A variety of vessels were formed from this obsidian, including a chalice from Kato Zakro, a dolium shell from Agia Triadha, fragments from Knossos with horizontal grooves below the rim, and imitations of Egyptian shallow carinated bowls (Warren 1969:135–136). In the Late Bronze Age, Gialian obsidian may have been directed to Crete by way of the Minoan settlement at Triandha on Rhodes (Warren 1975:103). This evidence suggests that artisans made particular artifacts from obsidian derived from specific sources, implying an intimate knowledge of the characteristics of the various types and the ability to acquire sufficient amounts to allow for specialization. The functional basis associated with multiple source exploitation has been suggested for the Classic Maya site of Tikal (Rice 1984:182). Only a society with complex, hierarchical organization could have fully implemented such a system. In both the Old and New Worlds, this occurred after the appearance of nascent states. Renfrew argues that the Aegean obsidian trade was not profitable enough in itself to have stimulated this development, but it does reflect the organizational capacity of state-level societies to administer such activities when social complexity did evolve (Renfrew et al. 1968:330).

Flint versus obsidian

The utilization of different lithic resources reveals aspects of the Bronze Age economy. Little exotic flint is present even at the Bronze Age and historic period sites in the southern Argolid, where the use of local raw material formed one part of the internal system. The most characteristic type of exotic flint at Neolithic Franchthi Cave is a very high-quality material called honey flint because of its rich amber color. The source of this flint is not known, but may be as far away as Bulgaria and Romania (Perlès 1987b), and involved the

Aegean in trade with Central Europe (Sherratt's "margins"). Bronze Age levels at Tsoungiza in the Nemea Valley have yielded substantial amounts of high-quality flint of various colors and its source is presumed to be nearby. Flint has proved resistant to various sourcing methods that stress trace element analysis (Foradas 1994; Ives 1984; Luedtke 1978, 1992; Vickery 1983).

The better flint blades in the southern Argolid Neolithic and the fine, parallel-sided flint blades in the Early Bronze Age were imported. This is clear from the absence altogether of cores, debitage, or debris of the same materials as the large blades (Runnels 1983, 1985a). The honey flint blades at Neolithic Franchthi Cave were retouched until exhausted, presumably because supplies were limited (Perlès 1987b). Perhaps a trade in finished flint blades existed at the same time as the obsidian trade from Melos. Until the geological sources of the exotic flints have been identified, it is not possible to comprehend fully the workings of this trade, or to relate the flint trade to the obsidian exchange system.

During the Bronze Age, the use of flint and chert dropped off drastically as obsidian became increasingly available. The rather poor quality of the local cherts would have limited their value as trade materials and precluded their use in the increasingly complex exchange patterns involving obsidian and the igneous and metamorphic rocks from different areas used as millstones (Runnels 1981, 1985b). In WST terms, local cherts played no role in interregional trade and thus remained an item for internal consumption only; low-value bulk items failed to move beyond the peripheries or margins of the system.

The increasing dependence on imported obsidian over locally abundant cherts reflects a scheduling shift in which the inhabitants of southern Greece placed greater emphasis on interregional trade as a means of expanding their resource base. The decision-making process may have involved two levels. First, since people traveled considerable distances to acquire a variety of goods (e.g., seasonally available foods, pottery), obsidian could be added to the list, even though its procurement probably would not have been the initial motive for such trips. Second, since abundant quantities of high-quality obsidian could be brought back from such general expeditions, residents could choose to ignore the chert, whose acquisition costs would have been minimal and which would otherwise have been part of a more efficient strategy. In this instance, a change in procurement scheduling for various exotic materials led to increased access to obsidian. Distance to the source outweighed advantages of obsidian (ease of knapping, sharp edges, availability of large chunks) until other activities took people to Melos on a regular basis. This aspect of the obsidian trade demonstrates its embedded nature as a bulk commodity in local and interregional exchange. Knappers, at least those in coastal sites in the northeastern Peloponnese, chose to work obsidian almost exclusively once the supply became more regular. Despite its availability, local chert in much of southern Greece is highly fractured and difficult to knap. Efficiency in this case is measured as production time, when a superior material is made available.

A closer look at data from several sites demonstrates the points made above. The chert used by ancient inhabitants of Agios Stephanos in southern Lakonia is generally of high quality and ranges widely in color. The precise source of the high-quality chert at the site is difficult to determine because various sources exist and current tests cannot clearly discriminate among them. It is unlikely, however, that chert quarries were as distant as Melos (but see above concerning possible sources for the Argolid honey flint), the putative source of all the obsidian. Yet obsidian dominates the assemblage, an indication of the inhabitants' desire to fulfill certain needs in a specific fashion. I have suggested (Kardulias 1992) that the exchange of chert and obsidian was probably only a minor part of the economic network, and was undoubtedly secondary to the acquisition of vital commodities such as metal and foodstuffs.

One might expect an increase in the percentage of obsidian at Bronze Age sites, since it is far superior to local stone sources in the Argolid for the production of large blades. This trend is clearly in evidence at Franchthi Cave by the Late Neolithic (Perlès 1991), and is dramatically reflected in survey site F32, one of the major Early Bronze Age settlements in the southern Argolid. Obsidian constitutes 98.7% (2106 pieces) and flint constitutes 1.3% (28 pieces) of the lithic industry at F32, demonstrating a clear shift in emphasis from the situation in earlier periods (Kardulias and Runnels 1995:107). For the Late Helladic/Mycenaean, the situation is similar in some respects. Of the fourteen sites with Mycenaean sherds, nine also have lithics: obsidian constitutes 68.8% of the assemblage (table 10.1). Even though the distribution of rock type is not as skewed as at F32, preference for obsidian is clear.

Did the occupants of individual sites undertake separate procurement journeys or did certain larger sites regulate the flow of obsidian? Much has been made of

TABLE 10.1. Late Bronze Age pottery and lithics from the Argolid survey.

SITE	SHERDS	LITHICS	
		Obsidian	*Chert*
F5	257	14	5
E74	151	4	10
F4	93	22	10
B21	79	- - -	- - -
B41	76	4	1
E13	72	6	7
A6	60	23	3
E9	52	- - -	- - -
C11	38	11	2
B38	35	- - -	- - -
B25	34	- - -	- - -
E5	27	2	2
F21	22	2	0
C3	20	- - -	- - -
TOTAL		88	40
		68.8%	31.2%

this issue in studies of Mesoamerican obsidian trade. Drennan (1984) suggests that during the Formative period, obsidian acquisition in the region was of such a small scale (5 kg/person/year) that no elaborate exchange network was necessary or even feasible. Only during the Classic period, with its complex socioeconomic structure, did obsidian become one focus of a large-scale commercial system. At Teotihuacan, for example, there is evidence of obsidian workshops the products of which were traded far afield (Millon 1967), although this view has been challenged (Clark 1986). Although the situation in the Aegean is quite different in terms of the number of sources and the means of transport, perhaps some general analogy is applicable. Early scholars suggested that the obsidian trade was controlled by Phylakopi throughout the Bronze Age and contributed to the wealth of this town (Bosanquet 1904). Torrence (1986), however, has argued that extraction of raw material from the quarries was never systematically controlled. Rather, she postulates that individual expeditions from various islands and the mainland probably procured obsidian directly. This system of acquisition would certainly have been easy enough to implement for the inhabitants of mainland coastal sites, such as Lerna and the cluster of sites around the village of Fournoi in the southern Argolid (figure 10.1) (Jameson et al. 1994:348–366; van Andel and Runnels 1987:90–93).

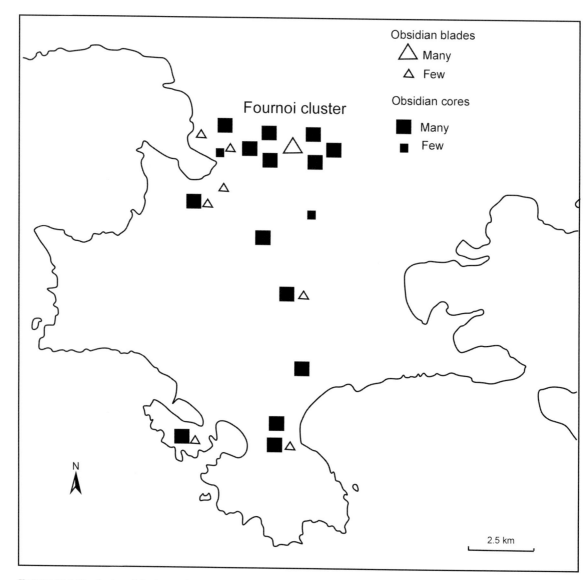

FIGURE 10.1 Distribution of obsidian artifacts in the Fournoi region of the southern Argolid, Greece. (Adapted from Jameson et al. 1994, figure 6.13.)

The distribution of obsidian on the Greek mainland may have followed several patterns. Torrence (1986:218–226) argues for "distribution without exchange," that is, simple reciprocal, noncommercial exchange, in the Neolithic and Bronze Age because of easy access to Melos from the mainland and other islands. She views obsidian in the Aegean as commercially insignificant. The data, I believe, suggest that the Bronze Age distribution pattern had a different cause. Perhaps because Torrence (1986) deals primarily with coastal sites, her assessment is accurate as far as it goes. Obsidian remained a relatively cheap commodity in the Bronze Age, but central places seem to have regulated its dispersal inland in the southern Argolid, and perhaps in Lakonia. As noted elsewhere, the distribution of obsidian during the Mycenaean period in the southern Argolid "suggests regulated dispersal within small regions from a central place" (Kardulias and Runnels 1995:93). These central places, however, were not the palaces, which instead focused on commodities with greater potential to generate wealth for the elite. This pattern is similar to that for obsidian in the Naco Valley, Honduras, during the Classic period. In this area peripheral to the Mayan core, the large site of La Sierra was the center of production for obsidian blades and pottery, which were then distributed throughout the valley (Schortman and Urban 1994:406).

With the advent of complex polities in the mid- to late third millennium BC, the potential for more regular, structured exchange ensued. The key question is if certain large sites in southern Greece came to dominate obsidian acquisition, becoming central clearinghouses through which the stone was distributed to other settlements in the peninsula. One avenue that may prove fruitful is the investigating the presence or absence of crested blades as indicators of on-site modification of nodules or large blanks into blade cores, as opposed to the importing of prepared cores from elsewhere, as Renfrew (1972:449) suggests. If crested blades are restricted to a few sites, production of blades occurred in a limited number of locations, and a model proposing the regulation of obsidian importation by large centers gains credibility. If, on the other hand, such pieces are widely distributed throughout the region, this pattern may reflect unrestricted access through a decentralized economic system (i.e., a continuation of the earlier system). In the southern Argolid, twenty-one sites yielded a total of fifty-eight crested blades, but only four sites yielded more than one specimen. Perhaps it is appropriate to identify F32, with thirty-four crested blades, tentatively as a major obsidian processing center that, if it did not control, certainly had a major input into the exchange network involving obsidian, and probably other commodities as well.

The distribution of cores and blades in the southern Argolid is another indicator of the importance of F32 (see table 10.1 and figure 10.1). Eleven sites have obsidian cores, but only five locations have more than one such core (F32, F6, and F19 are in close proximity to one another and may represent different activity areas in one site). Of the twenty-eight Bronze Age sites with obsidian blades (n = 304), only nine have ten or more pieces. The discrepancy in the percentages of Bronze Age cores and blades found at F32 may indicate that it was an important production site. Cores generally are not moved far from the center of production, whereas the blades, as finished products, could have been transported widely from F32 and thus created a more even distribution for this category. Agios Stephanos, with thirteen obsidian cores, thirty-one obsidian crested blades, and 534 obsidian blades, has numbers similar to F32 (Kardulias and Runnels 1995:106–108). An important point to note, however, is that these numbers far exceed those from Mycenaean palaces.

It is unlikely that inhabitants of inland sites such as Agios Stephanos engaged in direct journeys to Melos. Although situated near the coast, Agios Stephanos lies on a less direct route to Melos than the sites mentioned above. It is more plausible to posit an exchange network involving a central processing depot whose residents collected the obsidian in Melos, transported it to the mainland, and then distributed it to inland sites and to other places, such as Agios Stephanos, that had less access to the raw material. Local resources, such as lapis Lacedaemonius and foodstuffs, could have been exchanged for the obsidian. Such a system would explain the relatively small amount of obsidian at Agios Stephanos. It is possible that central processing depots existed in certain areas. Although the inhabitants of Agios Stephanos themselves may not have collected obsidian on occasional trips to Melos, in Lakonia there may have existed a central processing depot on the island of Elaphonisi, which lies on a more direct route to Melos (Hope Simpson and Dickinson 1979). Hope Simpson and Waterhouse (1961) noted considerable quantities of obsidian on the surface of six of thirteen sites on this island and the adjacent mainland.

Determining the amount of obsidian imported at any one time would aid in assessing the extent and intensity of exchange networks. Luedtke (1979) suggests this can be done by considering factors such as number of tools needed and the weight of the tools and associated debris. This approach offers an avenue for further research with Greek lithics. Torrence (1979) provided an early effort of this sort for the Aegean in her examination of the obsidian from an Early Minoan IIA deposit at Knossos. She estimated that twenty-three cores were completely exhausted in a "workshop." At an average starting weight of 0.82 kg per core, the total weight of the imported material would have been 18.86 kg. Even if this number represents the total procured in one season or a single expedition, the amount is not large, and certainly does not suggest that acquisition of stone was the key goal of commercial excursions.

CONCLUSION

As a commodity of local and regional but not international significance, lithics may address key aspects of domestic economy. Such tools were certainly important in the harvesting and threshing of grains, perhaps as early as the Neolithic (Kardulias and Yerkes 1996). The evidence comes from satellites of major Mycenaean sites and, rarely, from the palaces. The material from LH II levels at Tsoungiza in Nemea indicates the existence of a small hamlet with several families interacting in an egalitarian collaborative fashion (Wright et al. 1990). Unlike the southern trenches, in EU 10 and Harland's Trench L there are substantial quantities of obsidian hollow base points and chert tools. These quantities suggest local or on-site production of stone tools. The LH IIA ceramics, however, are the same as those from Mycenae and elsewhere in the Argolid and reflect centralized production. Wright et al. (1990:638) suggest that various sites in the Korinthia may have "served as administrative outposts of the palace, similar to Neopalatial Crete." Wright (1984:29) asks whether or not there were pressures on the Mycenaean system that encouraged self sufficiency and concentration on regional over more general economic activity. At Pylos he argues that in the late thirteenth century BC, changes in palace architecture may reflect the shift to direct oversight or supervision of certain industries by palace administrators. Palaima (1984a) also argues for a tightly controlled economy, while Tegyey (1984:77) suggests the presence of a "temple-economy" at Pylos (compare Lupack, chapter 6, this volume). This centralization evidently never affected stone tool manufacture. As Parkinson (1997, and chapter 9, this volume) has reported, very few lithics were found in and around the Palace of Nestor. Rather, he proposes that a major production center existed at the site of Romanou, near the coast. Evidence from elsewhere in Greece confirms this point. In the southern Argolid, there is no palatial structure, but there are many Late Bronze Age/Mycenaean sites. Lithic production debris is concentrated in a few central sites, with only finished blades and minimal debitage on sites in the interior. Torrence (1991:193) notes a similar pattern in northern Kea. Analysis of material from the Mycenaean citadel of Midea in the Argolid lends further support to the thesis of decentralized production of stone tools. Newhard (1996) argues that evidence for on-site knapping and stockpiling, both indicators of palatial control, is lacking at Midea. Lithics may be considered a type of staple good, one over which the palace maintained only minimal control (Shelmerdine 1997:567).

Despite the lack of centralized control of stone tool manufacture in Mycenaean times, assemblages from around the Aegean exhibit striking similarities. Torrence (1991:192) summarizes the situation: "Prismatic blades and the associated waste by-products of their manufacture are dominant, while the major retouched forms—points and denticulates—. . . . occur only rarely." She also notes that the abundant unmodified blanks (mostly blades) may have formed a major category of ad hoc tools. This pattern reflects the nonhegemonic nature of Mycenaean economies: no one polity could dominate its peers militarily or commercially, at least not for long. The regular contact with other regions encouraged certain common production techniques, but the palaces concentrated their efforts on certain commodities. Even in the small territories they occupied, they lacked both the ability and willingness to operate a full command economy.

Who produced the stone tools? This question concerns the larger issue of the level of specialization in the Mycenaean economy. What amount of debris would constitute evidence of a specialist working? Perhaps Mesoamerica can offer a relevant example. Clear evidence of specialized, full-time production exists at Colha (Belize), where the workshop area has deep deposits of debris. One Late Preclassic pit contained 603,000 flakes/m^3, and a Late Classic feature had 5 million flakes/m^3 (Shafer 1991:31). The other line of evidence is ethnographic and ethnoarchaeological. In recording the workshop of a modern Lacondon Maya flintknapper, John Clark (1991) found more than 100,000 flakes on the floor of the structure. No Mycenaean site has such quantities of debris. The closest figures come from satellite communities. In the southern Argolid, survey teams retrieved 3236 pieces of flaked stone (2985, or 92.2%, obsidian) from thirty-three sites with Bronze Age components (Kardulias and Runnels 1995:93). The tool types in this assemblage (denticulates/sickle elements, various scrapers, piercing tools, and so on) reflect probable use in agricultural contexts. Of the 1173 lithic artifacts recovered at Agios Stephanos, 1068 (90.9%) are obsidian; the tool types from this site also suggest agricultural activity. Numbers of lithic artifacts are comparable only at a few sites with palaces or large public structures. These sites include Phylakopi, Agia Irini, and Early Helladic Mallia (Torrence 1979; van Effenterre and van Effenterre 1969). The evidence from Lerna (Runnels 1985a), Agios Stephanos (Kardulias 1992), Midea (Newhard 1996), Kea (Torrence 1991), and elsewhere suggests production by part-time specialists. In the Mycenaean world system, the palace probably could not have exercised hegemonic control over all aspects of the economy; in the case of flaked lithics, it probably did not care to do so.

While Carothers (1992:280) argues for the presence of attached specialists (similar to Ventris and Chadwick's [1973:120] translation of a potter, a fuller, and an armorer as "royal" artisans; see chapter 4, this volume) at the palaces, the trades they practiced did not include flaked stone tool production; the Linear B documents are silent on this aspect of the economy (see chapter 9, this volume). That stone workers are not mentioned at all would suggest their trade was not under palatial supervision. Both the negative evidence and the presence of lithics at secondary and tertiary sites thus indicate noncentralized production.

The system for the manufacture of flaked stone lithics was decentralized, or at least not directly controlled by the palaces. It was in some ways a palimpsest of the larger international and interregional trade networks. The production of stone tools involved specialized craftsmen and some degree of regulation, at least in terms of the distribution of finished products inland from the coastal sites where raw material (obsidian, in particular) appeared in some abundance. Why was there such salutary neglect of lithic production by the palace administrators? Elites wanted to control those crafts that generated wealth. This in large part was due to the competition among the peer polities that made up the Mycenaean political landscape (Cherry 1986). Anything that offered an opportunity for such accumulation was closely regulated. For example, since textiles evidently made up an important component of the luxury trade, we find evidence in the Linear B texts for the palace control of large flocks, the weaving of the material under careful administrative scrutiny, and maintenance of the skilled workers out of palace stores. There is also evidence for the export of such textiles to foreign dignitaries. We also see this close control in the case of metal, especially bronze. The raw material, often in the form of ingots (note the quantities on the Ulu Burun shipwreck, which was probably destined for Cretan and mainland palaces) came to the centers, and was then assigned to bronzesmiths The finished products were carefully inventoried by the scribes and kept in storerooms. The same situation seems to hold for the production of perfumed oil, certain pottery, and other commodities (again, mostly precious items that provide low bulk and high value).

Some scholars have tried to make similar arguments for the importance of certain flakable rocks, especially obsidian. A common argument for years was that the affluence of Bronze Age Phylakopi on Melos was in part due to its proximity and control over the major obsidian quarries on the island (Bosanquet 1904). Torrence (1982, 1986) has demonstrated convincingly, however, that there is no evidence that the residents of Melos ever managed the obsidian quarries; in fact, she postulates relatively free access by seafarers from other islands and the mainland. Is this case an anomaly? Mellaart (1964:146) made the conventional argument for the wealth of Neolithic Çatal Hüyük: "One cannot possibly be wrong in suggesting that it was a well-organized trade that produced the city's wealth. Moreover it appears likely that the trade in obsidian was at the heart of this extensive commerce." As in the case of Melos, there is no evidence that the residents of Çatal Hüyük actually controlled the obsidian quarries; in fact, some of those sources are up to 250 km from the site (Redman 1978:184). In short, while the trade in obsidian was extensive and important, there is no reason to believe that groups near the quarries necessarily benefited from the trade to any great extent. Obsidian and other exotic, but not rare, rocks could be one symbol of elite status. This seems to be true for the Hopewell culture of the Ohio Valley; many burials of exalted individuals include elaborate ritual artifacts (e.g., oversized blades) made of obsidian from the Yellowstone Park region (Prufer 1964). The cultures of that western area, however, exhibit little in the way of affluence. While the obsidian trade was important, it was limited in the degree to which it affected economic fortunes.

Centralized control of flintknapping was impossible because this technology was so easily transported. In fact, flintknapping's mere presence at the internal level of the world system probably meant that it was little affected by fluctuations in the big system. Frank (1993) identified an A phase in the period 1500–1200 BC, followed by a B phase, 1200–1000 BC. The latter witnessed the decline in bronze casting and the decay of urban life; in some instances people shifted from urban to rural settlement. But the production of flaked stone tools continued unabated, at least in some areas. Although one could not become rich making stone tools, the implements did perform important tasks in the agricultural cycle.

The acquisition of flakeable stone during the Late Helladic/Late Bronze Age is thus an aspect of the economy that lacks great visibility in international trade. It was handled at the local and regional level and was outside the control of the palaces (certainly in the southern Argolid, Agios Stephanos, and Midea). Stone tools and raw material probably joined other commodities as they were exchanged in the Aegean sphere. But whereas bronze was treated as a critical material, stone was not, and its exchange and consumption were directed by forces other than the palace. Evidence from the southern Argolid suggests local elites may have fulfilled this administrative role. In reply to Sherratt's (1993) query, "What would a Bronze-age world system look like?" the Mycenaean world system was multitiered, with some central elements and activities and others decentralized.

CHAPTER 11

CRITIQUE

A VIEW FROM THE TABLETS

᠎᠎᠎᠎᠎᠎᠎

JOHN T. KILLEN

I AM DELIGHTED TO HAVE been asked to give my reactions as a Linear B specialist to the essays collected in this volume. If we are to make further progress in understanding the workings of Mycenaean polities, it is essential that there be continuous dialogue among text specialists, archaeologists, and ethnographers and that each side try to understand the other's evidence, methods of interpretation, and conclusions. It is extremely encouraging, therefore, that so many of the contributors have attempted to bridge the divide between disciplines and to compare their findings with those of their colleagues in other areas. I do not always agree with what the non-text experts have to say about the contents and significance of the Linear B documents, but I hope nonetheless that they will find my comments helpful, just as I have found it helpful to read their conclusions (and criticisms of Linear B specialists, including myself, writing on economic matters).

SIMILARITIES AND DISSIMILARITIES AMONG THE VARIOUS MYCENAEAN STATES

Several contributors have stressed the *dissimilarities* between the workings of the various Mycenaean kingdoms and have argued that we should avoid assuming that what holds good for one state necessarily holds

good for another. (In their introduction, the editors even go so far as to suggest that what they term "parallel systemic organization" is "a hypothetical and as yet unproved construction"; see chapter 2, this volume.) Such caution is commendable; there are certainly some differences between, for example, the organization of the textile industry at Pylos and at Knossos (Killen 1984b). On the other hand, we should not lose sight of the astonishing *similarities* among the centers, as revealed by the tablets. Not only are all the palaces alike in containing administrative records (tablets, sealings, and other documents) of a virtually identical type, with particularly close links in palaeographic terms between the tablets at mainland sites, the information on the documents is also remarkably similar, regardless of where they come from. The same system of numbers, weights, and measures is evidently in use at all the centers; there is no evidence of money, a market, or wages at any of the sites. As far as we can tell, all Mycenaean palaces organized their tax collection in a highly similar way (it is even possible that officials at Pylos and Knossos used the same tax tables [Olivier 1974]), and we find the same technical vocabulary for describing types of landholding and the same titles of dignitaries and administrators at several of the sites. Thus (to quote just a few examples from many), the term *ke-ke-me-na*, a technical description of land, occurs at Knossos, Pylos, and Tiryns (and land is measured in terms of seed [*pe-mo, pe-ma*] at Knossos, Pylos, Thebes, and Tiryns); the title *wa-na-ka*, /*wanax*/, "king," appears at Knossos, Pylos, and Thebes; and the terms *ko-re-te*, *du-ma*, and *a-to-mo*, all titles of local officials, occur at both Knossos and Pylos. Moreover, while we have only one possible reference in the archives of a Mycenaean palace to direct contact with another center (a reference at Mycenae to goods going to Thebes, probably—but not certainly—the Boeotian center), several names of "collectors" (perhaps members of the ruling elite in the various kingdoms) appear in more than one archive, suggesting at least the possibility that all these persons were members of a single ruling dynasty (Killen 1979b:176–179).

THE EXTENT OF THE PALACES' INVOLVEMENT IN THE ECONOMIES OF MYCENAEAN STATES

Writing in 1985, I argued that, given the information on the tablets, it was difficult "to avoid the conclusion that the role which the palaces played in the economy of Mycenaean states was not merely significant, but central and dominant," though I went on to stress that "caution is still certainly in order: as we have seen earlier, it may well be that the tablets give us an unbalanced picture of the state, and one in particular which exaggerates the importance of the role of the center in the workings of the economy" (Killen 1985:255). Several contributors have criticized this palace-centered view and have stressed the likelihood that there was a good deal of economic activity in Mycenaean kingdoms (like the production of coarseware pottery and lithics) in which the palace was not directly involved. I readily accept this criticism: the picture I gave in 1985 of economic activity in the Mycenaean states is certainly, I now think, too monochrome. It is important, however, not to downplay the extent or importance of palace involvement in the economies of these areas.

As I stressed in my 1985 paper (and as Paul Halstead also mentions in his contribution, chapter 7, this volume), some of the quantities mentioned in the archives at Knossos (over 10,000 units, perhaps about 800 tons, of wheat at *da-wo* in the south of the island; eighty to a hundred thousand sheep, scattered all over the center of Crete; and so on) betoken a major economic role for the palace, at least as far as these

commodities are concerned. Although it is less easy to estimate the extent of palatial economic activity in the case of Pylos, the *Na* flax tablets deal with contributions in this substance extracted from some one hundred villages and towns in the kingdom, while the *Ma* and other tablets show that the palace had the ability to levy taxes, in a variety of commodities, over what appears to be the length and breadth of the state. Nor, contrary to the belief of some scholars, is the palace content simply to assess the tax for a particular area (town or village), leaving its local representatives to arrange in detail how this should be provided. As is made clear by a record like *Nn 831*, which gives the detailed breakdown of the individual contributors of flax in the place *ko-ri-to*, the palace's interest in the taxation process does not stop simply at village chief level. Again, the figures on some of the personnel records at Pylos and Knossos show that the palaces played a major role in the deployment of labor in the kingdoms. (Since they are recording the personnel, the centers clearly have at least a degree of control over it.) Records of the textile industry at Knossos indicate the presence, in places all over the center and west of Crete, of comfortably in excess of one thousand women and their children, all working for the center (and there are likely to have been about seven hundred fifty women, and the same number of children, in the similar industry at Pylos [Chadwick 1988:76]); the *An o-ka* tablets at Pylos record arrangements for guarding the coasts of the kingdom that involved some eight hundred men in a number of different coastal areas; and a single tablet at Knossos (*B(1) 7034*) records a minimum of nine hundred men described as *o-re-i*, apparently "in the mountain."

In sum, then, while the palaces' involvement in economic and other activity in Mycenaean kingdoms was certainly selective, it would be a mistake, I believe, to suggest that in certain spheres it was not both widespread and deep.

DISCUSSION

I now turn to a number of more detailed issues, many of which specifically concern the interpretation of Linear B tablet information.

Comparison

In their introduction, the editors suggest that "if it is necessary to compare Mycenaean states to the ancient Near East, the best analogues seem to be in earlier periods (prior to 3200 BC) and in regions other than in the vicinity of Uruk" (see chapter 2). In my own experience, however, the closest analogies with Mycenaean texts are often to be found in records from the Ur III period (2150–2000 BC): significantly, I would suggest, a period of strong central control (Postgate 1994:42; see Cherry and Davis, chapter 12, this volume). (For the close similarities between the organization of textile production in the Ur III period and that of centrally controlled textile manufacture in the Mycenaean world, see, for example Killen [1979b], which draws heavily on H. Waetzoldt's [1972] admirable *Untersuchungen zur neusumerischen Textilindustrie*.)

Redistribution

Parkinson (chapter 9), it seems to me, provides an inadequate description of the role of redistribution in Mycenaean kingdoms. As I and others have noted (see, e.g., Killen 1985:283, n. 38; and chapter 7, this volume), a key activity of the Mycenaean centers was the *mobilization of resources*, the form of redistribution that involves the assembling of food (for rations) and working materials to enable dependent workers to involve themselves in highly specialized craft activity. (It is surely significant, as A. Morpurgo Davies [1979] has stressed, that once the Mycenaean palaces were destroyed, highly specialized craft production of the type recorded directly or indirectly in the tablets ceases to exist in the Greek world [and only returns in the Hellenistic and Roman periods, when major cities such as Alexandria provide a large enough market to support such specialization].)

Centralization and control

In chapter 9 (this volume), Parkinson also makes the claim that "all . . . specialized industries, with the exception of metalworking and some of the less specialized steps involved in textile production, occurred at the palace proper." In chapter 4 (this volume), however, Shelmerdine points out that even at Pylos, where much specialized textile work was concentrated at the center, we have evidence for specialized finishing workers (*a-ke-ti-ri-ja*, /*askêtriai*/) at *ro-u-so*, which, while it is clearly an important settlement, is not the palace itself. At Knossos, similarly, we have evidence for *askêtriai* at *da-wo* (near Phaistos), *da-*22-to* and *ra-su-to*. The place-names attested on the *As* and *V* records of men in scribal hands 103 and 115 suggest that male finishing workers (fullers) operated in a number of different areas in the kingdom.

It is therefore not possible to argue that because a craft activity attested archaeologically is decentralized, "it most likely operated independently of palatial control" (chapter 9, this volume). As Shelmerdine rightly puts it, "it is not the location of the work which will tell us [whether or not it is under palace control]".

In chapter 5, Small suggests that "territorial control of the Mycenaean polities remained centralized, barely moving beyond the palatial centers." Once again, this may well overstate the case. It is certainly true that our most detailed records of landholding at Pylos probably relate to areas close to the center, and that the same may be true at Knossos (see Killen 1987b). Note, however, that entries on the *Na* flax records at Pylos indicate knowledge by the center of the precise technical status of land held by individuals in various locations (see, e.g., *Na 926*, which records that the flax-producing land held by one *a₂-ku-mi-jo* at the village *pa-ka-a-ka-ri* is of the *aktiton* category) and that there are records at Knossos (at least one of them very detailed) of land held by "collectors" and the *lâwâgetâs* at a number of places well outside the center. See *F(2) 841*, a detailed record of land in the "ownership" of a "collector" *sa-pi-ti-nu-wo* at]-*ti-ja*, perhaps *do-ti-ja*, and Phaistos (Killen 1987b:174–177); *E 843*, a record of land or wheat attributed to the "collector" *e-me-si-jo* at various localities, including *pu-na-so* and *pa-na-so*; and *E(1) 288, E 846* and *E 1569*—all (it seems) records of land attributed to the *lâwâgetâs* (in the last case, land at *do-ti-ja*).

Finally, Small (chapter 5) goes on to argue, "The fact that this [tax] assessment is nonstaple and . . . that the assessment is tied to the productive demands of the palace workshops . . . demonstrates that the structure of the Pylian polity was probably closer to our concept of an estate that was reaching out beyond its borders to supply goods for its workshops." At Knossos, however, we have records of large quantities of wheat (probably in store and doubtless under the control of the palace) at places as far distant from Knossos as *da-wo*, near Phaistos (see *F(2) 852*). It does not seem inconceivable that if we had records of the wheat harvest at Pylos these would have shown a similar picture.

Linear B interpretations

The editors argue in their introduction (see chapter 2) that "local and provincial leaders who negotiated the transfer of such materials [that is, raw materials needed for the production of high-value prestige items] expected the corresponding return of a proportion of the finished goods manufactured by the state [under the so-called *ta-ra-si-ja* system].” Halstead (chapter 7) also describes the “disbursement of palatial craft goods outside the palaces and . . . the complementary acquisition by the palaces of local pottery and pulses.” In fact, however, the only possible references on the tablets to the distribution of (luxury) craft goods produced under the *ta-ra-si-ja* system to persons within the kingdoms are the mentions on storage records at Knossos of cloth described as *e-qe-si-ja*, one possible interpretation of which is “[cloth] for [distribution to] *hequetai*.” The *hequetai* (followers), however, appear to have their closest links with the central palace administration (and may well be members of the ruling elite). By contrast, the only distributions we know of to *local* officials (like the *ko-re-te-re*, who are “mayors” or the like in the provincial centers) appear to be all of nonmanufactured goods, like the commodity **154*, evidently some kind of skin, recorded on the Pylos tablet *On 300* as distributed to *ko-re-te-re* and other local officials.

Galaty (chapter 8) suggests that the Pylos record *Vn 130* deals with pottery vessels. One of the persons, however, mentioned on the tablet, apparently as supplying *a-ke-a₂*, plausibly interpreted as */angeha/* (jars or pails), is *a³-ki-e-u* of *a-pi-no-e-wi-jo*. It is difficult to believe that this is not the same *a³-ki-e-u* of *a-pi-no-e-wi-jo* as

is mentioned as the owner *vel sim.* of workers (*do-e-ro*, */doheloi/*, slaves) on the bronze-working record *Jn 605* (see line 10). Thus, it is more likely that *Vn 130* records the transfer of bronze vessels.

On the other hand, I find attractive Halstead’s suggestion (chapter 7) that few *o-no* records exist in the archives because these documents were customarily destroyed once the payments they recorded were made.

Finally, there is no evidence that any of the spices recorded on the tablets were imported, as suggested by Lupack (chapter 6). Some of the terms for spices found on the records are undoubtedly loan words, but there is nothing to confirm that any of the spices were not locally produced. Furthermore, as I have recently suggested (Killen 1993b), it may be that, far from sheep tending for the palace being a profitable activity (chapter 6), it was actually a liability. That little or nothing of the produce of the flock may have gone to the shepherd is suggested by the very demanding targets set for the production of the flocks on the *D* tablets at Knossos—certainly for lambs, and perhaps also for wool. Moreover, shepherds may have had to make good from their own resources any losses from the flocks they held.

CHAPTER 12

AN ARCHAEOLOGICAL HOMILY

卍卍卍卍卍卍卍

JOHN F. CHERRY AND JACK L. DAVIS

FACED WITH THE CHALLENGE of assimilating and commenting on a large set of archaeological conference papers, a colleague (Yoffee 1995) recently hit on the neat rhetorical device of framing his remarks in the form of a Mass, in the various parts of which he asked mercy on the discussant, gave thanks to the participants for their papers, affirmed commitment to certain methodologies, confessed archaeological sins, and sang a Hosanna to all the progress that had been made. Repeating such tropes here would be, so to speak, *de trop*. Still, this collection of papers, on which we have been invited to comment, likewise contains good news to be celebrated, as well as some weaknesses to admit. The comments are those of two archaeologists, trained largely in the classical tradition but with considerable exposure to, and sympathy for, anthropological goals. That we do not direct many remarks to the textual aspects of these papers should be construed not as lack of interest on our part but merely as a sensible division of labor with our learned fellow-commentator, John Killen.

EVANGELISM ACROSS THE GREAT DIVIDE

Publishers generally like to play down the fact that a book had its origins in a symposium or conference, but in the present case this actually seems something worth emphasizing. Held in the unforgettably bizarre ambiance of the Opryland Hotel, in Nashville, Tennessee (on which see Chippindale 1997:262–263), the session "Rethinking Mycenaean Palaces" at the 62nd Annual Meeting of the Society for American Archaeology had as its goal "the construction of an enhanced model of the Mycenaean state"—not the kind of language commonly heard at the meetings of the Archaeological Institute of America, which is the more usual meeting ground for groups of Aegean prehistorians. While it was not the first such gathering to bring archaeological and textual evidence to bear on the elucidation of the economy of the palaces of the Greek Bronze Age (compare Bintliff 1977; Hägg and Marinatos 1987), it was certainly the first to explicitly include scholars from anthropology in this endeavor. In light of the many misunderstandings and oversimplifications perpetuated by practitioners on both sides of the so-called "Great Divide" (as discussed in the co-editors' introduction; see chapter 2, this volume), organizing this session for the SAA, rather than AIA, meetings constituted an act of evangelism—preaching the gospel of methodological and theoretical cooperation, spreading the word that the classical versus anthropological dichotomy has been breaking down for some years, and urging anthropological archaeologists to have sufficient faith to cast off their blinkers and see the light that the rich, text-aided database on Aegean states can shed on comparative theory on the formation and operation of archaic states. It is a little reminiscent of an occasion some years ago when Colin Renfrew led a posse of (mainly) British archaeologists to the SAA meetings in Philadelphia with the avowed intention of convincing transatlantic colleagues that they should pay more attention to the rich archaeological record of Europe and to the distinctively European types of postprocessual theory emerging there (Renfrew and Shennan 1982). The success of that venture was, unfortunately, limited.

At the SAA meetings, there seems to have set in a steady decline of interest in archaeology beyond the Americas, at least to judge from our own sporadic observation of them over nearly thirty years, a decline also reflected in the publications and other activities of the SAA (see, e.g., remarks in the *SAA Bulletin*, vol. 15, no.5, made by one of the authors of this commentary). Informal tabulation of the 155 sessions and workshops held at the 1997 meetings revealed barely a dozen that could be said to have had anything to do with the Old World, and of these dozen, several dealt with Europe (mostly its very early prehistory) and one with the Near East, but none—except for this one—was devoted to any part of the Mediterranean or the Levant. This situation, of course, mirrors the structure of a survey course on Old World Archaeology in most North American anthropology departments: starting with East African hominids, but running out of both time and interest once the origins of domestication and urbanism in the Near East have been reached. If European prehistory somehow seems rather specialized and epiphenomenal, Mediterranean archaeology is simply not on the map. It is, of course, the special province of classical archaeology—a field regarded by many an anthropologist with a mixture of pity and scorn, usually owing to a knowledge of its practices and literature a generation or more out of date. (As an aside, we wonder if such parochialism may stem in part from the general absence in North America of programs or departments of *archaeology*, in which Old and New World archaeologies can meet face-to-face; see Wiseman 1998) Even this volume's editors, in their introduction, seem a trifle unfair in characterizing classical archaeologists as obsessed with "the peculiarities of artifact seriation and the linking of text with site" and, more generally, with a discredited brand of culture history that stands in contrast to anthropological archaeology's loftier aspirations of explaining cross-cultural variation and evolutionary process. Such

generalizations are unhelpful, because there are so many exceptions on either side. Both classical and anthropological archaeology, it should be remembered, have endured long periods of stultification.

It is not our intention here to join the stale debate over this disciplinary divide between classical and anthropological archaeology (compare Dyson 1993; Morris 1994; Snodgrass 1987:1–14; Spencer 1995; Renfrew 1980). We mention this blind spot on the part of anthropological archaeologists where Mediterranean archaeology is concerned only because it seems to us so unfortunate. They are missing out on some exciting work of impressive quality that can, and does, speak to "anthropological" questions and concerns of wide interest to archaeologists of all sorts. A better understanding, this book seems to say, will come from deeds, not words. Among the themes taken up in the pages of the present volume, for instance, we might mention the structure and functioning of clusters of early states, the investigation of staple and wealth finance, the archaeological recognition of prestige economies, the organization and distribution of craft production, the effective integration of texts and material culture in building more comprehensive models of the political economy, or the new perspectives made possible by the availability of high-intensity regional survey data. This last-named development, we feel, is particularly significant, and it very obviously underlies several papers in this volume (see chapters 3, 8, and 9, this volume). Over the past twenty years or more, not just Greece but the Mediterranean as a whole has witnessed staggering growth in archaeological survey, often strongly interdisciplinary in character. Some of it is not merely sound but methodologically and analytically pioneering, and it deserves to be widely known. The general indifference to such work on the part of New World archaeologists (see, e.g., Fish and Kowalewski 1990; Sullivan 1998) is therefore disappointing and puzzling.

What this volume represents, then, is a far cry from the usual rag-tag collection of conference papers, lumped together under some such generic title as "New Directions in Mediterranean Archaeology." It focuses tightly on a specific form of polity in a well-defined area and period, the Mycenaean states of Greece in the later Bronze Age, and it draws into dialogue several scholars trained or now teaching in anthropology (Galaty, Kardulias, Parkinson, Small), representatives of three or four generations of Linear B textual studies (Bennett, Killen, Shelmerdine, Bennet, Lupack), and archeologists actively pursuing fieldwork on the Aegean Bronze

Age (Bennet, Halstead, and the present authors). Even this rough categorization immediately falls apart when one considers how much crossover there is among the individuals concerned—Linear B experts actively involved in field survey, an anthropologist writing his doctoral dissertation on Aegean Bronze Age material, an archaeozoologist publishing on Mycenaean livestock texts, even Emmett Bennett—a founding grandfather of Linear B studies, though arguably the youngest in heart among all the contributors to this volume—pushing a wheelbarrow in the recent architectural restudy of the Palace of Nestor at Pylos. What better illustration could there be of Nigel Spencer's recent remark that "in much current research classical archaeology, ancient history, classics and anthropology are no longer running on narrow, completely parallel tracks without reference to each other or to other branches of archaeology" (1995:3).

COMPARISON AND COMBINATION OF EVIDENCE

A notable feature of this set of papers is that they focus not merely on Mycenaean kingdoms and their pala-tial centers but on one in particular—the Messenian kingdom of Pylos, administered from the so-called Palace of Nestor. This is no accident: a major interna-tional, interdisciplinary research enterprise there, the Pylos Regional Archaeological Project, has recently concluded, and a wealth of new information is now in the process of digestion and first publication (Davis 1998; Davis et al. 1997; Zangger et al. 1997). Three chapters (those of Bennet, Galaty, and Parkinson) depend on data derived from this project, and in fact more than half the volume's contributors have been directly involved in it in some way.

This concentration of interest offers some advan-tages, but at the same time it limits the opportunities for structured comparison between the various peer poli-ties elsewhere in the Mycenaean world. There is little discussion here of other states in the later Bronze Age southern Aegean, for instance those in the northeast Peloponnese and Boeotia (the current evidence from Attica and Laconia is now, and perhaps will remain, too sparse to be very helpful in this respect). Crete's Mycenaean kingdom (for which see now Driessen and Farnoux 1997; Driessen and Schoep 1999), for example, is rarely mentioned. In their introduction, the editors go to some lengths to emphasize the value

of a comparative, theoretical framework for studying Mycenaean polities as instances of the wider category of archaic states. Yet, aside from Kardulias's attempt to invoke "world systems" analysis and Small's use of Mesoamerican parallels to bolster his claim that we have fundamentally misconceived the character of the Mycenaean political economy, this volume in fact contains little such comparative analysis, either within or beyond the Mycenaean world. Its scarcity is all the more regrettable when one recalls that two analytical concepts that have been widely taken up by anthropo-logically oriented scholars of complex societies—the early state module (Renfrew 1975) and peer polity interaction (Renfrew and Cherry 1986)—arose precisely out of attempts to generalize about Aegean Bronze Age states.

The question here is not whether comparison itself is useful but what sorts of comparisons or analogies are justified or fruitful. A number of interesting and related issues are worth exploring a little. First, we generally agree with the assertion (made here, for instance, by Parkinson and Small) that the understandably enthusi-astic rush to interpret the Linear B texts following their decipherment in the early 1950s may have led to some hasty or ill-considered assumptions. Some examples of what we mean follow:

- The records from the various Mycenaean palaces bespeak an essentially uniform administrative organization.
- In Moses Finley's famous words, "the tablets reveal a massive redistributive operation, in which all personnel and all activities, all movement of both persons and goods . . . were administratively fixed" (1957: 135).
- This type of elaborately organized, redistributive palace economy—heavily centralized, minutely bureaucratic, with little scope for an independent citizenry— is one for which close parallels are thought to exist throughout many parts of the ancient Near East.

Let us take each of these points in turn, beginning with the first, on which the editors have focused par-ticular criticism. Killen (see chapter 11, this volume) is surely right to reaffirm the quite remarkable similari-ties between the various Mycenaean states (at least as seen through the lens of the Linear B documents)— parallelisms not confined only to such matters as the technicalities of the recording system or to the use of identical systems of mensuration (readily transferable technologies of administration) but extending also to higher order institutional features, such as the organization of landholding and taxation or the titles and functions both of top-level dignitaries and of local officials. What of the archaeological evidence? Does it, too, justify the assumption that whatever was happening at one center was happening elsewhere? We need to remind ourselves of the enormous gaps that still exist in the regional archaeological record relevant to the study of Mycenaean palaces, particularly the lack of spatially continuous, high-quality surface archaeology in the environs of most Aegean palatial centers. Even in the Pylian kingdom, only some 2% or 3% of the area probably controlled by the Palace of Nestor has yet been intensively surveyed; matters are only worse elsewhere (at Mycenae, for instance, since the Argive Plain has yet to be the target of any major survey). For Tiryns, Thebes, and indeed most other larger Aegean centers (such as Kato Zakros or Knossos on Crete), even their size cannot yet be estimated reliably from fine-grained data. The recent fieldwork at Pylos (Davis 1998; Davis et al. 1997; see chapter 3, this volume), which has radically revised our views of the size of this site and its growth through time, should be salutary in this respect. Such deficiencies in data are not entirely the result of lack of opportunity but also reflect the attitudes and priorities of Aegean prehistorians.

Notwithstanding such lacunae in the available data, it is the homogeneity and uniformity of Mycenaean culture that has always been regarded as one its most striking features, at least in its later phases (LH IIIA:2–LH IIIB). The attractiveness of the peer polity interaction approach is precisely to help specify a range of forms of interaction and cultural process that might lead to new institutions in society and to their progressive convergence among a group of interacting polities: warfare, competitive emulation, symbolic entrainment, the transmission of innovations, increased flow in the exchange of goods, and so on (Renfrew and Cherry 1986:8–10). It does not follow, however, that each region or each polity followed an identical trajectory toward statehood. We would underscore the exciting prospects for examining individual pathways toward complexity in various parts of the Mycenaean world—and they do clearly seem to have been different. How else to account for the remarkable cluster of half a dozen centers in the Argolid, the binary organization of the Pylian state, the seeming absence of strong polities in several regions (such as Laconia), the unique circumstance of Mycenaean incorporation of the entire state system of Minoan Crete, or the clear evidence that certain emergent centers of power and prestige that looked promising in the "formative" period (that is, before the end of LH II) suffered truncated political evolution and were stopped dead in their tracks, as Bennet, here and elsewhere (1995, 1999a), has discussed in the case of Messenia?

To point out that Mycenaean states varied in both size and complexity, and reached their final form along distinct pathways but under convergent processes is, however, no argument against comparison itself, only against premature generalization and oversimplifying assumptions of uniformity. The most productive strategy will involve the detailed individual study of different locales' development, as the means of isolating and evaluating variable causative factors affecting complexity. This, it seems to us, is the sense in which Galaty and Parkinson are urging us to think again—to reconstruct the economy from the bottom up, and from region to central place, in order to define more precisely what lies within, and what without, palatial control; to study how each palace functioned as an autonomous entity, before moving on to consider interaction between states; and to be strict with ourselves, so far as is possible, in segregating the data directly relevant only to a single palace and its region. That will not be an easy project, but from a heuristic perspective it is bound to be helpful. A comparable instance would perhaps be the liberating effects of the abandonment some years ago of the catch-all generalizing concept of "the Minoan-Mycenaean religion" (Nilsson 1950) and its replacement with the locally contextualized study of cult practice and ideology in different places and at different times, both Minoan and Mycenaean (Renfrew 1981a, 1985:11–26, 393–443; Wright 1994). Yet another instance, from much earlier in the development of Aegean prehistory as a field, is the fundamental separation of Aegean civilizations into Minoan versus Mycenaean (Fitton 1996; McDonald and Thomas 1990).

Turning now to the second of the assumptions listed above, the extent of palatial involvement in the economy and the nature of its redistributive activities, we need say less in light of John Killen's remarks. It is good to see that he is now willing to add nuance to his earlier characterization of the palaces' thoroughgoing economic dominance (Killen 1985) by allowing that their involvement was selective, yet still emphasizing the very impressive quantities of both goods and persons moving through the system. One significant stimulus for such a revision has been the work of Halstead, published in a series of important papers (especially 1988, 1992a, 1992b), some of whose salient points are crisply summarized in his present contribution. In an excellent demonstration of the advantages of first segregating clearly, and only later combining, radically different forms of evidence, Halstead used the comparison of archival and archaeological evidence to argue, very convincingly, that "a wide range of agricultural and craft production took place outside palatial control, and that a range of commodities entered or left the palace without being recorded by the Linear B bureaucracy" (1992a:65). The heavy hand of palace administration was somewhat lighter than we had supposed—although not, in our opinion, pace Small, hardly felt at all!

Some useful rethinking has also taken place on what is meant by "redistribution," much of it directly traceable to a seminal paper by Earle (1977), which itself reacts to and builds on earlier work by economic anthropologists such as Karl Polanyi and George Dalton. This rethinking has emphasized the importance in complex chiefdoms and archaic states of *mobilization*, whereby resources and personnel are marshaled with the primary goal of supporting the elite, either directly with foodstuffs or by the transformation through specialized craft activity of raw materials into high-value prestige items, with significant exchange value in reciprocal gift-giving among different elite groups. Trickle-down to lower political ranks, junior lineage members, provincial leaders, and so on, certainly occurs, but to a quite limited extent, so that much of what goes up, stays up. Such redistributive mechanisms as a means of underwriting state activities are perfectly familiar—to anthropological archaeologists, at least—as constituting a system of wealth finance. As applied to Mycenaean states, it is a conception far removed from the sort of simplistic picture of redistribution painted by Renfrew, admittedly now many years ago (1972), in which elites at central places served more or less as disinterested middlemen, altruistically brokering and furnishing facilities for exchanges between specialized producers and conveniently providing occasional subsistence relief to the populace at large.

This volume, therefore, makes an important contribution to Mycenaean studies in terms of the sophistication of writing about the political economy; the latter pages of the editors' introduction (see chapter 2, this volume) in particular offer a most welcome breath of fresh air. Importantly, key distinctions in their proposed models—such as localized versus state economic action, or restricted versus free circulation of wealth—have

been explored in some detail with real archaeological data in several of the papers herein (see chapters 8–10, this volume).

What, then, of the third assumption above, the relevance of Near Eastern parallels for Mycenaean state economies? We have a general sympathy with the charge, made at several points throughout the volume, that Aegean prehistorians have been rather myopic in limiting their search for analogues mainly to the Near East, chiefly because archival documentary evidence has been privileged over archaeological data. Building "an enhanced model of the Mycenaean state" obviously must set Aegean Bronze Age polities much more firmly in the comparative context of a broad range of preindustrial states, including New as well as Old World instances. But the characterization herein of ancient Near Eastern political economies as large-scale systems of statewide distribution itself seems outdated and unduly simplistic: much has happened in the forty years since Moses Finley turned to the "redistributive temple-palace economies" of the ancient Near East to provide some context for understanding the exciting new Linear B documents (see, e.g., Stein and Rothman 1994). Yoffee puts it well when he writes of early Mesopotamia:

> In these Mesopotamian city-states, there are no totalitarian Asiatic Modes of Production, oriental despotisms, monolithic controllers of production, temple-states, or all-knowing, all-seeing bureaucratic apparatuses of any kind. There are rather various kinds of elites and social orientations; while craftsmen work for great estates, independent entrepreneurs contract with those same organizations...Social groups and their leaders struggle for dominion or independence within the city-states and the city-states with each other. (1995:547)

More generally, has it not come to be appreciated that, except in the most totalitarian of regimes (Albania under Enver Hoxha, for instance), the acquisition, production, distribution, and consumption of different commodities constitute overlapping and intersecting spheres of action over which the state exercises quite variable authority in different parts of its territory, and as its own power base and requirements change over time? A state's aspirations and its practical ability to achieve them may be some way apart; the political economies of states operate within an environment that they control only partially. These are points that the present volume's editors fully realize and emphasize in their introduction and in their individual contributions.

These observations apply with equal force both to Aegean polities and to the generally larger Near Eastern states whose relevance the editors, in particular, have questioned, primarily on the grounds that they were bigger and more complex than the small-scale states of the Mycenaean mainland. The contrast has often been remarked before: Renfrew, for instance, comparing investment in religious monuments by Aegean Bronze Age civilizations and by those of the Near East or Egypt, described the formers' "very modest scale" as a curious feature (1977:114). This comment raises interesting general questions of spatial scale, and the spatial operation of power and dominance in states, which one of us (Cherry 1987) has explored in much greater detail elsewhere. It does not follow that territorially expansive states with more resources at their disposal are thereby enabled to impose their will and exercise command over the regional economy with a tighter fist: there are costs involved in transferring both resources and information, which are a function of the distances involved. Thus, while we commend the incorporation into the discussion of such New World polities as the Maya, Mixtec, or Zapotec, it would be a mistake, we think, to limit comparison only to state organizations similar in scale to the Mycenaean kingdoms. After all, many Classical Greek city-states, especially in Magna Graecia, occupied territories and supported populations that approached and sometimes even exceeded the size of their Bronze Age ancestors, yet they were constituted politically along such radically different lines that no one would propose them as direct analogues (compare, more generally, Nichols and Charlton 1997). As Flannery (1972) and many others have emphasized, it is the organization of centralized power and bureaucracy, as reflected, for example, in the structure of information flow and the hierarchies of decision making, that best captures the essence, and allows comparison, of state-level complex societies.

SOME PYLIAN REFLECTIONS

Despite the volume title's emphasis on palaces, the clear implication of most of the contributions is that, at this point, a better understanding will come, as the editors have said, from fitting "the Mycenaean center—and the economy that supported it—more firmly into a regional archaeological framework and into theoretical models of political, economic, and social structure" (see chapter 2, this volume). This is a call not only for enhanced models but also for different priorities and strategies in fieldwork. We know from the texts of (at least) three-tier settlement hierarchies in the Pylian and Knossian kingdoms, yet the detailed reconstruction of Mycenaean political geography remains elusive (see, most recently, Bennet 1999a), hampered by a positively embarrassing scarcity of evidence from excavations at Mycenaean towns, hamlets, or farmsteads. On the other hand, recent survey in the immediate area of the Palace of Nestor *has* produced archaeological evidence that seems to point to a three-tier hierarchy of settlement at the time of the Linear B texts (see Bennet 1998). This is where the regional perspective of archaeological survey takes on paramount importance, and its impact can be seen on almost every page of this book.

Yet even archaeologists who share an anthropological perspective on Greek prehistory have failed to take full advantage of the data already available, or that could easily be made available to them, for study of protohistoric palatial economies. We are thinking here principally of the general reluctance on the part of archaeologists—whether from the hither province of Classics or the further province of anthropology—to design programs of analysis for artifacts recovered by intensive surveys that would contribute to model building. Nearly all the publications of finds from Aegean regional projects that have appeared to date consist primarily of artifact descriptions, with very little spatial or quantitative analysis. We might add here that there exists plenty of poorly studied material from the central places themselves that could make significant contributions to our understanding. In the case of the Palace of Nestor, for example, the faunal assemblages remain essentially unpublished, as do the extensive deposits of ceramics and other finds from periods predating the palace itself (gaps now being addressed by studies in progress by Paul Halstead and Shari Stocker, respectively). This is why several papers included here, particularly those of Parkinson and Galaty, in our view represent a very positive step in the right direction. They take it for granted that there is much more to be learned from regional artifact assemblages than the simplistic equation of periods of occupation or function with dots on a map. We offer some thoughts on their conclusions, since we know this region and these data well.

Galaty, in his study of ceramic production and distribution in the Pylian kingdom, asserts that kylikes were wine-drinking vessels used in the ritual and political contexts of feasts. Of that, there can be little doubt, especially now that we have a better grasp on Mycenaean state banquets (Killen 1994) and a fuller appreciation of the social role of drinking, both in Mycenaean society (Wright 1995b) and more generally (Sherratt 1997). That kylikes would have been coveted prestige items, awarded by administrative elites to regional officials, however, is much more open to doubt. They are one of the most ubiquitous ceramic forms found by survey on Mycenaean-period sites. In the Pylos survey, in fact, kylikes were recovered at more than 90% of the sites with finds of the thirteenth century BC, and not only at the larger sites where one might expect to find administrative elites. If they are found so widely, it is hard to see them as quite so special as Galaty would have us believe (that is, that their symbolic resonance and ritual significance were such as to entail monopolistic palatial administrative control of kylix production)—although he himself argues that neither their widespread distribution nor their presence in domestic contexts need detract from their symbolic significance.

His conclusion that the regional pattern of production and distribution of fine drinking vessels differs from that of coarse tablewares accords with evidence elsewhere. The distribution of paste groups does seem to suggest substantial regional integration in ceramic exchange, a conclusion in line with those of other recent ceramic characterization studies. In the northeast Peloponnese, for example, considerable evidence is accumulating that both fine- and coarsewares were widely exchanged even before the emergence of Mycenaean palaces (Zerner 1993; Rutter 1995). We strongly suspect that the same will turn out to be true of western Messenia, when the Prepalatial pottery from the Palace of Nestor itself is fully analyzed. All of this suggests that regional exchange of pottery is likely to have been the status quo at the time the Mycenaean palaces were established. Galaty's conclusion, however, should be accepted only with some caution, in light of the fact that the coarsewares analyzed thus far derive mainly from sites that lie within the Pylian Hither Province, or very near to it, as in the case of Nichoria (see figures 3.1 and 8.2). Moreover, his contribution here is based on chemical characterization of only 310 ceramic samples from about eighteen sites. Many who work in provenance studies would emphasize that the firm characterization of just one individual ware, from a particular production site, in a specific period, requires at least twenty-five to thirty samples. We certainly appreciate the considerable difficulties of acquiring samples from Greece, as well as the expense and time

involved in their analysis, and we also accept that Galaty's stated intention is not to establish exact provenance but rather the broad outlines of regional structure in the production, distribution, and consumption of different classes of pottery. Making a start toward the clearer definition of such patterns is a very worthy goal and one in which a number of other scholars are now showing an interest (e.g., Gillis et al. 1997); nonetheless, we should not let our inferences run too far ahead of the solid data available to support them.

Did the Palace of Nestor in any way control the production of pottery during the thirteenth century? Galaty would say not, but in our view this question remains open. He notes that most of the kylikes he has analyzed are made of marine clays, that these offer decided advantages for drinking vessels, and that such clays were available in the vicinity of the palace. We apparently have a "royal potter" at Pylos who is granted land in Pakijane. We have one dominant chemical megagroup that includes kylikes and coarsewares. Why does this evidence not add up to the conclusion that regionally distributed production was supported by the palace itself? Does it really follow that, simply because the spatial pattern is decentralized, the industry in question was *not* under palatial control, and vice versa? It is presumably the lack of textual mentions of pottery that inclines us to the view that the palace was not much involved, if at all. Yet, as we all know, absence of evidence is not evidence of absence. How to deal with such silences in our texts is an intriguing issue that Shelmderdine (see chapter 4, this volume) also touches upon.

Textual silence also looms large in the evaluation of Parkinson's arguments. Like Galaty, his careful analysis has identified a very interesting pattern in the new Pylian regional survey data which suggests that obsidian reduction, and specifically the production of blades, was concentrated at just one site (Site I4, Romanou: figure 9.1). Such centralization of production is now a familiar pattern in prehistoric Greece, owing in part to the research of Kardulias, summarized in chapter 10, this volume. The pattern at Pylos is about as clear-cut as one might hope for, considering the sample size. Does it justify the broader conclusion, however reasonable, that the production and distribution of obsidian blades was organized outside the central authority of the palace bureaucracy? Indeed, why would an economy based on the control of prestige goods *not* be interested in controlling an exotic, nonlocal item such as obsidian? Might it not be another example of a spatially decentralized but nonetheless palatially controlled industry, like bronze working or several others noted by Shelmerdine? Considering the vagaries of preservation and the possibility that not every productive process in which the palace had an interest was closely monitored in writing, it is very hard to judge whether the lack of records is significant.

Parts of Parkinson's paper open wider vistas and provide links to issues also addressed in several other papers. He maintains, plausibly, that the internal economic organization of Pylos revolved very largely around the mobilization of resources to be employed for producing and acquiring prestige commodities and, furthermore, that palatial elites monopolized the acquisition and distribution of such exotic goods, whether obtained from abroad or produced under their sponsorship. Is this latter argument supported by the evidence? It is clear that objects and materials acquired outside the Pylian kingdom were used at the Palace of Nestor, but there are remarkably few clues as to how these objects got there. Similarly, there are few hints about what happened to prestige goods once they had been manufactured by dependent, specialized palace artisans. It is thus difficult to build an integrated model of the Mycenaean economy that relies on data from this one kingdom alone, as Galaty and Parkinson urged upon us in their introduction.

Parkinson focuses primarily on the mobilization of resources and labor, under palace sponsorship, to produce elite goods; but we can hardly ignore the international trade in exotica (treated—oddly, and without discussion—as an "independent and autonomous system" outside palatial control). It is worth asking what "international" actually means in the context of political organization in Greece in the thirteenth century BC. Should we limit ourselves, as does Cline (1994), to consideration of the pathetically few Egyptian, Hittite, Palestinian, or Mesopotamian objects that reached the Mycenaean kingdoms (not many more than one thousand items, and these spread over some fifty sites and several centuries)? This is, in any case, to ignore what may have been the most significant exotic item of all—metals. And if we are interested in competition for such exotica among Mycenaean elites, should we not consider that they could be (and no doubt were) acquired more frequently from areas within the borders of what is now the modern Greek state than from the Near East or Italy? What do we even mean by "foreign contacts"? The sorts of data Cline lists may be only one limited subset of the total external exchanges that a Mycenaean

state might have had. Moreover, if thirteenth-century BC Greece was not politically unified, and if large parts of the southern Aegean lay outside the direct control of any palatial system, is it not likely that exchange across state borders, closer to home, was actually far more significant for Mycenaean economies—and may also have resulted in the exchanges of technologies and ideologies that Kardulias (see chapter 10, this volume) envisions in his modeling of Aegean world systems?

We do not really know how prestige goods produced in Mycenaean palaces reached other sites. There exists remarkably little excavated data from residential second- and third-order sites, even in Messenia. Little attention has been paid to the study of excavated finds with a view to defining the types of relations between the Palace of Nestor and its hinterland which Parkinson's model presupposes must have existed (although we can look forward soon to new data from excavations and survey at Iklaina, almost certainly a second-order center in the Hither province of the kingdom of Pylos). Shelmerdine has noted the presence at Nichoria of miniature kylikes like those found in ritual contexts at the palace. Are the objects found in tholos tombs the products of palatial workshops? The arguments developed in Bennet's paper suggest that their use by local elites for display in such burials would largely have been curtailed. But what about prestige goods found in the monumental burials at, say, ancient Thouria? Where were these produced?

An intriguing aspect of Parkinson's paper is its suggestion concerning the collapse of the Mycenaean palaces. In fact, both Parkinson and Small suggest that Mycenaean palatial economies were fundamentally unstable: Parkinson, because the economy was excessively focused on wealth finance, and Small, because of the absence of substantial economic integration within a top-heavy kingdom, administered directly by a single dominant center (for example, the Palace of Nestor). Is there evidence that the taxation system employed at Pylos was alone "tied to the productive demands of the palace workshops"? Arguments about the nature of Mycenaean taxation must necessarily be based on documentary information. As Halstead outlines in his chapter, Pylian taxes consisted primarily of raw materials, but also included offerings for sacrifice or feasting, modest numbers of personnel, and obligations to pay some categories of tax "bound up with grants of land to certain officials and craftsmen" (compare also Perna 1999). Halstead notes that assessments were shared between contributing communities, a system arguably based on "historical convention." The language of taxation also seems to suggest that fiduciary responsibility ultimately lay with communities: assessments are listed by toponym, not individual, and office-holders in these communities who pay assessments can be identified only by the title of their office. Furthermore, the substantial parallelism in structure among the sets of documents that record taxations suggests that standard procedures for calculating assessments were used—that is, amounts were not individually negotiated. Finally, Small's assumption that major place-names do not represent districts seems to us to beg a serious question: If the principal toponyms assumed to represent districts do not represent districts, how then did the Palace of Nestor deal with the multitude of smaller sites in the territory it controlled, since we now know that such lower-order settlements were plentiful?

We confess considerable skepticism about these arguments that the Mycenaean palaces collapsed either because their economies were unduly concentrated on the production of prestige goods or because their bureaucracies were underdeveloped. One crucial piece of archaeological evidence that remains unexplained by either model, of course, is the substantial depopulation of Greece that occurred after the collapse, although, as Small suggests, a lack of economic integration might explain why Mycenaean palatial institutions failed to survive the Greek Dark Ages of the eleventh to eighth century BC. Nowhere is the evidence more clear than in Messenia in the territory of the former Mycenaean kingdom, and even at the site of the palace itself (see chapter 3, this volume): in the eleventh century BC, the entire area investigated by the Pylos Regional Archaeological Project was virtually empty of population. It was not just that the system at the Palace of Nestor collapsed; the very elites that Parkinson and Small imagine negotiated their status with the palace may no longer have existed. A more comprehensive model is surely needed to make sense of such facts.

ENVOI: AGAINST TOTALIZING

We come, lastly, to what Yoffee would call the Benedictus or Nunc Dimittis—or, in our less liturgically grand case, simply a final thought. Standing back from the contributions in this volume (and from their somewhat different preliminary oral versions in Nashville and the conversations that ensued), it strikes us that a thread that runs through most of them is a breaking down of what one might call the "totalizing" view of Mycenaean palaces. We mean this in several senses.

There is first the point, repeatedly made, that combining evidence from all the palaces so as to infer some totality, which we can call "the Mycenaean economy," may not be the best way of proceeding. A scissors-and-paste approach, utilizing evidence from wherever it happens to be available, results only in a semifictional generalized reconstruction that can have little validity in the case of any individual state. While there is nothing inherently wrong with identifying the Mycenaean state and its political economy as categories, we also need to deconstruct them, examine variability within them, compare and contrast trajectories of change, and proceed to more and better problem-oriented investigations.

Second, new evidence is eroding support for the notion that the palatial elite had either the ability or perhaps the need to exert total control over all aspects of production and consumption within a Mycenaean kingdom, in the sense that it has been envisaged by many Aegean scholars as a heavily bureaucratic and all-encompassing operation. In part, opinions about the scope and depth of such control vary in accordance with whether textual or archaeological evidence is allowed to have the upper hand; the editors, certainly, call for an end to the tyranny of the text. A more charitable view might be that there will always be major roadblocks when attempts are made to correlate in detail these two very different if equally lacunose forms of evidence. Certainly, it does not help to project onto the Mycenaean archaeological record, willy-nilly, ill-grounded analogies jerked out of time and place—whether feudal medieval Europe, Uruk-period Mesopotamia, or Zapotec Mexico. It is not enough to say merely "this state looks like that state"; we need to characterize specific modes of production, particular state strategies of mobilization and finance, and individual forms of symbolic structure.

Last—and now we are stretching the point somewhat—we detect a more realistic attitude to our aspirations for total understanding of how palaces worked, and what Mycenaean economies meant to those who participated in them. We need to be reminded that our knowledge is situationally constituted, and that our explanations and understanding have a specified context that relates to the history of all previous attempts to understand. Of one thing we can be sure: what seem to us now as fresh and exciting new perspectives and research agendas will appear to readers of future generations disarmingly naïve and hopelessly passé. Overarching metanarratives, of which we are often but dimly cognizant, drive our thinking, to a very considerable extent dictating the questions we now deem most worthwhile asking. It is, nonetheless, this dynamic process of developing explanations that is the aim of research, rather than attempts at closure by settling on some currently plausible, and comfortable, totalizing orthodoxy. By bringing fresh perspectives to bear on old problems and by challenging some cherished assumptions, this volume makes an important contribution to the essential open-endedness, and excitement, of Mycenaean studies.

POSTSCRIPT
TO THE 1999 EDITION

EMMETT L. BENNETT, JR.

I AM VERY GRATEFUL TO Michael Galaty and William Parkinson for letting me see this series of essays in manuscript, especially since I had not attended the sessions at which the papers were presented. I am, of course, also grateful to the contributors for the wide variety of opinions on the state of Mycenaean studies, which even lead to the question of whether there might be a better name and definition for those studies.

It is quite beyond my powers to provide critical comments on the several papers; the editors, in their introductory chapter, have done that well enough, as have those who provided responses. I must confess that some papers I understood immediately, and that there are others which I probably do not understand yet. The papers seem to me to fall in a characteristic mathematical distribution, not the Bell curve, but a curve "high on the ends, and low in the middle" (I come from Cincinnati, and from Carl Blegen's university, which may explain the geographic reference). I got something valuable from each of the papers. I am sure that this collection of essays will help bring a better, balanced understanding of the Mycenaeans who developed and used the writing system—with recognizable Greek nouns, verbs, adjectives, and names—that initiated a great revolution in 1952. One may hope that another significant development appears, with the encouragement of this collection of essays, in 2002.

Instead of comments on particular papers, or their topics, I propose to comment on a word that appears in almost every paper. It is, of course, already carefully considered by the editors, and I take as my text a portion from their introduction, from "Why Select the Topic of Mycenaean Palaces?": "[Palace] is a term used out of convenience, and to attempt to replace it would doubtless prove futile." Surely, some instances of the word "palace" will long resist eradication. For instance, we might consider the "Palace of Nestor" (in English and Greek) on the signs along the road that passes Ano Englianos. If we stuck to the Greek, we could spell it as a proper name "Anaktoron," skip "Nestor," and pretend we could not translate "Anaktoron" into another language. Or we could put up signs "Ano Englianos," and get those words into the Blue Guides. Our hosts, the city of Pylos and the town of Chora, are well satisfied with the name "Palace of Nestor," as they celebrate a "Nestoreia."

Maybe all we need to do is wait. Consider the "Palace of Minos" in Crete. Has it not become the name of a seminal book, and has not the site become, even in the guide books, simply "Knossos"?

The convenient place to start is in the dictionary. But surely we all have known the word from our childhood, and have a well-developed image of it in our heads; that, of course, is the trouble. Nevertheless, if we look in the *Oxford English Dictionary* for "palace," we will see that to use it for anything in 1500 BC, 1200 BC, 400 BC, or even 100 BC is anachronistic. The first meaning, which refers to the known origin of the word, is "the residence of a . . . sovereign." This comes from "Palatium," the house of Augustus on the Palatine Hill. The second meaning is "the official residence of an archbishop." If we kept these limited definitions in mind, we might eventually strip the word of unsuitable connotations. Still, the game would be lost in uproar should an American president begin to call his house the White Palace.

One strategy, consistent with the continued use of "palace," would be to discard the name of every Homeric hero, and bring about the elimination of any identification of this room or that as a "megaron" (if it had a chair in it, let it be called a "chair"), a "dungeon," a "prodromos," or an "archives room," with its equivalent of the "counting house" in which the king sits. Let them all be "room so-and-so," or better, "space 1, 2, 3. . . ." And because many place-names have been extracted form antiquity and reapplied to neighboring sites, let all excavated places bear the names they had not too long before 1800. These are very well known, and some are still in use.

One thing I think we must not do is find fault with our predecessors who, like Schliemann, looked for the palaces of Agamemnon, Odysseus, and Priam. Evans had no reason to doubt (until a few years later) that he had found the Palace of Minos. Blegen, in a very few days after the first shovel of earth, saw no difficulty in the name Nestor, no reason to prefer the earlier Neleus or the later Peisistratos. He clearly did not suppose that the Palaces at Mycenae, Ithaka, Troy, and Pylos were all of the same date just because Agamemnon, Odysseus, Priam, and Nestor were contemporaries in the epic. But the directors of excavations, who applied terms which now are impolitic, may themselves have been under constraints. When I was briefly assisting at Ano Englianos in 1954 there appeared in the earth-floored room I was working in two squarish blocks of purple stone. The workmen immediately called them "poly-thrones" and imagined the king and queen sitting on them and sipping their tea, though they are definitely uncomfortable as seats of any sort. Blegen found them to be simple bases for the posts holding up the timbers of the second floor.

I may add one other stratagem, suggested by the opportunities I recently had to assist both the Pylos Regional Archaeological Project (PRAP) and the Minnesota Archaeological Researches in the Western Peloponnese (MARWP). To keep the crew from the dangers of thinking anachronistically let them listen, as they drive in the four-wheeler, morning and evening, to and from the site, to cassettes of music, not from central England or southern United States but from the earliest recordings of the folk music of the archaeological region.

As I look back over the collection of essays and remember that they are intended to bring two related disciplines into something of a single channel, I am reminded of the history of my specialty, which has now had almost a century to grow up. It began only a little before 1900 and was for fifty years the province of archaeologists, who could at least make copies, describe, and make some graphic analysis of the material, and still not get very far. On the other hand were the crackpots. Naturally, those who weren't crackpots could be considered crackpots and find themselves not really eligible for institutional support. With the excellent discovery of texts at Pylos in 1939, there was enough material to make cryptographic analysis hopeful, and for ten years it was primarily the field of cryptographers, until they succeeded in finding the meanings of the signs and identifying the affinity of the language. Immediately all effort was directed at exploring the language, and linguists were kept very busy. They had much to argue about, and many theories to propose. But by 1975, say, they had just about exhausted the more accessible documents, and the new interest was in associating the texts the linguists had polished with archaeological sites, the economy, and the political structure of those who lived and wrote in what we innocently called palaces. This is still very much the character of Mycenology, except that what has been found out has given the linguists some new materials to work on and new theories to develop.

I am sure, therefore, that the working together of our various disciplines, such as is exemplified in this volume, will lead to significant advances in knowledge, in theory, in whatever our goal may turn out to be.

Despite these rather frivolous observations, I applaud the editors and the authors, and look forward confidently to continued discussions of the problems, and fruitful negotiations for the integration of the best scholarly approaches to them.

PART II

MYCENAEAN PALACES:
THE 2007 CONTRIBUTIONS

CHAPTER 13

CHARIOTS, INDUSTRY, AND ELITE POWER AT PYLOS

묘묘묘묘묘묘묘

ROBERT SCHON

By 1200 BC, the chariot already had a long history of use in the eastern Mediterranean and Near East. Fleets of thousands of chariots were deployed in warfare, as in the battle of Kadesh depicted on Ramses II's temple at Luxor and elsewhere. Other chariots, such as the ones found in Tutankhamun's tomb, were designed for high-speed racing (Sandor 2004). In terms of their technological sophistication and the level of managerial coordination required for their manufacture, chariots such as these rivaled the most grandiose monuments of their times (Sandor 2004). In the Aegean, the earliest evidence for chariots dates to the sixteenth century BC, and not long after, a distinct Aegean tradition of chariot design seems to have emerged (Catling 1968; Crouwel 1981). Less sophisticated in design than their eastern Mediterranean counterparts, Mycenaean chariots were nevertheless adequate for the needs of the rulers who commissioned their production. Chariots became powerful tools, both practical and symbolic, of the Mycenaean elite warrior class. On a practical level, they enhanced intrastate communication and provided a military advantage against anyone who did not have them. Symbolically, they helped situate the Mycenaean elite among their eastern Mediterranean peers while reemphasizing their position within local hierarchies.

The study of Mycenaean chariots can help scholars better understand the internal workings of Mycenaean society. Most discussions of Mycenaean chariots focus on their military functions. Such interpretations have relied primarily on textual references (especially Homer) and artistic depictions (Crouwel 1981; Drews 1993; Littauer 1972). While these sources have proved invaluable in reconstructing the potential uses of chariots in Late Bronze Age Greece, they are not without their drawbacks, as Homer and the visual arts tend to represent idealized, often anachronistic images of an incomplete range of potential uses. Some approaches have relied on the more complete evidence base in the Near East and have used analogy to reconstruct Mycenaean warfare and chariot use (Drews 1993; Ferrill 1985; Greenhalgh 1973, 1980). Such approaches tend to be flawed by their transliteration of Near Eastern traits to explain Mycenaean ways of doing things without adequate consideration of the particularities of Mycenaean culture and the Greek landscape. This transliteration is not limited to chariots but plagues many other explanations of social complexity in Bronze Age Greece (for discussion, see Cherry and Davis, chapter 12, this volume, and Parkinson, chapter 9, this volume). More recent scholarship deemphasizes the influence of Homer and the Near East, yet, with the exception of Piggott (1992), this scholarly corpus continues to focus on military applications of chariotry (Hanson 1999; van Wees 1992).

Little work has been devoted to the function of chariots as elite commodities in Mycenaean society. This chapter focuses on that very issue, examining first the hard evidence for the manufacture of chariots in a specific Mycenaean polity. The excavations at the Palace of Nestor at Pylos yielded both artifactual and textual evidence for chariot manufacture, and thus Pylos forms an optimal case study for this investigation. From there I explore the implication of this industry from the standpoint of production and consumption, and compare chariots to other industries controlled by the Palace of Nestor. This approach provides a more well-rounded picture of the social role of chariots and helps explain why the palace authorities placed such a high premium on their construction. In addition, by maintaining an internal focus on chariot use at Pylos, I hope to avoid the pitfalls of borrowing too heavily from the Mycenaeans' eastern peers. When chariot manufacture is compared with other industries controlled by the palace, it becomes clear that chariot manufacture complements the palace's other manufacturing interests while serving a common function as instruments of social power. The various industries controlled by the palace together offer a diversified set of carriers of elite ideology. They serve both to signal an individual's affiliation with the central authority at Pylos and to demarcate rank within the broader group of enfranchised Pylians.

THE MANUFACTURE OF CHARIOTS AT PYLOS

Blegen suggested early on that chariots were kept at the Palace of Nestor (Blegen and Lang 1958). He based his conclusion on limited yet convincing evidence. The palace's Linear B documents mention chariot parts explicitly, and one set of tablets, the *Sa* series, deals exclusively with chariot wheels. Blegen also inferred that chariot manufacture was centered in the Northeastern Building (Blegen and Rawson 1966). Subsequent scholars working on the issue have discussed chariots at Pylos only in the context of functional investigations of that structure (Bendall 2003; Tegyey 1984), treating chariot manufacture as one of a number of activities administered there.

In this chapter, I take a different approach and begin with the chariot industry itself. Resituating the discussion of chariot manufacture by using the Northeastern Building as a backdrop has two advantages. First, a focused investigation of the evidence for chariot manufacture at Pylos reveals new details about the industry. A more complete view of how chariots were manufactured at Pylos helps us better understand the practical and social importance of chariots in maintaining power in the Pylian polity. Second, as an addition to the list of industries already well investigated at Pylos, such as architecture, pottery, textile, and perfumed oils, an account of the chariot industry at Pylos adds to our growing understanding of how craft specialization was organized by palace authorities.

Raw Materials

Let us begin with a brief look at the raw materials that went into making a Mycenaean chariot. A detailed account appears in Crouwel's *Chariots and Other Means of Land Transport in Bronze Age Greece* (1981). The primary, and essential, raw materials that went into making a Mycenaean chariot were wood, leather, and bronze. Optional materials include gold, silver, and ivory, which would have been used for decoration. Wood formed the basic structure of the chariot. It was used to construct the frame of the box, the traction system, the yoke, the axles, and the wheels. The floor and screens of the box were made of leather, as were the bridle and reins. Leather was also used to pad and to bind together the wooden components of the traction system, the yoke, and the wheels. Bronze was employed in the wheel assembly to fasten the tires to the wheels, in the control mechanism, and as decoration. Organic compounds, used as adhesives and lubricants, would also have been required for a working chariot, but since we have no direct evidence for these materials, I leave them out of this study.

The artifactual evidence for these materials in the Northeastern Building is scant and ambiguous. Blegen reported two carbonized wooden planks from room 97 (Blegen and Rawson 1966:311). No leather has survived from the Northeastern Building. Pieces of bronze were found throughout the structure. Among the distinguishable remnants of bronze found in the building, a number of rivets and pins conceivably could have come from chariots. A few broken flat strips with rivets were found in room 99. They are concave on one side and convex on the other. Blegen concluded that they were from a bronze band that was part of a chariot, a corselet, or some other fixture in room 99 (Blegen and Rawson 1966:322).

More informative than the artifactual evidence are the Linear B tablets excavated in the Northeastern Building that contain references to the material components of chariots, summarized in table 13.1. The tablets mention raw materials such as bronze, animal

TABLE 13.1 Evidence for the material components of chariots at Pylos (AC = Archive Complex).

MATERIAL COMPONENT	TABLET	CONTEXT
Horse-chariots *i-qi-ja-i (a-qi-ja-i)*	*An 1282*	18 men are sent to work on them.
Wheels *a-mo-si*	*An 1282*	18 men are sent to work on them.
Wheels ⊕	*Sa 1313*	Listed as *we-je-ke-e*, "serviceable." Rest of the *Sa* set is in the AC.
Axles *a-ko-so-ne*	*Va 1323*	33 of them are in poor condition. *Vn 10* from the AC lists axles sent to the chariot workshop.
Beams *do-ka-ma-i*	*An 1282*	36 men are sent to work on them.
Wood	*Un 1314*	100 units of an unknown item, *pa-ra-we-'jo,'* are made of wood (*do-we-jo-qe*).
Yokes *ze-u-ke-si*	*Ub 1318*	3 pairs (*ti-ri-si*).
Halters *po-qe-wi-ja-i*	*An 1282*	5 men are sent to work on them.
Halters *po-qe-wi-ja*	*Ub 1315*	11 new pairs (*ne-wa*).
Reins *a-ni-ja*	*Ub 1315*	5 fitted with equipment (*te-u-ke-pi*); 6 Lousos type (*ro-u-si-je-wi-ja*); 3 saddlers' reins (*ra-pte-ri-ja*); 5 new without headbands (*ne-wa a-na-pu-ke*); 9 with 2 headbands; 2 other reins; 5 for cart animals (*a-pe-ne-wo*), 1 of which has headbands (*a-pu-ke*).
Bridles *we-ru-ma-ta*	*Ub 1318*	3 pairs.
Hides Sheep and goat ideogram	*Cn 1286*	Possibly *o-pi-ra-i-ja*, "hide with the hair left on" (Blegen and Lang 1958:190).
She-goats (hides or live?)	*Cn 1287*	11 she-goats total, given as payment or taken as assessment.
Rams	*Cc 1283, Cc 1285*	1 and 6 listed, respectively.
Goats	*Cc 1258, Cc 1284*	30 and 8 goats, respectively. *pe-re* on Cc 1284 suggests hides (see note 3).
Deerskin *e-ra-pi-ja, e-ra-ti-ja-o*	*Ub1316, Ub 1317*	8 hides owed (*o-pe-ro*) on each tablet.
Hides *di-pte-ra*	*Ub 1318*	Given to *au-ke-i-ja-te-we-i* (see also *An 1281* and *Fn 50*) to make saddlebags, straps, bindings, and panniers of basketry? Given to *me-ti-ja-no* for fastenings, *e-ru-ta-ra* "red" skins given to him for *a-re-se-si*. *wo-di-je-ja* receives pigskins, *we-e-wi-ja*, and rawhide, *wi-ri-no*, possibly for bridles (Ruijgh 1966:132). *a-pe-i-ja* receives pigskins with fringes, *u-po ka-ro*, and deerskin with pigskin underneath.
Hides	*Wr 1325*	He-goat ideogram.
Hides	*Wr 1328*	Oxhide, WI (contra Shelmerdine 1987:338, n. 21).
Hides	*Wr 1331*	Ram ideogram, *o-pa* on reverse.
Hides	*Wr 1332*	WI, *o-pa* on reverse.
Hides	*Wr 1334*	He-goat ideogram.
Bronze	*Ja 1288*	4.23 kg given to *ka-ra-wi-so* (contra Lang in Blegen and Lang 1958:190).

hides,[1] and wooden beams. They also list finished chariot parts such as wheels, reins, and axles. A number of clay seals with livestock ideograms provide further indirect evidence for the presence of hides in the Northeastern Building. The direct references to chariot parts demonstrate sufficiently that chariot manufacture was managed there. In the case of wooden beams (do-ka-ma-i), hides (di-pte-ra), and raw bronze (ka-ko), the evidence is somewhat conjectural. It is quite possible that many of the materials listed on these tablets were not destined to become parts of chariots. There are tablets from the Northeastern Building that refer to wood for spear shafts and hides for sandals, to give a couple of examples. Likewise, numerous bronze arrowheads were found in the building, and the bronze allotment on tablet Ja 1288 may have been used to make more of those. Regardless of the ultimate destiny of the specific raw materials listed on the tablets from the Northeastern Building, the tablets demonstrate conclusively that all of the major raw components (and some processed ones) required to construct a chariot passed through that structure. At least a few of these items were even stored there for an extended period of time. Despite some ambiguities, we can be confident that the headquarters of the chariot industry at Pylos was in the Northeastern Building.

In addition to materials, the manufacture of chariots required administration and labor. In this regard, the tablets are highly revealing. Table 13.2 summarizes the evidence for the workforce listed in the tablets found in the Northeastern Building. This workforce included unskilled laborers, specialist supervisors, and administrators. Anonymous laborers were recruited from numerous towns in the Pylian domain, in much the same way that the palace collected its taxes. Members of the elite also were involved in the industry. Such involvement may indeed be expected if the manufactured product was meant for elite consumption (Costin 1998; Spielmann 1998). On tablet An 1281, the names of a number of the supervisors can be cross-referenced to tablets that reveal their status and occupations. Au-ke-i-ja-te-we-i receives hides on Ub1318 (also found in the Northeastern Building), and tablet Fn 50 reveals that he has slaves.[2] Re-u-si-wo, o-na-se-u, po-so-ro, and ma-ra-si-jo are bronzesmiths by trade, as recorded on tablets Jn 692, Jn 658, Jn 601, and Jn 706, respectively. Nakassis (2005) has recently argued that a good number of bronzesmiths were members of the elite. They are listed on various tablets as landholders, shepherds of palatial flocks, and military officials.

Scholars have long recognized a connection between religion and industry in Mycenaean society (Lupack, chapter 6, this volume; Palmer 1963) and the manufacture of chariots at Pylos is no exception. Tablet An 1281 documents the connection of officials of the goddess "Potnia" with the chariot industry. Two loci of activity, as depicted on An 1281, are at Potnian shrines, one probably at Pylos, the other at po-ti-ja-ke-e. The shrine in front of the Northeastern Building, despite limited artifactual evidence, cannot be dissociated from the industrial activity taking place there. Priests and priestesses are also included among other members of the elite on the Qa series of tablets found in the Northeastern Building as recipients of *189, which may be a textile or some other elite gift.

Finally, a word about the scribes. At least ten scribes were at work recording materials in the Northeastern Building, and a few of them seem to have worked there exclusively (Melena 2000–2001; Palaima 1988). H26, whose work is preserved only in the Sa series—a set of tablets concerned with chariot wheels—may even have been permanently assigned to this industry. Ultimately, the evidence for scribal specialization is too meager to make any confident judgments, but we can assert securely that approximately one-third of the known palace scribes worked in the building. This fraction represents the largest bureaucratic workforce at Pylos outside of the Archives Complex.

Administration of the Northeastern Building

The tablets also provide insights into the manner in which the manufacture of chariots was administered. The administrators of the Northeastern Building tapped into many of the financial networks available to the palace. These included official transactions, such as general taxation (a-pu-do-si), individual contributions, work assignments (ta-ra-si-ja, o-pa), and payments (o-no), as well as less formalized ones.

General taxation, a-pu-do-si, is evident in the Ac series. These tablets refer to men and deerskins as o-pe-ro, "owed," the term generally used at Pylos for taxes. Taxes are collected from the sixteen main towns of the Pylian state. The taxes levied from each community were proportional, and Lang has noted the similarity in the proportions among the preserved tablets of the Ac series to those of the Ma series (Blegen and Lang 1958). The men assigned to chariot work on An 1282 were presumably recruited under this system.

TABLE 13.2 Evidence for chariot-related labor at Pylos.

HUMAN COMPONENTt	TABLET	CONTEXT
Anonymous workers	*Ac* Series	158 men recruited from 6 of the 16 towns. Tegyey (1984:69) extrapolates to 500+, if all 16 towns had been listed.
Anonymous workers	*An 1282*	Assigned in units of 18 to various chariot parts.
Named workers	*An 1281*	Assigned to named supervisors at 2 shrines of Potnia; 4 of these workers are bronzesmiths.
Named supervisors	*An 1281*	Receive workers at 2 shrines of Potnia; 3 of them are slave-owners; 1 of them receives hides on Ub 1318.
Bronzesmith	*Ja 1288*	*ka-ra-wi-jo*? receives an allotment of 4.23 kg.
Bronzesmiths	*An 1281*	*re-u-si-wo, po-so-ro, o-na-se-u, ma-ra-si-jo* assigned to supervisors (see above).
Leatherworkers	*Cn 1287?*	10 men, listed with she-goats; purpose uncertain.
Leatherworkers	*Ub 1318*	Men and women receiving skins for various tasks.
Miscellaneous craftsmen	*Un 1322*	Craftspeople receiving rations of wheat and/or figs. Those identified are not chariot workers, but others may be.
Priests, priestesses, and other elites	*Qa* Series	They receive *189, a garment or other prize.
Scribes	Not mentioned	Some work exclusively in the Northeast Building.

Linear B scholars often interpret the term *o-pe-ro* as indicative of taxation at Pylos (Bendall 2003). The term appears on *Un 1319* in association with wheat and on *Ub 1316* and *Ub 1317* in association with deerskins owed from the previous year. *O-pe-ro* might represent taxation in these cases; however, premodern states typically taxed communities, not individuals (Scott 1998), and thus these debts may be of a different nature. Considering the exigencies of hunting, an activity in which yields are unpredictable, it seems odd that anyone would be taxed in deerskins, but then again, that may explain why the previous year's assessment had not been met. Similarly, if the hides on *Cc 1258* and *Cc 1283-1285* reflect individual donations, then they too represent something other than a standard tax contribution (Bendall 2003).[3]

The *ta-ra-si-ja* system involved supplying craftspeople with raw materials and represented an obligation on the specialist to supply a finished good. *Ta-ra-si-ja* was associated with textiles and bronze at Pylos. Some bronzesmiths operated *a-ta-la-si-ja*— "without talasia"—and it is impossible to determine which alternative fits with the bronze allotment on *Ja 1288*. At Knossos, chariot wheels were manufactured under the *ta-ra-si-ja* system, so this is a possibility for

Pylos as well. More indirect evidence for *ta-ra-si-ja* is supplied by *Ub 1318*, which lists hides going to certain individuals to make finished goods. This certainly seems to be *ta-ra-si-ja* type of work, although the term is not written on the tablet.

O-pa may designate a type of work obligation related to raw materials or the "refurbishment" of finished goods (Killen 1999b; Melena 1983). It complements the *ta-ra-si-ja* system of allocation of resources to craftspeople (Shelmerdine 1987). *O-pa* work was performed on chariot wheels at Knossos (*So 4430*) and corselets at Pylos (*Sh 736*). In respect to livestock, *o-pa* may refer to the fattening of animals in preparation for sacrifice or the manufacture of leather goods (Killen 1999b). The term is inscribed on sealings in the Northeastern Building, and in three cases the sealing also contains the ideogram for hides (*Wr 1325, Wr 1331*, and *Wr 1332*).

In addition to receiving goods, either directly or via the central bureaucracy, the Northeastern Building was authorized to make payments. Such payments, like those made on *Un 1322*, are designated by the term *o-no* (Bendall 2003; Chadwick 1964).[4] Also, the *Qa* series may document the disbursement of elite gifts. Bendall (2003) has noted that all of the identifiable recipients of item *189* are elites, who also received land grants from the palace.

To summarize, the administration of the Northeastern Building utilized a number of economic mechanisms employed throughout the palace and possibly some less formalized mechanisms that are not attested to in the archives. These systems included general taxation, individual contributions, specific transactions usually associated with craftspeople, individual gifts, and payments for services. As with materials, we cannot assign all of the specific tablets discussed above to the manufacture of chariots, but we may assert that the managers of the chariot industry could have relied on the economic systems reflected in the tablets if they needed to. Not mentioned in the tablets from the Northeastern Building but clearly a part of this financial network was international trade. Bronze, silver, gold, and ivory were not indigenous resources at Pylos and had to have come from abroad. The tablets do not tell us about international trade, but the listing of these exotic materials and their actual presence as artifacts indicate at least that they were part of the chariot manufacturing process. The implementation of the entire range of financial systems demonstrates that the managers of the Northeastern Building had the full economic backing and authority of the palace behind them.

Based on the material and organizational evidence from the Northeastern Building, it is evident that chariot manufacture at Pylos was a highly centralized industry. But what does "centralized" mean in this case? While the palace monitored the allocation and collection of bronze to and from its affiliated bronzesmiths, their workplaces were dispersed (Smith 1992–1993). Leatherworking and woodworking, using materials easily available throughout the region, seem to have been decentralized crafts as well. Component parts of chariots would have been made in their respective workshops (bridles at leather workshops, bronze fastenings at bronzesmith shops), recorded by administrators at the Northeastern Building, and then taken to chariot assembly points such as the ones listed on *An 1281*.[5] Although they are in separate locations, the fact that these locations are Potnian shrines, run by religious personnel who were themselves clients of the palace (as indicated by their landholdings and gifts), is telling.

Such outsourcing does not threaten the monopoly held by the palace over chariot production because, for one thing, the manufacture of the most sophisticated component of the chariot, namely the wheel, remained in-house. The four-spoked chariot wheel required specialized skills to assemble and had to be made to high levels of tolerance to avoid failure (Brandt 1993; Piggott 1992). Pairs of wheels are often customized with exotic materials and assigned to individuals of high rank. The *Sa* tablets, all written by the same scribe (*H26*), record chariot wheels in various states of repair. One of these tablets (*Sa 1313*) was discovered in the Northeastern Building, while the rest of the set was found in the Archives Complex. We may infer that the tablets were originally written in room 98, where their associated wheels were kept, and then transferred to the Archives Complex once the work on them was completed (Shelmerdine 1987).

Horses are one part of the package I have not yet discussed in this chapter. The acquisition, training, and maintenance of a fit pair of horses might have been far more costly than the manufacture and maintenance of the chariot they pulled. Land is required for grazing, and the horses must be trained. We have very little evidence for horse rearing at Pylos. *Sa 22*, one of the chariot wheel tablets, lists a pair of horses. On tablet *Eq 03*, Kretheus (*ke-re-te-u*) receives five units of wheat on account of his horse (Ventris and Chadwick 1973:260). This information alone is not helpful, but when it is read in the context of the more complete set of horse-related tablets found at Knossos, we can fill in some gaps. At Knossos, individual charioteers were required to supply and maintain their own horses, but when need be, the palace supplied horses and feed for them. There may be a similar relationship at Pylos.

Although the loci of production were dispersed, centralization in this case depended on control of the industry, not its location. All aspects of chariot manufacture were in some way monitored by the palace. The Linear B term, *a-mo-te-jo-na-de* (on *Vn 10*), interpreted as "chariot workshop" (Shelmerdine 1999b) or "wheelwright's workshop" (Killen 1999b), may be an assembly point rather than a place where all aspects of chariot manufacture took place.[6] If the term refers to the Northeastern Building itself (Shelmerdine 1999b), it does so because the structure is a central hub of the industry or the location of wheel construction, not necessarily because it has *all* the characteristics of a workshop as archaeologists understand the term (Tournavitou 1988).[7] The fact that the Northeastern Building does not fit well into traditional workshop models is a symptom of the reliance on inflexible classificatory schemes to define industrial activity (such as Bendall 2003). Chariot manufacture, like many other industries at Pylos, was centrally administered but not necessarily centrally located. The managerial structure employed in the manufacture of chariots allowed the palace authorities to regionally outsource production without giving up control over it. I would argue further that the chariot industry, because of its complexity and scale, could not even have existed without such centralized supervision.

THE USES OF THE MYCENAEAN CHARIOT

To contextualize the social role of chariots in Pylos, I will briefly review how chariots were used in the polity. We may postulate four overlapping uses of chariots in Mycenaean Greece: warfare, elite bonding, communication, and status display. In all cases the outcome of their use is the same: they enhance the power of the central authority.

Most scholarly work concerning the use of chariots in warfare among the Mycenaeans has focused on the specific battle techniques employed. Three prevalent theories exist. The first, drawing on the tradition of Homeric scholarship and artistic depictions, limits their role to that of the "battle taxi" (Anglim et al. 2002; Littauer 1972; Littauer and Crouwel 1983). In this case, an elite warrior is transported to the battlefield, where he dismounts and begins to fight, without the fatigue caused by having to run to the action. He can also retreat to safety more quickly when the need arises. Such an "in-and-out" approach to battle is typical of warfare among chiefdoms (Gardner and Heider 1968). Another theory holds that the chariot was used in conjunction with a thrusting spear (Greenhalgh 1973). The Hittites used this technique (Drews 1993; Neve 1984), and Caesar writes about the Celts battling this way also (Anderson 1975; *Gallic Wars* 4.24.1; Greenhalgh 1973). Littauer and Crouwel (1983), however, basing their argument on the likely width of a chariot and length of a spear, have shown the impracticability of such a technique. A third hypothesis, posed by Drews (1993), sees chariots as mobile platforms for archers. This became the dominant method of chariot warfare in Egypt and the Near East during the Late Bronze Age. At Pylos, more than five hundred bronze arrowheads were stored in the Northeastern Building, and it is attractive to link them with the chariot industry there. These arrowheads were barbed (Blegen and Rawson 1966) and so likely were used for warfare and not hunting (Keeley 1996). Some Mycenaean warriors used heavy corselets, which would have been impractical in terms of mobility and

excessively tiring for uses other than archery (Littauer 1972). In light of the importance of keeping expensive horses out of harm's way and the general safety of fighting at a distance, this last technique would have been the most effective if the charioteer and archer could manage it. Crouwel (1981) and others assert, though, that the Greek landscape is just too bumpy for chariots to be used this way.

All three standard theories of chariot use in battle are problematic due to a combination of practical problems that would have inhibited their effectiveness and problems with the sources of evidence for them. Homer's value as a historical source is limited (Drews 1993; Greenhalgh 1973; van Wees 1994). Artistic depictions also idealize chariot warfare (see Drews 1993 on the Battle of Kadesh). In addition, most interpretations borrow heavily from artistic depictions from the Near East. Although chariots are depicted throughout Mycenaean art, we do not see similar battle tactics. What we do see are Mycenaeans with chariots fighting chariotless foes. Ultimately, we cannot determine a single prescribed technique for the use of Mycenaean chariots in battle, and their actual use could have been a combination of all three hypotheses (Anderson 1975; van Wees 1994).

Beyond specific battle tactics, we may be able to gain insight into the use of chariots at Pylos by examining the type of warfare in which they were deployed. Most approaches to Mycenaean warfare assume intergroup warfare between similarly equipped armies (Driessen 1999a; Greenhalgh 1973). Although this may be an accurate model for conflict between states, there are other possibilities at Pylos to consider. We may envision three nested scales of warfare in which Pylian soldiers participated: international (battles that took place outside the Aegean), interpolity (battles against another Mycenaean center), and territorial (battles involving the conquest of neighboring territories). Although the three levels of warfare are not mutually exclusive, our best evidence for Pylos speaks to the third scenario, that of territorial conquest.

Evidence for Mycenaean participation in international warfare is limited. Mycenaean soldiers (possibly mercenaries) are depicted on isolated sketches from Egypt and Anatolia (Cline 1995a; see chapter 17, this volume). In addition, chance finds of Mycenaean-type swords and textual references to the *Ahhiyawa* have been interpreted to represent Mycenaean soldiers abroad (Cline 1995a). In no case are Mycenaean soldiers associated with chariots. In light of transport costs and the need for standardization to facilitate repair and maintenance, it is more conceivable that if Mycenaean soldiers did use chariots outside Greece, they would have obtained them in the field.[8] On the home front, archaeologists have yet to identify any presence of foreign armies on Helladic soil.

On the regional level, the existence of massive fortifications at a number of centers, as well as Linear B tablets recording the muster of troops at Pylos, certainly indicates preparedness for invasion (Baumbach 1983), but we have yet to figure out what the archaeological correlates of interpolity warfare would be (Krzyszkowska 1999). If such warfare did occur, we would most likely find evidence for it in the Argolid, where the territorial boundaries of multiple centers abut each other. Such engagements, furthermore, probably would more often taken the form of sporadic raiding missions rather than battlefield standoffs between organized battalions. In such cases, chariots would not provide a decisive military advantage, although not having them would be disadvantageous. Interpolity warfare between Mycenaean centers, while likely, is still poorly documented, and the use of chariots in such warfare remains speculative.

There is stronger evidence for a more localized deployment of the Pylos chariot fleet. In Messenia, peer polity competition and power struggles involving localized warfare were likely until the late Middle Helladic to Late Helladic I. During LH I, the shift from local competition to regional conquest driven by Pylos had begun (Acheson 1999). Signs of the intensification of warfare among early complex societies include specialization of equipment and human resources, warlike ideology and iconography, and a shift from site-specific to regional defensive strategies (Haas 2001). These are all present at Pylos.[9] Furthermore, the construction of the Northeastern Building, and the centralization (if not creation) of the chariot industry at Pylos occurred during the same period (LH IIIB) that the palace was extending its territorial control into the Further province (Davis and Bennet 1999). When examined from this diachronic perspective, the intensification of military activities at Pylos appears to be part of a policy of territorial expansion. In the case of territorial conquest, chariots would have been used against a chariotless foe (the people living in eastern Messenia) and would have provided the greatest military benefit. Artwork reinforces this image. In no instance of Mycenaean art are chariot forces depicted fighting other chariot forces. Rather, chariots are depicted in battle dominating poorly equipped adversaries.[10]

The most common use of the Pylian chariot fleet, then, would have been at the subregional level against an ill-equipped adversary. Granted, the resolution of archaeological data decreases as spatial scales expand, and thus finer evidence at the local level may be anticipated. Nevertheless, a more localized focus on the military deployment of chariots has advantages. Borrowing from Renfrew (1975), we can model warfare as "action at a distance." Warfare and trade occupy overlapping networks of sociocultural interaction (Driessen 1999a; Keeley 1996). The frequency of engagements declines as distance from the home center increases and the associated costs increase. Although such a pattern does not preclude long-distance warfare, it does suggest that the localized mobilization of forces is more cost-effective.

The second potential use of chariots at Pylos was in elite bonding activities—military training, hunting, and racing. To control a chariot effectively, extensive training of both charioteer and horse is required. If access to chariots was restricted by the palace, chariot training would also have been restricted, and participation in such training would have strengthened social bonds among the elite. Using a horse in hunting was an essential element in its training (Morris 1990) and served to moderate its fear of other animals (Hyland 2003). Hunting per se was not solely an elite activity (Thomas 1999), but hunting by chariot would have been. An elite hunting party, chariots and all, is depicted in the megaron fresco at Tiryns (Morris 1990). Marinatos (1990) has argued for a possible link between the chariot depicted on the stelae from Grave Circle A at Mycenae and the lion hunt scene in the register below it, although emphasizing the symbolic value of the event. There is also one sealing from Pylos (*CMS I 302*) with a scene of a lion hunt by chariot. As with warfare, while we can be confident that chariots were used in hunting, the actual tactic employed remains elusive. The main quarry of Mycenaean hunters—wild boar, deer, and possibly lions—inhabited woodlands and thickets, where chariot riding might not have been feasible. It is possible that animals could have been chased into open terrain, where chariots would have assisted hunters in finishing them off.

Indirect evidence exists for chariot racing in Mycenaean culture. The chariot race at Patroklos's funeral in the *Iliad* receives more attention than all other events combined (Miller 2004). We can thus assume its prestige in Homer's Early Iron Age Greece, but not necessarily before then. Nevertheless, competitive racing seems a likely pastime. An LH IIIC amphora from Tiryns may depict a chariot race (Laser 1987; Miller 2004). Rather than being a release valve for aggression (contra Driessen 1999a), warlike sports have been shown to reinforce aggressive behavior in society (Sipes 1973). Chariot racing, as a means of training and prestige among the elite, would have been a natural outcome of the increased emphasis on warfare in Mycenaean ideology evident in LH IIIB. Although we have no concrete evidence for formalized chariot racing at Pylos, the need to train charioteers would have required some such activity. Elite bonding activities with chariots served two complementary purposes: first, they fostered the construction of elite identity through inclusive events, and second, they reinforced difference through exclusion of nonelites. Even if a noninitiate were to acquire a chariot, he would be unable to put it to good use.

"The fundamental infrastructure required for the exercise of . . . both organized and diffused power is communications. Without effective passing of messages, personnel, and resources, there can be no power" (Mann 1986:136). Chariots would have been a key component of the palace's communication networks. These networks governed the flow of goods and information.

The first step to understanding how chariots were used to foster communication within Pylian territory is to look at the road network. Scholars generally agree that the natural terrain of Greece is too rough for regular travel by wheeled vehicle. A road network is needed to maximize the benefits of all forms of wheeled travel. Early scholarship on Mycenaean road networks was, again, indebted to Homer (McDonald and Rapp 1972; Steffen 1884). Steffen, examining Late Bronze Age roads around Mycenae, argued that the roads were constructed purely for military defense, and specifically for chariot use (Hope-Simpson 1998; Mylonas 1966; Steffen 1884). The University of Minnesota Messenia Expedition volume even refers to them as "chariot roads" (McDonald and Rapp 1972). Scholars have since abandoned this unicausal explanation and have focused on road networks as a means to define territorial control and core areas (Hope-Simpson 1998; Jansen 1997, 2002). Most work has been done around Mycenae, where Late Bronze Age roads and bridges are best preserved. The primary function of Mycenae's road network was evidently to link settlements within its territory to each other and to the citadel; there is some evidence for interregional communication as well.

Although not as well preserved, a similar road network existed in Messenia. A regularly used network of dirt paths connecting major settlements in western Messenia probably had its origins in the Middle Helladic (Lukermann 1972). During the Late Bronze Age this network became more formalized, and some evidence of monumental roads remains. McDonald (1964) reconstructed a Pylian road network based on direct evidence from a few stretches of preserved Late Bronze Age roads, as well as by tracing roads of later periods that run past settlements and tholos tombs that were in use during the Late Bronze Age. Fant and Loy (1972) also took into account what the natural terrain would have allowed in supporting McDonald's reconstruction. In one case, a 1.9 km stretch of Late Helladic roadway near the modern town of Rizomilo leads toward the modern city of Kalamata and presents evidence for intraregional as well as interregional communication.

What might have been the relationship of chariots to the road network? The centralization of chariot manufacture, maintenance of the road network, and general expansion of Pylian influence into the Further Province come together to give us a picture of intensification of power by the palace that peaked during LH IIIB. The flow of people or goods to the palace, via ox-cart or pack animal, taxed or otherwise, was easier and swifter with roads and chariots. Chariots would have enhanced the supervision of this movement of goods by the elite. Decision making would also have been facilitated as agents of the palace authority, delivering messages, would have been better able to communicate with outlying secondary centers. As a result, chariots and the roads they traveled on would have strengthened palatial control over outlying territories.

Such forms of communication intensified control over the preexisting settlements within Pylos's territory. They also permitted control to be exercised over a greater area, and we have independent evidence for this result in the Further Province (Davis and Bennet 1999). Two possible models for the effect of enhanced communication within the polity emerge: (1) palatial elites were better able to supervise regional elites and maintain dominance over them, or (2) regional elites were enfranchised by the palace and regular communication, and travel to and from the palace enhanced their local status. Ultimately, the result for the palace was the same—greater power.

In addition to their practical value in enhancing the movement of goods and communicating political policy, the use of chariots on the intraregional road network had symbolic value. The display of elite commodities was an essential tool in communicating elite ideology. The spectacle of an elaborately dressed member of the warrior elite traversing the countryside at speed in a vehicle adorned with exotic materials reinforced the dominant position of the ruling class.

Summary

There exists evidence for a number of overlapping uses for the chariots manufactured at Pylos. These uses include warfare, elite bonding, communications, and status display. In all of their uses, chariots served the interests of the palatial elite, and did so mainly at the local and regional level. In his survey of the history of social power, Mann (1986) identifies four intersecting sources of social power that rulers employ to strengthen their authority: ideological, economic, military, and political (IEMP). Chariots functioned quite comfortably in each realm. As military tools, they were on the cutting edge of the Bronze Age arms race. Ideologically and politically, chariots were status symbols of the elite that differentiated them from non-chariot-riding people and enhanced reciprocal peer relations. As tools of communication, they could speed up and help secure economic transactions within the state.

CHARIOT MANUFACTURE AT PYLOS IN THE CONTEXT OF OTHER PALATIAL INDUSTRIES

Chariots are an important addition to other industries, such as textiles and perfumed oil, that have been well documented at Pylos (Killen 1984; Shelmerdine 1984, 1985). Chariots are a composite artifact, combining the work of craft specialists in wood, leather, metal, and animal husbandry. The elite nature of this artifact is reflected in the complex organization of its production and in the prestige afforded its possessors. The chariot, its rider, horses, and maintenance crew formed a "techno-social package-deal" (Piggott 1992) that served, reflected, and reinforced the power of the central authority. The other high-status items manufactured under palatial supervision served a similar purpose. So why add another? While chariots served a similar purpose to other elite status markers they did so in a manner that complemented the full set of Pylian elite status markers rather than simply repeating them.

Since they all served the interests of the central authority, it may be fruitful to examine chariots in the context of other industries centered at the palace. Here I will focus on a range of industries that are not only the best understood but also the most informative in terms of the overall purpose of the wealth finance system (D'Altroy and Earle 1985). These include monumental architecture, chariots, textiles, perfumed oils, and kylikes. Rather than focusing on the differences between the various industries, however, I prefer to treat these industries in unison, with the hope of shedding light on why the palace authorities should have invested so much effort in the production of elite status items in the first place. In terms of the context of production, all of these industries are "attached"—the mode generally employed in the production of luxury and wealth items (Costin 1991).[11] Attached production permits the sponsor (in this case, the palace) to control not only production but also distribution and, to a degree, consumption as well (Costin 1991). In fact, a few of these industries, chariot manufacture and perfumed oil in particular, were so attached that the layout of the palace was altered to accommodate them (Shelmerdine 1987; Wright 1984).

Other chapters in this volume have established the prevalence (though not the exclusive one) of wealth finance at Pylos (see, e.g., Halstead, chapter 7, and Parkinson, chapter 9). An examination of the elite industries established at the Palace of Nestor can help us understand why wealth finance was so critical to the maintenance of power. Systems of wealth finance are not adopted to manage surplus for the good of the general populace as protection against periodic shortages or to maximize the efficient exploitation of a heterogeneous ecosystem for the benefit of *Homo economicus* in the way that staple finance does. Rather, to explain wealth finance, we must turn to models of social action, as pioneered by Weber, that focus on the motivation of individual agents. In this case, the agents are the Mycenaean elites who controlled the Pylian polity. From a Weberian perspective, humans are motivated by a drive to maximize their power over nature and over other humans (Mann 1986; Weber 1978). The first relationship helps explain systems of staple finance and focuses on cooperative efforts such as the communal storage of surplus for periods of crisis. The second is competition based and is better suited to explaining wealth finance. In competition, people act to differentiate themselves from other people. In terms of Mann's IEMP model, we might presume that the items manufactured under palatial supervision were primarily economic sources of social power, but in fact, since we are dealing with a premonetary economy here, their primary purposes were equally social and ideological (Mauss 1990). True, the palace authorities assigned value to these goods, but they did not do so to lubricate local exchange mechanisms but to further their own ideological agenda (Voutsaki 1995b). The control of ideology allowed elites to legitimize and propagate social inequality. In this context, the elite status items manufactured under palatial supervision acted as markers of affiliation that legitimized and advertised the authority of the palatial elite. While they did so in different ways and in a variety of contexts, all of these items were symbols or emblems of the palace itself.

It has long been understood that there is a relationship between craft specialization and state formation (Renfrew 1972; Service 1962). Although a number of explanations for this relationship are possible, in the case of wealth finance systems, primacy must be given to craft specialization as a strategy related to enhancing political authority (Brumfiel and Earle 1987; Peregrine 1991). For ideology to function as a source of social power and, in turn, be an effective tool of the state, it must be materialized (DeMarrais et al. 1996). By dominating all phases of craft activity—production, distribution, and consumption—political authorities can control the materialization of ideology. The manufacture of elite goods—defined by their rarity, complexity, or as exotic materials—is an effective means to that end (Earle 1987).

For an object to be considered elite, it must contain a raw material that is not locally available (Helms 1979), it must require intense labor and technological sophistication to produce (Peregrine 1991), and its circulation must be restricted (Voutsaki 1995b); or the object must simply possess extraordinary symbolic significance (Voutsaki 1995b). These factors permit greater control of the items by the state. The objects manufactured under the supervision of the Palace of Nestor all shared at least some of these traits. Monumental structures, such as the palace and tholos tombs, were clear status markers: production costs were high, possession was restricted, and the message they conveyed was unambiguous. Furthermore, monuments often form the backdrop to rituals, which themselves are displays of elite ideology (DeMarrais et al. 1996). Chariots were difficult to produce, costly to maintain, and highly restricted. Certain textiles and perfumed oils similarly had restricted circulation and conveyed a message about the status of the wearer. Finally, I consider kylikes to be elite items not because of their inherent value but because their manufacture was perhaps centralized

(Galaty 1999a, 1999b, and chapter 8, this volume) and because they are associated with feasts, which are elite-sponsored activities (Wright 2004a).

Once the palace materialized its ideology in the form of its manufactured elite craft goods, the task remained to communicate this ideology to a target audience. As societies become increasingly complex, governance is enhanced by increased simplicity in ideological messaging (Yoffee 2005). Scott (1998) refers to this phenomenon as "legibility." Examples of legibility fostered by states include permanent last names, standardization of weights and measures, and cadastral surveys. While Scott's (1998) case studies are limited to the twentieth century AD and are rooted in "high modernist" ideals, Yoffee (2005) shows how some of these concepts are applicable to the ancient world. Pylos is no different: the three examples of legibility I cite above all appear on its Linear B tablets.[12] As for the palace's manufactured goods, similar items appeared throughout the polity in their nonelite forms (domestic architecture, ox-carts, plain oil, etc.). As a result, the language the palace used to communicate its ideological message was one that was already understood by the target audience.

The agents of this discourse were the enfranchised people, usually elites themselves, who received the goods, and the target audience consisted of people who either aspired to possess the items or, in the case of the highest status items, knew full well that they never would. The elite status items manufactured under palatial supervision covered a broad range of possibilities. No individual, possibly not even the wanax himself, could ever "possess" the palace or a tholos tomb on his or her own. At most, these items would have been shared among the top tier of society. At the other extreme, even a humble villager might someday possess a kylix as a souvenir of an elite feast that he or she attended. Chariots occupied a middle ground—clearly impossible for some to attain, while others, if they displayed loyalty and did well in the eyes of their superiors, might have been chosen to drive one.

Wobst's model of artifacts as instruments of information exchange offers a useful way to frame the symbolic value of chariots in comparison to other markers of elite status at Pylos. He defines information exchange as "all those communication events in which a message is emitted or in which it is received" (Wobst 1977:321). According to Wobst, humans use material culture to transmit messages, and vision is the primary sensory mode whereby artifactual messaging is accomplished. The power of visual messaging is that it can "establish the mutual *bona fide*, in visual mode, before any verbal contact has taken place or in the absence of any verbal contact. In this context, stylistic messaging defines mutually expectable behavior patterns and makes subsequent interaction more predictable and less stressful" (Wobst 1977:327). To establish power, a state must spread its ideological message to as many people as it can.

The effectiveness of an object as a transmitter of information depends on a number of factors, including the clarity of the message (measured by standardization and the distance at which the item becomes visible) and the context in which the message is displayed (familiar people or strangers) (Wobst 1977). To Wobst's criteria I add the intensity of the message (measured by the value and exclusivity of the item) and its frequency and range (factors that affect the number of potential messaging events).

In the case of Pylos, we may view the various elite status markers manufactured under palatial control as having the same fundamental message, namely, the palace authority was supremely powerful and affiliation with it carried great reward. Although the message was relatively uniform and redundant, the manner in which the palace elites utilized manufactured goods to disseminate it was quite varied. By diversifying the forms of its ideological message, the palace authority enhanced the overall efficiency by which this message was disseminated. The palace created its own network of symbolic communication.

We can gauge the strength and efficiency of this network by comparing unit costs (the cost of manufacturing an item), frequency (how many of such items are produced), range (the geographic spread of the items), and mobility (how easily the item moves around its range). Table 13.3 compares a number of elite status items manufactured under palatial supervision. These include the palace structure itself, tholos tombs (some of which continued to be used as symbols of authority through LH IIIB), chariots, elite textiles, perfumed oil, and kylikes.

Because each object has its own cost, frequency, range, and mobility, it occupies a different place in the network of symbolic communication. This place is determined by qualities inherent in the object, as well as by the value assigned to it by Pylian society. We cannot necessarily quantify this value, and it is not my goal to do so. What I do argue is that, taken as a whole, the set of palatially manufactured high-status markers conveys the palace's ideology better than any single item could. In light of the above variables, the palace structure is by far the most costly, but it is a single entity and is immobile, and thus, for the palace to be an effective conveyor of its message, the receptor (a person) must come to it. A stirrup jar full of perfumed oil is a weaker conveyor of the message, but since such jars are found in the thousands and as far afield as Egypt, they can convey the message of Pylian elitism with greater redundancy and over an extremely wide range. Chariots occupy a middle ground. They are far more costly to produce than perfumes but not as costly as a palace. At Pylos they number between one and two hundred, a quantity in between the solitary palace and the tons of stirrup jars. This brief analysis is only a starting point for a fuller study but should at least demonstrate the fruitfulness of comparing palatially manufactured items in terms of their potential to communicate state ideology.

CONCLUSIONS

In Late Bronze Age Greece, chariots were the ultimate elite status artifact. Their manufacture was efficiently supervised by Pylos's central authorities. Chariots were essential tools of conquest, they enhanced intrapolity communication, and they were valuable emblems of status. Although scholars have generally focused on the chariot as a tool of conquest, it was the effectiveness of the chariot in all three aspects of state strategy that made investment in the industry worthwhile (but see Piggott 1992 for the primacy of prestige). When compared with other industries controlled by the palatial elite, chariots, with their high value and high mobility, formed an effective addition to the set of carriers of elite ideology.

Acknowledgments. I thank James C. Wright and Mabel L. Lang, who supervised the thesis research on which this chapter is in part based, and Emma Blake, the volume editors, and an anonymous reviewer, who read and made insightful comments on an earlier draft.

NOTES

1. Whether some of these documents refer to hides or live animals is a contentious issue. The tablets are varied enough that some cases clearly imply one or the other, while in other cases either identification is possible.

2. *Mi-jo-pa₂* and *a-pi-e-ra*. Two men listed on *An 1281* also have slaves, who receive barley rations on tablet *Fn 50*.

3. I follow Duhoux's (1976), as opposed to Tegyey's (1984) and Bendall's (2003), interpretation of the Cc tablets

TABLE 13.3 Comparison of the potential for information exchange among items manufactured at the Palace of Nestor.

ITEM	UNIT COST	FREQUENCY	RANGE	MOBILITY
Palace	Very high	Only 1 in the polity	Locally visible	None
Tholos tomb	High, second only to the Palace	Few, scattered throughout the polity	Each one locally visible	None
Kylix	Very low	Thousands	Found throughout polity	Easily transported
Elite textile	Medium	Dozens?	Attached to a person	High
Perfumed oil	Low	Hundreds? Thousands?	Throughout the polity and abroad	Easily transported
Chariot	High	ca. 200?	Throughout the polity and occasionally beyond	Highly mobile and fast

as listing hides rather than live animals because of the use of *pe-re* on *Cc 1284*. Classical Greek uses the term αγο (to lead) for live animals and φερο (to carry) for skins. A similar distinction appears on *Tn 316*, where *pe-re* signals the carrying of *do-ra* "gifts" and *a-ke* refers to the conducting of *po-re-na*, specialized men and women. If *Cc1284* referred to live animals rather than hides, the scribe should have used *a-ke* rather than *pe-re*.

4. Gallagher (1988) has raised concerns over this translation in his thorough discussion of the term, and his interpretation of the word as "ass-load," a quasi-standardized quantity of goods, remains a possibility.

5. Since no place-name is associated with the shrine of *po-ti-ni-ja i-qe-ja* (the mistress of horses) it is possible that this shrine is at Pylos, perhaps at the Northeastern Building itself.

6. In Classical Greek, the term αρμοσις refers to the joining or fitting of items.

7. Alternatively, *a-mo-te-jo-na-de* may refer to one of the assembly points listed on *An1281*.

8. In general, Mycenaean chariots are considered less sophisticated in design than their Near Eastern counterparts, primarily because of the four-spoked wheel, which is not as sturdy as the six-spoked wheels used outside of Greece. Sandor (2004) has shown, though, that the Mycenaean engineers strengthened their wheels not by adding more spokes but by reinforcing the join between spoke and felloe.

9. See Snodgrass (1964) and Driessen (1999a) for specialized equipment, Nikolaidou and Kokkinidou (1997) for iconography, and Baumbach (1983) and Shelmerdine (1999b) for regional defense.

10. The most iconic image is that of the charioteer running over a prostrate enemy, as on the stele found above Shaft Grave V in Grave Circle A at Mycenae. The chariots on the wall painting in Hall 64 at Pylos do not appear to be actively engaged in the battle the way the foot soldiers are, but the fighting is clearly one-sided even without them (Davis and Bennet 1999; Lang 1969).

11. Costin's other three parameters—concentration, scale, and intensity—are relevant in terms of demarcating the divergent structures of these industries, but less so in establishing their unified purpose, which is my focus here.

12. See Lindgren (1973) and Nakassis (2006) for names, Bennett (1950) on weights and measures, and Bennett (1956) on landholdings.

CHAPTER 14

WHERE'S THE PALACE?

THE ABSENCE OF STATE FORMATION IN THE LATE BRONZE AGE CORINTHIA

DANIEL J. PULLEN AND THOMAS F. TARTARON

Those who held Mycenae's citadel,
And wealthy Corinth, and . . .
All these were commanded, a hundred ships,
By Lord Agamemnon, son of Atreus.

Homer, *Iliad* II.569–570, 576

IN A VOLUME DEVOTED to new ways of thinking about Mycenaean palaces, it is somewhat anomalous that our contribution addresses the lack of a palace in one region, the Corinthia. Based in part on our work in the eastern Corinthia as members of the Eastern Korinthia Archaeological Survey (EKAS), we characterize the search for a palace in the Corinthia and the discussion of the degree of control from Mycenae as fundamentally misguided. Although the question of why palaces emerged in regions such as the Argolid and Messenia has hardly been settled, there is a persistent assumption that Corinth's natural advantages should have set in train a process culminating in a palace-centered state. We question on theoretical grounds the evolutionary implications of this expectation, asking instead why a palace may *not* arise in such apparently advantageous circumstances. Further, by adopting a different scale of analysis and by taking a "coastscape" approach to human settlement and exploitation in the Aegean Late Bronze Age, we suggest that the Corinthia was not a center, as often presumed in light of the historical importance of the later polis of Corinth, and that Mycenae did not control the Corinthia during the Mycenaean period. Instead, we argue that the Corinthia was a *political* periphery, contested by competing polities centered at Mycenae (or the Argive Plain in general) and at Kolonna on Aigina in the Saronic Gulf. Ultimately Mycenae, with its greater resource base, eclipsed the island-based center on Aigina, despite the precocious rise of Kolonna in the Middle and early Late Bronze Age. In this chapter we outline an alternative model of political organization of the Late Bronze Age Corinthia. On a specific level, the model offers an explanation for the absence of a palatial center in the Corinthia in the Late Bronze Age. More generally, it utilizes the factors of scale, resource base, and modes of transportation to address interstate competition in the emergence of secondary, first-generation states, following Parkinson and Galaty's (2007) definition. Marcus's (1998b) Dynamic Model of states, with its oscillation between tight integration or consolidation, at one extreme, and loose confederation or dissolution at the other extreme is applicable here, as is a consideration of the adaptability of palatial organization to a stable socio-economic landscape (Haggis 2002). In this way we hope that our model not only is grounded in Aegean archaeology but also is applicable to cross-cultural studies of state formation.

THE CORINTHIA IN THE LATE BRONZE AGE

The lack of a Mycenaean palace in the Corinthia has long puzzled scholars (see figure 14.1 for places mentioned in the text). The conundrum is summarized by Rutter (2003:78) in a recent assessment of the site of ancient Corinth in the Late Bronze Age: "Why had Mycenae become so enormously rich by the beginning of the Mycenaean era, while Corinth had not? Surely Corinth was as well situated in terms of proximity to water and fertile agricultural land as Mycenae, and it was certainly better positioned to take advantage of trade." Despite the presence of several fortifications—Korakou, Perdikaria, Isthmia—no site has so far produced evidence for a palatial building like those known from Mycenae or Pylos. Arguing from this negative evidence and from texts such as Homer's "Catalogue of Ships," many scholars have posited that Mycenae exercised some form of direct control over the Corinthia. For instance, Salmon (1984:17–18) concludes:

The rich coastal plain was an obvious target for the rulers of Mycenae for its own sake; when the vital geographical position of the Isthmus is added to the equation, it is impossible to believe that the inhabitants of the Corinthia, settled as they were in numerous small and mostly defenceless communities, were able to retain their political independence. That does not of itself imply that they were drawn fully into the economic system of the Mycenaean palace; but if they were not, contemporary pressures would probably have created in the Isthmus region a dependent prince similar to those of Tiryns. The absence of a suitable centre for even such a ruler makes it probable that the Corinthia was directly exploited from Mycenae. The evidence of comparative wealth at Corinth and at Korakou probably marks the dwellings of subordinate officials of the Mycenaean kings.

We may recognize in these ruminations an Argolid- and mainland-centric perspective on the expansion of influence into the northern Corinthia. Rutter (2003)

FIGURE 14.1 Map of sites in the Saronic Gulf, Corinthia, and Argolid discussed in the text.

emphasizes the role of Mycenae in the recolonization of the Corinthian interior at sites such as Tsoungiza and Zygouries in the early Late Bronze Age, as demonstrated by excavations at these sites and by the Nemea Valley Archaeological Project, but the extension of control further to the north and east remains unproven. In the most comprehensive summary of Mycenaean activity in the Corinthia, Morgan (1999:347–367) maintains an Argolid/mainland-centric viewpoint, accepting the close relationship of Mycenae and the southwestern Corinthia, while cautioning against extending this control to the Corinthian coastal plain.

This formulation of the problem as simply one of degree of orientation toward the Argolid was, we admit, our initial approach to the Late Bronze Age Corinthia. After all, the Corinthia was indeed a part of Late Bronze Age Mycenaean culture; that much is clear from material culture such as ceramics. Mycenae began its expansion into the southwestern Corinthia at least by the early Late Helladic period. Excavations at Tsoungiza (Wright et al. 1990) and Zygouries (Blegen 1928) have documented the close associations of these communities with Mycenae. Both were resettled in the late Middle Helladic period, and their ceramics are closely related to those from Mycenae by LH IIA. The extensive road system emanating from Mycenae undoubtedly facilitated control over at least the southwestern region of the Corinthia (Hope Simpson 1998; Jansen 1997, 2002). Mycenaean settlements, cemeteries, and buildings existed elsewhere in the Corinthia, as seen in the cyclopean wall at Perdikaria in the EKAS survey zone and the fragment of a wall reported at Korakou (Blegen 1921:98). Parts of the so-called trans-Isthmian fortification wall are certainly Mycenaean, and some parts are walls (see Morgan 1999:362–365, 437–447 for a thoughtful assessment of the evidence), though other parts are more readily explainable as retaining walls for roads of the Mycenaean period. The recently discovered tholos tomb near Cheliotomylos, just west of Ancient Corinth, appears by the finds to be early (LH I or II); the presence of this tholos indicates one elite group asserting its presence early in the Late Bronze Age, but there is no evidence that this elite was successful in creating long-term control over any portion of the Northern Coastal Plain. But no fortified citadel like those in the Argolid has yet been identified in the Corinthia, and this has led most scholars to accept the notion of control of the Corinthia by the palace at Mycenae.

There are, however, other possible explanations for the lack in the Corinthia of a fortified citadel like those

of the Argolid. It is significant that, in contrast to the pattern detected in the Nemea and Berbati valleys, settlements on the Corinthian plain such as Perdikaria, Gonia, Korakou, and Aetopetra were probably occupied continuously from the beginning of the Bronze Age, and some have long histories of settlement during the Neolithic. Such longevity of settlement indicates a fundamental stability in the economic exploitation of the region in the *longue durée*. Neither EKAS nor prior investigators have detected archaeological evidence for the kind of differentiation in site size or content that might reflect the type of hierarchical relationships inherent to palace-based state systems. Instead, there is the appearance of multiple, local hierarchies or possibly heterarchies (Crumley 1995; Haggis 2002; Schoep and Knappett 2004). Considering the case of Prepalatial Crete, Haggis has argued that such systems are well integrated, that is, characterized by a "multiplicity of linkages between individuals, sites, and the landscape itself" (Haggis 2002:123), and are perhaps the most stable adaptations to Aegean landscapes. In contrast, palatial systems display high connectedness through regional political hierarchies rather than local relationships based on traditional land use and other social and economic interactions. As a result, they break down traditional structures and tend to be poorly integrated and inherently unstable. A well-integrated, heterarchical system that is stable within a local or regional landscape has no inevitable trajectory toward hierarchical complexity and may be able to resist the centralizing tendencies of a well-connected palatial system imposed from outside. In these observations we see one possible explanation for the Corinthia's missing palace.

COASTSCAPES, MARITIME TECHNOLOGY, AND HARBORS

To break the traditional continental fixation, we must turn in the direction of the sea. We advocate a "coastscape" approach as an aspect of landscape study that focuses on the coastal zone. The coastal zone, including both land and sea, has a peculiar property in that it is in a sense linear, with the inland "border" being continuous with contiguous land and the other border being discontinuous land (islands or other coasts) with intervening (and usually continuous) sea. This is fairly self-explanatory. In this perspective, however, the coast is seen not as a periphery to the contiguous inland zone but rather as a separate zone transitioning between the different worlds of land and sea. This explains the "scape" portion of the term coastscape, but what is the nature of this zone, how does it relate to its land and sea borders, and how has its use by societies changed through time?

These questions recall Broodbank's (1989, 2000) work on island archaeology, and indeed his characterizations of islands in the Cyclades are pertinent to the Saronic Gulf. As he remarks elsewhere (2000:41), much of the coastal area of the Peloponnese and Attica (among other areas) is "quasi-insular." In the Saronic Gulf we encounter islands, such as Aigina, peninsulas, such as Methana, and mainland regions that, because of their geographic isolation from the rest of the Peloponnese, function as islands. In the latter category we include areas such as the Hermionid, with its off-shore islands of Spetses, Dhokos, and Hydra, and the Troizenia, also with its island of Poros. Even today, transportation beyond the immediate region from many of these areas involves sea, not land, conveyance.

Broodbank (2000:75–76, 102–105) also points out that Aegean islands are not isolated land masses surrounded by empty sea; on the contrary, few areas in the Aegean are not within sight of other islands or mainland. Inter-island distances are short, often shorter than the length of one of the islands, and the travel distance between coasts of two opposing islands is often less than that to traverse a single island. Such is also the case in the Saronic Gulf, which possesses the added advantage that it is for all intents and purposes an inland sea, and in clement weather functions as a plain, allowing for direct-line connections throughout.

Broodbank (2000:81–91) further emphasizes the small-scale nature of Early Bronze Age Cycladic communities, and how few would have had the resources to mount enough men to power a longboat. Too often we who study the Bronze Age Aegean lose site of this simple demographic reality: these communities were small, as were the larger societies to which they belonged. What to our minds would be a simple task, such as mounting a longboat expedition, would have exceeded or greatly taxed the resources of most communities in the Early Cycladic period. Similar demographic constraints probably prevailed in the Saronic Gulf region and in later phases of the Bronze Age, though some of the mainland territories, such as the Troizenia, were well watered by springs and undoubtedly were well settled. The discovery by the Methana survey (Mee and Forbes 1997) of numerous sites in all phases of the Bronze Age shows that even one of the more inhospitable environments in the Saronic Gulf could be heavily exploited and settled. Still, settlements in the Aegean were never very large compared to those elsewhere in the eastern Mediterranean, and the regions under consideration in this chapter are not large.

One of the most obvious ways to utilize the coast is through harbors and other access to the sea. One finds built harbors and facilities in the historical periods in the Aegean, but in prehistory they tended to not have built features and installations, and may not have had an attached permanent settlement. Thus the archaeological problem arises of what exactly a prehistoric harbor should look like, absent permanent facilities such as piers, quays, docks, moles, seawalls, and breakwaters (for a recent typology of Bronze Age harbors, see Chryssoulaki 2005). Homeric descriptions of harbors suggest beaching of ships on a suitable sandy strand, but these are not always available. The other frequently mentioned setting is a sheltered bay, especially adjacent to a peninsula-based settlement. Much speculation has been generated by the West House fresco from Akrotiri, but even in these depictions the harbors appear as natural settings, unmodified by constructions: as Shaw (1990:433) concludes, "a need for [quays] had not yet developed in the Aegean." One of the few potential built facilities associated with a harbor function is Building P at Kommos (Shaw 1990), perhaps echoed in the ambiguous building on the north wall fresco of the West House; but again this facility has not modified the harbor itself. Constructed harbors for Late Bronze Age sites have been proposed at Pylos (Davis 1998:69–74) and elsewhere, but these usually involve human-induced geomorphological changes to create a "natural" harbor lacking docks and other built features characteristic of later harborworks.

Because the scale of long-distance Aegean voyaging in the prehistoric period was moderate and dependent on variable weather phenomena throughout the year, permanent, year-round facilities may not have been in great demand. We are interested particularly in harbors that may have been used only episodically, perhaps primarily for small boats that went no further than several kilometers up and down the coast, or, in the case of the Saronic Gulf, did not venture outside this relatively self-contained inland sea. Although we must consider the full range of activities and associated structures, facilities, and installations when considering movement by sea, including observation or monitoring points, navigational points, and protective or defensive installations, we nevertheless expect these harbors to exhibit low archaeological visibility. Moreover, many such harbors will have been rendered even less obtrusive through geomorphological processes, including local uplift and subsidence, as befell Lechaion and Kenchreai, the two famous ports of the ancient city of Corinth, or alluviation, as in the case of Miletos.

THE CONTRIBUTION OF EKAS

The Eastern Korinthia Archaeological Survey (1998–2002), under the co-direction of Timothy E. Gregory and Daniel J. Pullen and with Thomas F. Tartaron as field director, investigated selected parts of a 200 km² territory east of the ancient city of Corinth embracing the broad coastal plain at the Isthmus of Corinth and the rugged terrain of the Saronic coast and uplands south of the Isthmus (figure 14.2) (Tartaron, Gregory, et al. 2006). Because the Corinthia is situated at a natural crossroads and node for travel by land and sea, it was inevitable that trade, transportation, and

interconnections would form an essential part of a landscape study such as EKAS. We conceived of the eastern Corinthia as not just the fertile coastal plain dominated by Acrocorinth but as a larger area that included the large Sofiko peninsula to the southeast, projecting toward the island of Aigina. Was this area a part of the Corinthia? This question, while appropriate to a mainland, Corinth-based perspective, misses some of the very issues that EKAS sought to investigate, among them the interaction of the eastern Corinthia with areas "outside"—that is, beyond the coast. Our initial design and fieldwork were inspired by the mainland orientation described above, but the discovery of two prehistoric harbor sites on the Saronic coast, Vayia, a fortified Early Bronze Age settlement, and Korfos-*Kalamianos*, a seaside town of the Late Bronze Age, prompted us to reevaluate our (main)land-biased framework. We turn now to data obtained by EKAS from both inland and coastal areas that allow us to address the absence of a palatial state in the Corinthia.

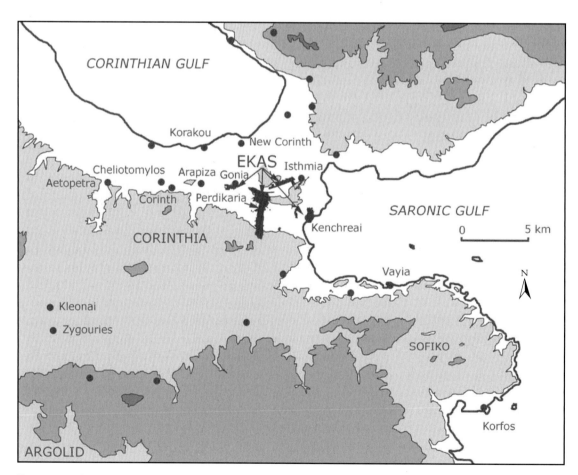

FIGURE 14.2 The eastern Corinthia in the Bronze Age. The EKAS survey territory is indicated. Dots indicate other Bronze Age sites.

The Northern Coastal Plain

Intensive survey performed by EKAS confirms a Bronze Age settlement pattern for the northern Corinthian plain that is characterized by long-term occupation of a few places (figure 14.3). This nucleated settlement pattern is perhaps an outgrowth of a landscape of several small Neolithic settlements spaced roughly equally apart, exploiting similar settings on the northern, uplifted edges of ancient marine terraces. Most Bronze Age sites are intervisible with one or more others in a string stretching from Aetopetra in the west to Kenchreai and Isthmia in the east. What is particularly significant is that the EH III and MH periods are well represented at many of the sites (Lambropoulou 1991:144), as is the EH I period, suggesting continuous occupation. This pattern is in contrast to those seen in the Berbati and Nemea valleys, Zygouries, and the southern Argolid, where there is a dramatic decline in number of settlements from EH II to MH—even abandonment, in the case of Tsoungiza and the Nemea Valley—indicating discontinuous settlement (Forsén 1992).

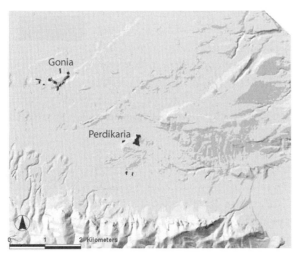

Neolithic

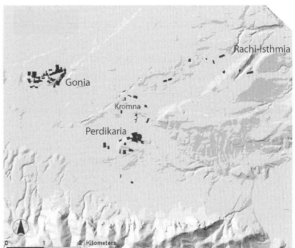

Early Bronze Age

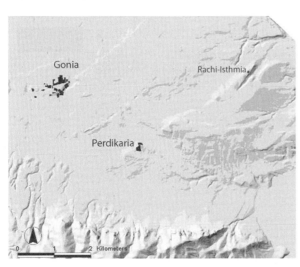

Middle Bronze Age

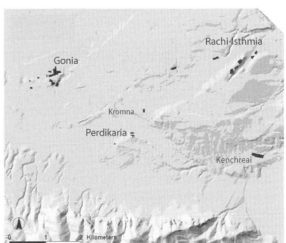

Late Bronze Age

FIGURE 14.3 Evidence for long-term stability and continuity of settlement systems in the northern Corinthian plain. EKAS survey units with ceramics identified to period are indicated.

Within this prehistoric landscape, the sites of Perdikaria and Gonia are good examples of long-occupied sites. At Perdikaria, material from the Middle, Late, and Final Neolithic periods was identified, as well as from EH I and II, MH, and LH periods. Only EH III material was not identified during the EKAS fieldwork, but this lack of ceramics identified as EH III may be accounted for in part by their low "visibility" in landscape studies and in part by limits placed on collection of material for later analysis (see Tartaron, Gregory, et al. 2006 for EKAS field methods). We would not be surprised if further work at Perdikaria produced material datable to this underrepresented, short period (circa 150–200 years). Gonia (Blegen 1930), to the northwest of Perdikaria, also has material from the Middle Neolithic through at least LH IIIB (but perhaps not from the latest sub-phase of the Late Bronze Age), yet the two sites are only 3 km apart. Korakou (Blegen 1921), occupied continuously from EH I through LH IIIC, is approximately 3 km northwest of Gonia, on the Corinthian Gulf coast. All three sites are intervisible. Such close, regular spacing of sites with similar long histories of continuous settlement and little indication of domination by one over another indicates a stable socioeconomic landscape, one that is well integrated, in Haggis's (2002) terms.

Coasts and Harbors

Instead of thinking of harbors and the coast as the periphery of a mainland-centered landscape, we began to look at the entire Saronic Gulf as a region of coastscapes, landscapes, and islands enmeshed in networks of interaction in prehistory. One component of EKAS was an explicit effort to model the location and use of harbors and the adjacent coastal zones in prehistory, using GIS, geomorphological studies, and archaeology (for details, see Rothaus et al. 2003; Tartaron et al. 2003). Our systematic search of the rugged and relatively unexplored eastern coastline of the Corinthia is one of the first such explorations in Greece. We located numerous small inlets that may have been used in an opportunistic fashion for anchorage in favorable (seasonal) conditions, and in a few cases we found clear evidence of exploitation in the Bronze Age.

Near the small harbor of modern Korfos, adjacent to a seemingly unpromising cape known as Trelli (Madness), the harbor model pointed us to the locality of Kalamianos. There we discovered a submerged harbor and a coastal town of the Late Bronze Age. Mycenaean ceramics cemented into submerged beach rock associated with tidal notches indicated local subsidence in episodic tectonic events of what had been a well-protected harbor of that period. On the adjacent land, architectural remains cover at least 7 ha. Much of this architecture exhibits a masonry style that is recognizably "cyclopean," typical of Mycenaean construction (Type III according to Loader's [1998] typology). This combined information substantiated our identification of Kalamianos as a major, previously unknown and unsuspected Mycenaean harbor. Atop a nearby hill is another prehistoric site, with evidence of FN, EH I, and EH II as well as LH remains, the latter again including characteristic Mycenaean architecture. A modern road leading up this hill has cut through a Mycenaean building, dated by a nearly complete tripod cooking pot that evidently had fallen out of the scarp. The view from the hilltop encompasses more than 180 degrees, from Attica south to Aigina, Methana, the Epidauria, and the southern Corinthia. This expansive viewshed is certainly one advantage of the site. Our discoveries in the vicinity of Korfos were incidental to intensive geomorphological work and did not occur in the context of an archaeological investigation. We reported these finds immediately to the Greek Archaeological Service and returned in 2007 to initiate archaeological fieldwork involving mapping of both surface and underwater remains, testing for archaeological deposits, and further geomorphological studies.

The search for harbors explicitly is a coastscape approach, for though a harbor occupies a liminal land/sea interface, it is also intimately connected with other, noncontiguous places. In searching for harbors on the coasts of the Corinthia, we also turn our gaze beyond the Corinthia to regions and places connected via the sea to our coastal sites, especially other harbors. This approach immediately broadens the region under consideration and increases the scale of our analysis from the Corinthia proper to the Saronic Gulf as a whole.

AIGINA AND THE SARONIC GULF IN THE BRONZE AGE

Viewing the Corinthia not from a mainland perspective in relationship to the neighboring Argolid but rather as part of the Saronic Gulf involves a change in scale and perspective. By adopting this wider perspective, we can begin to examine how the Corinthia interacted with, or was integrated with, neighboring regions. It is at this larger scale that we can more clearly model emerging polities in the Middle and Late Bronze Age.

The Saronic Gulf is essentially a small, nearly enclosed sea, in the shape of an ellipse roughly 80 by 55 km in diameter, with the site of Kolonna located nearly at its center. Standing at the site of Kolonna, or at any spot on the more hospitable northern and western shores of the island of Aigina, one is surrounded by land, with some water intervening—from the highest point on Aigina only about 20% of the horizon is open water with no nearby coastline. This is a phenomenological point that almost certainly would have influenced how Aiginetans perceived their world.

The Saronic Gulf has not often been considered a geopolitical unit, especially in Aegean prehistory, in large part because of the lack of identifiable palatial centers and the presumption that the coasts surrounding the Saronic were associated more with land-based polities than with each other. Despite our earlier criticism of reliance on Homer, it is interesting that in the famous Catalogue of Ships he identifies Diomedes' contingent as coming from Tiryns, Hermione, Asine, Aigina, Mases, and Epidauros—all ports on the Argolic or Saronic Gulfs—as well as from Argos and Troizen, both of which were close to the sea and had nearby ports (*Iliad* 2.559–568, trans. Lombardo 1997). Siennicka (2002) has recently drawn attention to the Saronic Gulf as a region, though she does adopt a mainland orientation in discussing the coasts as portions of mainland regions. But as she stresses, Kolonna on Aigina undoubtedly was the most important site in the Saronic Gulf.

Others have recognized the importance of Kolonna, including Niemeier (1995) and Rutter (2001), but they have not always identified explicitly the role of Kolonna in the emergence of Mycenaean polities, as we do here. By the later Early Bronze Age Kolonna had become, as Rutter notes, a very different type of site, one whose fortification walls were matched only by those at, perhaps, Troy and by the Middle Helladic Kolonna was a site "without peer on the mainland" (Rutter 2001:126, 130). The massive fortification walls, the widespread distribution of so-called Aiginetan ware ceramics, and the early shaft grave (Kilian-Dirlmeier 1997) all point to a major center of economic and political power in the Middle Bronze Age. Kolonna is certainly the central place in the Saronic Gulf, and the surrounding mainland, at least until the rise of Athens and Corinth in the historic periods.

The growing body of evidence from Kolonna indicates that, like Agia Irini on the island of Kea, Kolonna had major contacts throughout the Aegean in the Middle Bronze Age. Niemeier (1995) suggests that a Minoan-style ashlar block with a double axe mason's mark, reused in the Late Roman wall at Kolonna, indicates the presence of a monumental structure of Minoan style at Middle Bronze Age Kolonna. Such evidence as this, as well as the early shaft grave, leads Niemeier to posit that Kolonna was the first "state" in the Aegean outside of Crete.

As an island-based center, Kolonna undoubtedly utilized maritime technology. Some of the rare representations of boats outside Crete earlier than those in the famous Theran frescoes of the Late Bronze I period (see Wedde 2000 for Aegean ship imagery) are found on large jars from Kolonna (Siedentopf 1991). These apparently show rowed longboats, and one of those has clear representations of spears, suggesting a militaristic use. Wedde's (2000) analysis of the Kolonna representations suggests these vessels were among the largest of their kind in the Aegean, and despite the ambiguous depiction of propulsion methods, he links them to the sailing ships on the Akrotiri frescoes (sailing ships that are also paddled). Whatever the mode of propulsion used by the Kolonna boats, the symbolic meaning of those ships, whether emblematic or narrative (Wedde 2000:177–178), is crucial. Such visual projections of maritime technology provide, we maintain, clues to Kolonna's importance in the emergence of states in the Aegean.

When one considers the development of ship technology in the Bronze Age, the ability of Kolonna to dominate the Saronic becomes clear. Early ships of the third millennium BC were primarily paddled canoes or, in rare cases, longboats. In a single day, a paddled canoe could cover distances on the order of 10 km out and 10 km back (20 km in a single direction), compared to 40–50 km for a longboat, or 20–25 km out and 20–25 km back (Broodbank 2000:101–102). Thus Kolonna, utilizing longboats as its contemporaries in the Cyclades did, could reach nearly any part of the coast of the Saronic Gulf in one day, including the east coast of the Corinthia (figure 14.4). Moving beyond the Saronic, the range of longboats based at Agia Irini on Kea, a site approximately 80 km distant, or a two-day trip via longboat from Kolonna, would have just met the range of longboats based at Kolonna, at the southern tip of Attica, while the range of longboats based in the Argolic Gulf at, for example, Lerna or Tiryns, both ports during this time, would not have overlapped the range of longboats setting out from Kolonna. Kolonna may have had no meaningful competition in the Saronic Gulf, or any obstacle to control of Saronic coasts and

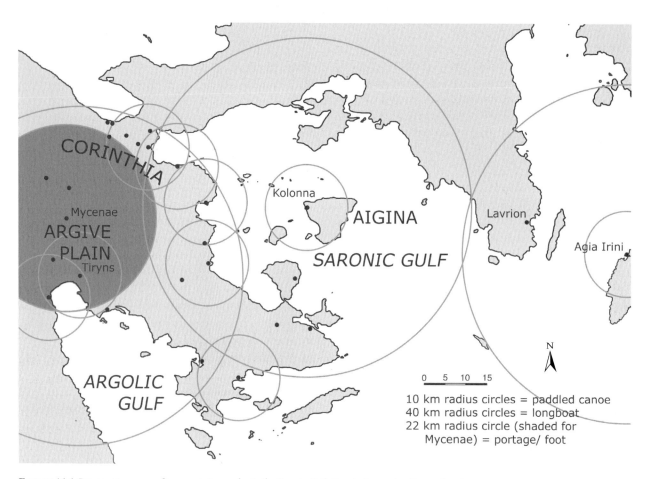

FIGURE 14.4 Comparative ranges of transportation modes in the Saronic Gulf. Dots indicate other Bronze Age sites

all maritime traffic in and out of coastal settlements. If so, no settlement in the Corinthia would have been in a position to gain control of trade with the outside world through the Saronic Gulf.

Kolonna's effective control of the Saronic Gulf undoubtedly played a role in the establishment of two fortified Early Bronze Age sites we discovered recently (Tartaron, Pullen, et al. 2006). One of these, Vayia, is a harbor site that visually dominated the entire western Saronic Gulf, including all the coast of the eastern Corinthian plain as well as southern Attica, the precise region that was not visible from Kolonna; the other site, Vassa, dominates one land route from the Epidauria to the northernmost harbor on the Epidaurian coast at Nea Epidauros. Vassa could be conceived of as a border settlement, perhaps as an outpost of Kolonna. While our surface survey of Vayia cannot answer the question of whether Vayia was an outpost of Kolonna (a position we favor) or whether Vayia was established to counteract the power of Kolonna, it is obvious that a mainland-based explanation limited by traditional conceptions of the Corinthia would not raise this issue.

Sailing technology, introduced to the Aegean apparently no later than the end of the Early Bronze Age, radically transformed transportation and communications. Though it is a replica of a much later sailing ship, sailing times of the *Kyrenia II* give us some idea of the magnitude of distances that could be covered by ancient sailing vessels. The *Kyrenia II* was able to achieve a speed of over 22 km/hour with favorable winds (speed of 11.98 knots for 5.8 hours over a distance of 69.49 nautical miles; Cariolou 1997:94). Voyage times in the Saronic Gulf under sail were likely reduced to a fraction of what they had been under paddling or rowing. Likewise, the new sailing technology would have greatly increased the distances achievable in single-day trips. And, perhaps more important, cargoes could have been significantly increased (e.g., the twenty tons of copper ingots on the Uluburun ship).

It is precisely at this time, the beginning of the Middle Bronze Age, that Minoan and Minoanizing pottery began to appear in quantities at sites such as Agia Irini (Davis 1979), Kolonna, and Lerna (Rutter 2001:124–126) and throughout the mainland (Peloponnese and central

Greece), Saronic Gulf, and southern Cyclades. It is also at this time that ceramic exports from Aigina began to appear in a wide region, indicating the extent of Kolonna's influence or at least connections. Our current understanding of the distribution of Aiginetan pottery indicates much overlap with Minoan and Minoanizing pottery, though the distribution of Aiginetan pottery is not as extensive (e.g., little Aiginetan pottery has been identified in the Cyclades; see Rutter 2001:127, figure 12). Though Attica, especially the mines at Lavrion, is often thought of as the object of the "Western String" trade route (Davis 1979, 2001 [1992]:24–26), it should be remembered that the Saronic Gulf is also easily accessible from central Crete via the same route, or via the small island of Velopoula (Parapola) between Spetses and Melos (Agouridis 1997:12) or from western Crete via the Laconian coast and Kythera. Two of the most strongly fortified sites of the Middle Bronze Age Aegean are situated near the ends of both branches of the Western String trade route, Agia Irini and Kolonna.

THE EMERGENCE OF MYCENAEAN POLITIES: COMPETITIVE FIRST-GENERATION STATES

The process of emergence of Mycenaean states is not well understood by any means, and most scholars today would not assume a single path to complexity. Apart from the Pylian kingdom, documented in some of its operations through the Linear B archives from the palace and known through the University of Minnesota Messenia Expedition and the Pylos Regional Archaeological Project, we have little understanding of the internal dynamics or development of Mycenaean polities. These processes are particularly perplexing in the Argive Plain, given the numerous fortified citadels, some of which exhibit all the trappings of being centers in their own right (e.g., Tiryns, Midea). In this chapter we are not so much concerned with these internal dynamics as we are with the emergence or nonemergence of Mycenaean states in particular regions.

Parkinson and Galaty (2007), following Marcus's Dynamic Model of archaic states (Marcus 1998b), make important methodological distinctions between primary or "pristine" and secondary states, and among first-, second-, and third-generation states. In this model, the crucial factor is not whether a state is primary or secondary, but whether it is of the first generation in a

region. Mycenaean states developed on the periphery of and later than Minoan states, which themselves developed on the periphery of and later than those of the eastern Mediterranean, and thus both by definition are secondary states. But by considering them as first-generation states in their regions, we can better examine the processes for the emergence of either Minoan or Mycenaean states. Sufficient for our purposes here is to accept the establishment of multiple Minoan states on Crete, perhaps with competing interests throughout the Aegean and Mediterranean.

The evidence from Kolonna indicates that it was one of the earliest first-generation states outside of Minoan Crete: the extensive trade networks, domination of the Saronic Gulf, the early shaft grave, the monumental fortifications, and the proposed Minoan-style (monumental?) building all point to this. Kolonna's sphere of influence (using as a minimum the one-day 40 km longboat range) is also on the route from the Lavrion metal sources to the Argive Plain. Kolonna's development into a state occurs in the Middle Bronze Age, slightly later than the emergence of polities on Crete.

Less clear as a candidate for state-level status is Agia Irini, the most important site on the Western String of islands leading from central Crete to the Lavrion metal deposits. Minoan influence, including Linear A administrative documents and Minoan metrology, is certainly apparent, but whether this Minoan influence indicates Minoan control (as in the frequently invoked "Minoan thalassocracy") is doubtful. Rather, this is most likely an indication of the local elite adopting the "superior" technology and culture of Crete (Wiener's [1984] "Versailles effect").

By the early Late Helladic period, Mycenae had begun to expand its control from the Argive Plain to the southwestern Corinthia, as seen in Argive LH IIA pottery at Tsoungiza and Zygouries. Though Mycenae was apparently not the only center to develop in the Argive Plain, its ability to mobilize wealth, as seen in the Shaft Graves, outstripped the ability of other centers in the Argive Plain to do the same (Voutsaki 1995a; Wright 1995a). Mycenae was perhaps able to convert a regional staple-finance-based economy into a tributary or wealth-financed economy in large part because of its control of these agricultural lands. As Parkinson and Galaty (2007; see also chapter 1) note, Mycenaean states utilized a network system of political economy (Blanton et al. 1996), whereby individuals in power monopolize access to exchange relationships involving prestige goods and knowledge.

Mycenae did not have to use the Western String for transport to or from Crete; western Crete was readily accessible via the Laconian coast, Kythera, and Antikythera. Using the longboat's one-day distance of 40 km, the entire Argolic Gulf would lie within the territory of the ports of Tiryns, Nauplion, Asine, or Lerna. Sailing technology, however, would increase the distances achievable in a single day. While Kolonna was well situated to control the Saronic Gulf, it was not well situated to control areas beyond. It would have been quite feasible for ships sailing from the Argolic Gulf toward the east coast of Attica (the area of Lavrion) or Agia Irini to completely bypass the Saronic Gulf. Likewise, it would have been quite feasible for ships to sail directly to central Crete via the string of islets stretching from Spetses to Melos.

The scale and size of Mycenaean states are pertinent to this discussion. Renfrew (1975, 1987) suggested territories of circa 1500 km^2 (circa 22 km radius) for his Early State Modules (a term now supplanted by "archaic state"), an estimate based in part on Minoan Crete

and Mycenaean Greece. This territorial extent also approximates the estimated distance covered by human or animal portage on land in a day (20 km in one direction; a circle of such size would cover 1256 km^2). In the case of Mycenae (figure 14.5), much of a circle of 22 km radius centered on the citadel would be land, and a high percentage of that land would be either the Argive Plain or the Berbati/Limnes Valley, but would also include the Nemea and Zygouries valleys. Thus, within a day's walk of the citadel are extensive agricultural lands. A circle of 22 km radius centered on Kolonna would cover mostly water, with only Aigina, Methana, Angistri and southern Salamis within this orbit—nowhere near as much agricultural land as was available to Mycenae within the same size territory.

Defining territories using land-based measures is not, however, satisfactory for the insular site of Kolonna. As the sole mode of transportation for Kolonnans beyond Aigina was by boat, the longboat range of 40 km provides a better estimate for the size of territory reachable in one day. A circle of 40 km radius covers

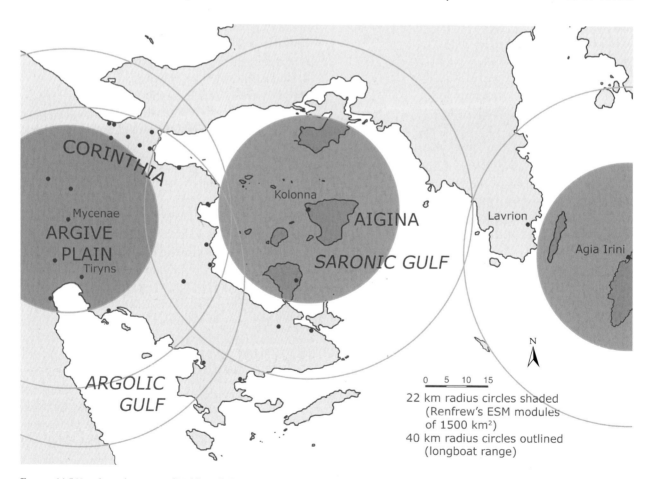

FIGURE 14.5 Hypothesized territories of Middle Helladic–Late Helladic polities in the Argolic and Saronic gulfs (22 km and 40 km radius circles). Centers have been identified at Mycenae and Tiryns (Argolic Gulf), Kolonna (Saronic Gulf), and Agia Irini (Western String/Cyclades). Dots indicate other Bronze Age sites.

approximately 5000 km², but in the case of Kolonna, about half of such a circle would encompass water, and most of the land would be at the margin of the circle (the mainland areas), beyond a 25 km radius. It is thus possible to suggest that the differing modes of transport available in the late Middle Helladic and early Late Helladic periods to Kolonna and Mycenae dictated vastly different sizes of territory.

The Corinthian plain lies just at the edge of both the 20 km straight-line distance from Mycenae and the 40 km distance from Kolonna—that is, it is not in either territory. Thus we should assign to the Corinthian plain the role of peripheral, not core, region. No single community in the Corinthia could circumvent Kolonna's domination of the Saronic Gulf to exploit external contacts (e.g., with Mycenae) in a bid to dominate neighboring sites. The site of Korakou, located at a harbor on the Corinthian Gulf, and therefore outside the proposed spheres of influence of Kolonna and Mycenae, is so far the only potential Mycenaean "center" on the Corinthian plain. In Blegen's excavations there were no indications of any substantial structure that could be termed palatial, though there are suggestions of a fortification wall (Blegen 1921:98)—but such walls are found also at Perdikaria and at Isthmia. Such walls most likely date to the later Late Helladic period, not to the late Middle Helladic/early Late Helladic period, a period critical for the development of states outside of Crete. The tholos at Cheliotomylos, while indicating the presence of one elite group early in the Late Helladic period, does not seem to have led to this site becoming a center in the later Late Helladic period.

Some evidence that the emergence of a state in the Late Bronze Age Corinthia was inhibited by a combination of local long-term stability and a balance of power between Kolonna and Mycenae may be found in the results of the EKAS intensive survey. In the northern Corinthian plain, Middle Helladic and Late Helladic pottery fabrics are varied in color and treatment, but most appear to be of local manufacture. Yet the similarity of decorative schemes and motifs leaves no doubt that the Corinthians of the Isthmus were well connected with the wider Mycenaean world, and rarely sherds are from vessels that were imported from the Argolid. Along the Saronic coast, at sites like Vayia and Kalamianos, a "Saronic" fabric tempered with volcanic rock fragments likely to have come from Aigina and Methana appears already in the later Neolithic and continues through the earlier part of the Bronze Age. Large pieces of andesite of Aiginetan origin litter the surface at Kalamianos and

other sites on the eastern Corinthian coast. Much of this stone may have arrived as ballast in visiting ships, or as raw material to be processed into ground stone implements. We may hypothesize from this admittedly preliminary information that the Corinthia maintained its strong local culture throughout the Bronze Age, while simultaneously feeling substantial influence from powerful states to the south and east.

CONCLUSION

In this chapter we have considered factors of scale and absolute size of territory, the effects of changing modes of transportation, and the stability of long-term occupation in analyzing the emergence of Mycenaean states in the Peloponnese and Saronic Gulf. Mycenaean polities emerged as competitive first-generation secondary states on the periphery of other secondary states (Minoan Crete). One factor not taken into account here is the appearance of other centers in the Saronic Gulf; a few early Late Helladic sites demonstrate features of elite political centers, including tholos tombs (e.g., Magoules, on the mainland at Galatas opposite Poros), while other Late Helladic sites have religious establishments (e.g., Agios Konstantinos on Methana, Apollo Maleatas at Epidauros) or perhaps even a palace (the Athenian Acropolis).

We offer two explanations for the absence of a Mycenaean palace in the Corinthia. First, the striking continuity of settlement at a few, nucleated sites in the northern Corinthian plain from the later Neolithic to the latter stages of the Late Bronze Age may be interpreted as evidence for long-term social and economic stability in a heterarchical arrangement, with no inevitable trajectory toward a complex hierarchical polity. This conclusion is antithetical to the evolutionary thinking that has dominated the discussion in the past. Second, any movement toward greater hierarchical complexity was simultaneously inhibited by a balance of power between land- and sea-based states, for which the Corinthia functioned as a peripheral zone. When we look beyond the mainland of the Argolid-Corinthia to consider the Corinthia as part of the larger Saronic world, we perceive that the domination of the Saronic Gulf by Kolonna prevented Corinthian communities on the Isthmus and on the Saronic coast from mobilizing independent access to external communication via the sea. It would not have been easy for Mycenae, held in check in the Saronic Gulf, to control events in the northern Corinthia by means of overland connections alone; however, the Argolid offered a "back door" route beyond the reach of the maritime power at Kolonna, which eventually was formalized through the LH III system of roads radiating from the citadel at Mycenae.

After the Bronze Age, the Corinthia developed into a center, undoubtedly because of its strategic position on the Corinthian Gulf with its access to the Adriatic and Italy, sources of the much sought-after new metal, iron. The sociopolitical landscape of Iron Age Greece is very different from that of its Bronze Age ancestor, and it is only in the Iron Age that the once peripheral territory of the Corinthia developed into a state.

Acknowledgments. We would like to thank EKAS colleagues R. Rothaus and J. Noller for discussing aspects of the harbor study, C. Ward for help with maritime technology, and W. Parkinson for providing a copy of Parkinson and Galaty (2007), as well as for many discussions of Aegean states over the last few years. Some of the ideas presented here were first presented by Pullen at the Mycenaean Seminar at the Institute of Classical Studies in May 2005, and we thank O. Krzyszkowska, C. Broodbank, and J. Bennet for that opportunity.

CHAPTER 15

MYCENAEAN NORTHERN BORDERS REVISITED

NEW EVIDENCE FROM THESSALY

🏛🏛🏛🏛🏛🏛🏛

VASSILIKI ADRIMI-SISMANI

THE EARLY TWENTIETH-CENTURY EXCAVA-TION of the two already known Neolithic settlements at Dimini and Sesklo, and their exemplary publication by Christos Tsountas (1968 [1908]), helped focus archaeological research in Thessaly on the Neolithic period (*La Thessalie* 1994, I). Research into the Mycenaean civilization of Thessaly was restricted. However, of the excavations that continued, the most important were those conducted by Verdelis at Pteleos (Verdelis 1952, 1953, 1954) and those conducted by Theocharis at the Kastro of Volos (Theocharis 1956, 1957, 1960a, 1961; cf. Batziou-Eustathiou 1998).

Until recently, Thessaly was considered part of the periphery of the Mycenaean world, while different opinions were expressed about its relations to the Mycenaean palatial centers of southern Greece. Specifically, it was claimed that the Mycenaean habitation of Thessaly, which began in LH II and flourished in LH III, had only a commercial character and that these settlements were abandoned after the collapse of the Mycenaean civilization (Wace and Thompson 1912:155). Hansen (1933:107) claimed that the Mycenaean period in Thessaly was a period of decline. So, until the 1990s, Thessaly was not included in the Mycenaean world. In her review of the palatial Bronze Age of southern and central Greece, Shelmerdine (1997:537–539) refers briefly to the finds from the area of the "Kastro" of

Volos and follows the northern limit of Mycenaean geographic scope as defined in Rutter's review of the Prepalatial Bronze Age. Rutter (1993:758) draws a border that extends from the mouth of the Spercheios River in the east to the southeastern corner of the Gulf of Arta in the west. Feuer identified, in 1983 and again in 1994, about one hundred Mycenaean sites in Thessaly and noted that 80% of the Mycenaean pottery was made locally. Despite that, in 1999 he still argued that Thessaly belonged to the periphery of the Mycenaean world, which he limited to southern Greece, even when he claimed that the area of ancient Iolkos had tighter bonds with the Mycenaean core than had other areas of the periphery (Feuer 1999:11).

Excavations in Thessaly over the past few decades have revealed, however, a powerful and healthy Mycenaean presence, an important, well-structured community that had been integrated into the Mycenaean world, and not just for reasons of commerce. Surveys indicate a large number of widespread, small settlements, without any fortification, continuing from those dated to the Middle Helladic (Hope Simpson and Dickinson 1979:272–298). Mycenaeans, according to Desborough, arrived in Thessaly from the sea mainly through the harbor of Iolkos (Desborough 1964:28). One group moved onto the plain of Larissa and thence to northern Thessaly, while another settled on the central plain of Pharsala. Surveys have been conducted in northern and eastern Thessaly by Feuer (1983:24–32) and by the Ephorate of Antiquities of Larissa (Gallis 1992), while the Late Helladic sites in the eastern and southern areas of the Pagasetic Gulf (plain of Pherae, plains of Almyros and Sourpi) have been surveyed and published by the IG' Ephorate of Prehistoric and Classical Antiquities in collaboration with the Italian Archaeological School (A. Intzesiloglou 1997), as well as by the Netherlander Institute and the IG' Ephorate of Prehistoric and Classical Antiquities (Reinders 2003). A movement of Mycenaean sites to the edges of the plains to the east and west has been demonstrated, while new evidence of Mycenaean material has turned up in southwestern Thessaly, in Philia, Kierion, Palamas, Agnantero, and elsewhere (Chadjiagelakis 1996, 1997, 1998:445–448), as well as in the important early tholos tomb of Georgikon (Theocharis 1960b:171; cf. M. Intzesiloglou 1997:478–480).

In this chapter, starting with the settlements located at the bay of Volos in the Magnesia district, including the important Late Helladic settlement found at Dimini, I show that Thessaly belonged to the Mycenaean world (figure 15.1). Actually, the area surrounding the inlet of the Pagasetic Gulf and the valley around the plain of Volos extending to Lake Karla (the ancient Lake

Voiveis) seem to have been especially well populated during LH III. Significant Late Helladic settlements have been detected in this area (Pherai, Aerino, Megalo Monastiri, Petra, Agios Athanasios), as well as in the area around Lake Karla and on the plain of Almyros (Thebes Phthiotidai, Magoula of Aïdinion, Pyrassos, Zerelia, Pteleos). Thus, we can assume that Magnesia during the Late Helladic was divided into three districts: one that included the settlements around the head of the Pagasetic Gulf, with a capital at Iolkos, controlling the harbor and plain of Volos, a second situated in the valley of Karla, controlling the plain and with Pherai as a capital, and a third controlling the Almyros plain, with Pteleos as a capital.

However, no Mycenaean presence has been confirmed yet at eastern Pelion, where myth places the reign of Philoctetes and ancient Olizon. A Mycenaean presence is, however, supported in the northern Sporades by, for example, a rich LH IIIA built tomb with *dromos* that was uncovered on the southeastern coast of the Sporadic island of Skopelos at Staphylos (Platon 1949); it had been built at the same time as the "Kasanaki" tomb that was revealed by the ring road of Volos (Adrimi-Sismani 2005). The tomb at Staphylos contained two burials and various grave goods (vases, figurines, beads, seal beads, bronze jewels

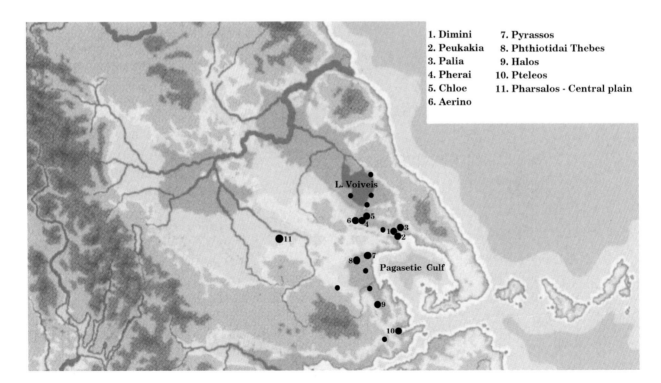

1. **Dimini**	7. **Pyrassos**
2. **Peukakia**	8. **Phthiotidai Thebes**
3. **Palia**	9. **Halos**
4. **Pherai**	10. **Pteleos**
5. **Chloe**	11. **Pharsalos - Central plain**
6. **Aerino**	

FIGURE 15.1 Map of Thessaly showing principal sites mentioned in the text.

and weapons, a bronze axe, and a gold sword-hilt). Another Mycenaean site was located at Kephala on Skiathos (Intzesiloglou 2000:350), which saw continuous habitation through the Neolithic and Early, Middle, and Late Helladic periods. Finally, our knowledge about the Mycenaean presence in Thessaly has been significantly improved by the excavations undertaken in Dimini, where a large Mycenaean palatial center has been discovered.

PAGASETIC GULF, ANCIENT IOLKOS

The Mycenaean settlement at Dimini

The Mycenaean settlement at Dimini was discovered in the last few decades and its excavation has provided a reliable picture of urban organization at a Mycenaean town in Thessaly. In particular, a rescue excavation conducted in 1977 east of the Neolithic settlement brought to light for the first time Mycenaean remains associated with the two already known tholos tombs uncovered at the end of the nineteen century and beginning of the twentieth century (Lolling and Wolters 1886; Michaud 1971:936).

Over the past twenty years (1977–1997), many additional rescue excavations have been conducted in the area east of the Neolithic settlement. Specifically, two Early Helladic strata containing sherd material and a vase, as well as deposits dated to the Middle and Late Helladic, were revealed overlying a Late Neolithic (Rachmani phase) layer (Adrimi-Sismani 2002). In addition, Middle Helladic architectural remains were uncovered on the plain lying east of the Neolithic site, along with Minyan ware, similar to the pottery that Tsountas had found in the Middle Helladic cist graves on the top of the hill at Dimini (Tsountas 1968 [1908]:126–152).

A Mycenaean settlement was founded at the end of the fifteenth century BC on the plain situated east of the hill. The settlement covered an area of about 10 ha and flourished during the fourteenth and thirteenth centuries BC, a period of expansion for the Mycenaean civilization (Adrimi-Sismani 2000, 2002). Geomorphological study of the deposits demonstrated that the sea had penetrated the plain during the second millennium BC, forming a deep channel, called "Iolka" by Hesychios. Zangger (1991) confirms this observation about the coastline during the Mycenaean period. Today, the deposits of the river Xerias have elongated the distance between Dimini and the coastline to 3 km. A few fragmentary LH I–II architectural remains have been revealed and associated with matte-painted polychrome ware of the Middle Helladic style. At the end of the fifteenth century BC (LH IIB), a large pottery kiln (diameter 3.80 m) was constructed to the east of the settlement, where a cist tomb of the same period had been found (Adrimi-Sismani 1999:131–142). The kiln was used until the beginning of the fourteenth century BC (LH IIIA), at which point the first buildings were built along a north-south road through the settlement. Between 1977 and 1997, eleven blocks of Mycenaean houses were excavated. They had been built in two main architectural phases, in LH IIIA and LH IIIB, as indicated by the architectural finds and the fine decorated pottery (reaching 10% of the total), which is quite similar to pottery from the Argolid.

Each of these houses covers a surface area of 60–80 sq m and is aligned along the road (figure 15.2). They are freestanding domestic constructions and, unlike the houses of the settlements in southern Greece, do not share walls. The first five excavated houses clearly had a domestic function and were built along the central road (Adrimi-Sismani 1994:17–44), which at that point was 4.5 m wide and paved with earth and small pebbles. The road was uncovered up to a length of 95 m. It is flanked by stone walls that sometimes serve as external walls of houses, thereby restricting immediate access, a fact that indicates that the road served other needs.

The rectangular houses are based on stone foundations and had mud brick superstructures. They had multiple rooms around courtyards containing wells. One house had a main room with a hearth and two smaller rooms at the back. On a fenced corner in one of these rooms a clay wheel–made painted figurine of an ox was found and perhaps an altar, finds pointing to the existence of a domestic shrine (Adrimi-Sismani 1994:31, plate 8). Many of the houses had rooms covered with white and ocher plaster. These rooms were used for storage, as indicated by pithoi, or as specialized working areas, as indicated by tools. All the houses contained clay baths; traces of a drainage system covered with slab stones were detected in several cases.

At the end of the thirteenth century BC, the settlement had a clear urban plan and a well-organized community, with central planning and craft specialization. Though it is difficult to estimate the exact population size, Dimini does offer the most complete picture of an organized Late Helladic settlement in eastern coastal Thessaly.

Plan of the Mycenaean settlement "Iolkos"

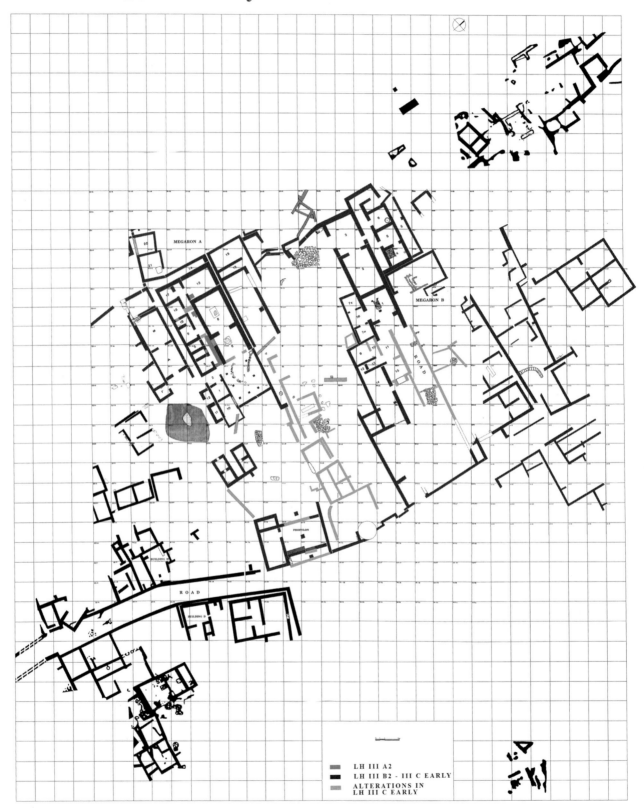

FIGURE 15.2 Plan of the Mycenaean settlement at Dimini.

At the end of the thirteenth century BC, after the destruction of the settlement, part of it was restored, but finally, at the beginning of the twelfth century BC, it was fully depopulated. It appears that the people living near the ruins made some repairs and then abandoned the settlement. Traces of this last phase, subsequent to the destruction, are difficult to detect, as modern cultivation has disturbed the layer located 0.20 m under the present ground surface. However, pottery that can be dated after the LH IIIC early period was not found, even in these disturbed deposits.

From 1997 onward, the electromagnetic research conducted at Dimini under the auspices of the Institute of Mediterranean Studies, led by Apostolos Sarris, has defined the borders of the settlement: from the pottery kiln to the east, in an area where possible workshops existed, to the Seskliotis river to the north (confirmed by Kambouroglou's geological research), to the Neolithic settlement to the west, and to the low hills to the south (Sarris 2001:15).

Systematic excavations conducted during the past five years have proved the accuracy of the geophysical research and uncovered a building complex of great importance, with two megaron-type, parallel buildings dubbed Megaron A and Megaron B (see figure 15.2).

These buildings possibly shared a common central courtyard.

Megaron A consists of two main wings of rooms divided by a long corridor and is framed by three wings of smaller rooms, identified as storage rooms (Adrimi-Sismani 1999:131–142). Megaron B was constructed in a similar way, with a wing of storage rooms running alongside the central megaron (figure 15.3).

The construction of this large building complex on the slope of the hill in a less prominent location is quite interesting, since no additional Late Helladic architectural remains have been found on top of the hill, except a small part of a building at the southwestern edge of the central court. This is probably a Late Helladic building, since limestone slabs of Middle Helladic tombs have been used in its foundations. Unfortunately, the first excavator (Stais 1966 [1901]) provided no detailed information, and no Late Helladic deposits were saved that could be dated with accuracy. However, the area at the top of the hill is not large enough to support a building complex of that size, and so it was placed on the slopes. The Late Helladic cist tombs found by Tsountas at the top of the hill in the southwestern courtyard (Tsountas 1968 [1908]:125–152) perhaps prevented use of the building of this area as an administrative center.

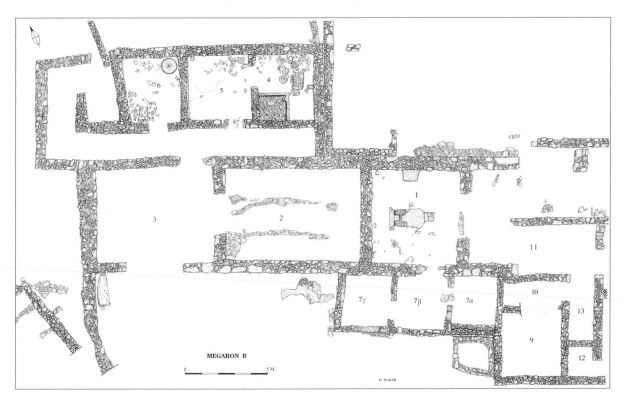

FIGURE 15.3 Plan of Megaron B at Dimini.

The choice of this specific area, the slope of the hill, provided control of the plain and Pagasetic Gulf and enough space to construct a complex building. After a large, flat surface was formed by cutting the slope, a new, complex building covering an area of 3000 sq m was built over an older LH IIIA megaron that had been destroyed by fire. The first large building, Megaron A, includes a central megaron, and its 1-m-thick walls could have supported an upper floor. These walls were covered with white and red plasters, while the floors were made of strong lime plaster mixed with pebbles.

The north wing of Megaron A consists of three large rooms and an open peristyle court with five or seven columns covered with white lime plaster, of which only the bases are preserved. White plaster that has been located on the floor only around the roofed peristyle indicates that the central area was open.

The south wing, contemporary with the north one, consists of ten small rooms that run parallel to the four rooms of the north wing and a large ramp that leads to a so-called waiting room before entering the central complex. The rooms of the south wing were used for the preparation and storage of food (rooms 4 and 5) and for small-scale manufacture of goods (rooms 9, 19, 18, and 17). Apart from pottery rubbers, ten molds and the necessary tools for manufacturing jewelry were also found. The most significant find in this wing with the storage rooms was part of a stone weight inscribed with Linear B (figure 15.4) (Adrimi Sismani and Godart 2005).

The roof of Megaron A was probably double-pitched and covered with clay tiles. Fragments of rough "tiles" with rounded corners were found on the narrow corridor between Megaron A and the wings of storerooms A and B, along with parts of a clay drain pipe; the pipe ends at a small ditch to the northeastern edge of a prostoon. To the same roof belongs a large clay funnel bearing intensive signs of use (Blegen and Rawson 1966:figure 171, 7–8; Tournavitou 1999:836). Megaron A therefore appears to preserve evidence of a central drainage system.

South of Megaron A is a wing of workshops where an intact large lead vessel was found. Another wing of storerooms was excavated north of Megaron A, where pithoi were found in situ.

To the east lies a small, freestanding building with four small rooms whose function is difficult to ascertain. It was probably a guard house. A propylon leading to Megaron A was located at the end of the main road that runs through the settlement.

FIGURE 15.4 Stone weight with Linear B inscription.

The second building complex, Megaron B, has the same orientation as Megaron A and the same structure (see figure 15.3). It is a central building with thick masonry (more than 1 m thick) that was built over older deposits. It had stone foundations and a superstructure of mud bricks, and consists of three contemporary rooms. To the east, a deep prostoon with two strong pilasters leads through a 2.80-m-wide door to a small prodomos where a large clay H-shaped altar existed with an elliptical low platform to the east (room 1). The entire construction bears intensive traces of fire and different layers of what may be the remains of burnt liquids. Behind, at the left and right of the base of the clay construction, two triangular mud bricks with circular holes were preserved up to a height of 0.40 m. A large intact painted mug found in front of the altar indicates that libations probably took place there, as do the cups with the remains of burnt animal bones uncovered in the three small attached side rooms connected by a small entrance (rooms 7a–c). In the easternmost room (room 7a), a bench built of stones is situated along the south wall. Behind the prodomos, access to the two large rooms (2 and 3) is possible only through room 3. It is difficult to understand why the prodomos does not connect with the rooms at the back, which are particularly large and were built at the same time. North of these three central rooms (rooms 1–3) of Megaron B lies a wing of storage rooms (rooms 4–6).

Megaron B was destroyed by an intense fire. The extensive and thick layer of destruction that consists of carbonized wood, burnt mud bricks, and burnt clay had not been disturbed at all until the moment of excavation and lies over an important quantity of pottery. In room 3, in front of the door that leads to the storage rooms, were also uncovered a large lead vessel, melted due to the severe fire, and a large Aeginetan tripod cooking pot, broken and totally burnt. Both vessels give the impression that they were pulled over toward the door at the time of destruction in order to be taken away. Also in room 3 many large fragments of wood were uncovered, remnants of beams that fell when the roof collapsed. The smaller pieces of wood have been identified by P. Kuniholm of Cornell University as olive and pine, while the main beam was made of a big oak trunk. The fire hardened the plaster covering the walls of the rooms and also baked the mud bricks of the upper part, which are well preserved in room 3.

The pottery from the destruction layer is in general typical of the LH IIIB2–IIIC Early period and is contemporary with pottery from the destruction layers in other Mycenaean centers in southern Greece, such as Mycenae, Tiryns, Pylos, Thebes, and Midea (Blegen and Rawson 1966; Demakopoulou 2003; Mountjoy 1997:109-137; Podzuweit 1978; Walberg 1998). This pottery consists mostly of fine plain vases, like plain carinated kylikes, shallow angular bowls, small cups, amphoras, hydriai, jugs, and tripod cooking pots. Among the decorated pottery are deep bowls of groups A and B, with paneled decoration and sometimes monochrome interiors, stemmed bowls, ring-based kraters, globular stirrup jars, round and straight-sided alabasters, and mugs.

Before discussing the issue of chronology, I will complete the description of this wing, which brought to light more important data related to its organization and function. In the storage rooms (rooms 4–6) were found a large quantity of vases. In storage room 5 were found drinking vessels for feasts, such as funnel-shaped or angular kylikes, cups, mugs, bowls, spoons, and askoi. These vessels, usually unpainted, were found on shelves, and clay analysis (conducted by K. Christakis, University of Bristol) showed they had not been used. Decorated pottery was also found in the same room, such as a spouted lekanis decorated with bands, an amphoriskos, a cooking pot, a large Canaanite amphora (Bass 1986:275; Shaw 1986:fig. 58a; Xenaki-Sakellariou 1985:134) with potter's marks, and a large unpainted stirrup jar. Storage vases for oil and wine were also found in situ in storage room 4, among them large piriform jars that were internally coated with wax (as determined by K. Christakis), perhaps to keep their contents in excellent condition; large unpainted kraters and hydriai; amphoras and smaller vases; kalathoi, and the like. Of special interest is a decorated rhyton (Mountjoy 1999:674–675) and part of an ivory comb, found in the same storeroom, along with wooden trunks, straw baskets, and specially paved rooms for the storage of fruits, as the carbonized seeds of olive trees and grapes show. Cereals (wheat and barley) were stored in storage room 6 in large pithoi placed in the ground and were poured using small clay scoops uncovered beside the vases. Some of the pithoi had already been removed outside of room 6, and maybe this fact points to an impeding economic decline just before the destruction. On the floor of the corridor leading to the storage room, two small tripod cooking pots (Tournavitou 1992a:201–202), an unpainted hydria, a large mug decorated with lozenges, an intact stone tripod spouted vase (Demakopoulou 1998), a rubber with millstone, and a triangular stone weight were uncovered in situ. A decorated lekythos dates with certainty this group of pottery to the LH IIIC early period (Mountjoy 1994:148). A large quantity of pottery was uncovered in a long room behind the storage rooms and mainly consists of vessels for food preparation and consumption. These vessels held traces of animal bones, fish, and oysters, and help identify this room as a kitchen. Food consumption or feasting may have taken place in rooms 2 and 3. It seems that in the kitchen, food was prepared in cooking amphoras and Aeginetan cooking pots, meat was grilled on spits (*krateutes*), and bread was baked on perforated clay trays. Cups, lekanis, and mugs were used in the next phase. The large number of kylikes, found scattered all over the place, indicates the consumption of liquids in small and large quantities, with ladles used to pour the liquids from larger to smaller vessels. All these indicate that feasting ceremonies which took place in Megaron B involved a large number of participants.

If the secondary rooms of Megaron B are easily identified as storage rooms or food preparation rooms, it is more difficult to identify the main rooms. Room 1, with the large clay construction at the center, the stone base, and the burnt liquids, may be considered a cult center, if the clay construction was indeed an altar and despite the lack of worship objects such as large clay figurines. If we assume that there was enough time before the destruction to remove the worship implements, then the small rooms (7a–g) with the stone bench and mugs containing burnt bones may have supported cult practices taking place in this sanctuary. Before the entrance to room 3 we uncovered a large limestone slab with cavities and in front of it sixteen small figurines, the position of which is reminiscent of cult activities and offerings.

The precise time of the destruction of Megaron A and B is fixed, according to radiocarbon dates from the Greek Laboratory for Archaeometry at the National Center for Scientific Research "Democritus," at the end of the thirteenth to beginning of the twelfth century BC (1292 and 1132 ± 34 BC). These destruction dates are similar to those from the other known Mycenaean centers of Greece. According to pottery evidence, destruction took place at the end of LH IIIB2 and at the beginning of the LH IIIC early period (Mountjoy 1994:144–145). These rooms were then abandoned. The inhabitants left the area and did not try to remove the debris, as they did in Megaron A, or to restore Megaron B. Instead, they built small rooms on a debris level eastward that were inhabited temporarily. In Megaron A, they closed off the prostoon, transforming it into a habitation area after building a hearth. They

also repaired its floor with inferior-quality plaster. This fact gave us the opportunity to study what happened in the Mycenaean settlement of Dimini immediately after the destruction. We have recently discovered that extensive repairs had been made throughout the settlement for the purpose of providing quick shelter to the people, and not just in restricted areas. That is why we see the secondary use of the large doorsteps (LH IIIA and IIIB buildings) and the quick construction of small shelters on top of the destruction deposits. Many small rooms were created in spaces that previously had not been used as living areas (interior courts), either through minor rearrangements of buildings that had not collapsed (Megaron A and propylon) or by levelling the deposits of the collapsed building and building small-scale structures instead. Obviously, the urban model has changed, since there are no large-scale buildings representing the settlement's administrative, economic, and religious center.

To examine the duration of the postdestruction repairs, we assembled the pottery from the floors of the reinhabited rooms and compared it with the pottery from the rest of the rooms that had not been reinhabited, as well as with the debris of Megaron B. The first conclusion from this comparison is that there is no chronological differentiation, despite the architectural repairs. Consequently, we conclude that the reoccupation of part of Megaron A and the new constructions took place on a relatively small scale and lasted for a short period of time following the destruction of the LH IIIC early period.

The second conclusion from the comparison is that in the stratum with the reinhabitation deposits in the area of the two megara, there are two pottery categories that are completely absent from the destruction layer. These are a gray pseudo-Minyan ware and a handmade burnished ware (Adrimi-Sismani 2006:85–110), which was uncovered only in the reinhabited rooms of Megaron A and in the open courts between Megara A and B. It will be interesting to see if we observe the same phenomenon in the area of the common houses. Pseudo-Minyan vases bring to mind the gray Middle Helladic Minyan pottery that had been manufactured at Dimini until the beginning of the Late Helladic and used through LH IIIA, although the shapes and manufacturing technique are different. They usually have a carinated body, and the usual shapes are the one-handled carinated kantharoi and shallow angular bowls and amphoras, while the gray Minyan kylix is totally absent. Dimini's handmade burnished ware differs from the handmade pottery manufactured throughout the entire Late Helladic period and used primarily in secondary contexts; it demonstrates new, original shapes and manufacturing processes. It consists of shallow carinated bowls with two horizontal handles and outgrowths on the lip, substantial vertical vases, vases with two vertical cylindrical handles at the height of the neck, shallow bowls with extremely carinated bodies and dotted decorations, and tubular vases with rope decorations that have parallels at Tel Kazel, also dated to the beginning of the twelfth century BC.

The majority of the Mycenaean pottery found in the same stratum with the pseudo-Minyan and the handmade burnished ware is typical of the pottery of the LH IIIC early period. However, some small differences were detected in the decoration of some vases that represent this period's basic pottery types, mostly the deep bowls of group A and B. Three categories of vases are observed that are slightly different from those that have been found in the destruction layer.

A first category consists of deep bowls of group A and B with external decoration, like in those of the destruction layer, and a monochrome interior, which for the first time now bears a reserved circle on the base. This feature is also observed at other Mycenaean sites of northern Greece, but they date generally to the LH IIIC early period.

A second category is characterized by the presence of exterior band decorations in deep bowls (FS 284, BE 25958, 25957) and monochrome interiors, but without reserved circles on their bases (the same is observed in stemmed deep bowls). Shallow angular bowls (FS 294) also belong in this category. They appear in this stratum for the first time bearing band decorations on their rims, bodies, and bases, without spiral motifs in the interior of the base. Spiral motifs appears a little later at other sites around the Pagasetic Gulf (Batziou-Eustathiou 1998).

In a third category are deep bowls with unpainted exteriors and monochrome interiors with unpainted circles on their bases.

These bowls coexist with the typical deep bowls of groups A and B, stemmed deep bowls, deep bowls with rosette decorations, the painted deep bowls that continue to be basic pottery types at the beginning of the LH IIIC early period, the kylikes, stirrup jars (FS 173), hydrias, amphoras (FS 69), jugs (FS 110), and the high globular alabastron and the conical bowl.

The pottery of the phase that follows the destruction is characterized by simplified decoration and, along with the pseudo-Minyan pottery and handmade burnished ware, represents the conditions that emerged after the destruction of Dimini's Mycenaean settlement: these forms imply an effort to mass produce simple, cheap pots necessary for daily life. Many theories have been proposed for the provenance of this pottery, which was thought to come either from northwestern Greece, the Morava valley, Italy, or Asia Minor.

To summarize these conclusions, just before its destruction at the end of LH IIIB2, the Mycenaean settlement of Dimini was highly organized and had an urban plan analogous to that of other well-known Mycenaean centers of central and southern Greece (cf. Adrimi-Sismani 2002), with which it was in contact, as indicated by similarities in pottery decoration and manufacture (within the so-called Mycenaean *koine*) and the exchange of products. The Mycenaean settlement at Dimini offers a reliable picture of the urban organization of Mycenaean settlements in Thessaly. Small organizational differences can be noted from place to place, but there was also the intention to mark social rank through the construction of a central, large-scale complex that combined habitation areas, spaces for storing agricultural products (and products acquired through exchange), craft production (e.g., metal and ivory workshops), and sacred spaces. The settlement at Dimini combines all the features of an administrative, financial, and religious center, and consequently it is the only settlement in Thessaly that clearly displays organizational and social elements (such as social ranking) of a true center. A ruling class that had knowledge of Linear B and was in touch with the rest of the Mycenaean world—with which there were exchanges, as attested by the raw materials (ivory stone-seals), Canaanite amphoras, the large stirrup jars, and so forth—lived in this complex. A whole city developed around it, with central planning and social ranking. The settlement's economy was based on intensive cultivation, animal breeding, and organized artisanship. The extremely fertile plain of Dimini and the low hills south of the settlement favored the development of agriculture and pastoralism. Artisanal pottery production and specialized workshops supported trade exchanges. Artisan activities inside the complex are indicated by grinding stones and molds, specifically by a double-faced mold (Reinholdt 1987:8–10, figure 2e) found along with all the necessary implements for jewelry production. Finally, although we have not yet discovered a Linear B archive, the Linear B specimen we do have shows that writing was in use during the Mycenaean period at Dimini, and indicates the presence of an accounting system that monitored the movement of products manufactured in the complex. The early presence of a megaron, from the end of the fifteenth century BC, connected with the Dimini A ("Lamiospito") tholos tomb, proves that from an early period there was a local ruling class in Dimini, as is found also at the other neighboring Mycenaean settlements—Pevkakia and Kastro Volos (Palia) (Batziou-Eustathiou 1998)—which were founded at the same time as Dimini near the inlet of the Pagasetic Gulf. The Mycenaean center of Dimini developed at the northern edge of the Mycenaean world and, along with the sites of Pevkakia and Kastro Volos (Palia), functioned together to control maritime communications and trade with the rest of the Aegean, as well as the exchange of the products of the Thessalian plain.

The Mycenaean settlements at Pevkakia and the Kastro of Volos

At Pevkakia, a coastal Mycenaean settlement has been investigated (see figure 15.1). Scholars have interpreted this settlement as the protected harbor of ancient Iolkos. Theocharis identified this site with Mycenaean Neleia, founded by Neleus, brother of Pelias and Aeson (Theocharis 1957:65). A continuous occupation has been observed from the Recent Neolithic to LH IIIB2, at the end of which the settlement was abandoned. Four typical LH IIIA2–IIIC houses and an LH IIB–IIIA1 cemetery have been found in that area (Batziou-Eusthatiou 1998; Wolters 1889:262). Pevkakia's settlement was abandoned at the same time as Dimini, at the LH IIIB2–IIIC early period.

The Mycenaean settlement at Kastro Volos (Palia) (see figure 15.1) is located at the entrance to the modern town of Volos, a short distance from the sea. Like Dimini, it was founded at the end of the fifteenth century BC, above rich Middle Helladic deposits. The area was identified in 1901 by Tsountas with the Mycenaean Iolkos mentioned in the *Iliad*'s "Catalogue of Ships" (Tsountas 1901). In 1911, Arvanitopoulos made reference to Mycenaean ruins. In 1956, Theocharis started a systematic excavation of the area that located parts of buildings from the fifteenth century BC that had been destroyed by a powerful fire. Because of the high quality of its construction, one of these buildings was identified by the excavator as the Palace of Iolkos, despite fragmentary architectural remains owing to later deposits above it, principally those of a medieval castle. There were two construction phases evident in this building, in

LH IIIA and LH IIIB2, when this second building was also destroyed by an intense fire (buildings: Theocharis 1956:119, 1957:54,1960a:49, 1961:45; tombs:/Avila 1983; Batziou-Eustathiou 1985:7–71, 1998). Of the three Mycenaean settlements in Volos district, this is the only one that was continuously inhabited, and it seems that after Dimini and Pevkakia were destroyed, Kastro Volos took full control of the plain and the coast of the Pagasetic Gulf. It seems very probable that, at the end of the twelfth century BC, segments of the populations from the neighbouring settlements moved to Kastro Volos. The habitation continues at Kastro Volos (Palia) after the LH IIIC early period, and the settlement, organized along different structural lines during the LH IIIC middle period, seems to suffer from the outbreak of hostilities within a society where there is no single ruling family, as is depicted on the sub-Mycenaean "warrior" krater. This late occupation of the site permits us to observe not only the continuity of the Mycenaean tradition but also the simultaneous presence and coexistence of elements of the Protogeometric period.

It is obvious that the importance of the Mycenaean occupation in the area goes back to the LH III period, since the large-scale buildings found in the area are contemporary with the large tholos tomb of Kapakli, one of the earliest tholos tombs in Magnesia, which has been found to the north of the Kastro hill. This tomb is built on flat ground, with a northeast-oriented walled road. The entrance (stomion)—2.40 m high, 5.50 m deep, and 2.30 m wide—was found completely obstructed by two walls and stones, with earth filling the gaps. The chamber has a diameter of 10 m and its conserved height is 4 m. Pelon (1976:243) thought that this tomb was similar to those of Messenia and Marathon. A vase for burning perfumes and two other vases from LH IIIA were found inside the tomb, and they form a terminus ante quem for its use. Avila (1983:5–60) postulated LH IIIA (fourteenth century BC) as the main period of use, which continued until LH IIIB (thirteenth century BC), despite all previous publications that dated the tomb to LH IIB (Kourouniotis 1906).

In general, the beginning of LH III is characterized by the first construction of large-scale buildings (Kastro Volos, Dimini) and tholos tombs (Kapakli, Lamiospito, Kasanaki) in the area of the Pagasetic Gulf (see figure 15.9). In fact, except for a pyxis from Kastro Volos, there is no Mycenaean pottery in the area dated to the LH I and LH IIA periods, while this pottery appears in general throughout the whole of Thessaly in the LH

IIB period. However, reconsideration of the evidence shows that in all probability, during these two phases at the beginning of the Mycenaean period, we have matte-painted pottery, especially polychrome ware, which continues to be fabricated during the late Middle Helladic period and used in this area. In any case, the boundary between the last phases of the Middle Helladic (Adrimi n.d.b) and the first phases of the Late Helladic period are indistinguishable. What excavation data do make clear, however, is that at the end of the Middle Helladic, there is a rising ruling class, as attested by the 156 Middle Helladic tombs at Sesklo, the 18 similar tombs at Dimini, the 36 at Pevkakia, and the five or six found at Kastro Volos. Analogous architectural remains found at Kastro Volos and Dimini, as well as around the inlet of the Pagasetic Gulf, testify that this social class, which continuously and progressively adopted the new systems of wealth organization characteristic of the Mycenaeans of southern Greece, was able in LH IIIA to found great Mycenaean centers, as indicated by large complex buildings and the tholos tombs. This fact points to a smooth transition from the Middle Helladic to LH I–IIA, since the two periods actually merge into each other, with types of tombs and pottery having their origins in the preceding phase.

Archaeological evidence for the fifteenth, fourteenth, and thirteenth centuries BC shows that from the three sites developed around the port of the Pagasetic Gulf, which provided a safe entrance to the Aegean, only at Dimini have administrative, financial, and religious functions been detected and proved to exist. So, it seems that of the various local forces that from the beginning of the fifteenth century BC fought to dominate the Pagasetic Gulf, the final winner—in the thirteenth century BC—was the wanax of Dimini. He seems to have held administrative and religious power, and it also seems that he had his own "royal artisans" who served his needs and professional expectations, and whom he may have personally supervised. To supply his workshops, for example when access to raw materials was constrained, he did not hesitate to organize overseas expeditions. The memory of one such expedition might have formed the basis for the myth of Jason and the Argonauts, with laborers starting from Iolkos to search for raw materials along the unexplored shores of the Black Sea.

The evidence from tholos tombs

The power and wealth of Dimini during the fourteenth and thirteenth centuries BC is further indicated by the

FIGURE 15.5 The "Lamiospito" tholos tomb at Dimini.

two tholos tombs built near the settlement. The Dimini A ("Lamiospito") tholos tomb (LH IIIA–B) is located almost 300 m to the west of the Mycenaean settlement (figure 15.5) (Lolling and Wolters 1886, 1887). It has a dromos with northeast orientation (13.30 m long and 3.30 m wide), side walls, and an obstruction wall at its end. The lintel is formed by four stones. The entrance (stomion) is 3.60 m high and 2.85 m deep, and the tholos has a diameter of 8.50 m. It is built with rough limestone blocks of various shapes and small size, with small stones filling the gaps. The floor, made of well-beaten earth, was covered with a fine layer (0.005 m) of ashes and coals. A sequence of five rows of mud bricks (0.55 m high and 0.50 m wide) runs around the base of the tholos, and on the right side of the tomb, over a pit with four dog burials. The tomb contained burials, and among the rare finds were semiburnt jewels made of glass and ivory, small golden discs, and weapons of bronze (now in the National Archaeological Museum).

The Dimini B ("Toumba") tholos tomb (figure 15.6), built at the western foot of the hill with the Neolithic finds, is dated to the thirteenth century BC, a little later than the Dimini A tomb (Stais 1966 [1901]). It is also a

FIGURE 15.6 The "Toumba" tholos tomb at Dimini

large-scale tholos tomb. It has a dromos (16.30 m long and 2.30 m wide) with a northeast orientation and an obstructing wall 15.30 m in from the stomion. The lintel is made of three stones. The tholos diameter is 8.30 m and is conserved to a height of 3.80 m. It is made from a lower row of large stones and an upper structure of rough schists of various shapes, without connecting material. In the northern part of the tholos, a rectangular construction (3.63 m long, 1.40–1.60 m wide) has been found leaning against the wall, probably for placement of the funeral bed. According to Stais (1966 [1901]), the construction was covered with stone slabs lying across the side walls and a wooden beam across the middle. The tomb was pillaged. Small golden and glass jewels are among the rare finds.

Another tholos tomb was recently revealed during work on the ring road of Volos, at the locality of Kasanaki, in a Final Neolithic stratum that had been used for a long time as a cemetery. The tomb was built of an alluvial conglomerate material brought from the neighbouring river of Xerias. This tomb and the cemetery to which it belongs cannot be easily associated with one of the three well-known settlements founded near the inlet of the Pagasetic Gulf. The

tomb is situated at a distance of more than 3 km from Kastro Volos, and even further from Dimini, whereas a distance of about 1.5 km between a tholos tomb and its associated settlement is considered reasonable. The distance between the Kasanaki tomb and the settlement of Kastro Volos is, however, rather unusual. We must take into account that the four tholos tombs—Dimini A, Dimini B, Kapakli, and Kasanaki—are situated west or southwest of a Neolithic settlement. Perhaps this is not a coincidence; it may be that this placement is related to the worship of ancestors. However, only archaeological data deriving from the tholos tomb at Kasanaki provide evidence for local beliefs related to burial customs, since in this tomb a secondary burial custom has been detected.

Kasanaki's tomb was found intact, except for a part of the tholos keystone, which was removed by the digging machine. It consists of the chamber, with a diameter of 6.70 m and a height of 6.50 m. The stomion is 3.85 m long with an intact dry-stone barrier, and the partially excavated dromos bears successive coatings of reddish clay along its sides. The vault was built according to the corbelled system, with large worked schist blocks on the base, particularly rough stones in the superstructure, and small schist wedges in the interstices.

The monument has an imposing, monumental façade that reaches a height of 6.40 m. The façade comprises the entrance, the relieving triangle, a stone beam that bears seven incised symbols (four large and three smaller ones), and a monolithic slab with inscribed rosettes and volutes, followed by a wall and two stone slabs.

Four shaft-graves had been dug into the chamber's floor and covered with a thin layer of sand, followed by another thick layer of ashes mixed with carbon, carbonized wood, disturbed burned and unburned human bones, and parts of the funeral offerings (vases, jewelry, etc.). Traces of fire are observed on the walls of the stomion and the tholos itself. The central shaft grave, with an imposing 4-m-long covering slab, was found completely empty, filled with earth and sand, while in the others there were accumulations of human bones burned partially or even totally, burnt pieces of wooden planks, and remains of burnt funeral offerings (similar to remains found in small pits along the perimeter of the tholos).

Excavation data show that seven dead, five adults— one 40-year-old female, another 18-year-old female, and three males aged about 25–30 years—and two children, aged about eight years, had been buried in the tholos tomb, accompanied by pottery, gold, glass, and faience jewelry, one large gold finger ring with a bezel made of ivory fabricated in the cloisonée technique, more smaller rings, one copper dagger, gold and glass plaques, seal stones made of agate and rock crystal, clay figurines (*kourotrophoi*), and golden sheets with holes that had probably belonged to the decoration of the deceased's clothes or burial shroud. Copper artifacts are absent. In general, Kasanaki's offerings are similar to those from Kapakli (Avila 1983:figures 4–7; Kourouniotis 1906:figures 12–15) and Dimini A (Lolling and Wolters 1886, 1887). The similarities in the finds and the architectural features of these tholos tombs are expected, since all are located near the Pagasetic Gulf, where the Late Helladic settlements of Kastro Volos, Dimini, and Pevkakia are also located. Similar finds of gold and glass have also been discovered inside Thessalian chamber tombs at Megalo Monastiri (Theocharis 1964a) and Pherai (Arachoviti 2000), as well as in southern Greece, especially the "Aidonia Treasure," which dates to the same period (*Ho Thissauros tôn Aidoniôn* 1998). According to the research of P. Guerra (Centre de Recherche et de Restauration des Musées de France), the gold used for the manufacture of Kasanaki's jewelry came from the alluvial deposits of a river that has not yet been identified.

The key to understanding Kasanaki's funeral practices is the fact that bones of the same dead, as well as similar sherds, were found in different graves. Twenty-four decorated and plain vases accompanying the tholos burials—mainly piriform jars, alabasters, stirrup jars, one-handled painted carinated cups, one-handled cups, and kylikes—that date from LH IIIA1 until LH IIIA2 indicate that the dead had belonged to a ruling class and that the tholos tomb had been used for a long period of time, perhaps by members of the same family. Drinking or libation ceremonies took place immediately after the deposition of the corpse. Afterward the dead were put in shaft graves, which were then covered by either a large gravestone or a slab. It seems that there was the intention to re-use the tomb, and that is why they proceeded to cremate the disarticulated bones at 300 degrees C. The remains of the pyres were swept into the three shaft graves as well as into the small, shallow peripheral pits. The rest of this burned mixture was scattered all over the interior of the tholos tomb. During this ceremony, undertaken at the same time for all of the dead, people performed libations and burned perfumed oils in bowls that were perhaps put on an offering table. Eighteen plain vases—cups, angular bowls, and carinated kylikes—that date from LH IIIA

to LH IIIA2 were found above the burned stratum. We note that Democritus radiocarbon dates fix the two periods of use of the Kasanaki tomb to the fourteenth century BC (1520–1400) and the thirteenth century BC (1435–1330), respectively. In general, the tholos tomb at Kasanaki provides some evidence of local beliefs related to burial customs, since in this tomb a secondary burial custom has been detected. Similar funeral customs were observed in the contemporary Kapakli and Dimini A tholos tombs (Avila 1983:15–60, figures 4-7; Lolling and Wolters 1886:438–444).

THE VALLEY OF KARLA: PHERAI, AERINO, PETRA, AND AGIOS ATHANASSIOS

Leaving the Pagasetic Gulf and heading inland, we pass through the modern town of Velestino—the ancient town of Pherai—and the now drained lake of Karla, ancient Voiveis. The myth of Admetus and Alceste is connected with Pherai, while the name of the city is mentioned in the "Catalogue of Ships" (*Iliad*, B, 711–715). Pherai's plain with its low hills and the extended Lake Voiveis created a perfect environment for the expansion of Late Helladic settlements, as confirmed also by Homer: "οἳ δὲ Φερὰς ἐνέμοντο παραὶ Βοιβηΐδα λίμνην, Βοίβην καὶ Γλαφύρας . . . τῶν ἦρχ᾽ Ἀδμήτοιο φίλος παῖς ἕνδεκα νηῶν Εὔμηλος" (Pherai predominated in the region of the lake Voiveis, over Boibe, Glaphyrai, . . . where ruled Eumelos, the beloved son of Admetos, with eleven boats) (*Iliad*, B, 711–714). Recent excavations have brought to light many settlements around Lake Voiveis and on the plain of Pherai. They are of different size, and some may be satellites of a central site. In that case, the main settlement of the area must be Pherai, and the others probably constituted mainly agrarian settlements connected with specific crops (cereals, olive trees, vineyards) or with the exploitation of certain natural resources, such as those of the lake. Mycenaean Pherai contains high Late Helladic deposits found on the top of those of the Middle Helladic period. The site occupies a large area situated around the site of the Bakali Magoula and Kastraki hillock (Arachoviti 1988; Doulgeri-Intzesiloglou 1994; Kakavogiannis 1977). Recent excavations (Arachoviti 2000) show that LH III was a prosperous period for the Pherai settlement. Six LH III cist graves and four pit graves have been investigated around the Magoula Bakali (Arachoviti 2000:359; Intzesiloglou 1990, 2000). In addition, a group of seven intact chamber tombs, with *dromoi* and vaulted roofs, dating from LH IIB–IIIB (1400–1225 BC), with indication of intensive use during LH IIIA (1400–1300 BC), have been investigated in the area of Magoula Bakali. They contained many funeral offerings, such as necklace beads, bronze jewels, figurines, seal beads, clay vases, and the like (Arachoviti 2000:359; Intzesiloglou 1989:figures 132–133, 1990:figures 96–97). Pherai's chamber tombs constitute typical examples of this type of funerary monument, largely used in Greece from the LH IIA period (1500–1460 BC). Their modest contents assign them to common families that, however, lived in a flourishing society.

Not far away from Pherai is the Aerino district, situated on the low hills north and east of Dervisi Castle. A research project in that area found a Late Helladic settlement, built over an Early Helladic and Middle Helladic occupation, in a place with sufficient water, natural fortification, and at the intersection of the ancient roads that crossed the Pherai region (Arachoviti 2000:364–365). In addition, many LH III tombs—simple pit graves, cist graves and two rare rectangular built tombs (Arachoviti 2000:367)—have been excavated that belonged to a large cemetery of the Mycenaean, Protogeometric, and Geometric periods. Nine small-scale tholos tombs dating from LH IIIA to LH IIIC (Arachoviti 2000:367–368), along with tholoi of the Protogeometric and Geometric periods, testify to continual use of the area for funeral purposes.

Most of the Aerino Mycenaean tholos tombs had dromoi that had been carved into earth with mostly southern orientations. These tombs contained many dead, and most of them also had cavities from which concentrations of bone had been removed (*anakomidai*). There was a great quantity and variety of funeral offerings (clay vases and figurines, bronze and iron jewelry, glassmass beads, faience, semiprecious stones, gold, sealing beads, weapons), which points to a relatively large and important Mycenaean settlement.

A series of Late Helladic settlements founded near Lake Voiveis indicates population growth during this period. The site of Petra, situated on three hills 3 km northeast of the modern village of Stephanovikeion, near the shore of Lake Voiveis, demonstrates continuous occupation from the Middle Helladic to the end of LH IIIB, and probably also LH IIIC. A "Cyclopean" fortification wall, 5 m thick, that remains unidentified surrounds the highest hill (Grundmann 1937:60; Liagouras 1963). The site was identified (Hope Simpson and Dickinson 1979:280) with Homeric

Voiveis, mentioned in the Homeric Catalogue of Ships. Meanwhile, recent finds from the district of Karla testify to the presence of an important LH settlement somewhere around the lake.

A cemetery of small tholos tombs arranged in rows and close to each other, and dated to LH IIIA and B periods (fourteenth to thirteenth century BC), was investigated at the Koriphoula site, inside an occupation level of the Recent Neolithic and Middle Helladic periods (Adrimi-Sismani n.d.a). The tombs, which are 1.40 m to 1.92 m high and 1.50 to 2.50 m in diameter, are built according to the "ekforic" system, with rough stones and without connecting material. Their entrances were obstructed, and their dromoi had stone side walls and east-west orientations. They contained five to twenty dead, so families probably used them for a long time, as in Pherai-Aerino. The dead had been placed on their backs or in a semiflexed position and had funeral gifts arranged around them (clay vases and figurines, seal stones). Concentrations of the oldest bones (*anakomidai*) were found at the edges of the tholos room or in pits along the side walls. At the Tsigenina site in the Karla district, an intact tholos tomb (tomb I) was revealed, built inside a Middle Helladic house. It contained twenty skulls, an intact skeleton, many *anakomidai*, and funeral gifts (alabasters, jars, spindle whorls, buttons, and many beads).

Cist tombs belonging to a Mycenaean cemetery of the same period were also found in the area of Karla. The dead were lying in a semiflexed position, usually without funeral gifts.

In general, all these cemeteries are without doubt connected to the Mycenaean settlement that has been investigated on the northwest side of the same hill, beside the shore of Lake Voiveis, and perhaps also to the Mycenaean settlement on Agios Athanasios hill.

A group of LH IIIA and IIIB chamber tombs has been investigated west of Magoula Mega Monastirion (Theocharis 1964a). They have chambers and dromoi, and contain many rich finds, including vases, golden rosettes, golden beads, a clay figurine of a chariot (a funeral offering in a child's burial), jewels made of glassmass, nineteen double beads among many others of different shapes, a golden ring with a sealing-decorated surface, three seal stones, two pieces of an ivory comb, and many lead bars. Also to be noted are the ruins of a Mycenaean settlement that were found nearby, west of the Mega Monastirion village. The settlement corresponding to the tombs was almost certainly a flourishing center of Mycenaean culture.

ALMYROS PLAIN:PYRASSOS, THEBES PHTHIOTIDAI, HALOS, PTELEOS

Returning to the Pagasetic Gulf, south of the region of ancient Iolkos, we find a series of important Late Helladic sites. On top of a hill, next to the harbor of the modern town of Nea Anchialos, an important Mycenaean stratum of LH III (Lazaridis 1968:31, 1969:37–39; Theocharis 1959:59) has been identified with the ancient town of Pyrassos (Strabo IX, 435), mentioned in the *Iliad* (B 659). A little further to the west (circa 4 km) of Anchialos, on the Volos–Almyros road and next to the village of Mikrothebes (ancient Thebes Phthiotidai), figurines and Mycenaean sherds were found within a Geometric-period stratum (Arvanitopoulos 1907:166; Stählin 1906:5). In addition, part of a Mycenaean construction and Mycenaean figurines and other small finds were found recently in the same area. Between Mikrothebes and the modern town of Almyros, on the so-called Krokion Plain, pottery of LH IIIB was located in Magoula Aidiniotiki, along with sherds belonging to the Recent Neolithic and the Eearly Helladic period (Arvanitopoulos 1907:171; Theocharis 1959:60). Also, many Late Helladic sites have been found near Almyros. A bronze ring was found at the Magoula Almyriotiki site (Alin 1962:145), along with LH IIIA pottery. At the Magoula Zerelia site (Hunter 1953:33, 35), identified with the ancient town of Iton, excavations by the British School at Athens uncovered a stratum containing Late Helladic sherds (twelfth century BC). A carved LH IIIA and IIIB chamber tomb was investigated at the Mamalaiika site near Kato Maurolofos, northwest of Almyros (Malakassioti 1992). At the neighbouring Sourpi Magoula (Wace and Thompson 1912:10, no. 71) traces of a Late Helladic occupation were located. Finally, at the Voulokaliva site, a large cemetery was investigated covering from the LH IIIB and IIIC to the Archaic and Hellenistic periods (Malakassioti and Mousioni 2001:353–368).

These finds support an important Mycenaean presence in this region and point to important sites for future investigation. At nearly all the above-mentioned sites, as in the case of Iolkos, there are traces of earlier Middle Helladic occupation. The richness of the local Mycenaean society is indicated by the five tholos tombs found a little bit to the south, next to the modern village of Pteleos. They have relatively small dimensions, and four of them are built at the foot of the acropolis of Gritsa, near a tell containing remains of a Middle Helladic occupation (Theocharis and Chourmouziadis 1968:269; Verdelis 1953). The tombs date from LH IIIA2, and most of them were used simultaneously through the LH IIIC1 early period. The best preserved has a dromos with a northeast orientation, an entrance 1.85 m high and 1.02–1.20 m wide, and a lintel made of two slabs. The entrance is obstructed with a stone wall, while the tholos masonry consists of long slabs filled with earth. The tholos diameter is about 4 m, while its original height is presumed to have been 4.50 m. Bones and many other finds were uncovered, such as clay vases, seal stones, golden beads, beads made of faience, spindle whorls, ivory jewelry, samples of cosmetic powder, and two spearheads. Three Middle Helladic cist graves were found belowground in the interior of another tomb, while among the finds there was a small, sub-Mycenaean amphora and two Protogeometric oinochoai. Long-term use of the site for funeral purposes is therefore testified, as also at site three, which was used during LH IIIC and was still in use during the Protogeometric period. Finally, two pit graves of the LH I and LH II periods were found in the same area. They contained jugs, oinochoai, and other Minyan ware.

CENTRAL PLAIN: PHARSALOS

In the central plain of Thessaly an important Mycenaean presence has also been noted. The modern town of Pharsala is built on top of ancient Pharsalos, identified with the Homeric Phthia, hometown of Achilles (*Iliad* I, 155). At the Phetich-Tzami site there is a continuous occupation dated from the Neolithic period to recent times, with a Mycenaean acropolis and traces of houses over Middle Helladic ruins (Verdelis 1954). Important traces of occupation have been uncovered also near the site of Phyllos (Theocharis 1960c). Two chamber tombs with dromoi and a cist grave covered with a tumulus, all spoiled, also have been investigated in the region. They contained pottery and finds of the LH IIIA period (Theocharis 1964b; Verdelis 1955:135). Two small, built graves with dromoi that were investigated northeast of the village of Agios Antonios contained pottery of LH IIIC and an E-type sword (Theocharis 1966a). Finally, Late Helladic sherds were found at another seven sites in the Pharsala region (Tsini, Ktouri Magoula, Tsaggli, Gynaikokastro, and Rhachi).

A series of Mycenaean sites has also been reported near the modern town of Karditsa, like the Pyrgos Kieriou hill, identified with ancient Arne (Chadjiagelakis

1996, 1997; Theochari 1959:69). In addition, a large-scale LH II–LH III tholos tomb and traces of others have been investigated 700 m to the southwest of the modern village Georgikon, near the village of Tsaousi (Intzesiloglou 1997; Theocharis 1960b). Sporadic LH IIB or IIIA1 finds have been made in Sophades (Alin 1962:141; Hunter 1953:19, 159), while LH IIIB vases and figurines have been found at the Philia site (Theocharis 1963, 1965:312; Pilali-Papasteriou and Papaeuthimiou-Papanthimou 1983).

More to the north, an LH IIIA stratum has been uncovered at Trikki, near the modern town of Trikala (Theocharis 1966b). A tumulus found at the Exalophos site contained at least two Mycenaean cist graves. The pottery dates one of them to LH IIIC (Theocharis 1968). In addition, a cemetery with cist graves has been investigated beside the village of Agrilia, at Chasia, at the north end of the Thessalian plain (Theocharis 1968:293). Some of these graves contained Late Helladic pottery, along with locally manufactured pottery, and they date to 1200 BC. Finally, several Late Bronze Age IIB–IIIC tombs were excavated nearby the modern village of Agnantero, situated along the road that leads from the modern town of Karditsa to Trikkala (Chadjiagelakis 1998).

CONCLUSION

Based on observations from the study of Mycenaean settlements and the presence of Mycenaeans in Thessaly, and keeping in mind the Late Helladic settlement at Dimini, I argue that Thessaly should be considered part of the Mycenaean world. Surveys and recent excavations within the framework of large-scale public works have located many Late Helladic settlements, supporting the idea of a population influx in Thessaly during that period, during which new settlements were founded on the Thessalian plain (figure 15.7).

All of the settlements seem to have no fortifications, a fact pointing to a secure and steady social environment for the Mycenaean inhabitants of Thessaly. The concentration of population in sites around the Pagasetic Gulf emphasizes the importance of economic exchange, which must be considered as organized as that of the Mycenaean cities of southern Greece. Apparently, their economic system relied on trade and exchange, and also on agricultural activities and pastoralism.

The Mycenaean settlement at Dimini provides a reliable picture of the urban organization of Mycenaean cities in Thessaly. This settlement integrates all the elements of an administrative, financial, and religious

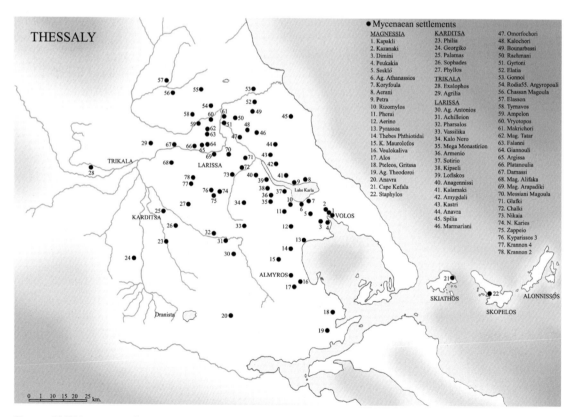

FIGURE 15.7 Mycenaean settlements in Thessaly.

center, and consequently it is the only settlement in Thessaly that clearly offers elements of organization and social hierarchy indicative of a true central place. It most probably functioned together with Pevkakia and Kastro Volos (Palia) to control maritime transfers and trade and the exchange of products of the Thessalian plain with the rest of the Aegean.

Since these three settlements were founded on top of rich Middle Bronze Age strata, there was probably continuous social development from the Middle to the Late Bronze Age. The settlement at Pevkakia must be considered a mere harbor installation, since no large complex or tholos tomb has ever been located there. As far as the other two sites are concerned (Kastro Volos, Dimini), the presence of a ruling class is confirmed by the large-scale building complexes founded in LH IIIA and by the occurrence of tholos tombs. Based on these structures, these three sites may have formed a political unit that maintained full control not only of the Pagasetic Gulf but of the Magnesian Plain as well. The settlements that developed on the plain of Karla and on the plains of Pharsalos and Larissa remained beyond the control of this center. Meanwhile, because of their dependence on the Pagasetic Gulf for trade and exchange purposes, we must accept that they were not as well organized politically as those settlements that developed around the inlet of the Pagasetic Gulf and constituted the center of Iolkos.

This center of Iolkos was destroyed in LH IIIB2, as also happened to the Mycenaean centers in southern Greece. Indeed, this same phenomenon also connects Thessaly to the rest of the well-known Mycenaean world. Habitation continued only at Kastro Volos (Palia) after the LH IIIC early period, and the settlement, organized along different structural lines during the LH IIIC middle period, seems to have suffered from an outbreak of hostilities in a society lacking evidence of a single ruling family, such as that depicted on the sub-Mycenaean "warrior" krater.

From the early Mycenaean period, the history of the Mycenaean presence in Thessaly is strongly marked by complex funerary practices and monuments (figure 15.8). The most impressive among them are associated with the tholos tombs, which can be divided into large-scale and smaller constructions, probably indicative of two different levels of social or political power. It is

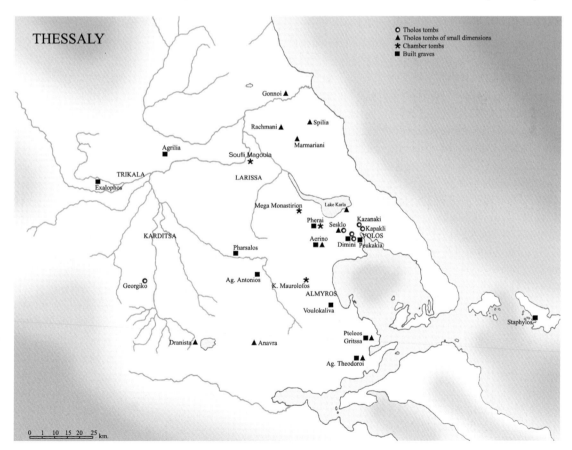

FIGURE 15.8 Mycenaean tombs in Thessaly.

FIGURE 15.9 Mycenaean settlements and tombs in the inlet of the Pagasetic Gulf.

significant that four large-scale tholos tombs—Kapakli, Kasanaki, Dimini A, and Dimini B—are located in the vicinity of the inlet of the Pagasetic Gulf (figure 15.9), the most powerful region of Thessaly ruled by Iolkos, and the fifth one is located in Georgikon, at the western edge of the Thessalian plain. Many other, smaller tholos tombs have been discovered in Thessaly (see figure 15.8). In particular, a group of ten small tholoi has been located recently around Lake Karla (ancient Voiveis), nine were recently found at Aerino, and five were excavated in 1952 at Pteleos, by Verdelis. All these tombs date from early LH IIIA to LH IIIC and were probably linked to single ruling families of those regions. Small tholos tombs continue to be built and used during the Early Iron Age in Thessaly, as shown by the examples of Pherai, Voulokalyva, Halos, Marmariani, Argyropouli, and Ano Dranista (see figure 15.8). The Protogeometric tholos tombs are of smaller dimensions, similar to the smaller category of Mycenaean tholoi. This continuity is also made clear by the fact that one of the Pteleos Mycenaean tholos tombs was re-used during the Protogeometric period, as also happened at Pherai and Aerino.

Chamber tombs are also located in many parts of Thessaly, as at Mega Monastirion, Pherai (Tachoula's field), and Kato Maurolophos (see figure 15.8). In the large quantity and great variety of funerary offerings found with them, these tombs bear similarities to the small tholos tombs, implying that the deceased individuals buried in the chamber tombs probably belonged to the same social rank as those buried in the small tholos tombs. It seems that the small tholos tombs in Thessaly replaced chamber tombs. In fact, compared with southern Greece, fewer chamber tombs were constructed in Thessaly. This is perhaps due to different geological and pedological conditions in southern versus northern Greece. Furthermore, built tombs with dromoi (Staphylos, Aerino, Dimini, Pevkakia) and cist and simple pit graves (see figure 15.8) with few funerary offerings were found close to many settlements and provide evidence of the burial practices of people at lower levels of the social hierarchy. The tombs normally contain inhumations, though there is one example of two second-degree cremations. The tombs were used for many years and may have been family monuments used for multiple generations, as made clear by the removal of the bones of the older burials.

In conclusion, Mycenaean Thessaly, apart from the humble funeral monuments of common individuals, displays the same social history as the rest of the Mycenaean world: the flourishing and subsequent destruction of a culture that reached a high degree of political and economic complexity, with wealth concentrated in the hands of certain social groups, which constructed important palatial complexes and impressive funeral monuments.

CHAPTER 16

RALLYING 'ROUND A "MINOAN" PAST:

THE LEGITIMATION OF POWER AT KNOSSOS DURING THE LATE BRONZE AGE

JAN DRIESSEN AND CHARLOTTE LANGOHR

INHERITING THE KINGDOM OF HEAVEN

FOR AT LEAST FIFTY generations—and probably many more than that—the site of Knossos had been a place of ritual gatherings and ceremonies of various kinds and a source of different types of power when, at the end of the Late Minoan IA period—variously dated to the end of the seventeenth or the end of the sixteenth century BC—its central building was briefly abandoned. Crete was going through its darkest period ever. The eruption of Santorini and its consequences dislodged Cretan society and decimated its population, destroying ritual sites, ceremonial centers, and entire settlements (Driessen and Macdonald 1997). When the (volcanic) dust settled again in LM IB–II, the ruins of the Knossian building were cleared away, its walls were patched up and adorned, and its storerooms were again filled with man-sized pithoi. Numerous workshops producing ivory, faience, and metal objects, as well as textiles, swords, and chariots, sprang up around the main edifice. But instead of priestesses, dancers, and athletes, dozens of officials wielding either a stylus or a sword (and probably both) now moved around the building, managing the daily business of palace, town, and hinterland, writing down their findings on clay tablets in a linear script not unlike that used before the troubles.

Perhaps for the first time in its long history, however, the building now served as the residence of a chief administrator who appropriated what seems originally to have been a religious title, wanax. The wanax probably yielded a vast array of secular and religious powers that emanated from, were legitimized by, and reflected on the building and the place. It was, perhaps for the first time in its history, a real palace, the abode of a living ruler. There are indications that this type of personal power originated before the final LM IB troubles (Drappier and Langohr 2004). The new regime paid considerable attention to military matters, and with good reason, since the palace and site would suffer a series of destructive events over the next two hundred years, perhaps following a separate sequence of events from the rest of the island (Hatzaki 2004:124). One of these events during the mature fourteenth century was more serious. During these years the building would, in one way or another, remain operational, gradually changing its appearance until it was finally abandoned to become a place of the past—a real p(a)lace of memory—during the thirteenth century BC. After six thousand years of continuous occupation, the focus of the Knossian settlement would relocate more to the north, the palace site perhaps becoming an *also*—a sacred grove (Coldstream 1973:181, n. 1).

This is where the power of Knossos lay, in its timeless history and grandiose past as a cosmological center for the entire island and beyond (Soles 1995). The new master of Knossos could see the signs and traces of this glorious history all over the tell: orangey Neolithic mud-bricks and incised sherds, sturdy Prepalatial terrace walls, impressive Protopalatial gypsum orthostats, and sumptuous Neopalatial ruined mansions. He who ruled Knossos could boast he ruled the island (figure 16.1).

This introduction serves to set the scene for the central thesis of this chapter, namely, that the local, "Minoan" past was used, during the advanced Late Bronze Age (LM IB–IIIB), to consolidate power as part of a strategy of legitimation in the formation and maintenance of a new regime that also appropriated the allegiance of the remaining or new elites by promoting a series of integrative mechanisms, which appear in both our archaeological and epigraphic sources (cf. Burke 2005). We use the word Minoan here consciously, assuming that, for the Late Bronze Age Knossians of the LM IB–IIIA2 period, the local past represented a specific identity marker that united Cretans of various regional and plausibly ethnic affiliations (Broodbank 2004). The term, of course, is as anachronistic as "Mycenaean."

TIME AND TABLETS

No discussion of Late Bronze Age Crete (LM IB–IIB) can avoid the question of the date of the final destruction of the palace of Knossos and its associated tablets (Dickinson 1994:21–22; Driessen 1990:5–7; 1997; Shelmerdine 1992; Rehak and Younger 1998:150, 152, 160). No straightforward answer is possible or perhaps needed. Arguments have been advanced for both an early, LM IIIA2 date (e.g., Popham 1970) and a later, LM IIIB1 date (e.g., Hallager 1977) for the final destruction of the palace. The latest generation of archaeologists working at Knossos seems to stick to Popham's date (Hatzaki 2004, 2005), although others would prefer a slightly later date, around 1350 BC (Warren 1991:36) or 1325 BC (Macdonald 2005:207). This would be the moment Knossos ceased to have an operational palace and workshops. But it was not yet the end of the building as such, since several of its rooms were cleared and used as storage rooms and cult areas during LM IIIB. It is possible that the palace once again changed function, becoming something like a temple estate, similar to *pa-ki-ja-na* in the Pylian kingdom. The town, too, continued to be occupied, although on a less impressive scale with respect to the quality of its houses, public amenities, and size (Hatzaki 2004, 2005).

That some Linear B administration accompanied this last phase seems likely and is implied by the presence of similar Linear B tablets dated to LM IIIB1 at Chania (Hallager et al. 1990, 1992). The Knossian tablets that belong to this phase deal mainly with textiles and the storage of stirrup jars (figure 16.2) (Haskell 2005). In view of the destruction deposits encountered, however, it seems sensible to date most of the other tablets to an LM

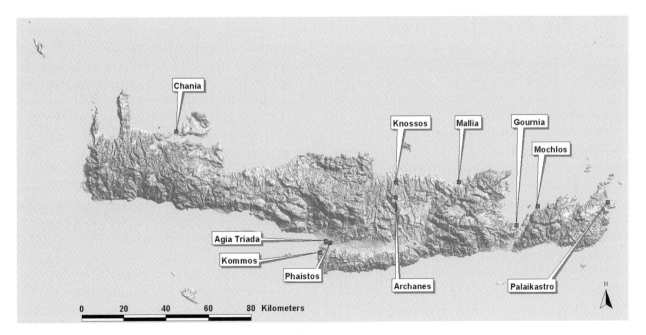

FIGURE 16.1 Map of Crete showing main LM II–III sites. (Courtesy of S. Soetens.)

FIGURE 16.2 Knossos: "late" Linear B tablet K700 with inventory of stirrup jars, the main type of storage after the LM IIIA2 destruction. (Courtesy of J.-P. Olivier.)

IIIA2 destruction, and to date a few minor tablet deposits, such as that from the Room of the Chariot Tablets, to earlier destructions in LM II or IIIA1, for which there is plenty of corroborative archaeological evidence (Driessen 1990, 1997; Firth 1996–1997:75, 2000–2001:154–281 passim; contra Hallager 2005). Information gained from the study of the Linear B tablets, therefore, can be applied to the entire advanced Late Bronze Age.

The stereotypic administrative system that was used throughout the Aegean administrative centers, whether on Crete or on the Greek mainland, suggests that the script and procedures, once invented, seldom changed or adapted to shifting regional or historical environments, although some minor modifications did occur (Driessen 2001a). In view of these different types of evidence, we argue that a wanax may no longer have been present at Knossos after LM IIIA2, or that he was demoted and perhaps became dependent on Chania or another center in south-central Crete (Banou 2005:157, n. 18, 169; Haskell 2005:esp. 215–219).

With the decipherment of Linear B, however, Mycenaean studies somehow derailed. Identity of script between Crete and the mainland quickly became equated with identity of language and, rapidly thereafter, with identical ethnic affiliation—all tainting henceforth the reconstruction of historical processes. Mycenaeanization, like Minoanization (Broodbank 2004), is a complex cultural phenomenon. While trying to avoid overgeneralizing, we suggest it is better to undertake a tentative reconstruction of Knossos and Crete during the advanced Late Bronze Age than to focus solely on the Knossos tablets or on matters of ethnicity. The term "Mycenaean Crete" is applicable only if we use it to describe a new cultural identity, without the implication of ethnicity. That said, if the presence of Mycenaeanizing cultural signifiers does not mean Mycenaeans were physically present, then the opposite must also be true: the physical presence of Mycenaeans does not mean that the culture cannot still have been Minoan.

ADOPTING AND ADAPTING THE BUILDING

In contrast to other "palaces" on the island, the building at Knossos not only was reused during LM II, it was also embellished on a scale surpassing earlier investments (contra Popham 1987). It remains unclear whether the building was not damaged at all because of an earlier abandonment or whether it was entirely cleaned out after a chimerical LM IB destruction. A series of studies have detailed the architectural history of the West Wing, showing how changes and modifications after MM II were always gradual and discreet (Begg 1987; Driessen 1990; Driessen and Macdonald 1997; Hallager 1977, 1987b; Macdonald 2005; Panagiotaki 1999). In LM II–IIIA1, the only real architectural change may have been the addition of the North-West Stairs, providing immediate access to the upper floors of the West Wing (Macdonald 2005:209; but see Driessen 1995:80).

One novelty that occurred during LM II was the use of gypsum for the embellishment of the building. This material also shows up predominantly in the construction of more private structures of this period, as in the Gypsum House near the Stratigraphical Museum or the Southwest House, where it is used in a Minoan Hall—again, a deliberate attempt to link to an earlier architectural tradition (Driessen 1999b:228–229, with more examples). Gypsum was used conspicuously for earlier constructions at Knossos (Chlouveraki 2002), but within the palace its popularity during LM II–IIIA1 is striking. The seat in the Throne Room is also made with gypsum and is likely to date to LM II (Driessen 1999b:229, n. 11). Gypsum, which was used for the production of monumental stone vases in imitation of the contemporary Palace Style vessels (Warren 1965, 1967), also appears conspicuously in two tombs that have been attributed to this period at Knossos: the Isopata Royal Tomb (Evans 1906) and in the *dromos* of the tholos tomb at Kefala (Hutchinson 1956; Preston 2005). The latter also yielded a Linear A inscription. Incidentally, brief Linear A inscriptions still occur in a few discrete contexts during LM II–III, almost all in funerary or ritual contexts (Schoep 2002:20; Whittaker 2005b:esp. 31).

A second significant innovation was the punctual decoration of the palace facades with fine limestone rosette friezes (Moser 1986:19–23) (figure 16.3). Antithetical half-rosettes and triglyph friezes—a new LM IIIA1 feature where stone is concerned—may have reflected earlier symbolism, as reflected by

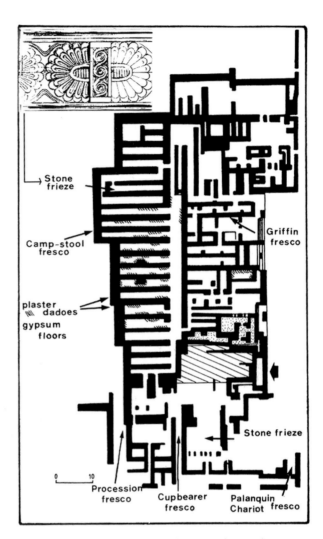

FIGURE 16.3 Palace of Knossos: major decorative scheme in the West Wing (after Driessen 1990) and stone frieze.

some miniature frescoes and sealings (e.g., Master Impression; see summary in Bietak 2000:37; Macdonald 2005:180), but in this context they adorned the major entrances to the palace and were probably emblematic of the palace of Knossos itself. The most recently identified fragments come from the area of the South House (Evely 2003:173), where they probably ended up as a result of the LM II–IIIA1 destruction of the south part of the palace. The motif was soon to be adopted by mainlanders, especially at Mycenae and Tiryns, both in palatial and in funerary domains. The benches in the Knossian throne room (Hood 2000:204; Moser 1986:24–25) were similarly decorated. This use suggests they date to the same early reconstruction, but it also underlines how gypsum and antithetical rosettes formed part of a single representational strategy (figure 16.4).

FIGURE 16.4 Palace of Knossos: gypsum throne with half-rosette frieze and griffin fresco in the Throne Room. (Drawing by M. Cameron. Courtesy of the British School at Athens.)

FIGURE 16.5 Camp Stool fresco. (Drawing by M. Cameron. Courtesy of the British School at Athens.)

A third decorative scheme, heavily influenced by the "Minoan" past, was embodied in the monumental frescoes. An important series of wall paintings has been dated to this phase (Hood 2000, 2005; Marinatos 1996). Most important, the West Porch was redecorated during LM II–IIIA1 with a bull fresco, repeating two earlier identical compositions on the same spot (Macdonald 2005:218). In view of its late survival, we suggest that the bull relief fresco adorning the North Entrance Passage also dates to the same phase. Bull iconography (Hallager and Hallager 1995) clearly refers to the past, as does the Procession fresco (including the Cupbearer), by repeating a scheme already attested at Akrotiri and later emulated in the mainland palaces. The Palanquin and Charioteer frescoes, which perhaps originally formed a single composition, seem to be more innovative, although the existence of chariots in LM I is attested in seal iconography as well. (Chariots would also form part of another strategy, discussed later in the chapter.) The Campstool fresco (including *La Parisienne*; figure 16.5), which may have adorned an entrance vestibule connected to the Northwest Stairs, probably also should be dated to an advanced stage of this phase. Some scholars have placed it even later because of the representation of a long-stemmed kylix (Hood 2000:206, 2005:62), but we assume the length of the stem to have been necessitated by the hand that holds it.

The fresco depicts a banquet scene, undoubtedly a common Cretan practice that was reactivated under the new regime (Borgna 2004). Indeed, some recent studies have argued that the earlier Cretan "palaces," laid out around a central court, were first and foremost monuments used for formalized religious and ceremonial practices related to storage and consumption in which rituals were performed by walking elaborate processional roads (Day and Wilson 2002; Driessen 2002, 2004; Melas 1995). The presence of fine ritual libation vessels in the Knossian Room of the Stone Vases, including some that date to LM II–IIIA1 (Driessen 1990:83–85, nn. 281–292; Warren 1967, 1969:132, 1979:106), shows that during this transitional period, the palace continued these types of practices, which are otherwise well known from the LM IB Treasury in the Zakros palace. Pictorial evidence from Aghia Triada, such as the *Piccola Processione*, possibly of LM II date, and the LM IIIA1 *Grande Processione*, reinforces the idea that similar practices remained important (Cucuzza 2003:205; Militello 1998:317–318).

Perhaps even more than in earlier times, the Camp Stool fresco shows that individual members of the elite were tied to the palace by the practice of communal feasting and banquets, during which meat sacrifices were distributed and quantities of wine were consumed. This is illustrated clearly by the importance of more distinctive personal drinking vessels, at first the Ephyraean goblets and later the kylikes, champagne cups, and kraters. The tablets provide clear evidence for such practices (see Killen 1994, 1998a).

Finally, the Griffin fresco and incurved altars that heraldically frame the seat in the Throne Room repeat Cretan religious symbols known from Akrotiri and, in fragmentary form, at Tell D'Aba, Tel Kabri, Malia, and elsewhere (Immerwahr 2000:485; Marinatos 1986:61, n. 15, 64, n. 71, 1993:154; recent reconstruction and references in Bietak 2005:89, plate 14.1; see also figure 16.4). The Knossian griffins are dated variously to LM IA (Bietak 2005:89), LM IB (Niemeier 1986), or LM II

(Macdonald 2005:116). We prefer the later date because of their overall compositional resemblances to pottery and seal designs of this phase. The presence of griffins on one of the short sides of the slightly later Hagia Triada sarcophagus has recently been interpreted along similar lines, as a symbol of royalty (Cucuzza 2003).

The fourth decorative scheme is the Palace Style (figure 16.6) and the monumental vases it adorns. The most common motifs—papyrus, palm trees, double axes, marine elements, architectural motifs, rosettes—had been used previously but were now placed ornamentally in an entirely new and different syntax (Hiller 1995; Niemeier 1985). The vases, in contrast to the frescoes to which they directly refer, had the advantage of being portable decorative devices. As with many other things, this style also would soon make it to the mainland.

The most impressive association of these four elements—gypsum, antithetical rosettes, monumental frescoes, and the Palace Style—occurs in the "throne room." Architectural framing goes back to Middle Minoan III times (Macdonald 2003:41; Panagiotaki 1999), if not earlier (Mirié 1979; Niemeier 1987; Reusch 1958), and rooms with benches are also well

represented in Cretan Protopalatial and Neopalatial architecture, especially at Haghia Triada (Kopaka 1990). But the inclusion of a special permanent seat that evidently was used frequently, framed by ritual iconography, is entirely new and would receive monumental imitation on the mainland in monuments such as the Lion Gate or on the fronts of some of the tholoi. Heraldic imagery was, however, already present in earlier Knossian iconography, as shown by the high-relief griffins tethered to columns from the fill above the North-South Corridor, dated perhaps to LM IA or LM IB (Hood 2005:75–76). There is thus no reason to assume this is an exogenous element.

The "throne room" does not turn the Knossos building into a Mycenaean palace either culturally or ethnically. The Linear B tablets notwithstanding, the building never was and did not become a Helladic-type palace, regardless of the date of the tablets or of the destruction of the palace. Indeed, where form and internal organization are concerned, it compares poorly to its mainland homonyms. Ashlar masonry, stone friezes, and frescoes are external embellishments that eventually would also characterize mainland palatial buildings. But these embellishments occurred only where a distinct, locally generated internal organization was followed that explicitly expressed the idea of royalty (e.g., Kilian 1988a). In Knossos, the latter is absent. This absence must have been intentional, since megaron structures or Helladic-inspired architectural arrangements do occur on the island from this period onward—for example, at Building A and B at Plati (Hayden 1987:211–213), the LM IIIA2 (early) Megaron ABCD at Haghia Triada (Cucuzza 1997; Hayden 1987:213–216), and at Building He at LM IIIB Gournia (Hawes 1908; Hayden 1987:210–211).

The throne room at Knossos, despite its name, is not placed at the end of an access system similar to the megaron in mainland palaces but blurs discretely into a Cretan and especially Minoan environment. Again, it could be argued that the building was adopted and adapted, but without changes to its traditional appearance and essence. It remained, or rather was turned into, a typical "Minoan" monument that now served as the hub of a newly established state system. Incidentally, 149 of the pithoi preserved in the West Magazines effectively date to this LM II–IIIA1 period (Christakis 2005:77), an observation that allows the reconstruction of an extremely dynamic actor. This stored wealth was incrementally used to acquire foreign metals and exotica, as we argue later. The redistribution, however, may no longer have served feasts for the entire society but only for the loyal elites (through banquets and gifts of weapons and costumes) and for attached specialist artisans who produced for the elite. In the following, LM IIIA2–B period, storage would be solely in large stirrup jars, as shown also by one of the Knossos tablets.

If we accept that the Knossos palace served as a rallying point because of its intergenerational power, then the massive investments made in the palace and surrounding town—in contrast to the squatter occupation that characterizes LM II–IIIA1 occupation at other sites—become more comprehensible. The power strategies they used allowed the wanax to use the place to legitimate his claim as the rightful heir to "Minoan" traditions—an amalgamation of various cultural traits that now were made distinctive. Local references to the past are similarly obvious and telling. For example, the LM IIIA1/2 constructions at Hagia Triada (the Megaron, the Sacello, and the Stoa FG) were deliberately placed over the remains of the Neopalatial mansion and developed around the earlier paved Piazzale dei Sacelli (Cucuzza 2001:172, 2003:204–222, esp. 220; La Rosa 1997:263). These constructions underline the continuing importance of various ceremonies and the importance of this part of the settlement as a religious and political focus of the LM III town. In fact, the LM IIIA2 Megaron ABCD at Haghia Triada uses several other elements blatantly referring to a Minoan past, including masons' marks, a specific type of column base in Room E, paving slabs set in mortar, a double window, and a gypsum bench with triglyph designs (Burke 2005:410). Quartier Nu at Malia, constructed during the advanced LM IIIA2 phase, has a central court—a Minoan idiom par excellence (Driessen and Farnoux 1994). At sites such as Malia, Kommos, and Palaikastro, to give just some examples, all reoccupation took place within older buildings, and new constructions are rare. In this respect, local tendencies repeated Knossian practices. This repetition occurs in other forms of material culture as well. For example, pottery studies suggest that local centers during LM II–IIIA1 imitated or imported contemporary Knossian vessels (Viannos area: Banou and Rethemiotakis 1997; Mochlos: Smith 2002; Kommos: Arvanitakis 2005; Haghia Triada: D'Agata 1999a, 1999b; Malia: Farnoux 1997; Rethymnon area: Andreadaki-Vlasaki and Papadopoulou 1997; Chania: Hallager 1990).

Many recent studies underline that it is not so much a Mycenaean influence that one should seek in the advanced Late Bronze Age settlements on Crete as

a Knossian or simply a local influence (Bennet 1987; Brogan et al. 2002; Kanta 1980:163–198, 2001:67; MacGillivray 1997:esp. 193; Smith 2002, 2004, 2005; Soles 1999a, 1999b; Tsipopoulou 1995:177, 1997, 2005:306). Sites such as Chania, Malia, the Mochlos-Myrsini-Tourloti area, Palaikastro, and those of the Mesara emulated and adopted Knossian features during LM II, IIIA1, and IIIA2. Knossos itself may have borrowed from a variety of sources, including the Greek mainland, Egypt, and an artificially reanimated and constructed "Minoan" past. With the palace of Knossos having been seriously damaged in LM IIIA2, Knossos also lost its position as an inspiration for the rest of the island, and local-regional traditions once again were reactivated.

FASHIONABLE IN FRONT OF A PHAROAH?

The aforementioned frescoes, especially those of the Procession Corridor, compare well with the depiction of *Keftiu* in the Tombs of the Nobles in Egyptian Thebes, especially those of the tomb of Rekhmire, where the codpieces of the tribute bearers were painted over with kilts so as to appear similar to those depicted in the tomb of Menkheperrasonb. Rehak (1996, 1998) traced the kilt to the Middle Bronze Age, so here, too, an old symbol may have been reactivated and given a new meaning, explicitly identifying members of the new Knossian elite (Driessen 1998–1999:88). Several authors have commented on the sheer number of Egyptian imports, especially during the LM II–IIIA1 period (references in Phillips 2003). Connections of different kinds existed between Egypt and Crete from at least the Old Kingdom/EM II times onward, and Egyptian stone vessels, as well as different types of raw material (ivory, gold, others), arrived in Crete (Warren 1995:12). Exchange intensified during the second millennium, and imported Egyptian artifacts corresponding to the Eighteenth Dynasty, are well represented on Crete. Phillips (1991) has argued for a change in consumption patterns after the end of LM IB, when the Minoans switched their attention to glass vessels. For the first time, jewelry and scarabs also appear, especially in funerary assemblages (Cline 1987; also Phillips 2005:456–457) of the core area, at Knossos-Sellopoulo (Popham et al. 1974), Archanes-Tholos A (Phillips 2003), and Haghia Triada (Cucuzza 2002; La Rosa 2000). Even the limestone sarcophagus used at the latter site is considered a reference to contemporary Egyptian practices (Burke 2005; Cucuzza 2002; see also Hiller 1999:esp. 368). In the advanced LM IIIA2 phase the number of imports diminishes, but they occur more widely throughout the island, and they no longer appear at Knossos, a sign that the place may have lost its dominant position and that regionally constituted groups now used a similar status package to express their identity (Cline 1997; Phillips 2005:457). It seems fair to assume that this craving for Egyptian imports implies that the new elite of Crete were looking "to forge new links with the emerging international superpower of the time: Egypt" (Rehak 1998:49). As such, it represents another means of distinction and a strategy of legitimation pursued by a social group, at first confined chiefly to Knossos (Cline 1987, 1995c:94–95, nn. 33–34).

EXPERIMENTING WITH DEATH

The information on Cretan Neopalatial funerary practices remains conspicuously unrepresentative to the extent that it has been suggested that excarnation or burial at sea took place (Driessen and Macdonald 1997:71; Marinatos 1993:231; Rehak and Younger 1998:110–111). A remarkable exception is represented by the reuse of Protopalatial tombs in the cemetery of the Knossian harbor town of Poros, where LM IA and IB burials are accompanied by what must originally have been relatively rich offerings, including gold rings, fancy pottery, weapons, and other precious goods (Dimopoulou 1994, 1999; Muhly 1992; Rethemiotakis and Dimopoulou 2003), that announce practices that did not become common until the next phase. At Poros, burials still took place within a Cretan-type chamber tomb that presented a communal character. But the attention given to personal ornaments represented a new behavior that might be attributed to merchants from the north.

During the next phase, LM II, pit caves, regular chamber tombs, shaft graves and tholoi were introduced or reactivated, and many of the practices were aligned with those on the mainland, especially in the Argolid (Alberti 2004), including individual primary burial, monumental architecture, and the deposition of specific wealthy assemblages that included an almost standardized collection of metal vases and weapons, seals, jewelry, and exotica.

This phase also saw the establishment or reactivation of a spatial connection between settlement and cemetery, which were linked by processional routes. This connection existed in earlier Pre- and Protopalatial times but seems to have been less important in Neopalatial times. Driessen and Schoep (1999) and Preston (1999, 2004a, 2004b) have suggested that the innovative mortuary practices found during LM II at Knossos are the result of active, strategic, and largely internally focused decisions of an elite that exploited the potential of the tomb for status display and assertion. They adapted and experimented with an ostentatious burial symbolism, borrowed from beyond the island, as one of the competitive strategies and opportunities available in the political vacuum left by the LM IB collapse. As argued by Niemeier (1983:226, 1985:204–216), many of the practices observed have indigenous Cretan antecedents.

Depositional practices and selectivity criteria operating in the funerary domain were henceforth also used as an integrative tool, made possible through the use of funeral processions and banquets (Perna 2001). Hatzaki (in D'Agata and Moody 2005:142) has also drawn attention to the possibility that ritual feasting (as indicated by kylikes and shallow cups) took place during LM II in the Temple Tomb at Knossos and may have been intended to deliberately reactivate earlier Neopalatial practices involving conical cups. We may also wonder whether Late Bronze Age Cretan tholoi, beginning with the one at Kephala in Knossos, also are not a convenient mating of local Cretan and mainland customs that may have been acceptable to Cretans as a traditional form of burial but that simultaneously expressed conspicuous consumption for those acquainted with mainland burial practices (Kanta 1997; but see O.T.P.K. Dickinson's response to Rutter 2005:53). The presence of similar LM II–IIIA1 burial assemblages elsewhere, as at Phaistos (Kalyvia) and now at Chania (new excavations in 2004; M. Vlasaki, personal communication), shows that right from the beginning, the Knossian renaissance covered a larger area. After this phase of experimenting with a rather innovative funerary ritual, it was adopted in a simplified form during the next phase of LM IIIA2-B at a large number of other Cretan sites (Perna 2001:128–129; Preston 2004a:327–331). But whereas experimentation characterized LM II burials and relative uniformity characterized LM IIIA1, considerable local variation again emerged during LM IIIA2-B, perhaps suggesting experimentation with mortuary symbolism by regional elites after the collapse of Knossos (Preston 2004a).

WHAT OF THE KYLIX?

Three types of vessels are regarded as characteristic of LM II: the flat alabastron, the Palace Style jar, and the Ephyraean goblet (Rehak and Younger 1998:153). The first two were unambiguous developments of local shapes. The Ephyraean goblet is usually seen as a new, intrusive form, adopted in LM II Crete (Popham 1984:165) from an earlier, LH IIB mainland form (French 1997). The goblet was immediately imitated and produced at Knossos and also at Chania (Hallager 1990), although fabric, treatment, technological features, and decorative motives often reflected typical Cretan manners that differed from imported mainland examples (French 1997:151; Mountjoy 1983:270). As argued by Borgna (2004), the Cretan elite, with the specific aim of legitimizing their status and establishing their power, used the Ephyraean goblet—and later, from LM IIIA1 on, the kylix and the krater—as a competitive device in practices of commensality. But whereas the latter were probably larger in scale and extremely ritualized in earlier times, as illustrated perhaps by deposits such as those at Nopigia or east of the palace at Galatas, they became now more limited to elite groups and were more politically charged. Future studies should indicate whether the Knossian elite was inspired to add a more individual dimension following a recognized mainland drinking practice (Borgna 2004) or whether this was also already a local practice (Wright 1995b). We interpret this innovative drinking vessel—even if it ultimately derived from the mainland—not as the sign of a "Mycenaean" presence at Knossos but as a deliberate choice in a larger strategy of legitimation. This strategy supported the formation and maintenance of a new regime at Knossos that mixed a desire for distinction with reference to former experience, as the particular Cretan manufacture of this category of pottery suggests (see also Smith 2002, 2004, 2005 for a comparable analysis but with a regional perspective).

THE STYLUS IS MIGHTIER THAN . . .

The main remaining question is why *Minoan* Crete modified its writing system to reflect a Greek language. The usual answer is that *Mycenaean* Greeks occupied the island either during or after the crisis years of LM IB, the period around 1450 BC, as part of a grand strategy on the part of Greek mainlanders to conquer the entire Aegean. This view is still accepted today but has been adapted in the light of new data (Macdonald 2005:195–223). Others find evidence for the establishment of Mycenaeans on the island only from LM IIIA2 on, at the time of their largest expansion and possible takeover of many areas in the Aegean and eastern Mediterranean (e.g., Hallager 1978, 1987b; Niemeier 1984:214), when they may have been helped by Egyptians (e.g., Cline 1987, 1995c:94, 1997).

Language, writing, and administration, however, can be used as weapons or tools of oppression, control, and exclusion, helping to create an effective communication system that is essential for any territorial state. There are ample signs to suggest that they were used to this effect on Crete, together with a set of other tools. Indeed, although Linear A and Linear B have a lot in common, Linear B appears to be a more integrated and uniform script, used with great success and effect to record the new ways in which economic data were gathered, processed, and stored, as Palaima (1984b, 1987b) has shown. The change in administrative language also provided an excellent opportunity to reform a whole array of accounting procedures, including ways of measuring goods.

Language was the means, not the end. Whoever took control of Knossos may well have deliberately changed the language as part of a political strategy, so that administrative reforms could be made that allowed tighter control. In this hypothesis, Linear B Greek was launched as the script and language of the new palace elite and a criterion, which a certain f(r)action of Cretans had to fulfill if they wanted to climb the hierarchical ladder. The use of another language—either one that was not so different (Renfrew 1998) or one that many Cretans were quite familiar with after centuries of contact—would have helped create a new power basis for a small, privileged group. There are historical parallels—Shulgi, Ahmose, fourteenth-century Ugarit, Charlemagne, Ataturk—of powerful individuals, in their attempts to crush surviving elite aspirations and tighten their grip on the government, introducing reforms affecting standards of measure, administrative language and practice, the military, and the territorial and fiscal organization of the state, all of which formed part of a larger framework of political control mechanisms.

Perhaps the change from a "Minoan" to a "Mycenaean" language was not such a revolution after all, if two other possibilities are considered. First, the Cretan language may not have differed that much from Greek, as some scholars have tried to argue (Duhoux 1998; Faure 1995; Renfrew 1998), and second, the different Cretan regions may have used a variety of languages or dialects during the Neopalatial period (Schoep 2002:158, table 3.24 on the rarity of Linear A words, apart from *kuro* and ritual formulas, attested at more than one site, and on the earlier use of two scripts, Cretan-Hieroglyphic and Linear A). This being the case, the shift to another, unifying language would have made administration easier (Driessen 2000:161–164). Of course, writing as such has little effect on the process of administration, and several empires used administrative systems without being literate (Driessen 1994–1995). Writing, however, allows a much larger quantity of data and number of transactions to be processed and to be situated in time and place.

Moreover, as part of a wider framework of political control mechanisms, writing has two advantages: it is an elite system difficult to master, and, in contrast to legally binding seals, it is impersonal. These two features make writing an ideal instrument for recording information and as a device of political power. It comes as no surprise, then, that the restriction on Linear B, both as a medium and geopolitically, was paralleled by similar restrictions on elite architecture, fresco decoration, formal burial, artisan production, and the general use of symbols during and after LM IB at Knossos. All were deliberate attempts to confine resources socially to the political elite.

SWORDS AND SHEEP, OR, COERCIVE FORCE AND ECONOMIC ORGANIZATION

Recent studies have stressed that the Knossian and Pylian states, as well as the other mainland kingdoms, pursued different power strategies, with the economy of the Knossos kingdom being primarily geared toward the acquisition and accumulation of prestige goods, especially metal vases and weapons, through its intensification of a power strategy that centered on sheep and textiles (Driessen 2001a; Halstead 1990, 1999a, 2001). At the same time, there may have been a change from an earlier, more cattle-oriented economy to an almost exclusively sheep-based economy, with the specific intention of producing wool. This is indicated in the Linear B tablets and by recent zoological studies showing changes in the age and sex of the animals at

slaughter (Halstead 2003). These changes, as Cherry (1988) has noted in a different context, are indications of "specialised pastoralism on a massive scale . . . with a strong element of state intervention." The increased stress on herding ultimately served to enhance elite control over foreign exchange, since the wool would be converted into high-class textiles used in exchange as a means to obtain foreign metal (Doxey 1987) and other exotica. Most of the Cretan countryside would have remained outside the political influence of Knossos, serving only as an occasional supply ground for cattle raids and tribute extraction. This would explain the relatively smaller number of toponyms that appear in the Knossos tablets, especially given the size of the island, and the much higher number at Pylos, an indication of the different ways in which local and regional control was exercised in the two kingdoms. The Knossos tablets also show that agriculture and land tenure were to some extent ancillary, serving to supplement the staple finance of the center, since it needed foodstuffs as payments for (part-time?) attached personnel, especially those working in the textile industries. Textiles could be converted into metals, which in turn could be converted into symbolically charged objects. The shift from intensive agriculture and trade to sheep made it easier for the Knossian elite to control this specific sector of the economy.

Control of this industry seems largely to have occurred by coercive force, explaining the massive attention given to military matters in the Knossos tablets, especially those that are hypothetically dated to the earlier phase of the administration (LM II–IIIA1) and those that would be contemporary with the warrior tombs at Knossos, Chania, and Kalyvia. Warfare was a central source of political power and elite identity during the LM II–IIIA period, and male status was tied to personal weaponry. Weapons were symbols of distinction and were the prerogative of a restricted group. The administration had good reason to take an interest in the production of swords (R-tablets) and chariots (S-tablets) in particular. By controlling both the manufacture of weapons through attached specialization and the distribution of the finished products, the palace could effectively control and manipulate access to weapons.

The connections between and among weaponry, power, metal wealth, and prestige are unambiguous. Decorated weapons made excellent gifts for gods (as at Symi) and for men because they were an ideal way to transfer precious metals. At the same time, they functioned as status and prestige symbols (see also Baboula 2000). Decorated swords and spearheads probably formed part of a gift obligation system, linking both internal and external elites to the central palace authority at Knossos. The detailed description of decorated swords and chariots in the Knossian tablets may indeed suggest that these were manufactured by palace workshops to serve as alliance gifts.

The importance of chariots is suggested by their presence on Knossian frescoes and on the Hagia Triada sarcophagus. Apart from status symbols and war machines, they may also have had cultic and ceremonial functions. For example, they could have been used in high-status funerary processions, as in later Greek history (Perna 2001). The distinctions in the types, quality, and quantity of military symbolism implied by funerary goods, particularly jewelry and weapons, undoubtedly denote differences in hierarchical status (Driessen and Macdonald 1984; Hewitt 1993; Kilian-Dirlmeier 1985, 1988; Matthäus 1983). These tombs therefore should be interpreted above all as the tombs of officials in the palace administration, who were buried with the insignia of their rank and status. Not all warrior burials are rich, and many of the weapons in them are clearly utilitarian. This seems to imply individualized status associated with warfare. Actual and status warrior burials make sense only if we assume the burials were used to express prestige and conspicuous consumption and the weapons were used to imply competition between living groups. We therefore suggest that, apart from its social connotations, warfare on Crete was one of the different political strategies of the Knossian elite, allowing the application of coercive force to concentrate wealth, which meant sheep and textiles, as indicated in the Linear B tablets.

CONSTRUCTING IDENTITY

In this chapter, we have deliberately steered away from using the word "Mycenaean" in discussing the advanced Late Bronze Age of Crete. We have proposed a new

reading of the evidence, recognizing cultural markers to which we have applied the term "Minoan." We regard the term as a label covering an artificial creation of an emblematic cultural package by Late Bronze Age Knossians that consisted of a variety of references used to construct a new identity. References were primarily to a local Cretan past, but now, and perhaps for the first time, with a unifying function that incorporated the different regional identities and tendencies that may have existed during Neopalatial times. This new identity also borrowed specific elements from the mainland, especially where administrative language and military status burials were concerned, but also from further afield, such as Egypt and the Near East. The most intriguing element, however, is the considered and strategic use of the past by the Knossian elite with the appropriation and subsequent reinvention and reuse of particular elements that triggered the memory of, and nostalgia for, the glory of times past as part of a legitimizing strategy. As in many other ancient societies, the past was a powerful tool (Bradley 2002; Van Dyke and Alcock 2003). The same would happen on Crete again, at the very end of the Bronze Age (Tsipopoulou 2005; Whittaker 2005a) and during the Iron Age (Coldstream 2000). We believe this process had started already in LM IB, before or during the fires that struck the island causing widespread destruction.

Acknowledgments. In the first edition of this volume, John F. Cherry and Jack L. Davis mentioned the absence of any discussion of "Crete's Mycenaean kingdom." The present chapter is an attempt to make up for this lacuna, and we thank the editors for their invitation to collaborate, and especially for their patience. We have deliberately stayed clear of chronological discussions, but advances both in regional pottery studies and in absolute chronology may soon show that certain features observed happened synchronously rather than diachronically. We thank M. Vlasaki-Andreadaki, C. F. Macdonald, I. Schoep, C. Broodbank and especially T. F. Cunningham for their assistance. C. Langohr acknowledges the support of the Belgian FNRS.

CHAPTER 17

RETHINKING MYCENAEAN INTERNATIONAL TRADE WITH EGYPT AND THE NEAR EAST

ERIC H. CLINE

URING THE PAST TWO decades, since the late 1980s, and especially in just the past few years, most scholarly thinking on the extent of Mycenaean trade and contact with Egypt and the Near East during the Late Bronze Age seems to have done an abrupt about-face. Perhaps I am misreading the recent publications on this topic, but it seems that many archaeologists, philologists, and ancient historians have rethought the issue and are now generally in agreement that the Mycenaeans and Minoans must have been in contact—perhaps even frequent contact—with Egypt and the Near East (Anatolia, Mesopotamia, and the Levant) during the second millennium BC.

More than one person has wondered aloud, in both private and public conversations with me, whether this new academic take on the ancient trade and contact across the Mediterranean could be a "trickle-down effect" resulting from the publication of Martin Bernal's *Black Athena: The Afroasiatic Roots of Classical Civilization*, in 1987 and 1991. However, it seems more likely that the recent and detailed publication of the material evidence for such contacts has finally persuaded all but the most die-hard opponents that the Aegean, Egypt, and the Near East were in continuous contact with each other throughout the Late Bronze Age (see, e.g., Cline 1994; Lambrou-Phillipson 1990; Phillips 1991). Indeed, as Guy Bunnens (1999:130–131) has recently written,

"The subject of the relations between the Aegean world and the East, including Egypt, seems to have found increasing favor over the past twenty years. M. Bernal's *Black Athena* . . . is a sign, more than a cause, of this renewed interest."[1]

In the interests of full disclosure, I would single out especially the contributions in the volume resulting from a conference we convened in Cincinnati in 1997 (Cline and Harris-Cline 1998). There we initially thought that the very question of contacts would be a topic of great debate, but as it turned out, the participants did not question whether, or even to what extent, the Aegean was in contact with Egypt and the eastern Mediterranean during the second millennium BC. Instead, the prevailing attitude was that such contacts were commonplace. The more interesting questions now lie in the realm of the impact and implications of such contacts and how our current theoretical tools, approaches, and analyses can be used to explain and investigate the influences and ideas that came along with such contacts.

The study of Aegean international contacts and trade has thus truly begun to come of age, at long last. Finally, there is no longer a single question—Was there contact and trade?—but now rather a series of questions, including: What were the mechanisms of transmission? What other influences and cultural ideas might have been exchanged along with the material objects? These are questions that still remain to be answered, and so, in this brief contribution, I would simply like to review our major categories and types of evidence for those who have not yet jumped on the Late Bronze Age trade bandwagon, and briefly to reiterate again the main points that result from such a study of the available data.[2]

EVIDENCE FOR MYCENAEAN FOREIGN RELATIONS WITH EGYPT AND THE NEAR EAST

As I have pointed out previously elsewhere (Cline 1999), there are several different categories of evidence available for those investigating the nature of Aegean trade and contact with Egypt and the Near East. Here we will consider only those that are specifically appropriate to the Mycenaean involvement in such affairs: (1) Egyptian and Near Eastern objects (hereafter Orientalia) found in Late Bronze Age contexts on the Greek mainland; (2) Mycenaean pottery and other artifacts found in Late Bronze Age contexts in Egypt, Anatolia, Syria-Palestine, Cyprus, and Mesopotamia; (3) Bronze Age paintings and documents from Egypt and the Near East that may show or mention Mycenaean goods, people, or interactions with the Greek mainland; and (4) Linear B tablets, found at Pylos and Mycenae, that contain textual references possibly resulting from contact with Syria-Palestine, Cyprus, Egypt, Anatolia, Mesopotamia, and perhaps elsewhere in the eastern Mediterranean.

Orientalia in Late Bronze Age contexts on the Greek mainland

FINDS BY CHRONOLOGICAL PERIOD

Of the nearly 1000 imported Egyptian and Near Eastern objects found in good Late Helladic/Late Minoan I–IIIC contexts, approximately one-quarter (circa 258 imports) are on the Greek mainland. Although nearly as many (circa 251 imports) are on Crete, the chronological distribution is intriguingly different between the two Aegean regions.

With regard to specific contexts in the Late Bronze Age (figures 17.1 and 17.2), there are 37 Orientalia in specific LH I–II contexts on the Greek mainland (compared to 94 such objects in LM I–II contexts on Crete). Although there are only 18 Egyptian and Near Eastern objects on the Greek mainland in specific LH IIIA contexts, there is a dramatic shift during the following

periods, when 116 Egyptian and Near Eastern objects are found in specific LH IIIB contexts and 51 such objects are found in specific LH IIIC contexts on the Greek mainland. (Additional imports are in generic LH III contexts and nonspecific LH IIIA–B contexts.)

This, it may be noted, is in direct contrast to the situation on Crete, where there are 107 imported Egyptian and Near Eastern objects in LM IIIA contexts but only seven in LM IIIB contexts, and none in LM IIIC contexts. It appears that the Mycenaeans of mainland Greece either took over or became the focus of the trade routes leading to and from Egypt and the Near East by the beginning of LH IIIB. This may or may not have had anything to do with the Mycenaean occupation of Knossos and Crete at approximately this same time (Cline 1997).

It should also be noted that Mycenae, Tiryns, and Boeotian Thebes together account for more than 90% (107 of 116) of the Orientalia found in LH IIIB contexts on mainland Greece. Most of the 38 imports found at Boeotian Thebes in these contexts are from a single hoard of imported cylinder seals and are probably an anomaly. However, those found at Mycenae and Tiryns come from a variety of origins and are probably a better representation of the cosmopolitan nature of the trade at the time: of the 44 such imports at LH IIIB Mycenae, 27 are from Syria-Palestine, 15 are from Egypt, and two are from Mesopotamia, while of the 25 such imports at LH IIIB Tiryns, 13 are from Syria-Palestine and 12 are from Cyprus. It is still of interest to note the paucity of Cypriot artifacts at Mycenae and of Egyptian objects at Tiryns, and to wonder whether there were explicit trading connections between specific Mycenaean polities or kings and explicit Egyptian or Near Eastern areas, for example, between Mycenae and Egypt, Tiryns and Cyprus, or Thebes and Mesopotamia (Cline 1994:87, 91–92). We should note again also the almost complete lack of imported Orientalia at the site of Pylos.

MESOPOTAMIA

If we now look briefly at the areas of origin of the Orientalia in Late Bronze Age contexts on the Greek mainland, approximately 41 Mesopotamian objects have been found in good LH I–IIIC contexts at mainland Greek sites, including Mycenae, Pylos, Kakovatos, Thorikos, Perati, and Boeotian Thebes. These objects are primarily beads, plaques, and pendants made of blue glass, and cylinder seals made of lapis lazuli and other semiprecious stones.

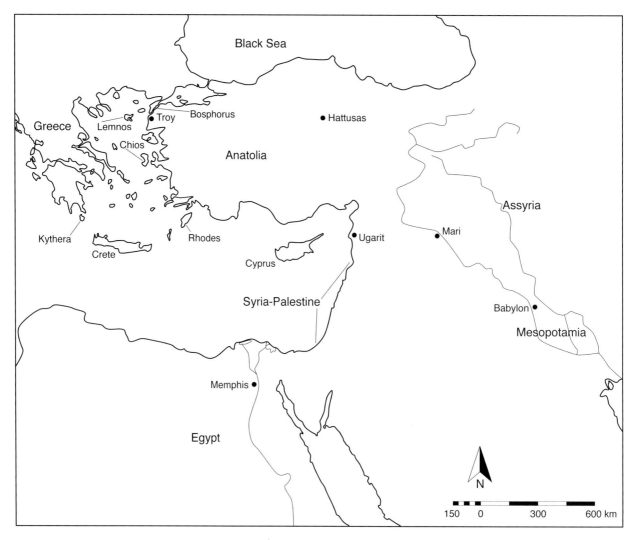

FIGURE 17.1 Map of eastern Mediterranean with regions and major sites mentioned in the text. For Greece and Crete, see Figures 1.1 and 16.1.

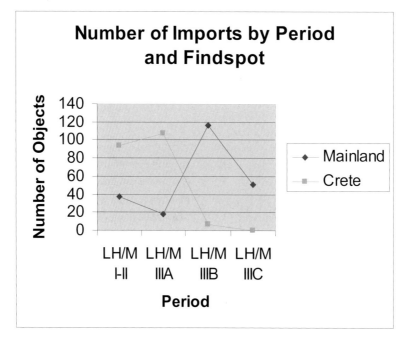

FIGURE 17.2 Eastern Mediterranean imports to Crete and mainland Greece through time.

Nineteen of these 41 objects, or nearly half, are Mesopotamian cylinder seals that were found as part of a cache of 38 faience and lapis lazuli cylinder seals in a context dating to the LH IIIB1–2 period (circa 1220 BC) within the New Kadmeion at the site of Boeotian Thebes. This cache represents the largest single group of imported seals found in the Aegean area. Included are seven seals of various Mesopotamian styles dating from the Early Dynastic III to the Old Babylonian periods (circa 2500–1700 BC) and 12 Kassite seals from Babylonia (thirteenth century BC). One is of faience, one is of stone, and 17 are of lapis lazuli.

The cylinder seals are extremely important in terms of indicating connections between Mesopotamia and the Aegean, however indirectly, toward the end of the Late Bronze Age. All of the seals are engraved with a scene of one kind or another, and many are inscribed. The most important of these is a cylinder seal made of deep blue, and very pure, lapis lazuli, with a scene in which a god, perhaps Marduk, rises between two mountains, grasping a stream in either hand. The accompanying inscription reads "Kidin-Marduk, son of Sha-ilimma-damqa, the *sha reshi* official of Burra-Buriash, king of the world" (Cline 1994:catalogue no. 203; translation following Brinkman 1981:73–74). Burra-Buriaš is the Kassite king Burna-Buriaš II, known from the Amarna letters in Egypt and from texts in his native city of Babylon, where he ruled circa 1359–1333 BC.

Of all the possibilities that have been previously suggested to account for the presence of these seals at Boeotian Thebes, the hypothesis that they were the raw stock of a local craftsman seems most likely, in part because of the abraded nature of the surface on many of the cylinder seals, suggesting either previous or imminent reuse and in part because of the local Mycenaean nature of the majority of the other artifacts in the New Kadmeion. Other suggestions, such as Porada's hypothesis that the seals represent a gift of one mina of lapis lazuli sent by King Tukulti-Ninurta I of Assyria to the king of Thebes during the latter part of the thirteenth century BC, or Lambrou-Phillipson's idea of a resident Syria-Palestinian craftsman in Thebes, seem less likely (see Cline 1994:25–26, with additional discussion and references).

EGYPT

The Egyptian imports in the Late Bronze Age Aegean include transport amphorae, storage jars, jugs, bowls, and vases in ceramic, stone, and glass, as well as scarabs and figurines of faience, frit, and steatite. More than half of these objects are functional items rather than trinkets, imported consistently over the course of the Late Bronze Age. The perishable trade goods, including perhaps grain, textiles, and metals sent between the two areas, must also be taken into account. Although these goods have long since disappeared, they are depicted in Egyptian tomb paintings and are occasionally mentioned in written texts.

Of the 236 Egyptian objects found in good LH/LM I–IIIC contexts, 75 are on the Greek mainland. Although more than 80% of the Egyptian imports in the LH/LM I–II Aegean found their way to Crete rather than mainland Greece (67 of 82 objects), even this large percentage is misleading, for many of the objects found outside Crete, including a number in the Shaft Graves at Mycenae, appear to have reached their final destinations via Crete. Eventually the situation turned in favor of the Mycenaeans, but not until the LH IIIB period.

Of the 46 Egyptian imports found in LH/LM IIIA contexts across the Aegean area, only eight have been found on the Greek mainland. From the LH/LM IIIB period on, however, there is a change in the distribution pattern of Egyptian imports in the Late Bronze Age Aegean, for virtually all Egyptian imports in the LH/LM IIIB–C Aegean are found on the Greek mainland: 18 of 22 in LH/LM IIIB contexts and 25 of 37 in LH/LM IIIC contexts. This concentration probably reflects the dominant status of the Mycenaeans in the Aegean during this time, but it is important to note that such Egyptian imports are found at a limited number of sites: of the 18 in LH IIIB contexts, 15 are at Mycenae; of the 25 in LH IIIC contexts, 24 are at the site of Perati in eastern Attica, whose cemetery consists primarily of tombs dated to the LH IIIC period.

It is conceivable—to judge from the numerous Egyptian imports found in LH IIIB contexts and the LH IIIB exported vessels found in Egypt (discussed later)—that Egypto-Aegean trade was flourishing during the Nineteenth Dynasty, in particular during the time of Ramses II. However, as noted, the majority of the Egyptian imports in LH IIIB contexts have been reported from Mycenae and the Argolid. This distribution might be an accident of discovery and could change with further excavations of LH IIIB sites in Greece. It might also indicate precisely which Mycenaeans were trading with Egypt at this time, that is, those in the Argolid rather than in Messenia or Laconia. But it might also be the case that many of these Egyptian objects actually arrived during the LH IIIA period and remained in circulation through the LH IIIB period (see discussion in Phillips 2007).

Among the objects that probably fall into this last category are faience plaque fragments, faience scarabs and seals, and a frit vase, all inscribed or painted with the cartouche of the Pharaoh Amenhotep III or his wife Queen Tiyi, who ruled circa 1391–1353 BC. Most have been found at Mycenae, one in an LH IIIA context and the others in LH IIIB contexts (see most recently Phillips in press; Phillips and Cline in press; previously, with references, Cline 1987, 1990, 1994:38–42, 1998.) A similar situation is found with two blue frit (Egyptian Blue) monkey figurines, each inscribed on the right shoulder with the cartouche of the earlier Egyptian Pharaoh, Amenhotep II. One, depicting a mother with her baby clinging to her belly, was found in an LH IIIA context at Tiryns. The other, depicting either a male or at least a female without an offspring, was found in a probable LH IIIB2 context at Mycenae. The uniqueness of these monkey figurines suggests that they originally arrived in mainland Greece as a set, only to be split up, used, and then buried at separate sites and at separate times (Cline 1991a).

The objects of Amenhotep III and his wife Queen Tiyi are even more unusual than the monkey figurines and are probably, at least in my opinion, to be linked in some way with the so-called Aegean List of Amenhotep III found at his mortuary temple at Kom el-Hetan back in Egypt, across the Nile River from modern-day Luxor. This unique list, which has been thoroughly discussed in recent years, has the names *Tanaja* (mainland Greece) and *Keftiu* (Crete), followed by 14 names of sites in the Aegean, including Mycenae, Nauplion, Kythera, Knossos, Kydonia, Phaistos, and Amnisos. Several of these sites have yielded objects of Amenhotep III and Queen Tiyi, leading to my own belief that this list may be an itinerary describing a route (or a specific voyage) to mainland Greece and Crete. At the very least, it is an indication that specific sites in the Bronze Age Aegean were sufficiently well known to the Eighteenth Dynasty Egyptians that they appear in Amenhotep III's mortuary temple in the company of major Near Eastern sites such as Hattusas, capital city of the Hittites (see again Phillips 2007; Phillips and Cline 2005; Cline 1987, 1990, 1994:38–42, and 1998. See now also Latacz 2004:130–133).

As I noted earlier, there was a change in the distribution of Orientalia from Crete to the Greek mainland by the LH/LM IIIB period. Thus, an Egyptian embassy

sent to the Aegean during the reign of Amenhotep III could have had a dual mission: to reaffirm connections with an old, valued trading partner (the Minoans on Crete) and to establish relations with a new, rising power (the Mycenaeans on mainland Greece). The large number of Egyptian objects, both inscribed and uninscribed, found at Mycenae suggests that this site may well have been the focal point of such an Egyptian embassy, and suggests further that there may have been a special relationship between Egypt and Mycenae.

SYRIA-PALESTINE

Of the 259 Syria-Palestinian imports found in good LH/LM I–IIIC contexts, about one-third (99 objects) are on the Greek mainland. Although nearly 50% of such imports in the LH/LM I–II Aegean found their way to Crete (10 of 21 objects), only 10% (2 of 21) found their way to mainland Greece (the other 9 objects were found on the Islands). This trend continued during the LH/LM IIIA period, when more than 80% of the Syria-Palestinian imports (43 of 53 objects) were deposited on Crete.

The situation is dramatically reversed in the LH/LM IIIB period, however, for of the Syria-Palestinian objects found in these contexts within the Aegean, 98% (54 of 55 objects) have been found on the Greek mainland, primarily in the Argolid. We may thus suggest that this turnaround is additional evidence that the Mycenaeans had gained control of the trade routes to the eastern Mediterranean by this time. Most notable is the sudden rise in faience objects, which accounts for 25 of these imports, of which 20 are faience vessels at Mycenae. The origin of some of these vessels has been the subject of heated debate, but the most recent studies indicate that a Syria-Palestinian origin for them is most likely (Peltenburg 1991). Once again three sites account for a majority of these Syria-Palestinian imports: in addition to 27 at Mycenae, there are 13 at Tiryns and eight at Thebes. In addition to the faience vessels, these imports include Canaanite jars and cylinder seals of various materials.

The majority of the Syria-Palestinian objects in good LH/LM IIIC contexts are also found on the Greek mainland (16 of 22 imports). These include Canaanite jar and other ceramic or terracotta vessel fragments, haematite weights, and an armor scale. While the number of objects imported during these years drops from the previous LH IIIB period—a decrease quite likely related to the troubles and disruptions occurring in the Near East at this time—we should also note again that not a single Syria-Palestinian import has been found on Crete in LM IIIC contexts.

CYPRUS

In all, there are some 176 Cypriot objects found in good LH/LM I-IIIC contexts. More than half of them are ceramic (104 of 176) and many of them are milk bowls, which represent the second most popular ceramic shape imported into the Bronze Age Aegean, behind only Canaanite jars. Of the 176 Cypriot imports, 40 have been found on the Greek mainland.

However, apart from a few (four in generic LH III contexts and two in LH IIIA1 contexts), Cypriot imports do not appear on the Greek mainland before the LH IIIB period. Then, just as we have seen was the case with the Egyptian and Syria-Palestinian objects, there is a sudden jump: 23 imports in LH IIIB contexts and 11 more in LH IIIC contexts. Moreover, the distribution is intriguing: of the 23 Cypriot imports in LH IIIB contexts, 12 are at Tiryns and 11 are at Thebes, while of the 11 Cypriot imports in LH IIIC contexts, nine are at Perati and two are in a hoard uncovered at Anthedon.[3] In other words, not a single Cypriot import has been found at either Mycenae or Thebes, in contrast to the Egyptian and Syria-Palestinian objects from the same periods of importation. This may imply some sort of selective distribution or importation either on the part of the exporting Cypriots, the importing Mycenaeans, or whoever was transporting these goods.

Thus the LH IIIB period represents the largest influx of Cypriot objects into mainland Greece (23 objects), with most found at Tiryns and Boeotian Thebes. The situation mirrors that of the Egyptian and Syro-Palestinian imports; once again the focus of importation apparently shifts from Crete to the mainland at the end of the LH/LM IIIA period. Thus, contrary to previous observations (as recently as Vagnetti and Lo Schiavo 1989:218), Cypriot imports do not peak in the LH IIIA period, followed by a marked decrease in LH IIIB. Rather, there is a change in orientation, from Crete to the mainland, after the LH IIIA period and a marked *increase* in imported goods during LH IIIB. These changes may be related to the possible Cypriot-oriented exportation of Mycenaean vessels with Cypro-Minoan potmarks at Tiryns and to the additional possibility of resident Cypriots at Tiryns (see earlier discussions in Hirschfeld 1990, 1992, 1996, 1999; Cline 1994:54, 61, 1999; now Maran 2004).

As noted above, by far the majority of Cypriot imports in LH IIIC contexts are found at Perati on the Greek mainland (9 of 11 objects); these are primarily gold earrings found in burial contexts, but they also include a tripod stand and several seals (of which two are actually in LH IIIB/C contexts). Why this should be so and why there are no ceramic imports from Cyprus found in these contexts is unclear; it is possible that the Aegean area was simply a series of mooring points and watering holes for Cypriot (or Syrian-Palestinian) ships heading further west, and that the real trade during these years was between the far reaches of the eastern and western Mediterranean.

ANATOLIA

Worked artifacts imported from Anatolia represent the smallest portion of the Orientalia found in the Late Bronze Age Aegean. As I have noted several times elsewhere, there are only about a dozen objects of probable Anatolian origin found in LH/LM I–III contexts anywhere within the Bronze Age Aegean. These are evenly split among items of ceramic, stone, and precious metal and are scattered both regionally and temporally, from LH/LM I–II to LH IIIC and from mainland Greece to Rhodes. Their manufacture dates span the spectrum of Hittite history, from the Old Kingdom to the end of the New Empire, and few can be linked to the activities of specific Hittite kings (Cline 1994:68; previously Cline 1991b).

Of these 12 previously identified objects of probable Anatolian origin which have been found in LH/LM I–III contexts, only four have been found on the Greek mainland: a silver "Smiting God" statuette reportedly from Nezero, Thessaly (but which was purchased by Sir Arthur Evans) and three at Mycenae: a gold pin, with its head in the shape of an Argali sheep, and a silver rhyton in the shape of a stag, both from Shaft Grave IV, and a steatite seal/bulla from LH IIIA2 Chamber Tomb 523 (see previously Cline 1991b and Cline 1994:catalogue nos. 18, 88, 237, and 716). This last object is perhaps now to be reidentified as a biconical seal, possibly with hieroglyphic Hittite/Luwian characters inscribed on it, much like the one recently found by Manfred Korfmann in level VIIb2 at Troy (see Hawkins and Easton 1996; Latacz 2004:49–51, 68–71, figure 11, with previous references). A similar seal at Perati previously identified as Cypriot (Cline 1994:catalogue no. 235) might also now be reconsidered and reclassified as an Anatolian import, although the possibility still remains that it is an imitation.

Put succinctly, as will be clear from the additional data presented below, there is still no good evidence for trade between Central Anatolian Hittites and Mycenaeans during the Late Bronze Age. Numerous hypotheses have been suggested in the past to account for this situation, including geographic and demographic problems, ignorance of existence, an accidental lack of discoveries, a lack of interest, and a trade in perishable goods, but none is particularly persuasive (see previously Cline 1991c, 1994:70–71, with a detailed discussion and additional references for each of these previous hypotheses).

Mycenaean pottery and artifacts in Egypt and the Near East

MESOPOTAMIA

Only a very few objects of possible Mycenaean manufacture have been unearthed in Late Bronze Age contexts in Mesopotamia: a sherd from a jar found at Babylon; a so-called Mycenaean-style copper ox-hide ingot found at Tell el Abyad (Dur Kurigalzu); and a circa 30-kilo block of Laurion (?) lead stamped with the seal of Tukulti-Ninurta I, king of Assyria circa 1244–1208 BC, found at Aššur (Cline 1994:26, with further references). Obviously, none of these objects is completely satisfactory as a Mycenaean export, and we may seriously doubt the probability of Mycenaeans having traveled to Mesopotamia on a steady basis during the Late Bronze Age.

EGYPT

In terms of the Mycenaean pottery found in Egypt, such ceramic vessels—which will have probably originally contained wine, oil, or perfume—are found throughout Egypt during the New Kingdom period. Ongoing excavations continue to increase the number of these objects, which now total more than 1800 vessels of various shapes and sizes and which appear to have been consistently imported throughout most of the fourteenth through twelfth centuries BC to more than 30 sites, from Marsa Matruh on the northwest coast to Sesebi in the far south.

It has long been known that LH IIIA2 ceramic vessels were present in reasonable quantities in Egypt, for example, at Amarna, Rifeh, Gurob, Sesebi, and now in the Memphite tomb of Aper-El, vizier to Amenhotep III and Akhenaten. It is possible, however, that LH IIIB vessels may have been imported in even greater numbers by the Pharaohs of the Nineteenth Dynasty.

For example, the LH IIIB vessels at Deir el Medina are almost certainly good Nineteenth Dynasty imports—Martha Bell reports that of these approximately 120 fragmentary Mycenaean vessels from Deir el Medina, "the bulk of the material seems to fall in LH IIIB, probably from the 19th Dynasty village" (Bell 1982:143–163, esp. 154, also 1985:77).

SYRIA-PALESTINE

Although the frequency of Aegean objects varies at different sites, most of Late Bronze Age Syria-Palestine presents a pattern consistent with continuous ceramic importation until approximately 1200 BC. There are more than 100 sites in Syria-Palestine at which Mycenaean vessels or artifacts have been found. A total of over 1800 vessels, primarily functional shapes, have been reported to date. However, the export of true Mycenaean pottery seems to have come to a virtual halt at the end of the LH IIIB period, for LH IIIC vessels found in the Near East are imitations made in Cyprus or Syria-Palestine (see references given in Cline 1994:49–50).

CYPRUS

Large quantities of Mycenaean and Minoan objects, including more than 4000 vessels, were exported to Cyprus throughout the Late Bronze Age, particularly during the LH III period. Mycenaean pottery in Cyprus reaches a peak during the LH IIIA1–2 period, which is perhaps surprising, since the peak of Cypriot exports to the Greek mainland does not occur before the LH IIIB period, but LH IIIB vessels have also been found at numerous sites on Cyprus, including Enkomi, Kourion, Kition, Kalavassos-Ayios Dhimitrios, Hala Sultan Tekke, Larnaka, and Episkopi (see references given in Cline 1994:61).

ANATOLIA

As for Aegean objects in Anatolia, as has long been known, Minoan and Mycenaean artifacts and architecture are fairly common along much of the western coast of Anatolia, ranging from single finds of ceramic vessels to indications of Aegean residents at Miletus. Aegean contacts with Troy and the Troad are well known, while recent evidence attests to Mycenaean penetration of the Bosphorus and to Mycenaean trade with the Black Sea region. Moreover, Aegean connections with southern Anatolia, long cast into doubt owing to lack of evidence, are now well attested to (Cline 1994:68, with previous references; Mee 1998; Niemeier 1998, 1999; Latacz 2004).

However, as has also been well documented in the past, there is little evidence for Aegean contact with the Hittite homelands in Central Anatolia during the Late Bronze Age. It is a fact that Aegean artifacts are extremely scarce in these Hittite homelands; decades of searching have yet to produce many finds, even at the Hittite capital city of Hattusas. The only Central Anatolian site to have Aegean pottery in any quantities is Masat, and even here there are only seven fragmentary LH IIIA2 and LH IIIB vessels, which might have reached the city only after Hittite control of the city had relaxed. All but one were found in a level dating to the thirteen century BC—a time, according to the excavator, when the city was possibly in the hands of the neighboring Kaška. It is worth noting again Sherratt and Crouwel's conclusion that there is "a strong inverse correlation between the amount of Late Helladic IIIA-B pottery and [the] degree of Hittite control" in Central Anatolia, and that my tentative suggestion in 1991 of a possible Hittite embargo against Mycenaean goods has yet to be disproved (Cline 1991c, 1994:68–74, with previous references; Sherratt and Crouwel 1987:345).

Egyptian and Near Eastern paintings and references showing or documenting contact with the Mycenaeans

MESOPOTAMIA

Although numerous texts document contact between the Minoans and Mesopotamians, particularly tablets found at Mari (Cline 1994:126–128, catalogue nos. D1–D12), only a single text might indicate contact between the Mycenaeans and Mesopotamia during the Late Bronze Age. This is the well-known thirteenth century BC treaty signed between the Hittite king Tudhaliya IV and Šaušgamuwa of Amurru. The treaty is concerned with the enforcement of an embargo against Assyria and its king, Tukulti-Ninurta I. Line IV 23 of this text is traditionally read, "let no ship of Ahhiyawa go to him . . ." (Güterbock 1983:136). Although Steiner (1989) called this translation into question, his suggestion was almost immediately repudiated, with several prominent scholars subsequently indicating their belief that the initial translation was more likely to be correct (see, e.g., Bryce 1999:343, n. 63; Lehmann 1991:111, n. 11; Niemeier 1998:25, n. 8; Singer 1991:171, n. 56). If this is a proper translation after all, it would indicate

a specific directive to blockade Ahhiyawan ships and to prevent the overland transportation of Ahhiyawan goods to Assyria. For those who equate the Ahhiyawans with the Mycenaeans, as I and many other scholars now do, this treaty should provide textual evidence for previous contact between the Mycenaeans and the Assyrians.

EGYPT

Paintings and literary references in Egypt during the New Kingdom period provide evidence for contacts with the Late Bronze Age Aegean (Cline 1994:108–120, catalogue nos. A1–A59), but most are concerned with *Keftiu*—probably the Egyptian name for the island of Crete and the Bronze Age Minoans. There are, however, a few specific occurrences of the term *Tj-n3-jj*—to be read Tanaja (possibly vocalized as a variation of *Danaoi)—which is most likely a specific reference to the Mycenaeans and Mainland Greece. These occur once in the fifteenth century BC, three times in the fourteenth century BC, and twice in the thirteenth century BC, specifically during the reigns of Thutmose III, Amenhotep III, and Ramses II. The most important of these is the occurrence of *Tanaja*, in the company of *Keftiu* and 14 other Aegean place names, in Amenhotep III's mortuary temple at Kom el-Hetan in Egypt.

Perhaps surprisingly, mainland Greece is not mentioned in the Amarna letters. Neither is Crete, for that matter; instead, the references to the Aegean appear elsewhere in Egypt during this period. Nevertheless, there is now possible evidence from Amarna itself for Mycenaeans in Egypt during this time. A fragment of papyrus originally excavated by Pendlebury at Amarna in the company of an LH IIIA2 late stirrup jar within the House/Chapel of the King's Sculptor depicts a group of what appear to be Mycenaean warriors rushing toward a fallen Egyptian, who is about to have his throat cut. The Mycenaeans wear Egyptian linen kilts but are identified by their distinctive boar's tusk helmets and ox-hide shields. What these Mycenaean mercenaries are doing in Egypt can only be guessed at, but they appear to be running to the aid of the fallen Egyptian, which some have suggested may signify some sort of alliance (Parkinson and Schofield 1993; Schofield and Parkinson 1994).

While literary references to the Aegean are common in Egypt during Ramses II's time, including two references to *Tanaja*, their significance is debated, for most of these were either usurped or copied from earlier lists. This is cause for at least an initial hesitation concerning the extent of contacts between Egypt and the Aegean during his reign. On the other hand, the Mycenaean pottery found in Nineteenth and Twentieth Dynasty contexts in Egypt and the 22 Egyptian objects found in LH/LM IIIB contexts in the Aegean indicate that such trade may have been ongoing and was perhaps at a level not seen since the days of Amenhotep III. It is possible that the mere existence of the lists of Ramses II reflects this continuing trade, but the lack of new lists may indicate that something changed, most likely the nationality of the sailors and merchants transporting the cargo and wares between Egypt and Mainland Greece.

SYRIA-PALESTINE

The mid-thirteenth-century BC Sinaranu text found in the archives at Ugarit bears witness to contacts and trade between the Aegean and Syria-Palestine during the LH/LM IIIB period and indicates that Ugarit was still functioning as a major emporium at that time; however, the text refers to contact with Crete rather than with the Greek mainland. Two other possible textual references to the Aegean found at Ugarit are also concerned with Crete rather than with the Greek mainland (Cline 1994:49–50, 120, catalogue nos. B1–B3). Until very recently, no paintings or textual references showing or documenting contact with the Mycenaeans had been discovered in Late Bronze Age Syria-Palestine. However, the first evidence for textual mentions of Myceneans in Canaanite documents has now been published, specifically in two letters (RS 94.2523 and RS 94.2530) found at Ugarit which date to the late 13th or early 12th century BC. These letters apparently contain a version of the Hittite word *Ahhiyawa* (see discussion below), used in these letters to refer to the "Hiyawa-men," and rendered into Akkadian as LÚ *hi-ia-ú-wi-i* (RS 94.2523) and both LÚ *hi-ia-a-ú* and LÚ.MEŠ *hi-ia-ú-wi-i* (RS 94.2530) (see Lackenbacher and Malbran-Labat 2005:237–238 and nn. 69, 76; Singer 2006:250–252).

CYPRUS

No paintings or textual references showing or documenting contact with the Mycenaeans have been discovered in Late Bronze Age Cyprus. However, one hopes that evidence of such contact, which is likely to have existed, will be found in the near future.

ANATOLIA

Apart from a possible representation of a Mycenaean warrior on a bowl of probable Hittite manufacture found at Hattusas, the only pictorial and textual representations from Anatolia that show or document contact with the Mycenaeans are the much debated Ahhiyawa texts from the Hittite archives at Hattusas (Cline 1994:121–125, catalogue nos. C1–C26). This is neither the time nor the place to rehash the old arguments, but it also now seems unnecessary, for Niemeier, among others, has put the debate to rest (Niemeier 1998, with previous references; see now also Hope Simpson 2003 and Latacz 2004). It is clear that Ahhiyawa can be none other than mainland Greece, and thus we have textual evidence for several centuries of contact, both peaceful and hostile, between the Hittites and the Mycenaeans.

Linear B words at Pylos and Mycenae of possible foreign origin or implying foreign contacts

Although Martin Bernal (1991:48–49, 482–482) may well have exaggerated the state of affairs in suggesting that there was a massive borrowing of Egyptian or Near Eastern words into Greek, it is true that a number of words in the Linear B texts found in the Aegean are of possible foreign origin or imply foreign contacts (see Cline 1994:128–131, catalogue nos. E1–E24).

Although there are two textual references to Egypt and the Egyptians in the Linear B texts found at Knossos (*mi-sa-ra-jo* = "Egyptian" and *a₃-ku-pi-ti-jo* = "Memphite" or "Egyptian"), there are no such references to Egypt in any of the texts on the Greek mainland.

There are, however, at least three possible Semitic loan-words found in the Linear B tablets at Pylos and Mycenae that may derive ultimately from Mesopotamia via Syria-Palestine: *ku-wa-no* = "blue glass or glass paste," *ka-ne-ja* = "reed," and *ko-no-ni-pi* = "part of the decoration of a jug and a chair" (Cline 1994:26, 131).

There are also six more possible Semitic loan-words found in the Linear B tablets at Pylos and Mycenae that may have arrived directly from Syria-Palestine: *sa-sa-ma* = "sesame," *ku-mi-no* = "cumin/caraway seed," *ku-pa-ro* and variations = "cyperus (a spice)," *ku-ru-so* and variations = "gold," *re-wo-te-jo* and variations = "lion," and *e-re-pa, e-re-pa-te-jo/-ja* and variations = "ivory" (Cline 1994:50, 128–130).

Of even greater interest, perhaps, are a few debated words in the Linear B texts at both Pylos and Knossos, which some have suggested as Syria-Palestinian gentilics, or personal names. These include *Pe-ri-ta* = "the man from Beirut," *Tu-ri-jo* = "the Tyrian (man from Tyre)," and *po-ni-ki-jo* = "Phoenician (man or spice)." *A-ra-da-jo* = "the man from Arad [Arvad]" is also found only in the tablets at Knossos (Cline 1994:50, 129; see previously Astour 1964:194, 1967:336–344).

In addition, the Linear B tablets found at Pylos and Mycenae (as well as Knossos) contain probable textual references to Cyprus, Cypriot goods, and possibly Minoan goods destined for Cyprus. The first term, *ku-pi-ri-jo* = "Cypriot," is used at Pylos as an ethnic adjective to describe individuals associated with sheepherding, bronze working, and mixed commodities, including wool, cloth, and alum. The second term, *a-ra-si-jo* = "Alašiya" or "Alašiyan," is most likely a reference to Cyprus, similar to the Akkadian *a-la-ši-ia*, Egyptian *'irs₃*, Hittite *a-la-ši-ia*, and Ugaritic *altyy*. It has been interpreted as an ethnic adjective or as a personal name, since it is used to designate a shepherd in one text found at Knossos. The term, however, also appears in connection with the Linear B word for oil, and thus may serve a second purpose by designating goods destined for or coming from Cyprus (Cline 1994:60, 130; see also Palaima 1991:280–281, 291–295).

Finally, there are a series of ethnic names interpreted as West Anatolian, primarily female workers, which are found in the Linear B texts at Pylos. All refer to areas located on the western coast of Anatolia. These are *Mi-ra-ti-ja* = "Miletus," *Ze-pu₂-ra₃* = "Halikarnassus," *Ki-ni-di-ja* = "Knidus," and *A-ˀ64-ja, A-ˀ64-jo* and variations = "Lydia (Asia)" or "Assuwa." Latacz (2004) has also recently suggested that there may be Trojan women mentioned on these Pylos tablets. It has been hypothesized that all of these women may have been captured during Mycenaean raids on the western coast of Anatolia (Cline 1994:68–69, 130–131; see most recently Latacz 2004:280–281, who cites Niemeier 1999:154 for additional occurrences of mentions in the Pylos tablets of women from Lemnos and Chios, as well as perhaps Troy or the Troad).

There may also be more such possible loan-words waiting to be discovered in the new Linear B tablets found at Boeotian Thebes in the 1990s.

CONCLUSIONS

The Orientalia found in Late Bronze Age contexts within the Aegean area, including those found on the Greek mainland, represent a significant body of evidence that may be utilized by scholars studying the trade and interconnections of the ancient Mediterranean. These imported objects consist of a variety of object types, shapes, materials, and areas of origin. Taken as a whole, they are far more than mere bric-a-brac. The scholar who dismisses these objects out of hand casts aside the only extant physical evidence left in the Aegean of the complex trading networks that connected the Mediterranean world during the second millennium BC.

However, these imports should not be considered simply on their own, for they can most profitably be used to supplement other extant data, in particular the textual and pictorial evidence from Egypt, Syria-Palestine, Anatolia, Mesopotamia, and the Aegean region itself. When utilized carefully in conjunction with these literary and pictorial data, the Orientalia can help to clarify our picture of the international trade and relations during the Late Bronze Age.

A number of tentative observations and conclusions may be made. First, trade was primarily directional to the major palatial centers of the Aegean, with secondary redistribution from those centers. Second, trade was primarily commercial, although some gift exchanges and reciprocity at the palatial level appear to have taken place as well. Third, the Greek mainland was the principal destination of the trade routes, or at least the objects, from Egypt and the Near East during the LH IIIB–C periods (thirteenth through mid-eleventh centuries BC), after Crete had been the primary destination in earlier periods. Fourth, the trade networks and diplomatic connections were apparently as complex and politically motivated in the ancient world as they are today, 3500 years later. Fifth, as I have suggested elsewhere for Crete and the Minoans (Cline 1999), I believe that the Orientalia found on mainland Greece and the Mycenaean objects found in Egypt and the Near East indicate that we should consider the Bronze Age Aegean not as simply "an adjunct to an eastern Mediterranean world system" (Kardulias 1995:342, 1996:1) but rather as an integral if geographically distant part of a "world system" of autonomous core regions linked via a trade network extending from the Aegean to the eastern Mediterranean and beyond. And finally, I would not be at all surprised to learn someday that it was the cutting of the trade routes to Egypt and the Near East that played a role—either major or minor—in the "systems collapse" I believe brought an end to Mycenaean society at the close of the Late Bronze Age.

The Late Bronze Age physical artifacts, along with the textual references, the inscriptions, and the wall paintings found in the Aegean, Egypt, and the eastern Mediterranean, all indicate that we must envision strong commercial and cultural interactions, both direct and indirect, between the Mycenaeans and the Canaanites, Kassites, Mitanni, Cypriotes, Assyrians, Egyptians, and, to a lesser extent, even the Hittites. They are conclusive proof that Greece and the Late Bronze Age Aegean cannot be studied in isolation, that contacts with Egypt and the Near East occurred and were probably even frequent. They provide tangible evidence of foreign contacts, ranging from the commercial transactions of independent merchants to emissaries sent from one royal court to another. Such exchanges occurred over a period of at least six hundred years, throughout the latter half of the second millennium BC. These interactions were not static but fluctuated with time and with the rise and fall of empires and kingdoms. The Orientalia found on mainland Greece and the Mycenaean pottery found in Egypt and the Near East remain as intriguing, tangible clues to what once was lively commerce and interaction.

NOTES

1. As an exception to the rule, see now Manning and Hulin 2005 for a deliberately minimalistic and, I believe, ultimately harmful interpretation of the available data. I would especially take issue with their statement that the "evidence base of 1,118 items [in Cline 1994] . . . [is] an inadequate, if not misleading basis from which to analyze trade" (p. 283). Since my 1994 catalogue represents all of the imported objects known to us at that time from the Late Bronze Age Aegean, it is certainly not inadequate, nor is it in any way misleading in and of itself. It is what it is. Regardless of whether there once were additional perishable items or other evidence "not represented in recovered artifact finds," as I agree there must have been, the fact is that these are the only extant objects we have. They must be taken into account in any discussion involving possible trade and contact between the LBA Aegean, Egypt, and the Near East; it does no good to disparage the only material evidence currently available to us. What one does with the data is a different matter; one can feel free to disagree with my subsequent hypotheses or suggestions based on those data, but to refer to the extant data as a "misleading basis from which to analyze trade" seems unduly minimalistic, misguided, and ingenuous.

2. This chapter represents a condensing and an updating of material originally presented in Cline 1994 and elsewhere. The material and interpretations presented here are focused on the imports found on the Greek mainland, just as Cline 1999 focused on the imports found on Crete and dealt specifically with Minoan contacts with Egypt and the Near East rather than with Mycenaean. In terms of the actual number of imports found on the Greek mainland in Late Bronze Age contexts, not much has changed since 1994 (although see now Maran 2004 for reports of a few new finds at Tiryns that have not yet been published and therefore are not included here). Unless otherwise specified, therefore, absolute numbers given below are taken from Cline 1994.

3. Note that Maran 2004 suggests that at least some of the Cypriot imports at Tiryns—the wall brackets characterized by a row of deep finger impressions on the vertical back portion—are actually local imitations. These objects have not yet been subjected to NAA or petrographic analysis to clarify their status as imports or local imitations (Maran, personal communication).

BIBLIOGRAPHY

𝍖𝍖𝍖𝍖𝍖𝍖

Acheson, P.

1999   The role of force in the development of early Mycenaean polities. In *POLEMOS: Le contexte guerrier en égée à l'âge du bronze. Actes de la 7e rencontre égéenne internationale*, edited by R. Laffineur, 97–102. Aegaeum 19. Liège: Université de Liège; Austin: University of Texas at Austin Program in Aegean Scripts and Prehistory.

Adrimi-Sismani,V.

1994   Mykenaiki poli sto Dimini: Neotera dedomena gia ten archaia Iolko. In *Neotera dedomena gia ten archaea Iolko: Praktika epistemonikes sinantisis, 12 Maiou 1993*, edited by Demotiko Kentro Istorias kai Tekmerioses, 17–44. Volos: Demos Volou.

1999   Mykenaikos keramikos klivanos sto Dimini. In *He peripheria tou Mykenaikou kosmou: Praktika A Diethnous epistemonikou Symposiou, Lamia 25–29 Septemvriou 1994*, edited by E. Froussou, 131–142. Lamia: Ekdosi ID' Eforias Proistorikon kai Klassikon Archaiotiton.

2000   *To Dimini sten Epoche tou Chalkou.* Unpublished Ph.D. dissertation, University of Thessaly, Volos.

2002   Archaia Iôlkos: Mia prôti proseggisi. In *Mnemeia tes Magnesias: Praktika Synedriou Anadeixe tou Diachronikou Mnemeiakou Ploutou tou Volou kai tes euryteres perioches (Volos, 11–13 Maiou)*, edited by Demotiko Kentro Istorias kai Tekmerioses, 94–107. Volos: Editions Volos.

2004–2005   Le palais de Iolkos et sa destruction. *Bulletin de Correspondence Hellénique* 128–129:1–54.

2005   Kasanaki tholos tomb. *Archaeological Reports of the British School of Athens* 50:59–61.

2006   He grisa pseudo-minya kai he stilvomeni cheiropoiete keramiki apo to mykenaiko oikismo tou Diminiou. In *To archaeologiko ergo ste Thessalia kai Sterea Ellada* I. Greek Ministry of Culture and the University of Thessaly. Volos: University of Thessaly.

n.d.a   Koriphoula. *Archaeologikon Deltion.* In press.

n.d.b   Dimini in the Middle Bronze Age. In *Proceedings of the "Messoeladika: Continental Greece in the Middle Bronze Age" International Colloquium, held by the French Archaeological Institute, the American School of Classical Studies and the Nederlanden Institute of Athens, Athens, March 8–12, 2006.* In press.

Adrimi-Sismani,V., and Godart L.

2005   Les inscriptions en Linéaire B de Dimini/Iolkos et leur contexte archéologique. *Annuario della Scuola Archeologica di Atene* 83, ser.3, no. 5, vol. I:47–69.

Agouridis, C.

1997   Sea routes and navigation in the third millennium Aegean. *Oxford Journal of Archaeology* 16:1–24.

Åkerström, Å.

1968   A Mycenaean potter's factory at Berbati near Mycenae. *Atti e Memorie del I Congresso Internazionale di Micenologia, Roma 1967. Incunabula Graeca* 25:48–53.

1987   *Berbati.* Vol. II, *The pictorial pottery.* Stockholm: Svenska Insititet i Athen; Göteborg: Paul Åströms Forlag.

Albers, G.

1994   *Spätmykenische Stadtheiligtümer: Systematische Analyse und vergleichende Auswertung der archäologischen Befunde.* British Archaeological Reports International Series 596. Oxford: British Archaeological Reports.

Alberti, L.

2004   The Late Minoan II–IIIA1 warrior graves at Knossos: The burial assemblages. In *Knossos: Palace, city, state. Proceedings of the conference in Heraklion organised by the British School at Athens and the 23rd Ephoreia of Prehistoric and Classical Antiquities of Heraklion, in November 2000, for the centenary of Sir Arthur Evans's excavations at Knossos*, edited by G. Cadogan, E. Hatzaki and A. Vasilakis, 127–136. British School at Athens Studies 12. Athens: British School at Athens.

Alden, M.

2001 *The prehistoric cemetery: Pre-Mycenaean and Early Mycenaean graves*. Well Built Mycenae 7. Oxford: Oxbow Books.

Alin, P.

1962 *Das ende der Mykenischen Fundstatten auf dem griechischen Festland*. Studies in Mediterranean Archaeology I. Lund: Paul Åströms Förlag.

Anderson, J.K.

1975 Greek chariot-borne and mounted infantry. *American Journal of Archaeology* 79:175–187.

Andreadaki-Vlasaki, M., and E. Papadopoulou

1997 LM IIIA:1 pottery from Khamalevri, Rethymnon. In *Late Minoan III pottery: Chronology and terminology. Acts of a meeting held at the Danish Institute at Athens, August 12–14, 1994*, edited by E. Hallager and B.P. Hallager, 111–151. Monographs of the Danish Institute at Athens 1. Athens: Åarhus University Press.

Anglim, S., P.G. Jestice, R.S. Rice, S.M. Rusch, and J. Serrati

2002 *Fighting techniques of the ancient world 3000 BC–AD 500: Equipment, combat skills and tactics*. London: Amber Books.

Arachoviti P.

1988 Velestino (Archaies Pherai). *Archaeologikon Deltion* 43B:248–249.

2000 Stoicheia archaeologikes drasis stis Pherais kai ten euryteri perioche tous ta teleutaia okto chronia. In *To Ergo tôn Ephoreiôn Archaeoteton kai Neoterôn Mnemeion tou HYP.PO. ste Thessalia kai ten euryteri perioche tes (1990–1998)*, edited by the Greek Ministry of Culture, 355–371. Volos: IG' Ephoreia Proïstorikôn kai Klassikôn Archaeoteton.

Arvanitakis, J.A.

2005 *The Neopalatial–Final Palatial transition at Kommos in southcentral Crete: Evidence for connections with Knossos and for the extent of Mycenaean influence in the LM II–IIIA1 ceramic record*. Ph.D. dissertation, University of Toronto.

Arvanitopoulos, A.

1907 En Pherais. *Praktika tes Archaeologikes Etaireias* 23:153–171.

1911 Archaia leophoros Pagasôn-Pherôn: Pithani thesis mykenaeôn taphon Minuôn Iolkou. *Praktika tes Archaeologikes Etaireias* 1911:301–303.

Astour, M.C.

1964 Greek names in the Semitic world and Semitic names in the Greek world. *Journal of Near Eastern Studies* 23:193–201.

1967 *HellenoSemitica*. 2nd ed. Leiden: E. J. Brill.

Aura Jorro, F.

1985 *Diccionario micenico I*. Madrid: Instituto de Filología.

Avila, R.

1983 Das Kuppelgrab von Volos-Kapakli. *Prähistorische Zeitschrift* 58:5–60.

Baboula, E.

2000 "Buried" metal in Late Minoan inheritance customs. In *Metals make the world go round: The supply and circulation of metals in Bronze Age Europe*, edited by C.F.E. Pare, 70–81. Oxford: Oxbow Books.

Banou, E.

2005 Late Minoan III Mochlos (East Crete) versus Late Minoan III Viannos (central-eastern Crete): Differences and similarities. In *Ariadne's threads. Connections between Crete and the Greek mainland in Late Minoan III (LM IIIA2 to LM IIIC). Proceedings of the International Workshop held at Athens, Scuola Archeologica Italiana, 5–6 April 2003*, edited by A.L. D'Agata and J. Moody, 146–184. Scuola Archeologica Italiana di Atene, Tripodes 3. Athens: Scuola Archeologica Italiana di Atene.

Banou, E., and G. Rethemiotakis

1997 Center and periphery: New evidence for the relations between Knossos and the area of Viannos in the LMII–IIIA periods. In *La Crète Mycénienne: Actes de la Table Ronde Internationale organisée par l'École française d'Athènes, 26–28 Mars 1991*, edited by J. Driessen and A. Farnoux, 23–57. *Bulletin de Correspondance Hellénique*, suppl. vol. 30. Paris: Diffusion de Boccard.

Barber, R.

1992 The origins of the Mycenaean palace. In *FILOLAKWN: Lakonian studies in honour of Hector Catling*, edited by J. Sanders, 11–23. London: The British School at Athens.

1999 Hostile Mycenaeans in the Cyclades? In *POLEMOS: Le contexte guerrier en Égée a L'Âge du Bronze*, edited by R. Laffineur, 133–139. Aegaeum 19. Liège: Université de Liège; Austin: University of Texas at Austin Program in Aegean Scripts and Prehistory.

Barlow, J., and P. Idziak

1989 Selective use of clays at a Middle Bronze Age site in Cyprus. *Archaeometry* 31:66–76.

Bass, G.

1986 A Bronze Age shipwreck at Ulu Burun (Kas): 1984 campaign. *American Journal of Archaeology* 90:274–275.

Batziou-Eustathiou, A.

1985 Mykenaika apo te Nea Ionia Volou. *Archaeologikon Deltion* 40:7–71.

1998 *He Hysteri Epoche tou Chalkou sten perioche tes Magnesias: To Kastro (Palia) kai ta Pevkakia).*

Unpublished Ph.D. dissertation, University of Thessaly, Volos.

Baumbach, L.

1983   An examination of the evidence for a state of emergency at Pylos c. 1200 B.C. from the Linear B tablets. In *Res Mycenaeae: Akten des VII. internationalen Mykenologischen Colloquiums*, edited by A. Heubeck and G. Neumann, 28–40. Göttingen: Vandenhoeck and Ruprecht.

Begg, D.J.I.

1987   Continuity in the West Wing at Knossos. In *The function of the Minoan palaces: Proceedings of the First International Symposium at the Swedish Institute at Athens, 10–16 June 1984*, edited by R. Hägg and N. Marinatos, 179–184. Stockholm: Paul Åströms Förlag.

Bell, M.R.

1982   The preliminary report on the Mycenaean pottery from Deir El Medina. *Annales du Service des antiquités de l'Égypte* 78:143–163.

1985   Gurob Tomb 605 and Mycenaean chronology. *Mélanges Gamal Eddin Mokhtar. Bd'E* 97(1):61–86.

Bendall, L.M.

2003   A reconsideration of the northeastern building at Pylos: Evidence for a Mycenaean redistributive center. *American Journal of Archaeology* 107:181–231.

2004   Fit for a king? Hierarchy, exclusion, aspiration and desire in the social structure of Mycenaean banqueting. In *Food, cuisine and society in prehistoric Greece*, edited by P. Halstead and J.C. Barrett, 105–135. Sheffield Studies in Aegean Archaeology 5. Oxford: Oxbow Books.

Bennet, J.

1985   The structure of the Linear B administration at Knossos. *American Journal of Archaeology* 89:231–249.

1987   The wild country east of Dikte: The problem of East Crete in the LM III period. In *Studies in Mycenaean and Classical Greek presented to John Chadwick*, edited by J. T. Killen, J. L. Melena, and J.-P. Olivier, 77–88. *Minos* 20–22. Salamanca: Ediciones Universidad de Salamanca.

1988a   Approaches to the problem of combining Linear B textual data and archaeological data in the LBA Aegean. In *Problems in Greek prehistory: Proceedings of the BSA Centenary Conference, Manchester, 14–18 April 1986*, edited by E.B. French and K. Wardle, 509–518. Bristol: Bristol Classical Press.

1988b   "Outside in the distance": Problems in understanding the economic geography of Mycenaean palatial territories. In *Texts, tablets, and scribes: Studies in Mycenaean epigraphy and economy offered to Emmett L. Bennett, Jr.*, edited by J.-P. Olivier and T.G. Palaima, 19–41. *Minos*, suppl. vol. 10. Salamanca: University of Salamanca.

1990   Knossos in context: Comparative perspectives on the Linear B administration of LM II–III Crete. *American Journal of Archaeology* 94:193–211.

1992   "Collectors" or "owners"? An examination of their possible functions within the palatial economy of LMIII Crete. In *Mykenaïka: Actes du 9e Colloque internationale sur les textes mycéniens et égéens*, edited by J.-P. Olivier, 65–101. *Bulletin de Correspondance Hellénique*, suppl. vol. 25. Paris: Diffusion de Boccard.

1995   Space through time: Diachronic perspectives on the spatial organization of the Pylian state. In *POLITEIA: Society and state in the Aegean Bronze Age*, edited by W.-D. Niemeier and R. Laffineur, 587–602. Aegaeum 13. Liège: Université de Liège; Austin: University of Texas at Austin Program in Aegean Scripts and Prehistory.

1998   The PRAP survey's contribution. In *Sandy Pylos: An archaeological history from Nestor to Navarino*, edited by J.L. Davis, 134–138. Austin: University of Texas Press.

1998–1999   *re-u-ko-to-ro za-we-te*: Leuktron as a secondary capital in the Pylos kingdom. In *A-NA-QO-TA: Studies presented to J.T. Killen*, edited by J. Bennet and J. Driessen, 11–30. *Minos* 33–34. Salamanca: Ediciones Universidad de Salamanca.

1999a   The Mycenaean conceptualization of space or Pylian geography . . . yet again. In *Floreant Studia Mycenaea: Akten des 10. Mykenologischen Kolloquiums 1995, Salzburg*, edited by S. Deger-Jalkotzy, S. Hiller, O. Panagl, and G. Nightingale, 139–142. Vienna: Österreichische Akademie der Wissenschaften.

1999b   Pylos: The expansion of a Mycenaean palatial center. In *Rethinking Mycenaean palaces: New interpretations of an old idea*, edited by M.L. Galaty and W.A. Parkinson, 9–18. Los Angeles: Cotsen Institute of Archaeology, University of California–Los Angeles.

Bennet, J., and I. Galanakis

2005   Parallels and contrasts: Early Mycenaean mortuary traditions in Messenia and Laconia. In *AUTOCHTHON: Papers presented to O.T.P.K. Dickinson on the occasion of his retirement*, edited by A. Dakouri-Hild and S. Sherratt, 144–155. British Archaeological Reports International Series 1432. Oxford: Archaeopress.

Bennet, J., and M.L. Galaty
1997   Ancient Greece: Recent developments in Aegean archaeology and regional studies. *Journal of Archaeological Research* 5(1):75–120.

Bennet, J., and C.W. Shelmerdine
2001   Not the Palace of Nestor: The development of the "Lower Town" and other non-palatial settlements in LBA Messenia. In *Urbanism in the Aegean Bronze Age*, edited by K. Branigan, 135–140. Sheffield Studies in Aegean Archaeology. Sheffield: Sheffield Academic Press.

Bennett, E., Jr.
1950   Fractional quantities in Minoan bookkeeping. *American Journal of Archaeology* 54: 204–222.

1956   The landholders of Pylos. *American Journal of Archaeology* 69:3–133.

Bergquist, B.
1988   The archaeology of sacrifice: Minoan-Mycenaean versus Greek. A brief query into two sites with contrary evidence. In *Early Greek cult practice*, edited by R. Hägg, N. Marinatos, and G. Nordquist, 21–34. Stockholm: Paul Åstroms Förlag.

Bernal, M.
1987   *Black Athena: The Afroasiatic roots of Classical civilisation. Vol. I. The fabrication of ancient Greece 1785–1985*. London: Free Association Books.

1991   *Black Athena: The Afroasiatic roots of Classical civilisation. Vol. II. The archaeological and documentary evidence*. New Brunswick, NJ: Rutgers University Press.

Bietak, M.
2000   Minoan paintings in Avaris, Egypt. In *The wall paintings of Thera: Proceedings of the First International Symposium at the Petros M. Nomikos Conference Center at Thera, 30 August–4 September, 1997*, edited by S. Sherratt, 33–42. Athens: Pergamos Editions.

2005   The setting of the Minoan wall paintings at Avaris. In *Aegean wall painting: A tribute to Mark Cameron*, edited by L. Morgan, 83–90. British School at Athens Studies 13. London: British School at Athens.

Binford, L.R.
1968a   Archaeological perspectives. In *New perspectives in archaeology*, edited by S.R. Binford and L.R. Binford, 5–32. London: Aldine.

1968b   Some comments on historical versus processual archaeology. *Southwestern Journal of Archaeology* 24:267–275.

1982   Objectivity–Explanation–Archaeology 1981. In *Theory and explanation in archaeology*, edited by C. Renfrew, M.J. Rowlands, and B. Seagraves. New York: Academic Press.

Bintliff, J.L., ed.
1977   *Mycenaean geography*. Cambridge: British Association for Mycenaean Studies.

Blanton, R.
1976   Anthropological studies of cities. *Annual Review of Anthropology* 5:249–264.

1978   *Monte Albán: Settlement patterns at the ancient Zapotec capital*. New York: Academic Press.

2004   A comparative perspective on settlement pattern and population change in Mesoamerican and Mediterranean civilizations. In *Side-by-side survey: Comparative regional studies in the Mediterranean world*, edited by S.E. Alcock and J.F. Cherry, 206–242. Oxford: Oxbow Books.

Blanton, R., G. Feinman, S. Kowaleski, and P. Peregrine
1996   A dual-processual theory for the evolution of the Mesoamerican civilization. *Current Anthropology* 37(1):1–14.

Blanton, R., S. Kowalewski, G. Feinman, and J. Appel
1981   *Ancient Mesoamerica: A comparison of change in three regions*. Cambridge: Cambridge University Press.

1982   Monte Albán's hinterland, part I: The Prehispanic settlement patterns of the central and southern parts of the valley of Oaxaca, Mexico. *Memoirs of the Museum of Anthropology* 15. Ann Arbor: University of Michigan Press.

1993   *Ancient Mesoamerica: A comparison of change in three regions*. 2nd ed. Cambridge: Cambridge University Press.

Blegen, C.W.
1921   *Korakou: A prehistoric settlement near Corinth*. Boston: American School of Classical Studies at Athens.

1928   *Zygouries: A prehistoric settlement in the Valley of Cleonae*. Cambridge, MA: Harvard University Press.

1930   Gonia. *Metropolitan Museum Studies* 3(1):55–80.

1937   *Prosymna: The Helladic settlement preceding the Argive Heraeum*. Cambridge: Cambridge University Press.

1975   Neolithic remains at Nemea. *Hesperia* 44:224–279.

Blegen, C.W., and M. Lang
1958   The Palace of Nestor excavations of 1957. *American Journal of Archaeology* 62:175–191.

Blegen, C.W., and M. Rawson
1966   *The Palace of Nestor at Pylos in western Messenia. Vol. I. The buildings and their contents*. Princeton, NJ: Princeton University Press.

Blegen, C.W., M. Rawson, W. Taylour, and W.P. Donovan
1973   *The Palace of Nestor at Pylos in western Messenia. Vol. III. Acropolis and Lower Town, tholoi, grave circles and chamber tombs, discoveries outside the citadel*. Princeton, NJ: Princeton University Press.

Blitzer, H.

1991 Middle to Late Helladic chipped stone implements of the southwest Peloponnese. Part I. The evidence from Malthi. *Hydra* 9:1–73.

1992 The chipped stone, ground stone, and worked bone industries. In *Excavations at Nichoria in southwest Greece. Vol. 2. The Bronze Age occupation*, edited by W. McDonald and N. Wilkie, 712–756. Minneapolis: University of Minnesota Press.

1995 Minoan implements and industries. In *Kommos: An excavation on the south coast of Crete. Vol. I. The Kommos region and houses of the Minoan town. Part I. The Kommos region, ecology, and Minoan industries*, edited by J.W. Shaw and M.C. Shaw, 403–536. Princeton, NJ: Princeton University Press.

Borgna, E.

2004 Aegean feasting: A Minoan perpective. In *The Mycenaean feast*, edited by J.C. Wright, 127–159. Princeton, NJ: American School of Classical Studies at Athens.

Borgna, E., and P. Càssola Guida

2005 Some observations on the nature of and modes of exchange between Italy and the Aegean in the Late Mycenaean period. In *EMPORIA: Aegeans in the Central and Eastern Mediterranean. Proceedings of the 10th International Aegean Conference, Athens, Italian School of Archaeology, 14–18 April 2004*, edited by R. Laffineur and E. Greco, 497–505. Aegaeum 25. Liège: Université de Liège; Austin: University of Texas at Austin Program in Aegean Scripts and Prehistory.

Bosanquet, R.C.

1904 The obsidian trade. In *Excavations at Phylakopi in Melos*, edited by T.D. Atkinson, 216–232. Journal of Hellenic Studies Occasional Paper 4. London: Macmillan.

Boyd, M.J.

2002 *Middle Helladic and Early Mycenaean mortuary practices in the southern and western Peloponnese*. British Archaeological Reports International Series 1009. Oxford: Archaeopress.

Bradley, R.

2002 *The past in prehistoric societies*. London: Routledge

Brandt, J.

1993 *The bicycle wheel*. 3rd ed. Palo Alto, CA: Avocet.

Branigan, K.

1987 The economic role of the first palaces. In *The function of the Minoan palaces. Proceedings of the Fourth International Symposium at the Swedish Institute in Athens, 10–16 June, 1984*, edited by R. Hägg and N. Marinatos, 245–249. Stockholm: Svenska Institutet i Athen.

1988 Some observations on state formation in Crete. In *Problems in Greek prehistory: Proceedings of the British School at Athens Centenary Conference, Manchester, 14–18 April 1986*, edited by E.B. French and K. Wardle, 63–71. Bristol: Bristol Classical Press.

1995 Social transformations and the rise of the state in Crete. In *POLITEIA: Society and state in the Aegean Bronze Age*, edited by W.-D. Niemeier and R. Laffineur, 33–42. Aegaeum 13. Liège: Université de Liège; Austin: University of Texas at Austin Program in Aegean Scripts and Prehistory.

Branigan, K., ed.

1998 *Cemetery and society in the Aegean Bronze Age*. Sheffield Studies in Aegean Archaeology 1. Sheffield: Sheffield Academic Press.

Braun, D.

1983 Pots as tools. In *Archaeological hammers and theories*, edited by J. Moore, 107–134. New York: Academic Press.

Brinkman, J.A.

1981 The Western Asiatic seals found at Thebes in Greece: A preliminary edition of the inscriptions. *Archiv für Orientforschung* 28:73–77.

Brogan, T.M., R.A.K. Smith, and J.S. Soles

2002 Mycenaeans at Mochlos? Exploring culture and identity in the LM IB to LM IIIA1 transition. *Aegean Archaeology* 6:89–118.

Broodbank, C.

1989 The longboat and society in the Cyclades in the Keros-Syros Culture. *American Journal of Archaeology* 93:319–37.

2000 *An island archaeology of the early Cyclades*. Cambridge: Cambridge University Press.

2004 Minoanisation. *Proceedings of the Cambridge Philological Society* 50:46–91.

Brumfiel, E.M.

1994 Factional competition and political development in the New World: An introduction. In *Factional competition and political development in the New World*, edited by E.M. Brumfiel and J.W. Fox, 3–13. Cambridge: Cambridge University Press.

Brumfiel, E.M., and T.K. Earle

1987 Specialization, exchange, and complex societies: An introduction. In *Production, exchange and complex societies*, edited by E.M. Brumfiel and T.K. Earle, 1–9. Cambridge: Cambridge University Press.

Bryce, T.R.

1999 *The kingdom of the Hittites*. Oxford: Clarendon Paperbacks.

Bunnens, G.

1999   Review of E.H. Cline, *Sailing the Wine-Dark Sea*. *Journal of the American Oriental Society* 119(1): 130–131.

Burke, B.

2005   Materialization of Mycenaean ideology and the Ayia Triada sarcophagus. *American Journal of Archaeology* 109:403–422.

Burton, J., and A. Simon

1993   Acid extraction as a simple and inexpensive method for compositional characterization of archaeological ceramics. *American Antiquity* 58(1):45–49.

1996   A pot is not a rock: A reply to Neff, Glascock, Bishop, and Blackman. *American Antiquity* 61(2):405–413.

Buxeda i Garrigós, J., R.E. Jones, V. Kilikoglou, S.T. Levi, Y. Maniatis, J. Mitchell, L. Vagnetti, K.A. Wardle, and S. Andreou

2003   Technology transfer at the periphery of the Mycenaean world: The cases of Mycenaean pottery found in central Macedonia (Greece) and the Plain of Sybaris (Italy). *Archaeometry* 45:263–284.

Buxeda i Garrigós, J., H. Mommsen, and A. Tsolakidou

2002   Alterations of Na, K and Rb concentrations in Mycenaean pottery and a proposed explanation using X-ray diffraction. *Archaeometry* 44:187–198.

Cann, J.R., and C. Renfrew

1964   The characterization of obsidian and its application to the Mediterranean region. *Proceedings of the Prehistoric Society* 30:111–133.

Cariolou, G.A.

1997   KYRENIA II: The return from Cyprus to Greece of the replica of a Hellenic merchant ship. In *Res Maritimae: Cyprus and the eastern Mediterranean from prehistory to Late Antiquity*, edited by S. Swiny, R.L. Hohlfelder, and H.W. Swiny, 83–7. ASOR Archaeological Reports 4. Atlanta, GA: Scholars Press.

Carlier, P.

1984   *La royauté en Grèce avant Alexandre*. Strasbourg: Association pour l'étude de la civilisation romaine.

1992   Les collecteurs sont-ils des fermiers? In *Mykenaika: Actes du 9e Colloque internationale sur les textes mycéniens et égéens*, edited by J.-P. Olivier, 159–166. *Bulletin de Correspondance Hellénique*, suppl. vol. 25.

Carothers, J.

1992   *The Pylian kingdom: A case study of an early state*. Ph.D. dissertation, University of California–Los Angeles. Ann Arbor: University Microfilms.

Carothers, J., and W. McDonald

1979   Size and distribution of the population in Late Bronze Age Messenia: Some statistical approaches. *Journal of Field Archaeology* 6:433–455.

Caskey, J.L.

1968   Lerna in the Early Bronze Age. *American Journal of Archaeology* 72:313–316.

1971   Investigations in Keos. Part I. Excavations and explorations, 1966–1970. *Hesperia* 40:359–396.

Catling, H.W.

1968   A Mycenaean puzzle from Lefkandi in Euboea. *American Journal of Archaeology* 72:41–49.

Catling, H., E. Richards, and A. Blin-Stoyle

1963   Correlations between composition and provenance of Mycenaean and Minoan pottery. *Annual of the British School of Archaeology in Athens* 58:94–115.

Catling, H., J.F. Cherry, R. Jones, and J.T. Killen

1980   The Linear B inscribed stirrup jars and west Crete. *Annual of the British School of Archaeology in Athens* 75:49–113.

Cavanagh, W.G.

1998   Innovation, conservatism and variation in Mycenaean funerary ritual. In *Cemetery and society in the Aegean Bronze Age*, edited by K. Branigan, 103–114. Sheffield Studies in Aegean Archaeology 1. Sheffield: Sheffield Academic Press.

2001   Empty space? Courts and squares in Mycenaean towns. In *Urbanism in the Aegean Bronze Age*, edited by K. Branigan, 119–134. Sheffield Studies in Aegean Archaeology 4. Sheffield: Sheffield Academic Press.

Cavanagh, W.G., and C. Mee

1990   The location of Mycenaean chamber tombs in the Argolid. In *Celebrations of death and divinity in the Bronze Age Argolid: Proceedings of the Sixth International Symposium at the Swedish Institute in Athens, 11–13 June, 1988*, edited by R. Hägg and G. Nordquist, 55–63. Stockholm: Svenska Institutet i Athen.

Chadjiagelakis, L.

1996   Akropoli Kieriou. *Archaeologikon Deltion* 51: 358–361.

1997   Akropoli Kieriou—Thesi Oglas. *Archaeologikon Deltion* 52:473.

1998   Agnantero. *Archaeologikon Deltion* 53:445–448.

Chadwick, J.

1957   Potnia. *Minos* 5:117–129.

1963   The Mycenae tablets III. *Transactions of the American Philosophical Society* 52(7):48–50.

1964   Pylos tablet Un1322. In *Mycenaean Studies: Proceedings of the Third International Colloquium for Mycenaean Studies held at "Wingspread," 4–8 September 1961*, edited by E.L. Bennett, 19–26. Madison: University of Wisconsin Press.

1972   The Mycenaean documents. In *The Minnesota Messenia Expedition: Reconstructing a Bronze Age regional environment*, edited by W. McDonald and G.R. Rapp, Jr., 100–116. Minneapolis: University of Minnesota Press.

1976 *The Mycenaean world*. Cambridge: Cambridge University Press.

1987 *Linear B and related scripts*. Berkeley and Los Angeles: University of California Press.

1988 The women of Pylos. In *Texts, tablets and scribes: Studies in Mycenaean epigraphy and economy offered to Emmett. L. Bennett, Jr.*, edited by J.-P. Olivier and T.G. Palaima, 49–93. *Minos*, suppl. vol. 10. Salamanca: University of Salamanca.

Chase-Dunn, C.

1989 *Global formation: Structures of the world-economy*. London: Basil Blackwell.

1992 The comparative study of world-systems. *Review* 15:313–333.

Chase-Dunn, C., and T.D. Hall

1991 *Core/periphery relations in precapitalist worlds*. Boulder, CO: Westview Press.

1993 Comparing world-systems: Concepts and working hypotheses. *Social Forces* 71:851–886.

1995 The historical evolution of world-systems. *Proto-soziologie* 7:23-34, 301–303.

1997 *Rise and demise: Comparing world-systems*. Boulder, CO: Westview Press.

Cherry, J.F.

1977 Investigating the political geography of an early state by multidimensional scaling of Linear B tablet data. In *Mycenaean geography: Proceedings of the Cambridge Colloquium 1976*, edited by J. Bintliff, 76–83. Cambridge: Cambridge University Press.

1981 Pattern and process in the earliest colonization of the Mediterranean islands. *Proceedings of the Prehistoric Society* 47:41–68.

1986 Polities and palaces: Some problems in Minoan state formation. In *Peer polity interaction and socio-political change*, edited by C. Renfrew and J.F. Cherry, 19–45. New York: Cambridge University Press.

1987 Power in space: Archaeological and geographical studies of the state. In *Landscape and culture: Geographical and archaeological perspectives*, edited by J.M. Wagstaff, 146–172. Oxford: Blackwell.

1988 Pastoralism and the role of animals in the pre- and protohistoric economies of the Aegean. In *Pastoral economies in Classical Antiquity*, edited by C. R. Whittaker, 6–34. Cambridge Philological Society, suppl. vol. 14. Cambridge: Cambridge University Press.

1990 The first colonization of the Mediterranean islands: A review of recent research. *Journal of Mediterranean Archaeology* 3:145–221.

Cherry, J.F., and J.L. Davis

1982 The Cyclades and the Greek mainland in LCI: The evidence of the pottery. *American Journal of Archaeology* 86:333–341.

1999 An archaeological homily. In *Rethinking Mycenaean palaces: New interpretations of an old idea*, edited by M.L. Galaty and W.A. Parkinson, 91–98. Los Angeles: Cotsen Institute of Archaeology, University of California–Los Angeles.

2001 "Under the scepter of Agamemnon": The view from the hinterlands of Mycenae. In *Urbanism in the Aegean Bronze Age*, edited by K. Branigan, 141–159. Sheffield Studies in Aegean Archaeology 4. Sheffield: Sheffield Academic Press.

Cherry, J.F., D. Morgomenou, and L.E. Talalay, eds.

2005 *Prehistorians round the pond: Reflections on Aegean prehistory as a discipline*. Ann Arbor, MI: Kelsey Museum of Archaeology.

Chippindale, C.

1997 Editorial. *Antiquity* 71:255–264.

Chlouveraki, S.

2002 Exploitation of gypsum in Minoan Crete. In *Interdisciplinary studies on ancient stone: ASMOSIA VI. Proceedings of the Sixth International Conference, Venice, June 15–18 June 2000*, edited by L. Lazzarini, 25–34. Padua: Bottega d'Erasmo Aldo Ausilio Editore.

Christakis, K.S.

2005 *Cretan Bronze Age pithoi: Traditions and trends in the production and consumption of storage containers in Bronze Age Crete*. Philadelphia: INSTAP/Academic Press.

Chryssoulaki, S.

2005 The imaginary navy of Minoan Crete: Rocky coasts and probable harbours. In *EMPORIA: Aegeans in the central and eastern Mediterranean*, edited by R. Laffineur and E. Greco, 77–90. Aegaeum 25. Liège: Université de Liège; Austin: University of Texas at Austin Program in Aegean Scripts and Prehistory.

Clark, J.E.

1986 From mountain to molehill: A critical review of Teotihuacan's obsidian industry. In *Economic aspects of prehispanic highland Mexico*, edited by B. Issac, 23–74. Greenwich, CT: JAI Press.

1991 Modern Lacandon lithic technology and blade workshops. In *Maya stone tools*, edited by T.R. Hester and H.J. Shafer, 266–265. Madison, WI: Prehistory Press.

Clark, J.E., and W. Parry

1990 Craft specialization and cultural complexity. *Research in Economic Anthropology* 12:289–346.

Cline, E.H.

1987   Amenhotep III and the Aegean: A reassessment of Egypto-Aegean relations in the 14th century BC. *Orientalia* 56(1):1–36.

1990   An unpublished Amenhotep III faience plaque from Mycenae. *Journal of the American Oriental Society* 110(2):200–212.

1991a   Monkey business in the Bronze Age Aegean: The Amenhotep II figurines at Mycenae and Tiryns. *Annual of the British School at Athens* 86:29–42.

1991b   Hittite objects in the Bronze Age Aegean. *Anatolian Studies* 41:133–143.

1991c   A possible Hittite embargo against the Mycenaeans. *Historia* 40(1):1–9.

1994   *Sailing the wine-dark sea: International trade and the Late Bronze Age Aegean.* British Archaeological Reports International Series 591. Oxford: Tempus Reparatum.

1995a   Tinker, tailor, soldier, sailor: Minoans and Mycenaeans abroad. In *POLITEIA: Society and state in the Aegean Bronze Age*, edited by W.-D. Niemeier and R. Laffineur, 265–283. Aegaeum 13. Liège: Université de Liège; Austin: University of Texas at Austin Program in Aegean Scripts and Prehistory.

1995b   "My brother, my son": Rulership and trade between the Late Bronze Age Aegean, Egypt and the Near East. In *The role of the ruler in the prehistoric Aegean: Proceedings of a panel discussion presented at the annual meeting of the Archaeological Institute of America New Orleans, Louisiana 28 December 1992, with additions*, edited by P. Rehak, 143–150. Aegaeum 11. Liège: Université de l'État à Liège; Austin: University of Texas at Austin Program in Aegean Scripts and Prehistory.

1995c   Egyptian and Near-Eastern imports at Late Bronze Age Mycenae. In *Egypt, the Aegean and the Levant: Interconnections in the second millenium BC*, edited by W.V. Davies and L. Schofield, 91–115. London: British Museum Press.

1997   A wrinkle in time: Orientalia and the Mycenaean occupation(s) of Crete. In *Ancient Egypt, the Aegean, and the Near East: Studies in honor of Martha Rhoads Bell, vol. I*, edited by J. Phillips, L. Bell, and B.B. Williams, 163–167. San Antonio: Van Siclen Publications.

1998   Amenhotep III, the Aegean and Anatolia. In *Amenhotep III: Perspectives on his reign*, edited by D. O'Connor and E.H. Cline, 236–250. Ann Arbor: University of Michigan Press.

1999   The nature of the economic relations of Crete with Egypt and the Near East during the Late Bronze Age. In *From Minoan farmers to Roman traders:*

Sidelights on the economy of ancient Crete, edited by A. Chaniotis, 115–143. Munich: G. B. Steiner.

Cline, E.H., and Harris-Cline, D., eds.

1998   *The Aegean and the Orient in the second millennium: Proceedings of the 50th Anniversary Symposium, Cincinnati, 18–20 April 1997.* Aegaeum 18. Liège: Université de Liège; Austin: University of Texas at Austin Programs in Aegean Scripts and Prehistory.

Coldstream, J.N.

1973   *Knossos. The Sanctuary of Demeter. Annual of the British School at Athens*, suppl. vol. 8. London: British School at Athens.

2000   Evans's Greek finds: The early Greek town of Knossos, and its encroachment on the borders of the Minoan palace. *Annual of the British School at Athens* 95:259–299.

Cooper, F.A.

1994   Minnesota archaeological researches at Pylos, 1991–1993 seasons. Available: http://marwp.cla.umn.edu/.

Cosmopoulos, M.B.

2006   The political landscape of Mycenaean states: *A-pu*[2] and the Hither Province of Pylos. *American Journal of Archaeology* 110:205–228.

Costin, C.

1991   Craft specialization: Issues in defining, documenting, and explaining the organization of production. In *Archaeological method and theory, vol. 3*, edited by M.B. Schiffer, 1–56. Tucson: University of Arizona Press.

1998   Introduction: Craft and social identity. In *Craft and social identity*, edited by C.L. Costin and R.P. Wright, 3–16. Archeological Papers of the American Anthropological Association 8. Arlington, VA: American Anthropological Association.

Costin, C., and Earle, T.K.

1989   Status distinction and legitimation of power as reflected in changing patterns of consumption in late prehispanic Peru. *American Antiquity* 54(4):691–714.

Crouwel, J.H.

1981   *Chariots and other means of land transport in Bronze Age Greece.* Amsterdam: Allard Pierson Museum.

Crumley, C.L.

1995   Heterarchy and the analysis of complex societies. In *Heterarchy and the analysis of complex societies*, edited by R.M. Ehrenreich, C.L. Crumley, and J.E. Levy, 1–5. Arlington, VA: American Anthropological Association.

Cucuzza, N.

1997   The North Sector buildings of Haghia Triada. *La Crète Mycénienne: Actes de la Table Ronde Internationale organisée par l'École française d'Athènes, 26–28 Mars 1991*, edited by J. Driessen and A. Farnoux, 73–84. *Bulletin de Correspondance Hellénique*, suppl. vol. 30. Paris: Diffusion de Boccard.

2001 Religion and architecture: Early LM IIIA2 buildings in the southern area of Haghia Triada. In *POTNIA: Deities and religion in the Aegean Bronze Age. Proceedings of the 8th International Aegean Conference Göteborg, Göteborg University, 12–15 April 2000*, edited by R. Laffineur and R. Hägg, 169–174. Aegaeum 22. Liège: Université de Liège; Austin: University of Texas, Program in Aegean Scripts and Prehistory.

2002 Osservazioni sui costume funerary dell'area di Festòs ed Haghia Triada nel TM IIIA1-A2 iniziale. *Creta Antica* 3:133–166.

2003 Il volo del grifo: osservazioni sulla Haghia Triada "Micenea." *Creta Antica* 4:199–272.

Dabney, M.K., P. Halstead, and P. Thomas

2004 Mycenaean feasting on Tsoungiza at ancient Nemea. In *The Mycenaean feast*, edited by J. Wright, 77–96. Princeton, NJ: American School of Classical Studies at Athens.

Dabney, M.K., and J.C. Wright

1990 Mortuary customs, palatial society and state formation in the Aegean area: A comparative study. In *Celebrations of death and divinity in the Bronze Age Argolid. Proceedings of the Sixth International Symposium at the Swedish Institute in Athens, 11–13 June, 1988*, edited by R. Hägg and G. Nordquist, 45–52. Stockholm: Svenska Institutet i Athen.

D'Agata, A.L.

1999a Dinamiche sociali, modelli culturali e indicatori etnici ad H. Triada nel TM III. L'evidenza offerta dalla ceramica. In *EPI PONTON PLAZOMENOI: Simposio italiano di Studi Egei dedicato a Luigi Bernabò Brea e Giovanni Pugliese Carratelli*, edited by V. La Rosa, D. Palermo and L. Vagnetti, 189–198. Roma: Scuola Archeologica Italiana di Atene.

1999b Hidden wars: Minoans and Myceaneans at Haghia Triada in the LM III period. The evidence from pottery. In *POLEMOS: Le contexte guerrier en Egée à l'Âge du Bronz., Actes de la 7e Rencontre égéenne internationale, Université de Liège, 15–17 avril 1998*, edited by R. Laffineur, 47–55. Aegaeum 19. Liège: Université de Liège; Austin: University of Texas Program in Aegean Scripts and Prehistory.

D'Agata, A.-L., and J. Moody, eds.

2005 *Ariadne's threads. Connections between Crete and the Greek Mainland in Late Minoan III (LM IIIA2 to LM IIIC). Proceedings of the International Workshop held at Athens at the Italian School in Athens, 5–6 April 2003.*

Scuola Archeologica Italiana di Atene, Tripodes 3. Athens: Scuola Archeologica di Atene.

Dalton, G.

1961 Economic theory and primitive society. *American Antiquity* 63:1–25.

D'Altroy, T., and R. Bishop

1990 The provincial organization of Inka ceramic production. *American Antiquity* 55:120–138.

D'Altroy, T., and T.K. Earle

1985 Staple finance, wealth finance, and storage in the Inka political economy. *Current Anthropology* 26(2):187–206.

Darcque, P.

2004 Les Mycéniens en dehors de Grèce continentale: La céramique et les autres témoignages archéologiques. In *La céramique mycénienne entre l'Égée et le Levant*. TMO 41. Lyon: Maison de l'Orient.

Davis, J.L.

1977 *Fortifications at Ayia Irini, Keos: Evidence for history and relative chronology.* Ph.D. dissertation, University of Cincinnati. Ann Arbor: University Microfilms.

1979 Minos and Dexithea: Crete and the Cyclades in the later Bronze Age. In *Papers in Cycladic prehistory*, edited by J.L. Davis and J.F. Cherry, 143–157. UCLA Institute of Archaeology Monograph 14. Los Angeles: University of California–Los Angeles.

1988 If there's a room at the top, what's at the bottom? *Bulletin of the Institute of Classical Studies of the University of London* 35:164–165.

2001 Classical archaeology and anthropological archaeology in North America: A meeting of the minds at the millennium? In *Archaeology at the millennium: A sourcebook*, edited by G.M. Feinman and T.D. Price, 415–437. New York: Kluwer Academic/Plenum.

2001 [1992] Review of Aegean prehistory I. The islands of the Aegean. In *Aegean prehistory: A review*, edited by T. Cullen, 19–94. *American Journal of Archaeology*, suppl. 1. Boston: Archaeological Institute of America.

Davis, J.L., ed.

1998 *Sandy Pylos: An archaeological history from Nestor to Navarino.* Austin: University of Texas Press.

Davis, J.L., S. Alcock, J. Bennet, Y. Lolos, and C.W. Shelmerdine

1997 The Pylos Regional Archaeological Project, part I: Overview and the archaeological survey. *Hesperia* 66:391–494.

Davis, J.L., and J. Bennet

1999 Making Mycenaeans: Warfare, territorial expansion, and representations of the other in the Pylian kingdom. In *POLEMOS: Le contexte guerrier en égée à l'âge du bronze. Actes de la 7e Rencontre Égéenne*

Internationale, edited by R. Laffineur, 105–118. Aegaeum 19. Liège Université de Liège; Austin: University of Texas at Austin Program in Aegean Scripts and Prehistory.

Davis, J.L., J. Bennet, and C.W. Shelmerdine

1999   The Pylos Regional Archaeological Project: The prehistoric investigations. In *MELETEMATA: Studies in Aegean archaeology presented to M.H. Wiener as he enters his 65th year*, edited by P.P. Betancourt, V. Karageorghis, R. Laffineur and W.-D. Niemeier, 177–186. Aegaeum 20. Liège: Université de Liège; Austin: University of Texas at Austin Program in Aegean Scripts and Prehistory.

Davis, J.L., and H.B. Lewis

1985   Mechanization of pottery production: A case study from the Cycladic islands. In *Prehistoric production and exchange*, edited by A.B. Knapp and T. Stech, 79–92. Los Angeles: University of California–Los Angeles.

Day, P.M.

1988   The production and distribution of storage jars in Neopalatial Crete. In *Problems in Greek prehistory: Proceedings of the BSA Centenary Conference, Manchester, 14–18 April 1986*, edited by E.B. French and K. Wardle, 499–508. Bristol: Bristol Classical Press.

1989   Technology and ethnography in petrographic studies of ceramics. In *Archaeometry: Proceedings of the 25th International Symposium*, edited by Y. Maniatis, 139–147. New York: Elsevier.

1999   Petrographic analysis of ceramics from the shipwreck at Point Iria. In *The Point Iria wreck: Interconnections in the Mediterranean ca. 1200 B.C. Proceedings of the International Conference, Island of Spetses, 19 September 1998*, edited by W. Phelps, Y. Lolos, and Y. Vichos, 59–75. Athens: Hellenic Institute of Marine Archaeology.

Day, P.M., and D.E. Wilson

2002   Landscapes of memory, craft and power at Pre-Palatial and Proto-Palatial Knossos. In *The Labyrinth revisited: Rethinking Minoan archaeology*, edited by Y. Hamilakis, 143–166. Oxford: Oxbow Books.

Day, P.M., D.E. Wilson, and E. Kiriatzi

1997   Reassessing specialization in prepalatial Cretan ceramic production. In *TEXNH: Craftsmen, craftswomen and craftsmanship in the Aegean Bronze Age*, edited by R. Laffineur and P. Betancourt, 275–289. Aegaeum 16. Liège: Université de Liège; Austin: University of Texas at Austin Program in Aegean Scripts and Prehistory.

de Fidio, P.

1977   *I dosmoi pilii a Poseidon*. Incunabula Graeca 65. Rome: Edizioni dell' Ateneo.

1982   Fiscalità, redistribuzione, equivalenze: Per una discussione sull economia micenea. *Studi Micenei ed Egeo-Anatolici* 23:83–136. Rome: Edizioni dell' Ateneo.

1987   Palais et communautés de village dans le royaume mycénien de Pylos. In *Tractata mycenaea: Proceedings of the Eighth International Colloquium on Mycenaean Studies*, edited by P. Ilievski and L. Crepajac, 129–149. Skopje: Macedonian Academy of Sciences and Arts.

1992   Mycènes et Proche-Orient, ou le théorème des modèles. In *Mykenaïka: Actes du 9e colloque internationale sur les textes mycéniens et égéens*, edited by J.-P. Olivier, 173–196. Bulletin de Correspondance Hellénique, suppl. vol. 25. Paris: Diffusion de Boccard.

2001   Centralization and its limits in the Mycenaean palatial systems. In *Economy and politics in the Mycenaean palace states. Proceedings of a conference held on 1–3 July 1999 in the Faculty of Classics, Cambridge*, edited by S. Voutsaki and J. Killen, 15–24. Cambridge: The Cambridge Philological Society.

Deger-Jalkotzy, S.

1983   Zum Charakter und zur Herausbildung der mykenischen Sozialstruktur. In *Res Mycenaeae*, edited by A. Heubeck and G. Neumann, 89–111. Göttingen: Vandenhoeck and Ruprect.

1996   On the negative aspects of the Mycenaean palace system. In *Atti e memorie del secondo congresso internazionale di micenolagia, Roma-Napoli, 14–20 ottobre 1991*, edited by E. DeMiro, L. Godart, and A. Sacconi, 715–728. Incunabula Graeca 98. Rome.

1998a   The Aegean islands and the breakdown of the Mycenaean palaces around 1200 B.C. In *Eastern Mediterranean: Cyprus–Dodecanese–Crete 16th–6th cent. B.C. Proceedings of the International Symposium. Rethymnon 13-16 May 1997*, edited by V. Karageorghis, and N. Stampolidis, 105–120. Athens: The University of Crete and the A.G. Leventis Foundation.

1998b   The last Mycenaeans and their successors updated. In *Mediterranean peoples in transition: Thirteenth to early tenth centuries BCE. In honor of Professor Trude Dothan*, edited by S. Gitin, A. Mazar, and E. Stern, 114–128. Jerusalem: Israel Exploration Society.

Deger-Jalkotzy, S., and M. Zavadil, eds.

2003   *LH III C chronology and synchronisms*. Vienna: Verlag der Österreichischen Akademie der Wissenschaften.

Demakopoulou, K.

1998   Stone vases from Midea. In *The Aegean and the Orient in the second millennium*, edited by E. H. Cline and D. Harris-Cline, 221–225. Aegaeum 18. Liege: Université de Liège, Histoire de l'art et archéologie de la Grèce antique.

2003   The pottery from the destruction layers in Midea: Late Helladic III B2 Late or Transitional Late Helladic II B2/Late Helladic IIIC Early? In *LH IIIC chronology and synchronisms*, edited by S. Deger-Jalkotzy and M. Zavadil, 77–92. Vienna: Verlag der Österreichischen Akademie der Wissenschaften.

DeMarrais, E., L.J. Castillo, and T. Earle

1996   Ideology, materialization, and power strategies. *Current Anthropology* 37(1):15–31.

Desborough, V. R. d'A.

1964   *The last Mycenaeans and their successors*. Oxford: Clarendon Press.

Dickinson, O.T.P.K.

1994   *The Aegean Bronze Age*. Cambridge: Cambridge University Press.

Diehl, R., and J. Berlo, eds.

1989   *Mesoamerica after the decline of Teotihuacan A.D. 700–900*. Washington, DC: Dumbarton Oaks.

Dimopoulou, N.

1994   Poros of Heraklion. *Archaeologikon Deltion* 49(2): 707–710.

1999   The Neopalatial cemetery of the Knossian harbour-town at Poros: Mortuary behaviour and social ranking. In *Eliten in der Bronzezeit. Ergebnisse zweiter Kolloquien in Mainz und Athen*, edited by I. Kilian-Dirlmeier and M. Egg, 27–36. Monographien des Römisch-Germanischen Zentralmuseums 43(2). Mainz: Verlag des Römisch-Germanischen Zentralmuseums.

Dixon, J.E., J.R. Cann, and C. Renfrew

1968   Obsidian and the origin of trade. *Scientific American* 218(3):38–46.

Dixon, J.E., and C. Renfrew

1973   The source of the Franchthi obsidians. *Hesperia* 42:82–85.

Donohue, A.A.

1985   One hundred years of the *American Journal of Archaeology*: An archival history. *American Journal of Archaeology* 89:3–30.

Doulgeri-Intzesiloglou, A.

1994   Oi neoteres archaeologikes ereunes sten periochi ton Pherôn. *Thessalia. Praktika Diethnous Synedriou, 15 chronia archaeologikes ereunas, 1957–1990. Apotelesmata kai prooptikes (Lyon, 17–22 Apriliou 1990)*, vol. B, edited by the Greek Ministry of Culture, 76–83. Athens: Kapon.

Doxey, D.

1987   Causes and effects of the fall of Knossos in 1375 B.C. *Oxford Journal of Archaeology* 6:301–324.

Drappier, G., and C. Langohr

2004   Iconographie du pouvoir en Crète minoenne. Vers la mise au point d'une méthodologie. In *Iconographie impériale, iconographie royale, iconographie des élites dans le monde gréco-romain*, edited by Y. Perrin, 19–47. Travaux du CERHI 1. Saint-Etienne: Publications de l'Université de Saint-Etienne.

Drennan, R.

1984   Long-distance movement of goods in the Mesoamerican Formative and Classic. *American Antiquity* 49:27–43.

Drews, R.

1993   *The end of the Bronze Age: Changes in warfare and catastrophe ca. 1200 B.C.* Princeton, NJ: Princeton University Press.

Driessen, J.

1990   *An early destruction in the Mycenaean palace at Knossos*. Acta Archaeologica Lovaniensia 2. Leuven: Katholieke Universiteit Leuven.

1994–1995   Data storage for reference and prediction at the dawn of civilization? A review article with some observations on archives before writing. *Minos* 29–30:329–356.

1995   Some observations on the modification of the access systems of Minoan palaces. *Aegean Archaeology* 2:67–85.

1997   Le Palais de Cnossos au MR II–III: Combien de destructions? In *La Crète Mycénienn: Actes de la Table Ronde Internationale organisée par l'École française d'Athènes, 26–28 Mars 1991*, edited by J. Driessen and A. Farnoux, 113–134. Bulletin de Correspondance Hellénique. suppl. vol. 30. Paris: Diffusion de Boccard.

1998–1999   *Kretes* and *Iawones*. Some observations on the identity of Late Bronze Age Knossians. In *A-NA-QO-TA: Studies presented to J.T. Killen*, edited by J. Bennet and J. Driessen, 83–105. *Minos* 33–34. Salamanca: Ediciones Universidad de Salamanca.

1999a   The archaeology of Aegean warfare. In *POLEMOS: Le contexte guerrier en égée à l'âge du bronze. Actes de la 7e Rencontre Égéenne Internationale*, edited by R. Laffineur, 11–20. Aegaeum 19. Liège Université de Liège; Austin: Program in Aegean Scripts and Prehistory.

1999b   The dismantling of a Minoan Hall at Palaikastro (Knossians go home?). In *MELETEMATA: Studies in Aegean archaeology presented to M.H. Wiener as he enters his 65th year*, edited by P.P. Betancourt, V. Karageorghis, R. Laffineur, and W.-D. Niemeier,

227–236. Aegaeum 20. Liège: Université de Liège; Austin: University of Texas, Program in Aegean Scripts and Prehistory.

2000   *The scribes of the room of the chariot tablets. Minos*, suppl. 15. Salamanca: Ediciones Universidad de Salamanca.

2001a   Center and periphery: Some observations on the administration of the kingdom of Knossos. In *Economy and politics in the Mycenaean palace state:. Proceedings of a conference held on 1-3 July 1999 in the Faculty of Classics, Cambridge*, edited by S. Voutsaki and J.T. Killen, 96–112. Cambridge Philological Society, suppl. vol. 27, Cambridge: Cambridge Philological Society.

2001b   History and hierarchy: Preliminary observations on the settlement pattern in Minoan Crete. In *Urbanism in the Aegean Bronze Age*, edited by K. Branigan, 51–71. Sheffield Studies in Aegean Archaeology 4. Sheffield: Sheffield Academic Press.

2002   "The king must die": Some observations on the use of Minoan court compounds. In *Monuments of Minos: Rethinking the Minoan palaces. Proceedings of the International Workshop "Crete of the Hundred Palaces?", Université Catholique de Louvain-la-Neuve, 14–15 December 2001*, edited by J. Driessen, I. Schoep, and R. Laffineur, 1–14. Aegaeum 23. Liège: Université de Liège; Austin: University of Texas Program in Aegean Scripts and Prehistory.

2004   The Central Court of the Palace of Knossos. In *Knossos: Palace, city, state. Proceedings of the conference in Heraklion organised by the British School at Athens and the 23rd Ephoreia of Prehistoric and Classical Antiquities of Heraklion, in November 2000, for the centenary of Sir Arthur Evans's excavations at Knossos*, edited by G. Cadogan, E. Hatzaki, and A. Vasilakis, 75–82. British School at Athens Studies 12. Athens: British School at Athens.

Driessen, J., and A. Farnoux

1994   Mycenaeans at Malia? *Aegean Archaeology* 1:54–64.

2000   "La Crète vaut bien une messe": Domination and "collaboration" on Mycenaean Crete. In *Proceedings of the International Cretological Congress, Vol. 1: Prehistoric and Archaic Greece*, edited by E. Periodos, A. Karetsou, T. Detorakis, and A. Kalokairinos, 431–438. Heraklion: Etairia Kritikon Istorikon Meleton.

Driessen, J., and A. Farnoux, eds.

1997   *La Crète Mycénienne: Actes de la Table Ronde Internationale organisée par l'École française d'Athènes, 26–28 Mars 1991*. Bulletin de Correspondance Hellénique, suppl. vol. 30. Paris: Diffusion de Boccard.

Driessen, J., and C.F. Macdonald

1984   Some military aspects of the Aegean in the late fifteenth and early fourteenth centuries B.C. *Annual of the British School at Athens* 79: 49-74.

1997   *The troubled island: Minoan Crete before and after the Santorini eruption*. Aegaeum 17. Liège: Université de Liège; Austin: University of Texas Program in Aegean Scripts and Prehistory.

Driessen, J., and I. Schoep

1999   The stylus and the sword: The role of scribes and warriors in the conquest of Crete. In *POLEMOS: Le contexte guerrier en Egée à l'Âge du Bronze, Actes de la 7e Rencontre égéenne internationale, Université de Liège, 15–17 avril 1998*, edited by R. Laffineur, 389–397. Aegaeum 19. Liège: Université de Liège; Austin: University of Texas Program in Aegean Scripts and Prehistory.

Duhoux, Y.

1976   *Aspects du vocabulaire économique mycénien*. Amsterdam: Adolf M. Hakkert.

1998   Pre-Hellenic language(s) of Crete. *The Journal of Indo-European Studies* 26:1–39.

Dyson, S.L.

1985   Two paths to the past: A comparative study of the last fifty years of *American Antiquity* and *American Journal of Archaeology*. *American Antiquity* 50:452–463.

1989   Complacency and crisis in late twentieth century classical archaeology. In *Classics: A discipline and profession in crisis?* edited by P. Culham, L. Edmunds, and A. Smith, 211–220. Lanham, MD: University Press of America.

1993   From new to New Age archaeology: Archaeological theory and classical archaeology. A 1990s perspective. *American Journal of Archaeology* 97:195–206.

Earle, T.K.

1977   A reappraisal of redistribution: Complex Hawaiian chiefdoms. In *Exchange systems in prehistory*, edited by T.K. Earle and J. Ericson, 213–229. New York: Academic Press.

1987   Chiefdoms in archaeological and ethnohistorical perspective. *Annual Reviews in Anthropology* 16:279–308.

Evans, A.J.

1906   *The prehistoric tombs of Knossos*. Archaeologia 59. London: B. Quaritch

1921   *The Palace of Minos: A comparative account of the successive stages of early Cretan civilization as illustrated by the discoveries at Knossos, Vol. 1*. London: MacMillan and Co., Limited.

Evans, J.D.

1964   Excavations in the Neolithic settlement at Knossos. *Annual of the British School at Athens* 59:132–240.

Evely, R.D.G.

2003 The stone, bone, ivory, bronze, and clay finds. In *Knossos: The South House*, edited by P.A. Mountjoy, 167–194. *Annual of the British School at Athens*, suppl. vol. 34. London: The British School at Athens.

Evely, R.D.G., and C. Runnels

1992 *Ground stone*. Well-Built Mycenae: The Helleno-British Excavations within the Citadel of Mycenae 1959–1969, fasc. 27. Oxford: Oxbow Books.

Fant, J.E., and W.G. Loy

1972 Surveying and mapping. In *The Minnesota Messenia Expedition: Reconstructing a Bronze Age regional environment*, edited by W.A. McDonald and G.R. Rapp, 18–35. Minneapolis: University of Minnesota Press.

Farnoux, A.

1997 Malia aux Minoen Récent II et IIIA1. In *La Crète Mycénienne. Actes de la Table Ronde Internationale organisée par l'École française d'Athènes, 26–28 Mars 1991*, edited by J. Driessen and A. Farnoux, 135–147. *Bulletin de Correspondance Hellénique*, suppl. vol. 30. Paris: Diffusion de Boccard.

Faure, P.

1995 Le caractère hellénique de la langue des Minoens. In *Proceedings of the 7th International Cretological Congress, vol. A1: Archaeology*, edited by N.E. Papadogiannakis, 317–327. Rethymnon: Iera Mitropolis Rethymnis and Aulopotamou.

Feinman, G.

1985 Changes in the organization of ceramic production in pre-hispanic Oaxaca, Mexico. In *Decoding prehistoric ceramics*, edited by B. Nelson, 195–223. Carbondale: Southern Illinois University Press.

2000 Dual-processual theory and social formations in the Southwest. In *Alternative leadership strategies in the Prehispanic Southwest*, edited by B.J. Mills, 207–224. Tucson: University of Arizona Press.

Feinman, G., and Neitzel, J.

1984 Too many types: An overview of sedentary prestate societies in the Americas. In *Advances in archaeological method and theory 7*, edited by M.B. Schiffer, 39–102. New York: Academic Press.

Ferrill, A.

1985 *The origins of war*. London: Thames and Hudson.

Feuer, B.

1983 *The northern Mycenaean border in Thessaly*. British Archaeological Reports International Series 176. Oxford: BAR.

1994 Mycenean Thessaly. In *Thessalia. Praktika Diethnous Synedriou, 15 chronia archaeologikes ereunas, 1957–1990. Apotelesmata kai prooptikes (Lyon, 17–22 Apriliou 1990)*, volume B, edited by the Greek Ministry of Culture, 211–214. Athens: Kapon.

1999 The Mycenaean periphery: Some theoretical and methodological considerations. In *He peripheria tou Mykenaikou kosmou: Praktika A Diethnous epistemonikou Symposiou, Lamia 25–29 Septemvriou 1994* (in Greek), edited by E. Froussou, 7–14. Lamia: Ekdosi ID' Eforias Proistorikon kai Klassikon Archaiotiton.

Finley, M.I.

1957 The Mycenaean tablets and economic history. *Economic History Review* 10:128–141. (Reprinted in *Economy and society in Greece*, edited by B.D. Shaw and R. Saller. London: Penguin, 1981.)

1973 *The ancient economy*. Berkeley and Los Angeles: University of California Press.

1981 *Early Greece. The Bronze and Archaic Ages*. New York: W.W. Norton.

Firth, R.J.

1996-1997 The find-places of the tablets from the palace of Knossos. *Minos* 31-32:7–122.

2000–2001 A review of the find-places of the Linear B tablets from the palace of Knossos. *Minos* 35–36:63–290.

Fish, S.K., and S.A. Kowalewski, eds.

1990 *The archaeology of regions: A case for full-coverage survey*. Washington, DC: Smithsonian Institution Press.

Fitton, J.L.

1996 *The discovery of the Greek Bronze Age*. Cambridge, MA: Harvard University Press.

Flannery, K.V.

1972 The cultural evolution of civilizations. *Annual Review of Ecology and Systematics* 3:399–426.

1995 Prehistoric social evolution. In *Research frontiers in anthropology*, edited by C.R. Ember and M. Ember, 1–6. Englewood Cliffs, NJ: Prentice Hall.

Flannery, K., and J. Marcus

1996 *Zapotec civilization: How urban society evolved in Mexico's Oaxaca Valley*. London: Thames and Hudson.

Foradas, J.G.

1994 *Chert acquisition for ceremonial bladelet manufacture at three Scioto Hopewell Sites: A test of the normative mineral composition method for sourcing cherts*. Ph.D. dissertation, Ohio State University. Ann Arbor: University Microfilms.

Forsén, J.

1992 *Twilight of the Early Helladics: A study of the disturbances in east-central and southern Greece towards the end of the Early Bronze Age*. Studies in Mediterranean Archaeology, Pocketbook 116. Jonsered, Sweden: Paul Åströms Förlag.

Foster, E.D.

1977   An administrative department at Knossos concerned with perfumery and offerings. *Minos* 16:19–1.

1981   The flax impost at Pylos and Mycenaean land-holding. *Minos* 17:67–121.

Frank, A.G.

1993   Bronze Age world system cycles. *Current Anthropology* 34:383–429.

Freidel, D.

1981   Continuity and disjunction: Late Postclassic settlement patterns in northern Yucatan. In *Frameworks for studying lowland Maya settlement patterns*, edited by W. Ashmore, 311–324. Albuquerque: University of New Mexico Press.

French, E.B.

1981   Cult places at Mycenae. In *Sanctuaries and cults in the Aegean Bronze Age*, edited by R. Hägg and N. Marinatos, 41–48. Stockholm: Svenska Institutet i Athen.

1997   Ephyrean goblets at Knossos: The chicken or the egg. In *La Crète Mycénienne: Actes de la Table Ronde Internationale organisée par l'École française d'Athènes, 26–28 Mars 1991*, edited by J. Driessen and A. Farnoux, 149–225. *Bulletin de Correspondance Hellénique*, suppl. vol. 30. Paris: Diffusion de Boccard.

1998   The ups and downs of Mycenaean 1250–1150 BCE. In *Mediterranean peoples in transition: Thirteenth to early tenth centuries BCE. In honor of Professor Trude Dothan*, edited by S. Gitin, A. Mazar, and E. Stern, 2–5. Jerusalem: Israel Exploration Society.

n.d.   *The room with the fresco complex.* Well Built Mycenae: The Helleno-British Excavations within the Citadel of Mycenae 1959–1969, fasc. 11. W. Taylour, E. French, and K. Wardle, series editors. Oxford: Oxbow Books. In press.

French, E., and K. Shelton

2005   Early palatial Mycenae. In *AUTOCHTHON: Papers presented to O.T.P.K. Dickinson on the occasion of his retirement*, edited by A. Dakouri-Hild and S. Sherratt, 175–184. British Archaeological Reports International Series 1432. Oxford: Archaeopress.

French, E., and K. Wardle, eds.

1988   *Problems in Greek prehistory.* Bristol: Bristol Classical Press.

Freter, A.

1994   The Classic Maya collapse at Copan, Honduras: An analysis of Maya rural settlement trends. In *Archaeological views from the countryside: Village communities in early complex societies*, edited by G. Schwartz and S. Falconer, 160–176. Washington, DC: Smithsonian Institute Press.

Friedman, J., and M.J. Rowlands

1977   Notes towards an epigenetic model of the evolution of "civilization." In *The evolution of social systems*, edited by J. Friedman and M.J. Rowlands, 201–276. London: Duckworth Press.

Froussou, E., ed.

1999   *I perifereia tou Mykinaikou kosmou. A' Diethnes Diepistimoniko Symposio, Lamia, 25–29 Septemvriou 1994.* Lamia: Ekdosi ID' Eforeias Proistorikon kai Klassikon Archaiotiton.

Furumark, A.

1941   *The Mycenaean pottery: Analysis and classification.* Stockholm: Kungl. Vitterhets, historie och antikvitets akademien.

Galaty, M.L.

1999a   Wealth ceramics, staple ceramics: Pots and the Mycenaean palaces. In *Rethinking Mycenaean palaces: New interpretations of an old idea*, edited by M.L. Galaty and W.A. Parkinson, 49–60. Los Angeles: Cotsen Institute of Archaeology, University of California–Los Angeles.

1999b   *Nestor's wine cups: Investigating ceramic manufacture and exchange in a Late Bronze Age "Mycenaean" state.* British Archaeological Reports International Series 766. Oxford: British Archaeological Reports.

2005   European regional studies: A coming of age? *Journal of Archaeological Research* 13:291–336.

2007   "There are prehistoric cities up there": The Bronze and Iron Ages in Northern Albania. In *Between the Aegean and the Baltic Seas: Prehistory across borders*, edited by I. Galanakis, H. Tomas, Y. Galanakis, and R. Laffineur, 133–140. Aegaeum 27. Liège: Université de Liège; Austin: University of Texas at Austin Program in Aegean Scripts and Prehistory.

Galaty, M.L., and W.A. Parkinson

1999   Putting Mycenaean palaces in their place: An introduction. In *Rethinking Mycenaean palaces: New interpretations of an old idea*, edited by M.L. Galaty and W.A. Parkinson, 1–8. Los Angeles: Cotsen Institute of Archaeology, University of California–Los Angeles.

Galaty, M.L., and W.A. Parkinson, eds.

1999   *Rethinking Mycenaean palaces: New interpretations of an old idea.* Los Angeles: Cotsen Institute of Archaeology, University of California–Los Angeles.

Gallagher, W.R.

1988   A reconsideration of *o-no* in Mycenaean Greek. *Minos* 23:85–106.

Gallis, K.I.

1992   *Atlas proistorikôn Theseon tes anatolikes thessalikes pediadas.* Larissa: Ypourgeio Politismou.

Gallou, C.

2005 *The Mycenaean cult of the dead*. British Archaeological Reports S1372. Oxford: Archaeopress.

Gamble, C.

1982 Leadership and "surplus" production. In *Ranking, resource and exchange*, edited by C. Renfrew and S. Shennan, 100–105. Cambridge: Cambridge University Press.

Gardner, R., and K.G. Heider

1968 *Gardens of war: Life and death in the New Guinea stone age*. New York: Random House.

Gilman, A.

1981 The development of social stratification in Bronze Age Europe. *Current Anthropology* 22:1–8.

Gillis, C.

1997 The smith in the Late Bronze Age: State employee, independent artisan, or both? In *TEXNH: Craftsmen, craftswomen and craftsmanship in the Aegean Bronze Age. Proceedings of the 6th International Aegean Conference, Philadelphia, Temple University, 18–21 April 1996*, edited by R. Laffineur and P.P. Betancourt, 533–537. Aegaeum 16. Liège: Université de Liège; Austin: University of Texas at Austin Program in Aegean Scripts and Prehistory.

Gillis, C., C. Risberg, and B. Sjöberg, eds.

1997 *Trade and production in premonetary Greece: Production and the craftsman (Proceedings of the 4th and 5th International Workshops, Athens 1994 and 1995)*. Jonsered, Sweden: Paul Åströms Förlag.

Gitin, S., A. Mazar, and E. Stern, eds.

1998 *Mediterranean peoples in transition: Thirteenth to early tenth centuries BCE. In honor of Professor Trude Dothan*. Jerusalem: Israel Exploration Society.

Godart, L.

1971 Les tablettes de la série Co de Cnossos. *Minos* 12:418–424.

1977 Les resources des palais mycéniens de Cnossos et Pylos. *Les Études Classiques* 45:31-42.

1992 Les collecteurs dans le monde Égéen. In *Mykenaïka: Actes du 9e Colloque internationale sur les textes mycéniens et égéens*, edited by J.-P. Olivier, 257–283. *Bulletin de Correspondance Hellénique*, suppl. vol. 25. Paris: Diffusion de Boccard.

Greenhalgh, P.A.L.

1973 *Early Greek warfare: Horsemen and chariots in the Homeric and Archaic ages*. Cambridge: Cambridge University Press.

1980 The Dendra charioteer. *Antiquity* 54:201–205.

Grundmann, K.

1937 Magoula Chatzimissiotiki. *Athenische Mitteilungen* 62:56–61.

Gunneweg, J., and H.V. Michel

1999 Does the different layout of the Late Bronze Age tombs at Laish/Dan and Akko in Northern Canaan reflect different trade relations? An instrumental neutron activation study on Mycenaean pottery. *Journal of Archaeological Science* 26:989–995.

Güterbock, H.G.

1983 The Hittites and the Aegean World. 1. The Ahhiyawa problem reconsidered. *American Journal of Archaeology* 87:133–138.

Haas, J.

2001 Warfare and the evolution of culture. In *Archaeology at the millennium: A sourcebook*, edited by T.D. Price and G. Feinman, 329–350. New York: Kluwer Academic/Plenum Publishers.

Hägg, R.

1990 The role of libations in Mycenaean ceremony and cult. In *Celebrations of death and divinity in the Bronze Age Argolid: Proceedings of the Sixth International Symposium at the Swedish Institute in Athens, 11–13 June, 1988*, edited by R. Hägg and G. Nordquist, 177–184. Stockholm: Svenska Institutet i Athen.

1992 Sanctuaries and workshops in the Bronze Age Aegean. In *Economics of cult in the ancient Greek world. Proceedings of the Uppsala Symposium, 1990*, edited by T. Linders and B. Alroth, 29–32. Boreas, Uppsala Studies in Ancient Mediterranean and Near Eastern Civilizations 21. Uppsala.

1995 State and religion in Mycenaean Greece. In *POLITEIA: Society and state in the Aegean Bronze Age*, edited by W.-D. Niemeier and R. Laffineur, 387–391. Aegaeum 13. Liège: Université de Liège; Austin: University of Texas at Austin.

1997 Religious syncretism at Knossos and in post-palatial Crete? In *La Crète Mycénienne: Actes de la Table Ronde Internationale organisée par l'École française d'Athènes, 26–28 Mars 1991*, edited by J. Driessen and A. Farnoux, 163–168. *Bulletin de Correspondance Hellénique*, suppl. vol. 30. Paris: Diffusion de Boccard.

Hägg, R., and N. Marinatos, eds.

1981 *Sanctuaries and cults in the Aegean Bronze Age: Proceedings of the First International Symposium at the Swedish Institute in Athens, 12–13 May 1980*. Stockholm: Svenska Institutet i Athen.

1987 *The function of the Minoan palaces*. Stockholm: Paul Åströms Förlag.

Hägg, R., and G. Nordquist, eds.

1990 *Celebrations of death and divinity in the Bronze Age Argolid: Proceedings of the Sixth International Symposium at the Swedish Institute in Athens, 11–13 June, 1988*. Stockholm: Svenska Institutet i Athen.

Haggis, D.C.

2002   Integration and complexity in the late Prepalatial Period: A view from the countryside in eastern Crete. In *Labyrinth revisited: Rethinking "Minoan" archaeology*, edited by Y. Hamilakis, 120–142. Oxford: Oxbow Books.

Hall, T.D.

1994   The case for a world-systems approach to civilizations: A view from the "transformationist" camp. *Comparative Civilizations Review* 30:30–49.

1996a   Finding the global in the local. In *Economic analysis beyond the local system*, edited by R. Blanton, P. Peregrine, T.D. Hall, and D. Winslow, 95–107. Lanham, MD: University Press of America.

1996b   World-systems and evolution: An appraisal. *Journal of World-Systems Research* 2:4. Available: http://csf. colorado.edu/wsystems/jwsr.html.

Hall, T.D., and C. Chase-Dunn

1994   Forward into the past: World-systems before 1500. *Sociological Forum* 9:295–306.

Hallager, B.

1990   LM II and Khania. In *Proceedings of the 6th International Cretological Congress, vol. A2*, edited by V. Niniou-Kindeli, 77–91. Chania: Filologikos Syllogos "O Chrysostomos".

Hallager, E.

1977   *The Mycenaean palace at Knossos: Evidence for final destruction in the LM IIIB Period.* Stockholm: Paul Aströms Förlag.

1978   The history of the palace at Knossos in the Late Minoan period. *Studi Micenei ed egeo-anatolici* 19:17–33.

1987a   The uniformity in seal use and sealing practice during the Late Helladic/Late Minoan III Period. In *Ariadne's threads: Connections between Crete and the Greek mainland in Late Minoan III (LM IIIA2 to LM IIIC). Proceedings of the International Workshop held at Athens, Scuola Archeologica Italiana, 5–6 April 2003*, edited by A.L. D'Agata and J. Moody, 244–265. Scuola Archeologica Italiana di Atene, Tripodes 3. Athens: Scuola Archeologica Italiana di Atene.

1987b   A harvest festival room in the Minoan palaces? An architectural study of the Pillar Crypt area at Knossos. In *The function of the Minoan Palaces*, edited by R. Hägg and N. Marinatos, 169–187. Stockholm: Paul Aströms Vörlag.

2005   The inscribed stirrup jars: Implications for Late Minoan IIIB Crete. *American Journal of Archaeology* 91:171–190.

Hallager, E., and B. Hallager

1995   The Knossian bull: Political propaganda in Neopalatial Crete? In *POLITEIA: Society and state in the Aegean Bronze Age. Proceedings of the 5th International Aegean Conference, University of Heidelberg, Archäologisches Institut, 10–13 April 1994*, edited by R. Laffineur and W.D. Niemeier, 547–556. Aegaeum 12. Liège: Université de Liège; Austin: University of Texas Program in Aegean Scripts and Prehistory.

Hallager, E., M. Vlasakis, and B. Hallager

1990   The first Linear B tablet(s) from Khania. *Kadmos* 29:24–34.

1992   New Linear B tablets from Khania. *Kadmos* 31:61–87.

Halstead, P.

1988   On redistribution and the Minoan-Mycenaean palatial economies. In *Problems in Greek prehistory: Proceedings of the British School at Athens Centenary Conference, Manchester, 14–18 April 1986*, edited by E.B. French and K. Wardle, 519–530. Bristol: Bristol Classical Press.

1990   Lost Sheep? On the Linear B evidence for breeding flocks at Knossos and Pylos. *Minos* 25-26:343–363.

1992a   The Mycenaean palatial economy: Making the most of the gaps in the evidence. *Proceedings of the Cambridge Philological Society* 38:57–86.

1992b   Agriculture in the Bronze Age Aegean: Towards a model of palatial economy. In *Agriculture in ancient Greece*, edited by B. Wells, 105–117. Stockholm: Svenska Institutet i Athen.

1993a   Lost sheep? On the Linear B evidence for breeding flocks at Mycenaean Knossos and Pylos. *Minos* 25–26:343–365.

1993b   Banking on livestock: Indirect storage in Greek agriculture. *Bulletin on Sumerian Agriculture* 7:63–75.

1995a   Late Bronze Age grain crops and Linear B ideograms *65, *120 and *121. *Annual of the British School at Athens* 90:229–234.

1995b   Plough and power: The economic and social significance of cultivation with the ox-drawn ard in the Mediterranean. *Bulletin on Sumerian Agriculture* 8:11-22.

1995c   From sharing to hoarding: The Neolithic foundations of Aegean Bronze Age society? In *POLITEIA: Society and state in the Aegean Bronze Age*, edited by W.-D. Niemeier and R. Laffineur, 11–20. Aegaeum 13. Liège: Université de Liège; Austin: University of Texas at Austin Program in Aegean Scripts and Prehistory.

1996   Pastoralism or household herding? Problems of scale and specialization in early Greek animal husbandry. *World Archaeology* 28: 20-42.

1998–1999   Text, bones, and herders: Approaches to animal husbandry in Late Bronze Age Greece. In *A-NA-*

QO-TA: Studies presented to J.T. Killen, edited by J. Bennet and J. Driessen, 149–190. *Minos* 33–34. Salamanca: Ediciones Universidad de Salamanca.

1999a Missing sheep: On the meaning and wider significance of O in Knossos sheep records. *Annual of the British School at Athens* 94:145–166.

1999b Mycenaean agriculture: The nature of palatial intervention. *Bulletin of the Institute of Classical Studies of the University of London* 43:211–212.

1999c Surplus and share-croppers: The grain production strategies of Mycenaean palaces. In *MELETEMATA: Studies in Aegean archaeology presented to Malcolm H. Wiener as he enters his 65th year*, edited by R. Laffineur and P.P. Betancourt, 319–326. Aegaeum 20. Liège: Université de Liège; Austin: University of Texas at Austin Program in Aegean Scripts and Prehistory.

1999d Towards a model of Mycenaean palatial mobilization. In *Rethinking Mycenaean palaces: New interpretations of an old idea*, edited by M.L. Galaty and W.A. Parkinson, 35–42. Los Angeles: Cotsen Institute of Archaeology, University of California–Los Angeles.

2001 Mycenaean wheat, flax and sheep: Palatial intervention in farming and its implications for rural society. In *Economy and politics in the Mycenaean palace states: Proceedings of a conference held on 1–3 July 1999 in the Faculty of Classics, Cambridge*, edited by S. Voutsaki and J.T. Killen, 38–50. Cambridge Philological Society, suppl. vol. 27. Cambridge: Cambridge Philological Society.

2003 Texts and bones: Contrasting Linear B and archaeozoological evidence for animal exploitation in Mycenaean southern Greece. In *Zooarchaeology in Greece: Recent advances*, edited by E. Kotjabopoulou, Y. Hamilakis, P. Halstead, C. Gamble, and P. Elefanti, 257–261. British School at Athens Studies 9. London: The British School at Athens.

Halstead, P., and V. Isaakidou

2004 Faunal evidence for feasting: Burnt offerings from the palace of Nestor at Pylos. In *Food, cuisine and society in prehistoric Greece*, edited by P. Halstead and J.C. Barrett, 136–154. Sheffield Studies in Aegean Archaeology 5. Oxford: Oxbow Books.

Halstead, P., and J. O'Shea

1982 A friend in need is a friend indeed: Social storage and the origins of social ranking. In *Ranking, resource and exchange*, edited by C. Renfrew and S. Shennan, 92–99. Cambridge: Cambridge University Press.

Hamilakis, Y.

1996 Wine, oil and the dialectics of power in Bronze Age Crete: A review of the evidence. *Oxford Journal of Archaeology* 15(1):1–32.

1998 Eating the dead: Mortuary feasting and the politics of memory in the Aegean Bronze Age societies. In *Cemetery and society in the Aegean Bronze Age*, edited by K. Branigan, 115–132. Sheffield Studies in Aegean Archaeology 1. Sheffield: Sheffield University Press.

Hamilakis, Y., and E. Konsolaki

2004 Pigs for the gods: Burnt animal sacrifices as embodied rituals at a Mycenaean sanctuary. *Oxford Journal of Archaeology* 23:135–151.

Hansen, H.

1933 *Early civilization in Thessaly*. Baltimore: Johns Hopkins University Press.

Hanson, V.D.

1999 The status of ancient military history: Traditional work, recent research, and on-going controversies. *The Journal of Military History* 63:379–413.

Harris, M.

1987 *Cultural anthropology*. 2nd ed. New York: Harper and Row.

Haskell, H.W.

2005 Region to region export of transport stirrup jars from LM IIIA2/B Crete. In *Ariadne's threads: Connections between Crete and the Greek mainland in Late Minoan III (LM IIIA2 to LM IIIC). Proceedings of the International Workshop held at Athens, Scuola Archeologica Italiana, 5–6 April 2003*, edited by A.L. D'Agata and J. Moody, 205–221. Scuola Archeologica Italiana di Atene, Tripodes 3. Athens: Scuola Archeologica Italiana di Atene.

Hatzaki, E.M.

2004 From Final Palatial to Postpalatial Knossos: A view from the Late Minoan II to Late Minoan IIIB town. In *Knossos: Palace, city, state. Proceedings of the Conference in Heraklion organised by the British School at Athens and the 23rd Ephoreia of Prehistoric and Classical Antiquities of Heraklion, in November 2000, for the Centenary of Sir Arthur Evans's Excavations at Knossos*, edited by G. Cadogan, E. Hatzaki and A. Vasilakis, 121–126. British School at Athens Studies 12. Athens: British School at Athens.

2005 Postpalatial Knossos: Town and cemeteries from LM IIIA2 to LM IIIC. In *Ariadne's threads: Connections between Crete and the Greek mainland in Late Minoan III (LM IIIA2 to LM IIIC). Proceedings of the International Workshop held at Athens, Scuola Archeologica Italiana, 5–6 April 2003*, edited by A.L. D'Agata and J. Moody, 64–95. Scuola Archeologica

Italiana di Atene, Tripodes 3. Athens: Scuola Archeologica Italiana di Atene.

Hawes, H.B., et al.

1908   *Gournia, Vassiliki and other prehistoric sites on the Isthmus of Hierapetra*. Philadelphia: American Exploration Society.

Hawkins, J.D., and Easton, D.F.

1996   A hieroglyphic seal from Troia. *Studia Troica* 6:111–118.

Hayden, B.

1987   Crete in transition: LMIIIA-IIIB architecture: A preliminary study. *Studi Micenei ed egeo-anatolici* 26:199–234.

Hein, A., Th. Beier, and H. Mommsen

2002   A complete chemical grouping of the Perlman/ Asaro Neutron Activation Analysis Databank on Mycenaean and Minoan pottery. In *Modern trends in scientific studies on ancient ceramics. Papers presented at the 5th European Meeting on Ancient Ceramics, Athens 1999*, edited by V. Kilikoglou, A. Hein, and Y. Maniatis, 143–150. British Archaeological Reports International Series 1011. Oxford: Archaeopress.

Hein, A., A. Tsolakidou, and H. Mommsen

2002   Mycenaean pottery from the Argolid and Achaia: A mineralogical approach where chemistry leaves unanswered questions. *Archaeometry* 44:177–186.

Helms, M.

1979   *Ancient Panama: Chiefs in search of power*. Austin: University of Texas Press.

1988   *Ulysses' sail: An ethnographic odyssey of power, knowledge, and geographical distance*. Princeton, NJ: Princeton University Press.

1993   *Craft and the kingly ideal: Art, trade, and power*. Austin: University of Texas at Austin.

Helmsley, L.

1991   Techniques of village pottery production. In *Cypriot ceramics: Reading the prehistoric record*, edited by J. Barlow, D. Bolger, and B. Kling, 215–220. University of Pennsylvania Museum Symposium Series, monograph 74.

Hewitt, S.

1993   *A study of Mycenaean and Minoan warrior burials in the Aegean from the period of the Shaft Graves to the fall of the Palace of Knossos*. Ph.D. dissertation, Queen's University at Kingston. Ann Arbor: University Microfilms.

Hiller, S.

1981   Mykenische Heiligtmer: Das Zeugnis der Linear B-Texte. In *Sanctuaries and cults in the Aegean Bronze Age*, edited by R. Hägg and N. Marinatos, 95–126. Stockholm: Svenska Institutet i Athen.

1988   Dependent personnel in Mycenaean texts. In *Society and economy in the Eastern Mediterranean*, edited by M. Heltzer and E. Lipinski, 53–68. Orientalia Lovaniensia Analecta 23. Louvain: University of Louvain.

1995   Der SM II-Palaststil: Ausdruck politischer Ideologie? In *POLITEIA: Society and state in the Aegean Bronze Age. Proceedings of the 5th International Aegean Conference, University of Heidelberg, Archäologisches Institut, 10–13 April 1994*, edited by R. Laffineur and W.D. Niemeier, 561–572. Aegaeum 12. Liège: Université de Liège; Austin: University of Texas Program in Aegean Scripts and Prehistory.

1999   Egyptian elements on the Hagia Triada sarcophagus. In *MELETEMATA: Studies in Aegean archaeology presented to M.H. Wiener as he enters his 65th year*, edited by P.P. Betancourt, V. Karageorghis, R. Laffineur and W.-D. Niemeier, 361–369. Aegaeum 20. Liège: Université de Liège; Austin: University of Texas Program in Aegean Scripts and Prehistory.

Hirschfeld, N.

1990   *Incised marks on LH/LM III pottery*. Master's thesis, Institute of Nautical Archaeology, Texas A&M University.

1992   Cypriot marks on Mycenaean pottery. In *Mykenaïka: Actes du IXe colloque international sur les textes mycéniens et égéens, Athènes, 2–6 octobre 1990*: 315B19, edited by J-P. Olivier, 315–319. *Bulletin de Correspondance Hellénique*, suppl. vol. 25. Paris: Diffusion de Boccard.

1996   Cypriots in the Mycenaean Aegean. In *Atti e memorie del Secondo Congresso Internazionale di Micenologia, Roma–-Napoli, 1–20 Ottobre 1991, vol. I*, edited by E. De Miro, L. Godart, and A. Sacconi, 289–297. Rome: Gruppo Editoriale Internatzionale.

1999   *Potmarks of the Late Bronze Age Eastern Mediterranean*. Ph.D. dissertation, University of Texas at Austin.

Hirth, K.

1989   Militarism and social organization at Xochicalco, Morelos. In *Mesoamerica after the decline of Teotihuacan A.D. 700–900*, edited by R. Diehl and J. Berloeds, 69–82. Washington, DC: Dumbarton Oaks.

1998   *Ho thissauros tôn aïdoniôn. Sphragides kai kosmemata tew Ysteris Epoches Chalkou sto Aigaeo. Mouseio Ellhnikes Archaeotetas. Melvourni, 9 fevr. 1998–22 fevr. 1999*. Athens: TAPA.

Hodder, I.

1977   Geographical techniques and Mycenaean geography. In *Mycenaean geography: Proceedings of the Cambridge Colloquium 1976*, edited by J. Bintliff, 27–39. Cambridge: Cambridge University Press.

1981   Pottery, production and use: A theoretical discussion. In *Production and distribution: A ceramic viewpoint*, edited by H. Howard and E. Thomas, 215–220. British Archaeological Reports International Series 120. Oxford: British Archaeological Reports.

Hood, M.S.F.

2000   Cretan fresco dates. In *The wall paintings of Thera: Proceedings of the First International Symposium, Petros M. Nomikos Conference Center, Thera, Hellas, 30 August–4 September 1997*, edited by S. Sherratt, 191–207. Athens: The Thera Foundation.

2005   Dating the Knossos frescoes. In *Aegean wall painting: A Tribute to Mark Cameron*, edited by L. Morgan, 45–81. British School at Athens Studies 13. London: British School at Athens.

Hooker, J.T.

1980   *Linear B: An introduction.* Bristol: Bristol Classical Press.

Hope Simpson, R.

1998   The Mycenaean highways. *Classical Views/Echos du Monde Classique* 42:239–260.

2002   The Mycenae roads and Mycenaean chariots. *Mouseion* 2(1):25–133.

2003   The Dodecanese and the Ahhiyawa question. *Annual of the British School at Athens* 98: 203–237.

Hope Simpson, R., and O.T.P.K. Dickinson

1979   *A gazetteer of Aegean civilisation in the Bronze Age. Vol. I. The mainland and islands.* Studies in Mediterranean Archaeology and Literature 52. Göteborg: Paul Åströms Förlag.

Hope Simpson, R., and H. Waterhouse

1961   Prehistoric Laconia: Part II. *Annual of the British School at Athens* 56:114–75.

Hunter, A.G.

1953   *The Bronze Age in Thessaly and its environs with special reference to Mycenaean culture.* Thesis, Oxford University.

Hutchinson, R.W.

1956   A tholos tomb in the Kephala. *Annual of the British School at Athens* 51:74–80.

Huxley, G.L.

1972   Small finds from deposits. In *Kythera: Excavations and studies*, edited by J.N. Coldstream and G.L. Huxley, 205–219. Park Ridge, NJ: Noyes Press.

Hyland, A.

2003   *The horse in the ancient world.* Gloucestershire: Sutton Publishing.

Ilievski, P.

1992   Observations on the personal names from the Knossos D tablets. In *Mykenaïka*, edited by J.-P. Olivier, 321–349. *Bulletin de Correspondance Hellénique*, suppl. vol. 25. Paris: Diffusion de Boccard.

Immerwahr, S.

2000   Thera and Knossos: Relations of the paintings to their architectural space. In *The wall paintings of Thera: Proceedings of the First International Symposium, Petros M. Nomikos Conference Center, Thera, Hellas, 30 August–4 September 1997*, edited by S. Sherratt, 467–490. Athens: Thera Foundation.

Intzesiloglou, A.

1989   Oikopedo M. Tachoula. *Archaeologikon Deltion* 44B:219–220.

1990   Velestino (Archaies Pherai) . *Archaeologikon Deltion* 45B:201–203.

1997   Helleno-Italiko Programma Epiphaneiakôn Ereunôn. *Archaeologikon Deltion* 52:497–498.

2000   Pherai–Peparethos–Skiathos: Merika stoicheia tou archaeologikou ergou mias oktaetias (1990–1998). In *To Ergo tôn Ephoreiôn Archaeoteton kai Neoterôn Mnemeion tou HYP.PO. ste Thessalia kai ten euryteri perioche tes (1990–1998)*, edited by the Greek Ministry of Culture, 345–353. Volos: IG' Ephoreia Proïstorikôn kai Klassikôn Archaeotiton.

Intzesiloglou, M.

1997   Georgiko–Xironeri. *Archaeologikon Deltion* 52: 478–480.

Isaakidou, V., P. Halstead, J. Davis, and S. Stocker

2002   Burnt animal sacrifice in Late Bronze Age Greece: New evidence from the Mycenaean "Palace of Nestor," Pylos. *Antiquity* 76:86–92.

Ives, D.J.

1984   Chert sources and identification in archaeology: Can a silk purse be made into a sow's ear? In *Lithic resource procurement: Proceedings from the Second Conference on Prehistoric Chert Exploitation*, edited by S.C. Vehik, 211–224. Center for Archaeological Investigations, Occasional Paper 4. Carbondale: Southern Illinois University Press.

Jacob-Felsch, M.

2000   Problems in Mycenaean chronology. *Hephaistos* 18:29–71.

Jameson, M., C. Runnels, and T. van Andel

1994   *A Greek countryside: The southern Argolid from prehistory to the present day.* Stanford: Stanford University Press.

Jansen, A.G.

1997   Bronze Age highways at Mycenae. *Classical Views/ Echos du Monde Classique* 41:1–16.

2002   *A study of the remains of Mycenaean roads and stations of Bronze-Age Greece.* New York: Edwin Mellen Press.

Johnson, G.A.

1973 *Local exchange and early state development in south-western Iran*. Anthropological Papers, Museum of Anthropology, University of Michigan, no. 51, Ann Arbor.

1980 Rank-size convexity and system integration: A view from archaeology. *Economic Geography* 56:234-247.

1981 Monitoring complex system integration and boundary phenomena with settlement size data. In *Archaeological approaches to the study of complexity*, edited by S. van der Leeuw, 144–189. Amsterdam: Universiteit van Amsterdam.

Jones, R.E., L. Vagnetti, S.T. Levi, J. Williams, D. Jenkins, and A. de Guio

2002 Mycenaean and Aegean-type pottery from northern Italy. Archaeological and archaeometric studies. *Studi Micenei ed Egeo-Anatolici* 44:221–261.

Jung, R.

2003 Late Helladic IIIC at the Toúmbes of Kastanás and Ólynthos—and the problems of Macedonian Mycenaean pottery. In *LH IIIC chronology and synchronisms: Proceedings of the International Workshop Held at the Austrian Academy of Sciences at Vienna, May 7th and 8th, 2001*, edited by S. Deger-Jalkotzy and M. Zavadil, 131–144. Vienna: Verlag der Österreichischen Akademie der Wissenschaften.

Kakavogiannis, E.

1977 Anaskaphikes Ereunes stis Pherais to 1977. *Archaeologika Analekta ex Athenôn* 2:174–187.

Kanta, A.

1980 *The Late Minoan III period in Crete: A survey of sites, pottery and their distribution*. Göteborg: Paul Aström Förlag.

1997 Late Bronze Age tholos tombs, origins and evolution: The missing links. In *La Crète Mycénienne: Actes de la Table Ronde Internationale organisée par l'École française d'Athènes, 26–28 Mars 1991*, edited by J. Driessen and A. Farnoux, 229–247. *Bulletin de Correspondance Hellénique*, suppl. vol. 30. Paris: Diffusion de Boccard.

2001 The cremations of Olous and the custom of the cremation in Bronze Age Crete. In *Cremation in the Bronze and early Iron Ages*, edited by N. Stampolidis, 59–68. Athens.

Karantzali, E.

2001 *The Mycenaean cemetery at Pylona on Rhodes*. British Archaeological Reports S988. Oxford: Archaeopress.

Karantzali, E., and M.J. Ponting

2000 ICP-AES analysis of some Mycenaean vases from the cemetery at Pylona, Rhodes. *Annual of the British School of Archaeology at Athens* 95:219–238.

Kardulias, P.N.

1992 The ecology of flaked stone tool production in southern Greece: The evidence from Agios Stephanos and the southern Argolid. *American Journal of Archaeology* 96:421–442.

1995 World systems theory and Aegean Bronze Age economy. *American Journal of Archaeology* 99:342 (abstract).

1999a Flaked stone and the role of the palaces in the Mycenaean world system. In *Rethinking Mycenaean palaces: New interpretations of an old idea*, edited by M.L. Galaty and W.A. Parkinson, 61–72. Los Angeles: Cotsen Institute of Archaeology, University of Calfiornia–Los Angeles.

1999b Multiple levels in the Aegean Bronze Age world-system. In *World systems theory in practice: Leadership, production, and exchange*, edited by P.N. Kardulias, 179–202. Lanham, MD: Rowman and Littlefield.

1999c Preface. In *World systems theory in practice: Leadership, production, and exchange*, edited by P.N. Kardulias, xvii–xxi. Lanham, MD: Rowman and Littlefield.

2001 Negotiated peripherality: Making incorporation work for you on the margins of world-systems. Paper presented at the 100th Annual Meeting of the American Anthropological Association, Washington, DC, 30 November 2001.

Kardulias, P.N., and C. Runnels

1985 Lithic artifacts from southern Greece: A short report on the Argolid Survey. *Old World Archaeology Newsletter* 9:2.

1995 The lithic artifacts. In *Artifact and assemblage: The finds from a regional survey of the southern Argolid, Greece*, edited by C. Runnels, chap. 4. Stanford: Stanford University Press.

Kardulias, P.N., and R.W. Yerkes

1996 Microwear and metric analysis of threshing sledge flints from Greece and Cyprus. *Journal of Archaeological Science* 23:657–666.

Kassianidou, E.

1995 The organisation of copper production in LBA Cyprus: Thoughts from a metallurgical perspective. Paper presented at the Seventeenth Annual Conference of the Theoretical Archaeology Group, University of Reading, 18–21 December 1995.

Keeley, L.H.

1996 *War before civilization*. New York: Oxford University Press.

Kelley, J.H., and M.P. Hanen

1988 *Archaeology and the methodology of science*. Albuquerque: University of New Mexico Press.

Kenoyer, J.
1995   Ideology and legitimation in the Indus state as revealed through symbolic objects. *The Archaeological Review* 4(1 and 2):87–132.

Kepecs, S., and M. Kolb, eds.
1997   *New approaches to combining the archaeological and historical records. Journal of Archaeological Method and Theory Special Issue* 4(3/4).

Kilian, K.
1981   *Ausgrabungen in Tiryns 1978, 1979.* Archäologischer Anzeiger 149–194.
1987   L'architecture des résidences mycéniennes: Origine et extension d'une structure du pouvoir politique pendant l'âge du bronze récent. In *Le système palatial en Orient, en Grèce et à Rome: Actes du Colloque de Strasbourg, 19-22 juin 1985,* edited by E. Lévy, 203–217. Strasbourg: Université des Sciences Humaines de Strasbourg.
1988a   The emergence of the wanax ideology in the Mycenaean palaces. *Oxford Journal of Archaeology* 7:291–302.
1988b   Mycenaeans up to date; trends and changes in recent research. In *Problems in Greek prehistory. Proceedings of the British School at Athens Centenary Conference, Manchester, 14–18 April 1986,* edited by E.B. French and K. Wardle, 115–152. Bristol: Bristol Classical Press.
1992   Mykenische Heiligtümer der Peloponnes. In *Kotinos. Festschrift für Erika Simon,* edited by H. Froning, T. Hölscher, and H. Mielsch, 10–25. Mainz: P. von Zabern.

Kilian-Dirlmeier, I.
1985   Noch einmal zu den "Kriegergräbern" von Knossos. *Jahrbuch des Römisch-germanischen Zentralmuseums* 32:196–214.
1988   Jewellery in Mycenaean and Minoan graves. In *Problems in Greek prehistory: Proceedings of the British School at Athens Centenary Conference, Manchester, 14–18 April 1986,* edited by E. French and K. Wardle, 161–172. Bristol: Bristol Classical Press.
1997   *Alt-Ägina IV.3: Das mittelbronzezeitliche Schachtgrab von Ägina.* Mainz: von Zabern.

Kilikoglou, V., Y. Maniatis, and A. Grimanis
1988   The effect of purification and firing of clays on trace element provenance studies. *Archaeometry* 30(1):37–46.

Killen, J.T.
1964   The wool industry of Crete in the Late Bronze Age. *Annual of the British School at Athens* 59:1–15.
1979a   The Linear B tablets and economic history: Some problems. *Bulletin of the Institute of Classical Studies of the University of London* 26:133–134.
1979b   The Knossos Ld(1) tablets. In *Colloquium Mycenaeum,* edited by E. Risch and H. Mühlstein, 151–181. Neuchâtel: Faculté des Lettres; Geneva: Librairie Droz.
1983   PY An 1. *Minos* 18:71–79.
1984a   Last year's debts on the Pylos Ma tablets. *Studi Micenei ed Egeo-Anatolici* 25:173–188. Rome: Edizioni dell' Ateneo.
1984b   The textile industries at Pylos and Knossos. In *Pylos comes alive. Industry and administration in a Mycenaean palace,* edited by C.W. Shelmerdine and T.J. Palaima, 49–64. New York: Archaeological Institute of America.
1985   The Linear B tablets and the Mycenaean economy. In *Linear B: A 1984 survey,* edited by A. Morpurgo Davies and Y. Duhoux, 241–305. Bibliothèque des Cahiers de l'Institut de Linguistique de Louvain 26. Cabay: Louvain-la-Neuve.
1987a   Bronzeworking at Knossos and Pylos. *Hermathena* 143:61–72.
1987b   Piety begins at home: Place-names on Knossos records of religious offerings. In *Tractata Mycenaea,* edited by P.Hr. Ilievski and L. Crepajac, 163–177. Skopje: Macedonian Academy of Science and Arts.
1988   Epigraphy and interpretation in Knossos WOMAN and CLOTH records. In *Texts, tablets and scribes: Studies in Mycenaean epigraphy and economy offered to Emmett. L. Bennett, Jr.,* edited by J.-P. Olivier and T.G. Palaima, 167–183. *Minos,* suppl. vol. 10. Salamanca: University of Salamanca.
1993a   Ke-u-po-da e-sa-re-u and the exemptions on the Pylos Na tablets. *Minos* 27–28:109–123.
1993b   Records of sheep and goats at Mycenaean Knossos and Pylos. *Bulletin on Sumerian Agriculture* 7:209–218.
1993c   The oxen's names on the Knossos Ch tablets. *Minos* 27–28:101–107.
1994   Thebes sealings, Knossos tablets and Mycenaean state banquets. *Bulletin of the Institute of Classical Studies of the University of London* 39:67–84.
1995a   Some further thoughts on "collectors." In *POLITEIA: Society and state in the Aegean Bronze Age,* edited by W.-D. Niemeier and R. Laffineur, 213–224. Aegaeum 13. Liège: Université de Liège; Austin: University of Texas at Austin.
1995b   A-ma e-pi-ke-re. *Minos* 29–30:329–333.
1996   Administering a Mycenaean kingdom: Some taxing problems. *Bulletin of the Institute of Classical Studies of the University of London* 41:147–148.
1998a   The Pylos Ta tablets revisited. In *Recherches récentes en épigraphie créto-mycénienne,* edited by F. Rougemont

and J.-P. Olivier. *Bulletin de Correspondance Hellénique* 122:403–443.

1998b   The rôle of the state in wheat and olive production in Mycenaean Crete. *Aevum* 72:19–23.

1999a   Critique: A view from the tablets. In *Rethinking Mycenaean palaces: New interpretations of an old idea*, edited by M.L. Galaty and W.A. Parkinson, 87–90. Los Angeles: Cotsen Institute of Archaeology, University of California–Los Angeles.

1999b   Mycenaean *o-pa*. In *Floreant Studia Mycenaeae: Akten des X Internationalen Mykenologischen Colloquiums in Saltzburg vom 1.–5. Mai 1995*, edited by S. Deger-Jalkotzy, S. Hiller, and O. Panagl, 325–342. Vienna: Verlag der Österreichischen Akademie der Wissenschaften.

2001   Some thoughts on TA-RA-SI-JA. In *Economy and politics in the Mycenaean palace states: Proceedings of a conference held on 1–3 July 1999 in the Faculty of Classics, Cambridge*, edited by S. Voutsaki and J. Killen, 161–180. Cambridge: The Cambridge Philological Society.

Knapp, A.B.

1986   *Copper production and divine protection: Archaeology, ideology and social complexity on Bronze Age Cyprus.* Studies in Mediterranean Archaeology and Literature, Pocketbook 42. Göteborg: Paul Åströms Förlag.

1993   Thalassocracies in Bronze Age eastern Mediterranean trade: Making and breaking a myth. *World Archaeology* 24:332–347.

Knapp, A.B., and J.F. Cherry

1994   *Provenance studies and Bronze Age Cyprus: Production, exchange, and politico-economic change.* Madison, WI: Prehistory Press.

Knappett, C.

2001   Overseen or overlooked? Ceramic production in a Mycenaean palatial system. In *Economy and politics in the Mycenaean palace states. Proceedings of a conference held on 1–3 July 1999 in the Faculty of Classics, Cambridge*, edited by S. Voutsaki and J. Killen, 80–95. Cambridge: The Cambridge Philological Society.

Kohl, P.L.

1989   The use and abuse of world systems theory: The case of the "pristine" West Asian state. In *Archaeological thought in America*, edited by C.C. Lamberg-Karlovsky, 218–240. New York: Cambridge University Press.

1992   The Transcaucasian "periphery" in the Bronze Age: A preliminary formulation. In *Resources, power, and interregional interaction*, edited by E.M. Schortman

and P.A. Urban, 117–137. New York: Plenum Press.

Konsolaki, E.

1991   Methana, Agios Konstantinos: B' Ephoreia Proistorikon kai Klassikon Archaioteton. *Archaiologikon Deltion* 46:71–74.

1995   The Mycenaean sanctuary on Methana. *Bulletin of the Institute of Classical Studies of the University of London* 40:242.

1997   Personal communication to Susan Lupack, April 10.

Kopaka, C.

1990   Des pièces de repos dans l'habitat minoen du IIème millénaire avant J.-C.? *L'habitat égéen préhistorique, Actes de la Table Ronde internationale tenue à l'Ecole Française d'Athènes, Athènes, 23-25 juin 1987*, edited by In P. Darcque and R. Treuil, 217–230. *Bulletin de Correspondance Hellénique*, suppl. vol.19. Paris: Diffusion de Boccard.

Korres, G.S.

1990   Excavations in the region of Pylos. In *EUMOUSIA: Ceramic and iconographic studies in honour of Alexander Cambitoglou*, edited by J.-P. Descœudres, 1–11. *Mediterranean Archaeology*, suppl. 1. Sydney: University of Sydney.

Kourouniotis, K.

1906   Anaskaphe tholo tou taphou en Volo. *Archaeologike Ephemeris* 29:212–240.

Kowalewski, S.

1982   The evolution of primate regional systems. *Comparative Urban Research* 9:60–68.

Krzyszkowska, O.

1992   Aegean ivory carving: Towards an evaluation of Late Bronze Age workshop material. In *Ivory in Greece and the eastern Mediterranean from the Bronze Age to the Hellenistic period*, edited by J.L. Fitton, 25–35. British Museum Occasional Paper 85. London: British Museum.

1997   Cult and craft: Ivories from the Citadel House area, Mycenae. In *TEXNH: Craftsmen, craftswomen and craftsmanship in the Aegean Bronze Age*, edited by R. Laffineur and P. Betancourt, 145–150. Aegaeum 16. Liège: Université de Liège; Austin: University of Texas at Austin

1999   So where's the loot? The spoils of war and the archaeological record. In *POLEMOS: Le contexte guerrier en égée à l'âge du bronze. Actes de la 7e Rencontre Égéenne Internationale*, edited by R. Laffineur, 489–496. Aegaeum 19. Liège Université de Liège; Austin: University of Texas at Austin Program in Aegean Scripts and Prehistory.

Kurjack, E.

1974 *Prehistoric lowland Maya community and social organization: A case study at Dzibilchaltun, Yucatan, Mexico.* Middle American Research Institute Publication 38. New Orleans: Tulane University.

Lackenbacher, S., and Malbran-Labat, F.

2005 Ugarit et les Hittites dans les archives de la "Maison d'Urtenu." Studi Micenei ed Egeo-Anatolici 47:227–240.

Laffineur, R., and P. Betancourt, eds.

1997 *TEXNH: Craftsmen, craftswomen and craftsmanship in the Aegean Bronze Age.* Aegaeum 16. Liège: Université de Liège; Austin: University of Texas at Austin Program in Aegean Scripts and Prehistory.

Laffineur, R., and E. Greco, eds.

2005 *EMPORIA: Aegeans in the Central and Eastern Mediterranean. Proceedings of the 10th International Aegean Conference, Athens, Italian School of Archaeology, 14–18 April 2004.* Aegaeum 25. Liege: Université de Liège; Austin: University of Texas at Austin Program in Aegean Scripts and Prehistory.

Lambrou-Phillipson, C.

1990 *Hellenorientalia: The Near Eastern presence in the Bronze Age Aegean ca. 3000- 1100 B.C. plus Orientalia: A catalogue of Egyptian, Mesopotamian, Mitannian, Syro-Palestinian, Cypriot and Asia Minor objects from the Bronze Age Aegean.* Göteborg: Paul Åströms Förlag.

Lambropoulou, A.

1991 *The Middle Helladic period in the Corinthia and the Argolid: An archaeological survey.* Ph.D. dissertation, Bryn Mawr College. Ann Arbor: University Microfilms.

Lang, M.

1969 *The Palace of Nestor at Pylos in western Messenia. Vol. II: The frescoes.* Princeton, NJ: Princeton University Press.

La Rosa, V.

1997 Aghia Triada à l'époque mycénienne: l'utopie d'une ville capitale. In *La Crète Mycénienne. Actes de la Table Ronde Internationale organisée par l'École française d'Athènes, 26–28 Mars 1991*, edited by J. Driessen and A. Farnoux, 249–266. *Bulletin de Correspondance Hellénique*, suppl. vol. 30. Paris: Diffusion de Boccard.

2000 To whom did the Queen Tiyi scarab found at Hagia Triada belong? In ΚΡΗΤΗ-ΑΙΓΥΠΤΟΣ. Πολιτισμικοί δεσμοί τριών χιλιετιών, Kriti - Aigyptos. Politismikoi desmoi trion chilietion, edited by A. Karetsou, 86–93. Athens: Heraklion Archaeological Museum.

Laser, S.

1987 *Sport und Spiel.* Archaeologia Homerica, vol. 3. Göttingen: Vandenhoeck and Ruprecht.

Latacz, J.

2004 *Troy and Homer: Towards a solution of an old mystery.* Oxford: Oxford University Press.

La Thessalie

1994 *La Thessalie. Quinze ans de recherches archéologiques, 1975–1990. Bilans et perspectives. Actes du Colloque International. Lyon, 17–22 avril 1990.* Vol. I. Greek Ministry of Culture. Athens: Kapon.

Lazaridis, P.

1968 Anaskaphai Neas Anchialou. *Praktika tes Archaeologikes Etaireias* 147:31–41.

1969 Anaskaphai Neas Anchialou. *Praktika tes Archaeologikes Etaireias* 148:37–49.

LeClaire, E.E.

1962 Economic theory and economic anthropology. *American Anthropologist* 64:1172–1203.

Leekley, D., and R. Noyes

1975 *Archaeological excavations in the Greek islands.* Park Ridge, NJ: Noyes Press.

Lehmann, G.A.

1991 Die "politisch-historischen" Beziehungen der Ägäis-Welt des 15.–13. Jh.s v. Chr. Zu Ägypten und Vorderasian: Einige Hinweise. In *Zweihundert Jahre Homer-Forschung: Rückblick und Ausblick*, Colloquium Rauricum 2, edited by J. Latacz, 105–126. Stuttgart and Lepizig: B.G. Teubner.

Lejeune, M.

1979 Sur la fiscalité Pylienne Ma. In *Colloquium Myceanaeum: Actes du sixième colloque international sur les textes Mycéniens*, edited by E. Risch and H. Muhlestein, 147–150. Neuchâtel: University of Neuchâtel.

Lewartowski, K.

1995 Mycenaean social structure: a view from simple graves. In *POLITEIA: Society and state in the Aegean Bronze Age*, edited by W.-D. Niemeier and R. Laffineur, 103–112. Aegaeum 13. Liège: Université de Liège; Austin: University of Texas at Austin.

2000 *Late Helladic simple graves: A study of Mycenaean burial customs.* British Archaeological Reports S878. Oxford: Archaeopress.

Liagouras, A.

1963 Stephanovikeion. Proin Chatzimissi. *Archaeologikon Deltion* 18:144.

Lindgren, M.

1973 The people of Pylos: Prosopographical and methodological studies in the Pylos archives. *Acta Universitatis Upsaliensis. Boreas, Uppsala Studies in*

Ancient Mediterranean and Near Eastern Civilizations 3:1–2.

Littauer, M.A.

1972   The military use of the chariot in the Aegean in the Late Bronze Age. *American Journal of Archaeology* 76:145–157.

Littauer, M.A., and J. Crouwel

1983   Chariots in Late Bronze Age Greece. *Antiquity* 57:187–192.

Loader, C.N.

1998   *Building in Cyclopean masonry, with special reference to the Mycenaean fortifications on Mainland Greece.* Studies in Mediterranean Archaeology, Pocket Book 148. Jonsered: Paul Åströms Förlag.

Lolling, H.G., and P. Wolters

1886   Das Kuppelgrab bei Dimini. *Athenische Mitteilungen* 11:435–443.

1887   Das Kuppelgrab bei Dimini. *Athenische Mitteilungen* 12:136–138.

Lolos, Y.G.

1987   *The Late Helladic I pottery of the southwestern Peloponnesos and its local characteristics.* Studies in Mediterranean Archaeology and Literature, Pocket Book 50. Göteborg: Paul Åströms Förlag.

1989   The tholos tomb at Koryphasion: Evidence for the transition from Middle to Late Helladic in Messenia. In *TRANSITION: Le monde égéen du Bronze moyen au Bronze récent. Actes de la 2e Rencontre égéenne internationale de l'Université de Liège, 18-20 avril 1988,* edited by R. Laffineur, 171–175. Aegaeum 3. Liege: Université de Liège; Austin: University of Texas at Austin Program in Aegean Scripts and Prehistory.

1994   *Pylos imathoeis. I protevousa tou Nestoros kai i gyro periohi.* Athens: Oionos Press.

2003   Cypro-Mycenaean relations ca. 1200 BC: Point Iria in the Gulf of Argos and Old Salamis in the Saronic Gulf. In *Sea routes: Interconnections in the Mediterranean 16th–6th c. BC. Proceedings of an international symposium held at Rethymnon, Crete, September 29–October 2, 2002,* edited by N.C. Stampolidi and V. Karageorghis, 101–116. Athens: The University of Crete and the A.G. Leventis Foundation

Lombardo, S., trans.

1997   *Homer. Iliad.* Indianapolis: Hackett Publishing.

Luedtke, B.

1978   Chert sources and trace-element analysis. *American Antiquity* 42:413–23.

1979   Quarrying and quantifications: Estimates of lithic material demand. *Midcontinental Journal of Archaeology* 4:255–266.

1992   *An archaeologist's guide to chert and flint.* UCLA Institute of Archaeology Archaeological Research Tools, no. 7. Los Angeles: UCLA.

Lukermann, F.E.

1972   Settlement and circulation: Pattern and systems. In *The Minnesota Messenia Expedition: Reconstructing a Bronze Age regional environment,* edited by W.A. McDonald and G.R. Rapp, 148–170. Minneapolis: University of Minnesota Press.

Macdonald, C.F.

1997   The prelude to Mycenaean Crete. In *La Crète Mycénienne: Actes de la Table Ronde Internationale organisée par l'École française d'Athènes, 26–28 Mars 1991,* edited by J. Driessen and A. Farnoux, 267–273. Bulletin de Correspondance Hellénique, suppl. vol. 30. Paris: Diffusion de Boccard.

2003   The palace of Minos at Knossos. *Athena Review* 3(3):36–43.

2005   *Knossos.* London: Folio Society.

MacGillivray, J.A.

1997   Late Minoan II and III pottery and chronology at Palaikastro: An introduction. In *Late Minoan III Pottery: Chronology and terminology. Acts of a meeting held at the Danish Institute at Athens, August 12–14, 1994,* edited by E. Hallager and B.P. Hallager, 193–207. Monographs of the Danish Institute at Athens 1. Athens: Åarhus University Press.

Mackenzie, D.

1898   Excavations in Melos, 1898, the successive settlements. *Annual of the British School at Athens* 4:11–36.

Malakassioti, Z.

1992   Thalamoeides Mykenaikos taphos ston Kato Mavrolopho Almyrou. In *Diethnes synedrio gia ten Archaia Thessalia ste mneme tou D. R. Theochari,* edited by the Greek Ministry of Culture, 267–271. Athens: Tameio Archaeologikon Poron kai Apalotrioseon.

Malakassioti, Z., and A. Mousioni

2001   Nea eurymata tes Hysteris Epoches tou Chalkou kai tes Epochis tou Sidirou sten Halo. In *Kauseis sten Epoche tou Chalkou kai ten Proimi Epochi tou Siderou,* edited by N.C. Stambolides, 353–368. Athens: Ypourgeio Politismou.

Maniatis, Y., and M. Tite

1978   Ceramic technology in the Aegean world during the Bronze Age. In *Thera and the Aegean world I,* edited by C. Doumas, 483–492. London.

Mann, M.

1986   *The sources of social power. Vol. I. A history of power from the beginning to A.D. 1760.* Cambridge: Cambridge University Press.

Manning, S.W., and L. Hulin
2005   Maritime commerce and geographies of mobility in the Late Bronze Age of the eastern Mediterranean: Problematizations. In *The archaeology of Mediterranean prehistory*, edited by E. Blake and A.B. Knapp, 270–302. Oxford: Blackwell Publishing.

Mantzourani, E.
1995   Vases and vessels in Aegean wall painting. In *Klados: Essays in honor of J.N. Coldstream*, edited by C. Morris, 123–141. London: Institute of Classical Studies.

Maran, J.
2001   Political and religious aspects of architectural change on the upper citadel of Tiryns. The case of building T. In *POTNIA: Deities and religion in the Aegean Bronze Age. Proceedings of the 8th International Aegean Conference Göteborg, Göteborg University, 12-15 April 2000*, edited by R. Laffineur and R. Hägg, 113–122. Aegaeum 22. Liège: Université de Liège; Austin: University of Texas Program in Aegean Scripts and Prehistory.
2004   The spreading of objects and ideas in the Late Bronze Age Eastern Mediterranean: Two case examples from the Argolid of the 13th and 12th centuries B.C. *Bulletin of the American Schools of Oriental Research* 336:11–30.

Marcus, J.
1974   The iconography of power among the Classic Maya. *World Archaeology* 6:83–94.
1989   From centralized systems to city-states: Possible models for the Epiclassic. In *Mesoamerica after the decline of Teotihuacan A.D. 700–900*, edited by R. Diehl and J. Berlo, 201–208. Washington, DC: Dumbarton Oaks.
1993a   *Mesoamerican writing systems*. Princeton, NJ: Princeton University Press.
1993b   Ancient Maya political organization. In *Lowland Maya civilization in the eighth century A.D.*, edited by J.A. Sabloff and J.S. Henderson, 111–172. Washington, DC: Dumbarton Oaks Research Library and Collection.
1998a   Note to editors, January 14.
1998b   The peaks and valleys of ancient states: An extension of the dynamic model. In *Archaic states*, edited by G.M. Feinman and J. Marcus, 59–94. Santa Fe: School of American Research Press.
2003   Recent advances in Maya archaeology. *Journal of Archaeological Research* 11(2):71–148.
2004   Primary and secondary state formation in southern Mesoamerica. In *Understanding Early Classic Copan*, edited by E.E. Bell, M.A. Canuto, and R.J. Sharer, 357–373. Philadelphia, PA: University

of Pennsylvania Museum of Archaeology and Anthropology.

Marinatos, N.
1986   *Minoan sacrificial ritual: Cult practice and symbolism*. Stockholm: Paul Åströms Förlag.
1990   Celebrations of death and the symbolism of the lion hunt. In *Celebrations of death and divinity in the Bronze Age Argolid: Proceedings of the Sixth International Symposium at the Swedish Institute at Athens, 11–13 June, 1988*, edited by R. Hägg and G.C. Nordquist, 143–148. SkrAth 4, XL, Stockholm.
1993   *Minoan religion: Ritual, image and symbol*. Columbia: University of South Carolina.
1996   The iconographical program of the palace of Knossos. In *Haus und Palast im alten Ägypten*, edited by M. Bietak, 149–157. Vienna: Verlag der Österreichischen Akademie der Wissenschaften.

Matoïan, V.
2003   Aegean and Near Eastern vitreous materials: New data from Ugarit. In *Sea routes: Interconnections in the Mediterranean 16th–6th c. BC. Proceedings of an international symposium held at Rethymnon, Crete, September 29–October 2, 2002*, edited by N.C. Stampolidi and V. Karageorghis, 151–162. Athens: The University of Crete and the A.G. Leventis Foundation.

Matson, F.
1972   Ceramic studies. In *The Minnesota Messenia Expedition: Reconstructing a Bronze Age regional environment*, edited by W. McDonald and G.R. Rapp, Jr., 200–244. Minneapolis: University of Minnesota Press.

Matthäus, H.
1983   Minoische Kriegergräber. In *Minoan Society. Proceedings of the Cambridge Colloquium 1981*, edited by O. Krzyszkowska and L. Nixon, 203–216. Bristol: Bristol Classical Press.

Mauss, M.
1990 [1966]   *The gift: The form and reason for exchange in archaic societies*, translated by W.D. Halls. London: Routledge.

McCallum, L.R.
1987   *Decorative program in the Mycenaean palace of Pylos: The megaron frescoes*. Ph.D. dissertation, University of Pennsylvania. Ann Arbor: University Microfilms.

McDonald, W.A.
1964   Overland communications in Greece during LHIII with special reference to southwest Peloponnese. In *Mycenaean Studies: Proceedings of the Third International Colloquium for Mycenaean Studies held at "Wingspread," 4–8 September 1961*, edited by

E.L. Bennett, Jr., 217–240. Madison: University of Wisconsin Press.

1975　　Excavations at Nichoria in Messenia: 1972–1973. *Hesperia* 44:69–141.

McDonald, W.A., and R. Hope Simpson

1969　　Explorations in southwest Peloponnese: 1964–1968. *American Journal of Archaeology* 73:123–177.

1972　　Archaeological exploration. In *The Minnesota Messenia Expedition: Reconstructing a Bronze Age regional environment*, edited by W. McDonald and G.R. Rapp, Jr., 117–147. Minneapolis: University of Minnesota Press.

McDonald, W.A., and G.R. Rapp, Jr., eds.

1972　　*The Minnesota Messenia Expedition: Reconstructing a Bronze Age regional environment.* Minneapolis: University of Minnesota Press.

McDonald, W.A., and C.G. Thomas

1990　　*Progress into the past. The rediscovery of Mycenaean civilization.* 2nd ed. Bloomington: Indiana University Press.

McDonald, W.A., and N.C. Wilkie, eds.

1992　　*Excavations at Nichoria in southwest Greece. Vol. II. The Bronze Age occupation.* Minneapolis: University of Minnesota Press.

Mee, C.

1998　　Anatolia and the Aegean in the Late Bronze Age. In *The Aegean and the Orient in the second millennium. Proceedings of the 50th Anniversary Symposium, Cincinnati, 18–20 April 1997*, edited by E.H. Cline and D. Harris-Cline, 137–148. *Aegaeum* 18. Liège: Université de Liège; Austin: University of Texas at Austin Program in Aegean Scripts and Prehistory.

Mee, C., and H. Forbes, eds.

1997　　*A rough and rocky place: The landscape and settlement history of the Methana Peninsula, Greece.* Liverpool Monographs in Archaeology and Oriental Studies. Liverpool: Liverpool University Press.

Melas, E.M.

1995　　Transcending the "palace": Kinship versus kingship, and the social dimension of Minoan ritual. In *Proceedings of the 7th International Cretological Congress, vol. A1: Archaeology*, edited by N.E. Papadogiannakis, 613–624. Rethymnon: Iera Mitropolis Rethymnis and Aulopotamou.

Melena, J.L.

1983　　Further thoughts on Mycenaean o-pa. In *Res Mycenaeae: Akten des VII. Internationalen Mykenologischen Colloquiums in Nürnberg vom 6. 10. April 1981*, edited by A.H. heubeck and G. Neumann, 258–286. Göttingen: Vandenhoeck and Ruprecht.

2000-2001　63 joins and quasi-joins of fragments from the Linear B tablets from Pylos. *Minos* 35:371–384.

Mellaart, J.

1964　　A Neolithic city in Turkey. *Scientific American* 210(4):94–104.

Michailidou, A., ed.

2001　　*Manufacture and measurement: Counting, measuring and recording craft items in early Aegean societies.* Research Centre for Greek and Roman Antiquity, National Hellenic Research Foundation. Paris: Diffusion de Boccard.

Michaud, J.P.

1971　　Dimini. *Bulletin de Correspondence Hellenique* 95:936–937.

Militello, P.

1998　　*Haghia Triada I. Gli affreschi.* Monografia della Scuola monografie della Scuola archeologica di Atene e delle missioni italiane in Oriente 9. Padua: Bottega d'Erasmo.

Miller, S.G.

2004　　*Ancient Greek athletics.* New Haven: Yale University Press.

Millon, R.

1967　　Teotihuacan. *Scientific American* 216(6):38–48.

Mills, B.J., ed.

2000　　*Alternative leadership strategies in the Prehispanic Southwest.* Tucson: University of Arizona Press.

Mirié, S.

1979　　*Das Thronraumareal des Palastes von Knossos: Versuch einer Neuinterpretation seiner Entstehung und seiner Funktion.* Saarbrücker Beiträge zur Altertumswissenschaft 26, Bonn.

Mommsen, H., T. Beier, and P. Åström

2003　　Neutron Activation Analysis results of six Mycenaean sherds from Hala Sultan Tekke, Cyprus. *Archaeology and Natural Science* 2:5–10.

Mommsen, H., A. Hein, D. Ittameier, J. Maran, and P. Dakoronia

2001　　New Mycenaean pottery production centres from eastern Central Greece obtained by Neutron Activation Analysis. In *Archaeometry issues in Greek prehistory and antiquity*, edited by Y. Bassiakos, E. Aloupi, and Y. Facorellis, 343–354. Athens: The Hellenic Society of Archaeometry and the Society of Messenian Archaeological Studies.

Mommsen, H., and J. Maran

2000-2001　Production places of some Mycenaean pictorial vessels: The contribution of chemical pottery analysis. *Opuscula atheniensia* 25–26:95–106.

Moody, J.

1987　　The Minoan palace as a prestige artifact. In *The function of the Minoan palaces. Proceedings of the Fourth International Symposium at the Swedish Institute in Athens, 10–16 June, 1984*, edited by R. Hägg and N.

Marinatos, 235–241. Stockholm: Svenska Institutet i Athen.

2005 "Drought and the decline of Mycenae" updated. In *AUTOCHTHON: Papers presented to O.T.P.K. Dickinson on the occasion of his retirement*, edited by A. Dakouri-Hild and S. Sherratt, 126–133. British Archaeological Reports IS1432. Oxford: Archaeopress.

Moore, A., and W. Taylour

n.d. *The ancillary areas of the cult centre*. Well Built Mycenae: The Helleno-British Excavations within the Citadel of Mycenae 1959–1969, fasc. 13. W. Taylour, E. French, and K. Wardle, series editors. Oxford: Oxbow Books. In press.

Morgan, C.

1999 *Isthmia 8: The Late Bronze Age settlement and Early Iron Age sanctuary*. Princeton, NJ: American School of Classical Studies at Athens.

Morpurgo Davies, A.

1979 Terminology of work and terminology of power in Greek and Linear B. In *Colloquium Mycenaeum*, edited by E. Risch and H. Mühlstein, 87–108. Neuchâtel: Faculté des Lettres; Genève: Librairie Droz.

1999 The morphology of personal names in Mycenaean and Greek: Some observations. In *Floreant Studia Mycenaea: Akten des X. Internationalen Mykenologischen Colloquiums in Salzburg vom 1.–5. Mai 1995. Band II*, edited by S. Deger-Jalkotsky, S. Hiller, O. Panagl, 389–405. Vienna: Österreichische Akademie der Wissenschaften.

Morris, C.E.

1990 In pursuit of the white tusked boar: Aspects of hunting in Mycenaean society. In *Celebrations of death and divinity in the Bronze Age Argolid: Proceedings of the Sixth International Symposium at the Swedish Institute at Athens, 11–13 June, 1988*, edited by R. Hägg and G.C. Nordquist, 149–156. Stockholm: Paul Åströms Förlag.

Morris, H.J.

1986 *An economic model of the late Mycenaean kingdom of Pylos*. Ph.D. dissertation, University of Minnesota.

Morris, I.

1994 Archaeologies of Greece. In *Classical Greece: Ancient histories and modern archaeologies*, edited by I. Morris, 8–47. New York: Cambridge University Press.

Morris, I., ed.

1994 *Classical Greece: Ancient histories and modern archaeologies*. New York: Cambridge University Press.

Moser von Filseck, K.

1986 Der Alabasterfries von Tiryns. *Archäologischer Anzeiger* 1986:1–32.

Mountjoy, P.A.

1983 The Ephyraean goblet reviewed. *Annual of the British School at Athens* 78: 265-271.

1986 *Mycenaean decorated pottery: A guide to identification*. Göteborg: Paul Åströms Förlag.

1994 *Grapte Mykenaike keramike*. Athens: Kardamitsas.

1997 The destruction of the palace at Pylos reconsidered. *Annual of the British School of Athens* 92:109–137.

1998 The East Aegean-West Anatolian interface in the Late Bronze Age: Mycenaeans and the Kingdom of Ahhiyawa. *Anatolian Studies* 48:33–67.

1999 *Regional Mycenaean decorated pottery*. Berlin: M. Leidorf.

Muhly, P.

1992 *Minoan carved graves at Heraklion Poros*. Athens: Archaeological Society.

Murphy, J.

1998 Ideologies, rites and rituals: A view of prepalatial Minoan tholoi. In *Cemetery and society in the Aegean Bronze Age*, edited by K. Branigan, 27–40. Sheffield Studies in Aegean Archaeology 1. Sheffield: Sheffield Academic Press.

n.d. Two studies, one conclusion: Social organization in south-central Crete during the Prepalatial Period. Unpublished manuscript, University of Akron.

Mylonas, G.

1959 *Agios Kosmas: An Early Bronze Age settlement and cemetery in Attica*. Princeton, NJ: Princeton University Press.

1966 *Mycenae and the Mycenaean age*. Princeton, NJ: Princeton University Press.

Nagao, D.

1989 Public proclamation in the art of Cacaxtla and Xochicalco. In *Mesoamerica after the decline of Teotihuacan A.D. 700–900*, edited by R. Diehl and J. Berloeds, 83–104. Washington, DC: Dumbarton Oaks.

Nakassis, D.

2005 *Craft specialists and the Mycenaean state: The case of the Pylian bronze-smiths*. Paper presented at the 106th annual meeting of the Archaeological Institute of America, San Francisco, CA.

2006 *The individual and the Mycenaean state: Agency and prosopography in the Linear B texts from Pylos*, Ph.D. Dissertation, University of Texas, Austin.

Nakou, G.

1995 The cutting edge: A new look at early Aegean metallurgy. *Journal of Mediterranean Archaeology* 8:1–32.

Neff, H., F. Bove, B. Lou, and M. Piechowski

1992 Ceramic raw materials survey in pacific coastal Guatemala. In *Chemical characterization of ceramic pastes in archaeology*, edited by H. Neff, 59–84. Madison, WI: Prehistory Press.

Neff, H., M. Glasscock, R. Bishop, and M. Blackman

1996   An assessment of the acid-extraction approach to compositional characterization of archaeological ceramics. *American Antiquity* 61(2):389–404.

Neve, P.

1984   Ein älter-hetitisches Relief von Büyükkale. In *Bogazköy VI: Funde aus den Grabungen bis 1979*. Berlin.

Newhard, J.M.

1996   The chipped stone assemblage from Midea: The 1990 season. Master's thesis, University of Cincinnati.

Nichols, D.L., and T.H. Charlton, eds.

1997   *The archaeology of city-states: Cross-cultural approaches*. Washington, DC: Smithsonian Institution Press.

Nicklin, K.

1979   The location of pottery manufacture. *Man* 14: 436–458.

Niemeier, W-D.

1983   The character of the Knossian palace society in the second half of the fifteenth century B.C.: Mycenaean or Minoans? In *Minoan society: Proceedings of the Cambridge Colloquium 1981*, edited by O. Krzyszkowska and L. Nixon, 217–236. Bristol: Bristol Classical Press.

1984   The end of the Minoan thalassocracy. In *The function of the Minoan palaces: Proceedings of the First International Symposium at the Swedish Institute at Athens, 10–16 June 1984*, edited by R. Hägg and N. Marinatos, 205–215. Stockholm: Paul Åströms Förlag.

1985   *Die Palaststilkeramik von Knossos, Stil, Cronologie und historischer Context*. Archäologische Forschungen 13. Berlin: Mann.

1986   Zur Deutung des Thronraumes im Palast von Knossos. *Mitteilungen des Deutschen Archäologischen Instituts, Athenische Abteilung* 101:63–95.

1987   On the function of the "Throne Room" in the palace at Knossos. In *The function of the Minoan palaces: Proceedings of the First International Symposium at the Swedish Institute at Athens, 1–16 June 1984*, edited by R. Hägg and N. Marinatos, 163–168. Stockholm: Paul Åströms Förlag.

1995   Aegina—first Aegean "state" outside of Crete. In *POLITEIA: Society and state in the Aegean Bronze Age*, edited by R. Laffineur and W.-D. Niemeier, 73–79. Aegaeum 12. Liège: Université de Liège; Austin: University of Texas at Austin Program in Aegean Scripts and Prehistory.

1998   The Mycenaeans in Western Anatolia and the problem of the origins of the Sea Peoples. In *Mediterranean peoples in transition: Thirteenth to early tenth centuries BCE. In honor of Professor Trude Dothan*, edited by S. Gitin, A. Mazar, and E. Stern, 17–65. Jerusalem: Israel Exploration Society.

1999   Mycenaeans and Hittites in war in Western Asia Minor. In *POLEMOS: Le Contexte Guerrier en Égée a l'Âge du Bronze*, edited by R. Laffineur, 141–155. Aegaeum 19. Liège: Université de Liège; Austin: University of Texas at Austin Program in Aegean Scripts and Prehistory.

Nikolaidou, M., and D. Kokkinidou

1997   The symbolism of violence in palatial societies of the late Bronze Age Aegean, a gender approach. In *Material harm: Archaeological studies of war and violence*, edited by J. Carman, 174–197. Glasgow: Cruithne Press.

Nilsson, M.P.

1950   *The Minoan-Mycenaean religion and its survival in Greek religion*. 2nd ed. Lund: Biblo & Tannen Booksellers & Publishers.

Nordquist, G.

1997   Male craft and female industry. Two types of production in the Aegean Bronze Age. In *TEXNH: Craftsmen, craftswomen and craftsmanship in the Aegean Bronze Age. Proceedings of the 6th International Aegean Conference, Philadelphia, Temple University, 18–21 April 1996*, edited by R. Laffineur and P.P. Betancourt, 533–537. Aegaeum 16. Liège: Université de Liège; Austin: University of Texas at Austin Program in Aegean Scripts and Prehistory.

Nosch, M-L.B.

2000   Acquisition and distribution: ta-ra-si-ja in the Mycenaean textile industry. In *Trade and production in premonetary Greece: Acquisition and distribution of raw materials and finished products. Proceedings of the 6th International Workshop, Athens 1996*, edited by Gillis, C., C. Risberg, and B. Sjöberg, 42–62. Jonsered: Paul Åströms Förlag.

Nur, A., and E.H. Cline

2000   Poseidon's horses: Plate tectonics and earthquake storms in the Late Bronze Age Aegean and eastern Mediterranean. *Journal of Archaeological Science* 27(1):43–63.

Olivier J.

1967   La série Dn de Cnossos. *Studi Micenei ed Egeo-Anatolici* 2:71–93.

1974   Une loi fiscale mycénienne. *Bulletin de Correspondance Hellénique* 98:23–35.

1984   Administrations at Knossos and Pylos: What differences. In *Pylos comes alive: Industry and administration in a Mycenaean palace*, edited by C.W. Shelmerdine and T.J. Palaima, 11–18. New York: Archaeological Institute of America.

1988 KN: Da-Dg. In *Texts, tablets and scribes. Studies in Mycenaean epigraphy and economy offered to Emmett. L. Bennett, Jr.*, edited by J.-P. Olivier and T.G. Palaima, 219–267. *Minos*, suppl. vol. 10. Salamanca: University of Salamanca.

1990 Les grands nombres dans les archives crétoises du deuxième millénaire. In *Pepragmena tou 6 diethnous kritologikou sinedriou A, 2*, edited by B. Niniou-Kindeli, 69–76. Khania: Filologikos Sillogos o Khrisostomos.

2001 Les "collecteurs": Leur distribution spatiale et temporelle. In *Economy and politics in the Mycenaean palace states: Proceedings of a conference held on 1–3 July 1999 in the Faculty of Classics, Cambridge*, edited by S. Voutsaki and J. Killen, 139–160. Cambridge: The Cambridge Philological Society.

Olsen, B.A.

1998 Women, children and the family in the Late Bronze Age: Differences in Minoan and Mycenaean constructions of gender. *World Archaeology* 29:380–392.

Palaima, T.G.

1983 Evidence for the influence of the Knossian graphic tradition at Pylos. In *Concilium Eirene XVI. Vol. 3, Section 4: Mycenaeological colloquium. Proceedings of the 16th International Eirene Conference*, edited by P. Oliva and A. Frolikova, 80–84. Prague.

1984a Scribal organization and palatial activity. In *Pylos comes alive. Industry and administration in a Mycenaean palace*, edited by C.W. Shelmerdine and T.J. Palaima, 31–39. New York: Archaeological Institute of America.

1984b Inscribed stirrup jars and regionalism in Linear B Crete. *Studi Micenei ed Egeo-Anatolici* 25:189–203.

1987a Preliminary comparative textual evidence for palatial control of economic activity in Minoan and Mycenaean Crete. In *The function of the Minoan palaces. Proceedings of the fourth international symposium at the Swedish Institute in Athens, 10–16 June, 1984*, edited by R. Hägg and N. Marinatos, 301–305. Stockholm: Svenska Institutet i Athen.

1987b Myceneaean seals and sealings in their economic and administrative contexts. In *Tractata Mycenaea: Proceedings of the Eighth International Colloquium on Mycenaean Studies, Ohrid, 15–20 September 1985*, edited by P. Ilievski and L. Crepajac, 249–266. Skopje: Macedonian Academy of Sciences and Arts.

1988 *The scribes of Pylos*. Incunabula Graeca 87. Rome: Edizioni dell'Ateneo.

1991 Maritime matters in the Linear B tablets. In *Thalassa: L'Egée préhistorique et la mer*, edited by R. Laffineur and L. Basch, 273–310. Aegaeum 7. Liège: Université de Liège; Austin: University of Texas at Austin Program in Aegean Scripts and Prehistory.

1995 The nature of the Mycenaean wanax: Non-Indo-European origins and priestly functions. In *The role of the ruler in the prehistoric Aegean: Proceedings of a panel discussion presented at the annual meeting of the Archaeological Institute of America, New Orleans, Louisiana 28 December 1992, with additions*, edited by P.Rehak, 119–142. Aegaeum 11. Liège: Université de l'État à Liège; Austin: University of Texas at Austin Program in Aegean Scripts and Prehistory.

1997 Potter and fuller: The royal craftsmen. In *TEXNH: Craftsmen, craftswomen and craftsmanship in the Aegean Bronze Age*, edited by R. Laffineur and P. Betancourt, 407–412. Aegaeum 16. Liège: Université de Liège; Austin: University of Texas at Austin Program in Aegean Scripts and Prehistory.

2000 Wannabe wanaks' power rise. *The Times* (London), Higher Education Supplement, June 9, 2000, 31.

2003 "Archives" and "scribes" and information hierarchy in Mycenaean Greek Linear B records. In *Ancient archives and archival traditions: Concepts of record-keeping in the ancient world*, edited by M. Brosius, 153–194. Oxford: Oxford University Press.

Palaima, T.G., and C.W. Shelmerdine

1984 Mycenaean archaeology and the Pylos texts. *Cambridge Archaeological Review* 3(2):76–89.

Palaima, T.G., and J.C. Wright

1985 Ins and outs of the archive rooms at Pylos: Form and function in a Mycenaean palace. *American Journal of Archaeology* 89:251–262.

Palmer, L.R.

1963 *The interpretation of Mycenaean Greek texts*. Oxford: Oxford University Press.

Palmer, R.

1992 Wheat and barley in Mycenaean society. In *Mykenaika. Actes du 9e colloque internationale sur les textes mycéniens et égéens*, edited by J.-P. Olivier, 475–491. Bulletin de Correspondance Hellenique supplementary volume 25. Paris: Diffusion de Boccard.

1994 *Wine in the Mycenaean palace economy*. Aegaeum 10. Liège: Université de Liège; Austin: University of Texas at Austin.

1995 Linear A commodities: A comparison of resources. In *POLITEIA: Society and state in the Aegean Bronze Age*, edited by W.-D. Niemeier and R. Laffineur,

133–155. Aegaeum 13. Liège: Université de Liège; Austin:University of Texas at Austin.

1998–1999   Models in Linear B landholding: An analysis of methodology. In *A-NA-QO-TA. Studies presented to J.T. Killen*, edited by J. Bennet and J. Driessen, 223–250. *Minos* 33–34. Salamanca: Ediciones Universidad de Salamanca.

1999   Perishable goods in Mycenaean texts. In *Floreant Studia Mycenaea: Akten des X. Internationalen Mykenologischen Colloquiums in Salzburg vom 1.–5. Mai 1995. Band II*, edited by S. Deger-Jalkotsky, S. Hiller, and O. Panagl, 460–485. Vienna: Österreichische Akademie der Wissenschaften.

2001   Bridging the gap: The continuity of Greek agriculture from the Mycenaean to the historical period. In *Prehistory and history: Ethnicity, class and political economy*, edited by D. Tandy, 41–84. Montreal: Black Rose Books.

2003   Trade in wine, perfumed oil and foodstuffs: The Linear B evidence and beyond. In *Sea routes: Interconnections in the Mediterranean 16th–6th c. BC. Proceedings of an international symposium held at Rethymnon, Crete, September 29–October 2, 2002*, edited by N.C. Stampolidis and V. Karageorghis, 125–140. Athens: The University of Crete and the A.G. Leventis Foundation.

Panagiotaki, M.

1999   *The central palace sanctuary at Knossos*. British School at Athens, supple. vol. 31. London: The British School at Athens.

Papadimitriou, N.

2001   *Built chamber tombs of Middle and Late Bronze Age date in Mainland Greece and the Islands*. British Archaeological Reports S925. Oxford: Archaeopress.

Papadopoulos, J.K., and R.M. Leventhal, eds.

2003   *Theory and practice in Mediterranean archaeology: Old world and new world perspectives*. Cotsen Advanced Seminars 1. Los Angeles: Cotsen Institute of Archaeology, University of California–Los Angeles.

Parkinson, R., and Schofield, L.

1993   Akhenaten's army? *Egyptian Archaeology* 3:34–35.

Parkinson, W. A.

1997   Chipping away at a Mycenaean economy. *Bulletin of the Central States Anthropological Society* 32(1):12–26.

1999   Chipping away at a Mycenaean economy: Obsidian exchange, Linear B, and palatial control in Late Bronze Age Messenia. In *Rethinking Mycenaean palaces: New interpretationsof an old idea*, edited by M.L. Galaty and W.A. Parkinson, 73–86. Los Angeles:

Cotsen Institute of Archaeology, University of California–Los Angeles.

Parkinson, W.A., and M.L. Galaty

2007   Primary and secondary states in perspective: An integrated approach to state formation in the prehistoric Aegean. *American Anthropologist* 109: 113-129.

Peacock, D.

1982   *Pottery in the Roman world: An ethnoarchaeological approach*. London: Longman.

Peatfield, A.

1992   Rural ritual in Bronze Age Crete: The peak sanctuary at Atsipadhes. *Cambridge Archaeological Journal* 2: 59–87.

Pelon, O.

1976   *Tholoi, tumuli et cercles funéraires. Recherches sur les monuments funéraires de plan circulaire dans l'Égée de l'âge du Bronze (IIIe et IIe millénaires av. J.-C.)*. Bibliothèque des Écoles Françaises d'Athènes et de Rome, 229. Paris: Diffusion de Boccard.

Peltenberg, E.

1991   Greeting gifts and luxury faience: A context for orientalising trends in late Mycenaean Greece. In *Bronze Age trade in the Mediterranean*, edited by N.H. Gale, 162–179. Jonsered: Paul Åströms Forlag.

Peregrine, P.

1991   Some political aspects of craft specialization. *World Archaeology* 23:1–11.

Perlès, Catherine

1987a   *Les industries lithiques taillées de Franchthi (Argolide, Grèce)*. Tome I: Présentation générale et industries paléolithiques. Bloomington: Indiana University Press.

1987b   Les industries du Néolithique précéramique de Grèce: Nouvelles études, nouvelles interpretations. In *Chipped stone industries of the early farming cultures in Europe*, 19–39. Warsaw: Archaeologia Interregionalis.

1990a   L'Outillage de pierre taillée néolithique en Grèce: Approvisionnement et exploitation des matières premières. *Bulletin de Correspondance Hellénique* 114:1–42.

1990b   *Les Industries lithiques taillées de Franchthi (Argolide Grèce), II, Les industries du mésolithique et du néolithique initial* (with contributions by P.C. Vaughan, C. Renfrew, and A. Aspinall). Excavations at Franchthi Cave, Greece, fasc. 5. Bloomington: Indiana University Press.

1990c   From stone procurement to Neolithic society in Greece. The David Skomp Distinguished Lectures in Anthropology, Department of Anthropology, Indiana University, February 1989.

1992   Systems of exchange and organization of production in Neolithic Greece. *Journal of Mediterranean Archaeology* 5(2):115–164.

Perna, K.
2001   Rituali funerary e rappresentazione del potere nella Creta del TM IIIA2/B. *Creta Antica* 2:125–139.

Perna, M.
1999   Emergenza e fiscalità a Pilo. In *POLEMOS: Warfare in the Aegean Bronze Age*, edited by R. Laffineur, 381–387. Liège: L'Université de Liège; Austin: University of Texas at Austin Program in Aegean Scripts and Prehistory.

Phelps, W., Y. Lolos, and Y. Vichos, eds.
1999   *The Point Iria wreck: Interconnections in the Mediterranean ca. 1200 B.C. Proceedings of the International Conference, Island of Spetses, 19 September 1998.* Athens: Hellenic Institute of Marine Archaeology.

Phillips, J.S.
1991   *The impact and implications of the Egyptian and Egyptianizing objects found in Bronze Age Crete ca. 3000–ca. 1100 B.C.* Ph.D. dissertation, University of Toronto.

2003   An unconsidered trifle. In *The synchronization of civilizations in the Eastern Mediterranean in the Second Millennium BC: Proceedings of the SCIEM 2000–Euroconference Haindorf, 2nd of May–7th of May 2001*, edited by M. Bietak, 545–550. Vienna: Verlag der Österreichischen Akademie der Wissenschaften.

2005   The last pharaohs on Crete. Old contexts and old readings reconsidered. In *EMPORIA. Aegeans in the Central and Eastern Mediterranean: Proceedings of the 10th International Aegean Conference, Athens, Italian School of Archaeology, 14–18 April 2004*, edited by R. Laffineur and E. Greco, 455–461. Aegaeum 25. Liège: Université de Liège; Austin: University of Texas Program in Aegean Scripts and Prehistory.

2007   The Amenhotep III 'plaques' from Mycenae: Comparison, contrast and a question of chronology. In *The synchronisation of civilisations in the Eastern Mediterranean in the second millennium B.C. III: Proceedings of the SCIEM 2000—2nd EuroConference, Vienna, 28th of May–1st of June, 2003*, edited by M. Bietak and E. Czerny, 479–493. Wien: Verlag der Österreichischen Akademie der Wissenschaften.

Phillips, J.S., and Cline, E.H.
2005   Amenhotep III and Mycenae: New evidence. In *Autochthon: Papers presented to O.T.P.K. Dickinson on the occasion of his retirement*, edited by A. Dakouri-Hild and E. S. Sherratt, 317–328. B.A.R. International Series 1432. Oxford: Archaeopress.

Piggott, S.
1992   *Wagon, chariot and carriage: Symbol and status in the history of transport.* London: Thames and Hudson.

Pilali-Papasteriou, A., and K. Papaeuthimiou-Papanthimou
1983   New archaeological research in the sanctuary of Philia (in Greek). *Anthropologika* 4:49–67.

Piteros, C., J.-P. Olivier, and J.L. Melena
1990   Les inscriptions en Linéaire B des nodules de Thèbes (1982): La fouille, les documents, les possibilités d'interpretation. *Bulletin de Correspondance Hellénique* 114:103–184.

Platon, N.
1949   O taphos tou Staphylou kai o minoikos apoikismos tes Peparethou. *Kretika Chronika* 3:534–573.

Podzuweit, C.
1978   Ausgrabungen in Tiryns 1976: Bericht zur spaetmykenische Keramik. *Archaeologischer Anzeiger* 49:471–498.

Polanyi, K.
1957   The economy as instituted process. In *Trade and market in the early empires*, edited by K. Polanyi, C.M. Arensberg, and H.W. Pearson, 243–270. New York: Free Press.

1968   *Primitive, archaic and modern economies*, edited by G. Dalton. Boston: Beacon Press.

Pool, C.
1992   Integrating ceramic production and distribution. In *Ceramic production and distribution: An integrated approach*, edited by G. Bey and C. Pool, 275–313. Boulder, CO: Westview Press.

Popham, M.R.
1970   *The destruction of the palace at Knossos.* Studies in Mediterranean Archaeology 12. Lund: Paul Aström Förlag.

1984   *The Minoan Unexplored Mansion at Knossos.* British School at Athens, suppl. Paper 17. London: British School at Athens.

1987   The use of the palace at Knossos at the time of its destruction. In *The function of the Minoan palaces: Proceedings of the First International Symposium at the Swedish Institute at Athens, 10–16 June 1984*, edited by R. Hägg and N. Marinatos, 297–299. Stockholm: Paul Åströms Förlag.

Popham, M.R., E.A Catling, and H.W. Catling
1974   Sellopoulo Tombs 3 and 4: Two Late Minoan graves near Knossos. *Annual of the British School at Athens* 69:195–257.

Postgate, J.N.
1994   *Early Mesopotamia: Society and economy at the dawn of history.* New York: Routledge.

Preston, L.
1999   Mortuary practices and the negotiation of social identities at LMII Knossos. *American Journal of Archaeology* 103:131–143.
2004a   A mortuary perspective on political changes in Late Minoan II–IIIB Crete. *American Journal of Archaeology* 108:321–348.
2004b   Final Palatial Knossos and Postpalatial Crete: A mortuary perspective on political dynamics. In *Knossos: Palace, City, State. Proceedings of the Conference in Heraklion organised by the British School at Athens and the 23rd Ephoreia of Prehistoric and Classical Antiquities of Heraklion, in November 2000, for the Centenary of Sir Arthur Evans's Excavations at Knossos,* edited by G. Cadogan, E. Hatzaki and A. Vasilakis, 137–145. British School at Athens Studies 12. Athens: British School at Athens.
2005   The Kephala tholos at Knossos: A study in the reuse of the past (with a contribution by R. Gowland). *Annual of the British School at Athens* 100:61–123.

Prufer, O.
1964   The Hopewell cult. *Scientific American* 211(6): 90–102.

Pulak, Cemal
1997   The Uluburun shipwreck. In *Res Maritimae: Cyprus and the Eastern Mediterranean from Prehistory to Late Antiquity. Proceedings of the Second International Symposium Cities on the Sea. Nicosia, Cyprus, October 18–22, 1994,* edited by S. Swiny, R.L. Hohlfelder, and H. Wylde Swiny, 233–262. Cyprus American Archaeological Research Institute Monograph Series 1. Atlanta, GA: Scholars Press.

Pullen, D.J.
1992   Ox and plough in the Early Bronze Age Aegean. *American Journal of Archaeology* 96:45–54.

Redman, C.L.
1978   *The rise of civilization.* San Francisco: W.H. Freeman.

Rehak, P.
1995   Enthroned figures in Aegean art and the function of the Mycenaean megaron. In *The role of the ruler in the prehistoric Aegean: Proceedings of a panel discussion presented at the annual meeting of the Archaeological Institute of America, New Orleans, Louisiana 28 December 1992, with additions,* edited by P. Rehak, 95–118. Aegaeum 11. Liège: Université de l'État à Liège; Austin: University of Texas, Program in Aegean Scripts and Prehistory.
1996   Aegean breechcloths, kilts and the Keftiu paintings. *American Journal of Archaeology* 100:35–51.
1998   Aegean natives in the Theban tomb paintings: The Keftiu revisited. In *The Aegean and the Orient in the Second Millennium: Proceedings of the 50th Anniversary Symposium, University of Cincinnati, 18–20 April 1997,* edited by E. Cline and D. Harris-Cline, 39–49. Aegaeum 18. Liège: Université de Liège; Austin: University of Texas, Program in Aegean Scripts and Prehistory.

Rehak, P. and J.G. Younger
1998   Review of Aegean Prehistory VII: Neopalatial, Final Palatial and Postpalatial Crete. *American Journal of Archaeology* 102:91–173.

Reinders, H.R.
2003   *Prehistoric sites at the Almirós and Soúrpi plains (Thessaly, Greece).* Koninklijke: Van Gorcum.

Reinholdt, C.P.W.
1987   *Untersuchungen zur Bronze und Früheisenzeitlichen Metallverarbeitung in Griechenland, Zyrean und Troia.* Ph.D. dissertation, University of Salzburg. Paris and London.

Renfrew, C.
1972   *The emergence of civilisation: The Cyclades and the Aegean in the third millennium BC.* London: Methuen.
1975   Trade as action at a distance: Questions of integration and communication. In *Ancient civilization and trade,* edited by J. Sabloff and C. Lamberg-Karlovsky, 3–59. Albuquerque: University of New Mexico Press.
1977   Retrospect and prospect. In *Mycenaean geography. Proceedings of the Cambridge Colloquium 1976,* edited by J. Bintliff, 108–122. Cambridge: Cambridge University Press.
1978   Trajectory discontinuity and morphogenesis: The implications of catastrophe theory for archaeology. *American Antiquity* 43:203–222.
1980   The great tradition versus the great divide: Archaeology as anthropology? *American Journal of Archaeology* 84:287–298.
1981a   Questions of Minoan and Mycenaean cult. In *Sanctuaries and cults in the Aegean Bronze Age,* edited by R. Hägg and N. Marinatos, 27–33. Stockholm: Paul Åströms Förlag.
1981b   The sanctuary at Phylakopi. In *Sanctuaries and cults in the Aegean Bronze Age,* edited by R. Hägg and N. Marinatos, 67–80. Stockholm: Paul Åströms Förlag.
1982a   Prehistoric exchange. In *An island polity. The archaeology of exploitation in Melos,* edited by C. Renfrew and M. Wagstaff, 222–227. Cambridge: Cambridge University Press.
1982b   Polity and power. In *An island polity. The archaeology of exploitation in Melos,* edited by C. Renfrew and

M. Wagstaff, 264–290. Cambridge: Cambridge University Press.

1984 Trade as action at a distance. Reprinted in *Approaches to social archaeology*, by C. Renfrew, 86-134. Edinburgh: Edinburgh University Press.

1985 *The archaeology of cult: The sanctuary at Phylakopi.* British School at Athens suppl. vol. 18. London: Thames and Hudson.

1987 Introduction: Peer polity interaction and socio-political change. In *Peer polity interaction and socio-political change*, edited by C. Renfrew and J.F. Cherry, 1–18. Cambridge: Cambridge University Press.

1994 The archaeology of religion. In *The ancient mind: Elements of cognitive archaeology*, edited by C. Renfrew and E. Zubrow, 47–54. Cambridge: Cambridge University Press.

1998 Word of Minos: The Minoan contribution to Mycenaean Greek and the linguistic geography of the Aegean Bronze Age. *Cambridge Archaeological Journal* 8:239–264.

2003 Retrospect and prospect: Mediterranean archaeology in a new millennium. In *Theory and practice in Mediterranean archaeology: Old World and New World perspectives*, edited by J.K. Papadopoulos and R.M. Leventhal, 311–318. Cotsen Advanced Seminars 1. Los Angeles: Cotsen Institute of Archaeology, University of California–Los Angeles.

Renfrew, C., J.R. Cann, and J.E. Dixon
1965 Obsidian in the Aegean. *Annual of the British School at Athens* 60:225–247.

Renfrew, C., and J.F. Cherry, eds.
1986 *Peer polity interaction and socio-political change.* Cambridge: Cambridge University Press.

Renfrew, C., J.E. Dixon, and J.R. Cann
1968 Further analysis of Near Eastern obsidians. *Proceedings of the Prehistoric Society* 34:319–331.

Renfrew, C., and S. Shennan, eds.
1982 *Ranking, resource and exchange.* Cambridge: Cambridge University Press.

Rethemiotakis, G., and N. Dimopoulou
2003 The "Sacred Mansion" ring from Poros, Heraklion. *Mitteilungen des Deutschen Archäologischen Instituts, Athenische Abteilung* 118:1–22.

Reusch, H.
1958 Zum Wandschmuck des Thronsaales in Knossos. In *Minoica: Festschrift zum 80. Geburtstag von Johannes Sundwall*, edited by E. Grumach, 334–358. Schriften der Sektion für Altertumswissenschaften 12. Berlin: Akademie-Verlag.

Rice, P.
1984 Obsidian procurement in the Central Peten Lakes region, Guatemala. *Journal of Field Archaeology* 9:363–373.

1987a Economic change in the lowland Maya Late Classic period. In *Specialization, exchange, and complex societies*, edited by E. Brumfiel and T.K. Earle, 76–85. Cambridge: Cambridge University Press.

1987b *Pottery analysis: A sourcebook.* Chicago: University of Chicago Press.

1996 The archaeology of wine: The wine and brandy haciendas of Moquegua, Peru. *Journal of Field Archaeology* 23:188–204.

Ridley, C., and K.A. Wardle
1979 Rescue excavations at Servia 1971–1973: A preliminary report. *Annual of the British School at Athens* 74:185–230.

Rothaus, R., E. Reinhardt, T. Tartaron, and J. Noller
2003 A geoarchaeological approach for understanding prehistoric usage of the coastline of the eastern Korinthia. In *Metron: Measuring the Aegean Bronze Age*, edited by K. Foster and R. Laffineur, 37–47. Aegaeum 24. Liège: Université de Liège; Austin: University of Texas, Program in Aegean Scripts and Prehistory.

Rougemont, F.
2001 Some thoughts on the identification of the "collectors" in the Linear B tablets. In *Economy and politics in the Mycenaean palace states: Proceedings of a conference held on 1–3 July 1999 in the Faculty of Classics, Cambridge*, edited by S. Voutsaki and J. Killen, 129–138. Cambridge: The Cambridge Philological Society.

Ruijgh, C.J.
1966 Observations sur la tablette Ub1318 de Pylos. *Lingua* 16:130–152.

Runnels, C.
1981 *A diachronic study and economic analysis of millstones from the Argolid, Greece.* Ph.D. dissertation, Indiana University.

1982 Flaked-stone artifacts in Greece during the historical period. *Journal of Field Archaeology* 9(3):363–373.

1983 Trade and communication in prehistoric Greece. *Ekistics* 302:417–420.

1985a The Bronze Age flaked stone industries from Lerna: A preliminary report. *Hesperia* 54:357–391.

1985b Trade and demand for millstones in southern Greece in the Neolithic and the Early Bronze Age. In *Prehistoric production and exchange: The Aegean and eastern Mediterranean*, edited by A.B. Knapp and T. Stech, 30–43. UCLA Monographs in Archaeology. Los Angeles: University of California–Los Angeles.

1988   Early Bronze Age stone mortars from the southern Argolid. *Hesperia* 57:257–272.

Rutter, J.B.

1993   Review of Aegean prehistory II: The Prepalatial Bronze Age of the southern and central Greek mainland. *American Journal of Archaeology* 97:758–774.

1995   *Lerna, a Preclassical site in the Argolid III: The pottery of Lerna IV.* Princeton, NJ: American School of Classical Studies.

2001   Review of *Rethinking Mycenaean palaces. American Journal of Archaeology* 105:345.

2001 [1993]   Review of Aegean prehistory II: The prepalatial Bronze Age of the southern Greek mainland. In *Aegean prehistory: A review*, edited by T. Cullen, 95–147. *American Journal of Archaeology* suppl. 1. Boston: Archaeological Institute of America.

2003   Corinth and the Corinthia in the second millennium B.C.: Old approaches, new problems. In *Corinth: The centenary 1896–1996*, edited by C.K. Williams and N. Bookidis, 75–83. Corinth 20. Princeton, NJ: American School of Classical Studies at Athens.

2005   Southern triangles revisited: Lakonia, Messenia, and Crete in the 14th–12th centuries B.C. In *Ariadne's threads: Connections between Crete and the Greek mainland in Late Minoan III (LM IIIA2 to LM IIIC). Proceedings of the International Workshop held at Athens, Scuola Archeologica Italiana, 5–6 April 2003*, edited by A.L. D'Agata and J. Moody, 17–50. Scuola Archeologica Italiana di Atene, Tripodes 3. Athens: Scuola Archeologica Italiana di Atene.

Sackett, L.H., V. Hankey, R.J. Howell, T.W. Jacobsen and M.R. Popham

1966   Prehistoric Euboea: Contributions toward a survey. *Annual of the British School at Athens* 61:33–112.

Saflund, G.

1980   Sacrificial banquets in the "Palace of Nestor." *Opuscula Atheniensia* 13:237–246.

Salmon, J.B.

1984   *Wealthy Corinth: A history of the city to 338 BC.* Oxford: Clarendon Press.

Sanders, W.

1989   Household, lineage, and state at eighth-century Copan, Honduras. In *The House of the Bacabs, Copan, Honduras*, edited by D. Webster, 89–105. Studies in Precolumbian Art and Archaeology, no. 29. Washington, DC: Dumbarton Oaks.

Sandor, B.

2004   The rise and decline of the Tutankhamun-class chariot. *Oxford Journal of Archaeology* 23:153–175.

Sarris, A.

2001   Mycenaean Dimini, Magnesia: Phase III. *Archaeotelescopika Nea* 4:11–15.

Schallin, A.-M.

1997a   The Late Bronze Age potter's workshop at Mastos in the Berbati Valley. In *Trade and production in premonetary Greece: Production and the craftsman. Proceedings of the 4th and 5th International Workshops, Athens 1994 and 1995*, edited by C. Gillis, C. Risberg, and B. Sjöberg, 73–88. Jonsered, Sweden: Paul Åströms Forlag.

1997b   Metallurgy, a divine affair? In *Trade and production in premonetary Greece: Production and the craftsman, Proceedings of the 4th and 5th International Workshops, Athens 1994 and 1995*, edited by C. Gillis, C. Risberg and B. Sjöberg, 139–172. Jonsered, Sweden: Paul Åströms Forlag.

1998   The nature of Mycenaean presence and peer polity interaction in the Late Bronze Age Cyclades. *Kea-Kythnos: History and archaeology. Proceedings of an International Symposium Kea-Kythnos, 22–25 June 1994*, edited by L.G. Mendoni and A. Mazarakis Ainian, 175–187. Meletimata 27. Paris: Diffusion de Boccard; Athens: Research Centre for Greek and Roman Antiquity, National Hellenic Research Foundation.

Schoep, I.

2002   *The administration of Neopalatial Crete. Minos* 17, suppl. Salamanca: Ediciones Universidad de Salamanca.

Schoep, I., and C. Knappett

2004   Dual emergence: Evolving heterarchy, exploding hierarchy. In *The emergence of civilisation revisited*, edited by J.C. Barrett and P. Halstead, 21–37. Sheffield Studies in Aegean Archaeology 6. Oxford: Oxbow Books.

Schofield, L., and R. Parkinson

1994   Of helmets and heretics: A possible Egyptian representation of Mycenaean warriors on a papyrus from El-Amarna. *Annual of the British School at Athens* 89:157-170.

Schortman, E., and P. Urban

1994   Living on the edge: Core/periphery relations in ancient southeastern Mesoamerica. *Current Anthropology* 35:401–430.

Scott, J.C.

1998   *Seeing like a state: How certain schemes to improve the human condition have failed.* New Haven: Yale University Press.

Service, E.R.

1962   *Primitive social organization.* New York: Random House.

Sgouritsa, N.

2005   The Aegeans in the Central Mediterranean: The role of Western Greece. In *EMPORIA: Aegeans in the Central and Eastern Mediterranean. Proceedings of the 10th International Aegean Conference, Athens, Italian School of Archaeology, 14–18 April 2004*, edited by R. Laffineur and E. Greco, 515–526. Aegaeum 25. Liege: Université de Liège; Austin: University of Texas at Austin Program in Aegean Scripts and Prehistory.

Shafer, H.J.

1991   Late Preclassic formal stone tool production at Colha, Belize. In *Maya stone tools*, edited by T.R. Hester and H.J. Shafer, 31–44. Madison, WI: Prehistory Press.

Shannon, T.R.

1996   *An introduction to the world-system perspective.* 2nd ed. Boulder, CO: Westview Press.

Shaw, J.W.

1986   Excavations at Kommos (Crete) during 1984–85. *Hesperia* 55:219–269.

1990   Bronze Age Aegean harboursides. In *Thera and the Aegean world III.I archaeology*, edited by D.A. Hardy, C.G. Doumas, J.A. Sakellarakis, and P.M. Warren, 420–436. London: Thera Foundation.

1997   Personal communication to Susan Lupack, March 15.

Shear, I.

1987   *The Panagia houses at Mycenae.* University of Pennsylvania Museum Monograph 68. Philadelphia: University of Pennsylvania.

2004   *Kingship in the Mycenaean world and its reflections in the oral tradition.* Prehistory Monographs 13. Philadelphia: Institute for Aegean Prehistory Academic Press.

Shelford, P., F. Hodson, M.E. Cosgrove, S.E. Warren, and C. Renfrew

1982   The sources and characteristics of Melian obsidian. In *An island polity*, edited by C. Renfrew and M. Wagstaff, 182–192. Cambridge: Cambridge University Press.

Shelmerdine, C.W.

1973   The Pylos Ma tablets reconsidered. *American Journal of Archaeology* 85:319–325.

1981   Nichoria in context: A major town in the Pylos kingdom. *American Journal of Archaeology* 85:319–325.

1984   The perfumed oil industry at Pylos. In *Pylos comes alive. Industry and administration in a Mycenaean palace*, edited by C.W. Shelmerdine and T.G. Palaima, 81-96. New York: Archaeological Institute of America.

1985   *The perfume industry of Mycenaean Pylos.* Studies in Mediterranean Archaeology and Literature, Pocket Book 34. Göteborg: Paul Åströms Förlag.

1987   Architectural change and economic decline at Pylos. In *Studies in Mycenaean and Classical Greek presented to J. Chadwick*, edited by J.T. Killen, J.L. Melena, and J.-P. Olivier, 557–568. *Minos* 20–22. Salamanca: Ediciones Universidad de Salamanca/Servicio Editorial–Universidad del País Vasco

1992   Historical and economic considerations in interpreting Mycenaean texts. In *Mykenaïka: Actes du IXe colloque international sur les textes mycéniens et égéens organisé par le Center de l'Antiquité Grecque et Romaine de la Fondation Hellénique de Recherches scientifiques et l'Ecole Française d'Athènes*, edited by. J-P. Olivier, 569–589. *Bulletin de Correspondance Hellénique*, suppl. vol. 25. Paris: Diffusion de Boccard.

1997   Review of Aegean prehistory VI. The palatial Bronze Age of the southern and central Greek mainland. *American Journal of Archaeology* 101:537–585.

1999a   Administration in the Mycenaean palaces: Where's the chief? In *Rethinking Mycenaean palaces: New interpretations of an old idea*, edited by M.L. Galaty and W.A. Parkinson, 19–24. Los Angeles: Cotsen Institute of Archaeology, University of California–Los Angeles.

1999b   A comparative look at Mycenaean administration(s). In *Floreant Studia Mycenaeae: Akten des X Internationalen Mykenologischen Colloquiums in Saltzburg vom 1.–5. Mai 1995*, edited by S. Deger-Jalkotzy, S. Hiller, and O. Panagl, 555–576. Vienna: Verlag der Österreichischen Akademie der Wissenschaften.

2001   The evolution of administration at Pylos. In *Economy and politics in the Mycenaean palace states: Proceedings of a conference held on 1–3 July 1999 in the Faculty of Classics, Cambridge*, edited by S. Voutsaki and J. Killen, 113–128. Cambridge: The Cambridge Philological Society.

Shelmerdine, C.W., and T.G. Palaima, eds.

1984   *Pylos comes alive: Industry and administration in a Mycenaean palace.* New York: Archaeological Institute of America.

Sherratt, A.

1993   What would a Bronze-Age world system look like? Relations between temperate Europe and the Mediterranean in later prehistory. *Journal of European Archaeology* 1(2):1–57.

1997   Cups that cheered: The introduction of alcohol to prehistoric Europe. Reprinted in *Economy and society in prehistoric Europe: Changing perspectives*, by A. Sherratt, 376–402. Princeton, NJ: Princeton University Press.

Sherratt, A., and S. Sherratt

1991 From luxuries to commodities: The nature of Mediterranean Bronze Age trading systems. In *Bronze Age trade in the Mediterranean*, edited by N.H. Gale, 351–386. Studies in Mediterranean Archaeology 90. Jonsered, Sweden: Paul Åströms Forlag.

Sherratt, E.S., and J.H. Crouwel

1987 Mycenaean pottery from Cilicia in Oxford. *Oxford Journal of Archaeology* 6:325–352.

Sherratt, S.

1999 E pur si muove: Pots, markets and values in the second millennium Mediterranean. In *The complex past of pottery: Production, circulation and consumption of Mycenaean and Greek pottery (sixteenth to early fifth centuries BC). Proceedings of the ARCHON international conference, held in Amsterdam, 8–9 November 1996*, edited by J.P. Crielaard, V. Stissi, and G. van Wijngaarden, 163–211. Amsterdam: J. Geiben.

2001 Potemkin palaces and route-based economies. In *Economy and politics in the Mycenaean palace states: Proceedings of a conference held on 1–3 July 1999 in the Faculty of Classics, Cambridge*, edited by S. Voutsaki and J. Killen, 214–238. Cambridge: The Cambridge Philological Society.

Siedentopf, H.

1991 *Alt-Ägina IV.2: Mattbemalte Keramik der mittleren Bronzezeit*. Mainz: von Zabern.

Siennicka, M.

2002 Mycenaean settlement patterns in the Saronic Gulf. *Swiatowit* 4(45):179–193.

Singer, I.

1991 A concise history of Amurru. In *Amurru Akkadian. Vol. II. A linguistic study*, edited by S. Izre'el, 135–195. Atlanta, GA: Scholars Press.

2006 Ships bound for Lukka: A new interpretation of the companion letters RS 94.2530 and RS 94.2523. *Altorientalische Forschungen* 33/2:242–262.

Sinopoli, C.

1991 *Approaches to archaeological ceramics*. New York: Plenum.

Sipes, R.G.

1973 War, sports and aggression: An empirical test of two rival theories. *American Anthropologist* 75(1):64–86.

Sjöberg, B.L.

2004 *Asine and the Argolid in the Late Helladic III period*. British Archaeological Reports S1225. Oxford: Archaeopress.

Small, D.

1998 Surviving the collapse: The oikos and structural continuity in Late Bronze Age Greece. In *Mediterranean peoples in transition: Thirteenth to early tenth centuries BCE*, edited by S.Gitin, A. Mazar, and E. Stern, 283–292. Jerusalem: Israel Exploration Society.

1999 Mycenaean polities: States or *estates*? In *Rethinking Mycenaean palaces: New interpretations of an old idea*, edited by M.L. Galaty and W.A. Parkinson, 43–48. Los Angeles: Cotsen Institute of Archaeology, University of California–Los Angeles.

Smith, J.

1992-1993 The Pylos Jn series. *Minos* 27–28: 167–259.

Smith, R.A.K.,

2002 *The tombs of Mochlos and Myrsini: Pottery and cultural regionalism in Late Minoan III Crete*. Ph.D. dissertation, Bryn Mawr College. Ann Arbor: University Microfilms.

2004 Late Minoan III Mochlos and the regional consumption of pottery. In *Crete beyond the palaces: Proceedings of the 2000 conference*, edited by L. Preston Day, M.S. Mook, and J.D. Muhly, 309-317. Philadelphia: INSTAP/Academic Press.

2005 Minoans, Mycenaeans and Mochlos: The formation of regional identity in Late Minoan III Crete. In *Ariadne's threads: Connections between Crete and the Greek Mainland in Late Minoan III (LM IIIA2 to LM IIIC). Proceedings of the International Workshop held at Athens, Scuola Archeologica Italiana, 5–6 April 2003*, edited by A.L. D'Agata and J. Moody, 185–199. Scuola Archeologica Italiana di Atene, Tripodes 3. Athens: Scuola Archeologica Italiana di Atene.

Snodgrass, A.M.

1964 *Early Greek armour and weapons: From the end of the Bronze Age to 600 B.C*. Edinburgh: Edinburgh University Press.

1985 The new archaeology and the classical archaeologist. *American Journal of Archaeology* 89:31–37.

1987 *An archaeology of Greece. The present state and future scope of a discipline*. Berkeley and Los Angeles: University of California Press.

Soles, J.S.,

1995 The functions of a cosmological center: Knossos in Palatial Crete. In *POLITEIA: Society and state in the Aegean Bronze Age. Proceedings of the 5th International Aegean Conference, University of Heidelberg, Archäologisches Institut, 10–13 April 1994*, edited by R. Laffineur and W.D. Niemeier, 405–414. Aegaeum 12. Liège: Université de Liège; Austin: University of Texas, Program in Aegean Scripts and Prehistory.

1999a The collapse of Minoan civilization: The evidence of the broken ashlar. In *POLEMOS: Le contexte guerrier en Egée à l'Âge du Bronze, Actes de la 7e Rencontre égéenne internationale, Université de Liège, 15–17 avril 1998*, edited by R. Laffineur, 57–65. Aegaeum 19.

Liège: Université de Liège; Austin: University of Texas, Program in Aegean Scripts and Prehistory.

1999b The ritual "killing" of pottery and the discovery of a Mycenaean telestas at Mochlos. In *MELETEMATA: Studies in Aegean Archaeology presented to M.H. Wiener as he enters his 65th year*, edited by P.P. Betancourt, V. Karageorghis, R. Laffineur, and W.-D. Niemeier, 787–793. Aegaeum 20. Liège: Université de Liège; Austin: University of Texas, Program in Aegean Scripts and Prehistory.

Spencer, N., ed.

1995 *Time, tradition and society in Greek archaeology: Bridging the "Great Divide."* London and New York: Routledge.

Spielmann, K.A.

1998 Ritual craft specialists in middle range societies. In *Craft and social identity*, edited by C.L. Costin and R.P. Wright, 153–159. Archeological papers of the American Anthropological Association number 8. Arlington, VA: American Anthropological Association.

Spyropoulos, T., and J. Chadwick

1975 *The Thebes tablets II. Minos*, suppl. vol. 4. Salamanca: University of Salamanca.

Stählin, D.

1906 Das Phthiotische Theben. *Athenische Mitteilungen* 31:5–9.

Stais V.

1966 [1901] Ai en Dimini Thessalias anaskafai. *Praktika tes Archaeologikes Etaireias* 79:37–40.

Stampolidis, N.C., and V. Karageorghis, eds.

2003 *Sea Routes . . . : Interconnections in the Mediterranean 16th–6th Century BC*. University of Crete/A. G. Leventis Foundation.

Stark, B.

1985 Archaeological identification of pottery production locations: Ethnoarchaeological and archaeological data in Mesoamerica. In *Decoding prehistoric ceramics*, edited by B. Nelson, 158–194. Carbondale: Southern Illinois University Press.

Steel, L.

1998 The social impact of Mycenaean imported pottery in Cyprus. *Annual of the British School at Athens* 93:285–296.

Steffen, B.

1884 *Karten von Mykenai*. Berlin: Dierich Reimer.

Stein, G.

1994a Introduction, part II. The organizational dynamics of complexity in greater Mesopotamia. In *Chiefdoms and early states in the Near East: The organizational dynamics of complexity*, edited by M. Rothman and G. Stein, 11–22. Madison, WI: Prehistory Press.

1994b Segmentary states and organizational variation in early complex societies: A rural perspective. In *Archaeological views from the countryside: Village communities in early complex societies*, edited by G. Schwartz and S. Falconer, 10–18. Washington, DC: Smithsonian Institution Press.

1998 Heterogeneity, power, and political economy: Some current research issues in the archaeology of Old World complex societies. *Journal of Archaeological Research* 6(1):1–44.

1999 *Rethinking world-systems: Diasporas, colonies, and interaction in Uruk Mesopotamia*. Tucson: University of Arizona Press.

Stein, G., and M. Blackman

1993 The organizational context of specialized craft production in early Mesopotamian states. *Research in Economic Anthropology* 14:29–59.

Stein, G., and M. Rothman, eds.

1994 *Chiefdoms and early states in the Near East: The organizational dynamics of complexity*. Madison, WI: Prehistory Press.

Steiner, G.

1989 "Schiffe von Ahhiyawa" oder "Kriegsschifte" von Amurru im Šauškamuwa-Vertrag? *Ugarit-Forschungen* 21:393–411.

Stoltman, J.

1989 A quantitative approach to the petrographic analysis of ceramic thin sections. *American Antiquity* 54(1):147–160.

1991 Ceramic petrography as a technique for documenting cultural interaction: An example from the Upper Mississippi Valley. *American Antiquity* 56(1):103–120.

Stos-Gale, Z.A., G. Maliotis, N.H. Gale, and N. Annetts

1997 Lead isotope characteristics of the Cyprus copper ore deposits applied to provenance studies of copper oxhide ingots. *Archaeometry* 39(1):83–123.

Sullivan, A.P., ed.

1998 *Surface archaeology*. Albuquerque: University of New Mexico Press.

Swiny, S., R.L. Hohlfelder, and H.W. Swiny, eds.

1997 *Res Maritimae: Cyprus and the eastern Mediterranean from prehistory to Late Antiquity*. ASOR Archaeological Reports 4. Atlanta, GA: Scholars Press.

Tainter, J.

1988 *The collapse of complex societies*. Cambridge: Cambridge University Press.

Talbott, P.

1984 Prospecting for clay. *Journal of the American Ceramic Society* 63(8):1047–1050.

Tartaron, T.F.

2001   Glykys Limin: A Mycenaean port of trade in Southern Epirus? In *Prehistory and history: Ethnicity, class and political economy*, edited by D.W. Tandy. Montreal: Black Rose Books.

2004   *Bronze Age landscape and society in Southern Epirus, Greece.* British Archaeological Reports S1290. Oxford: Archaeopress.

2005   Glykys Limin and the discontinuous Mycenaean periphery. In *EMPORIA: Aegeans in the Central and Eastern Mediterranean. Proceedings of the 10th International Aegean Conference, Athens, Italian School of Archaeology, 14–18 April 2004*, edited by R. Laffineur and E. Greco, 153–162. Aegaeum 25. Liege: Université de Liège; Austin: University of Texas at Austin Program in Aegean Scripts and Prehistory.

Tartaron, T.F., T. Gregory, D.J. Pullen, J.S. Noller, R.M. Rothaus, J. Rife, L. Tzortzopoulou-Gregory, R. Schon, W. Caraher, D. Pettegrew, and D. Nakassis

2006   The Eastern Korinthia Archaeological Survey: Integrated methods for a dynamic landscape. *Hesperia* 75: 453-523.

Tartaron, T.F., D.J. Pullen, and J.S. Noller

2006   *Rillenkarren* at Vayia: Geomorphology and a new class of Early Bronze Age fortified settlement in southern Greece. *Antiquity* 80:145–160

Tartaron, T.F., R.M. Rothaus, and D.J. Pullen

2003   Searching for prehistoric Aegean harbors with GIS, geomorphology, and archaeology. *Athena Review* 3(4):27–36.

Tartaron, T.F., and K.L. Zachos

1999   The Mycenaeans and Epirus. *I perifereia tou Mykinaikou kosmou. A' Diethnes Diepistimoniko Symposio, Lamia, 25–29 Septemvriou 1994*, edited by E. Froussou, 57–76. Lamia: Ekdosi ID' Eforeias Proistorikon kai Klassikon Archaiotiton.

Taylour, W.

1969   Mycenae, 1968. *Antiquity* 43:91–97.

1970   New light on Mycenaean religion. *Antiquity* 44:270–280.

Taylour, W., E.B. French, and K.A. Wardle, eds.

1981   Well Built Mycenae: The Helleno-British Excavations within the Citadel of Mycenae 1959–1969. Aris and Phillips.

Tegyey, I.

1984   The northeast workshop at Pylos. In *Pylos comes alive: Industry and administration in a Mycenaean palace*, edited by C.W. Shelmerdine and T.G. Palaima, 65–79. New York: Archaeological Institute of America.

Theochari, M.

1959   Ek tes Proïstorikes Trikkes. *Thessalika* 2:69–79.

Theocharis, D. R.

1956   Anaskaphai en Iolko. *Praktika tes Archaeologikes Etaireias* 69:119–130.

1957   Anaskaphai en Iolko. *Praktika tes Archaeologikes Etaireias* 1956:54–69.

1959   Pyrassos. *Thessalika* 2:29–68.

1960a   Anaskaphai en Iolko. *Praktika tes Archaeologikes Etaireias* 1960:49–59.

1960b   Tholotos taphos Georgikou. *Archaeologikon Deltion* 16:171.

1960c   Topographikai ereunai. *Archaeologikon Deltion* 16:186.

1961   Anaskaphai Iolkou. *Praktika tes Archaeologikes Etaireias* 72:45–54.

1963   Philia Karditsis. *Archaelogikon Deltion* 18:138.

1964a   Anaskaphai Mykenaikôn thalamoeidôn tafon para to Mega Monasterion Larissis. *Archaelogikon Deltion* 19:255–258.

1964b   Pharsalos. *Archaelogikon Deltion* 19:260.

1965   Hieron Athenas Itônias. *Archaelogikon Deltion* 20:311–313.

1966a   Agios Antonios Pharsalon. *Archaelogikon Deltion* 21: 253.

1966b   Anaskaphai en Trikke. *Archaelogikon Deltion* 21:247.

1968   O tymbos tou Exalophou kai he esbole tôn Thessalôn. *Archaeologika Analecta ex Athenôn* 1:289–295.

1981   *Neolithikos politismos.* Athinai: Morfotiko Idrima Ethnikis Trapezis.

Theocharis D.R., and G. Ch. Chourmouziadis

1968   Pteleos. *Archaeologikon Deltion* 23:269.

Thomas, C.G.

1976   The nature of Mycenaean kingship. *Studi Micenei ed Egeo-Anatolici* 17: 93–116.

Thomas, N.R.

1999   The war animal: Three days in the life of a Mycenaean lion. In *POLEMOS: Le contexte guerrier en égée à l'âge du bronze. Actes de la 7e Rencontre Égéenne Internationale*, edited by R. Laffineur, 297–306. Aegaeum 19. Liège: Université de Liège; Austin: University of Texas at Austin Program in Aegean Scripts and Prehistory.

Tomas, H.

2005   Mycenaeans in Croatia? In *EMPORIA: Aegeans in the Central and Eastern Mediterranean. Proceedings of the 10th International Aegean Conference, Athens, Italian School of Archaeology, 14–18 April 2004*, edited by R. Laffineur and E. Greco, 673–684. Aegaeum 25. Liege: Université de Liège; Austin: University of Texas at Austin Program in Aegean Scripts and Prehistory.

Torrence, R.

1979   A technological approach to Cycladic blade industries. In *Papers in Cycladic prehistory*, edited by J.L. Davis and J.F. Cherry, 66–86. UCLA Monographs in Archaeology 24. Los Angeles.

1982   The obsidian quarries and their use. In *An island polity*, edited by C. Renfrew and M. Wagstaff, 193–221. Cambridge: Cambridge University Press.

1984   Monopoly or direct access? Industrial organization at the Melos obsidian quarries. In *Prehistoric quarries and lithic production*, edited by J. Ericson and B Purdy. Cambridge: Cambridge University Press.

1985   Appendix C: The chipped stone. In *The archaeology of cult: The sanctuary at Phylakopi*, by C. Renfrew, 469–478. London: Thames and Hudson.

1986   *Production and exchange of stone tools: Prehistoric obsidian in the Aegean*. New Studies in Archaeology. Cambridge: Cambridge University Press.

1991   The chipped stone. In *Landscape archaeology as long-term history: Northern Keos in the Cycladic Islands*, edited by J.F. Cherry, J.L. Davis, and E. Mantzourani, 173–198. Los Angeles: UCLA Institute of Archaeology.

Tournavitou, I.

1988   Towards an identification of a workshop space. In *Problems in Greek prehistory. Proceedings of the British School at Athens Centenary Conference, Manchester, 14–18 April 1986*, edited by E.B. French and K. Wardle, 447–467. Bristol: Bristol Classical Press.

1992a   Practical use and social function: A neglected aspect of Mycenaean pottery. *Annual of the British School at Athens* 87:181–210.

1992b   The ivories from the House of Sphinxes and the House of the Shields: Techniques in a palatial workshop context. In *Ivory in Greece and the eastern Mediterranean from the Bronze Age to the Hellenistic Period*, edited by J.L. Fitton, 37–44. British Museum Occasional Paper 85. London: British Museum.

1999   Hearths in non-palatial settlement contexts. In *MELETEMATA. Studies in Aegean archeology presented to M.C. Wiener as he enters his 65th Year (Aegaeum 20)*, edited by P. Betancourt, V. Karageorgis, R. LAfinneur, and W. Niemeier, 833–840. Liege: Université de Liège, Histoire de l'art et archéologie de la Grèce antique.

Triadan, D., H. Neff, and M. Glascock

1997   An evaluation of the archaeological relevance of weak-acid extraction ICP: White mountain red-ware as a case study. *Journal of Archaeological Science* 24:997–1002.

Trigger, B.G.

1989   *A history of archaeological thought*. Cambridge: Cambridge University Press.

Tsipopoulou, M.

1995   Late Minoan III Sitia. Patterns of settlement and land use. In *Achladia. Scavi e ricerche della Missione Greco-Italiana in Creta Orientale (1991–1993)*, edited by M. Tsipopoulou and L. Vagnetti, 177–192. Incunabula Graeca 97. Rome: Gruppo Editoriale Internazionale.

1997   Late Minoan III reoccupation in the area of the palatial building at Petras, Siteia. In *Late Minoan III Pottery. Chronology and terminology. Acts of a meeting held at the Danish Institute at Athens, August 12–14, 1994*, edited by E. Hallager and B.P. Hallager, 209–257. Monographs of the Danish Institute at Athens 1. Athens: Åarhus University Press.

2005   "Mycenoans" at the Isthmus of Ierapetra: Some (preliminary) thoughts on the foundation of the (Eteo)cretan cultural identity. In *Ariadne's threads: Connections between Crete and the Greek Mainland in Late Minoan III (LM IIIA2 to LM IIIC). Proceedings of the International Workshop held at Athens, Scuola Archeologica Italiana, 5–6 April 2003*, edited by A.L. D'Agata and J. Moody, 303–330. Scuola Archeologica Italiana di Atene, Tripodes 3. Athens: Scuola Archeologica Italiana di Atene.

Tsountas, C.

1901   *Praktika tes Archaeologikes Etaireias* 23:42.

1968 [1908]   *Ai Proistorikai Akropoleis Diminiou kai Sesklou*, edited by the Ellenike Arxaeologike Etaireia. Athens: Sakellariou.

Tzedakis, Y., and H. Martlew

1999   *Minoans and Mycenaeans: Flavours of their time*. Greek Ministry of Culture/National Archaeological Museum/Kapon.

Vagnetti, L.

1998   Variety and function of the Aegean derivative pottery in the central Mediterranean in the Late Bronze Age. In *Mediterranean peoples in transition: Thirteenth to early tenth centuries BCE. In honor of Professor Trude Dothan*, edited by S. Gitin, A. Mazar, and E. Stern, 66–77. Jerusalem: Israel Exploration Society.

1999a   Mycenaeans and Cypriots in the Central Mediterranean before and after 1200 B.C. In *The Point Iria Wreck: Interconnections in the Mediterranean ca. 1200 B.C. Proceedings of the International Conference, Island of Spetses, 19 September 1998*, edited by W. Phelps, Y. Lolos, and Y. Vichos, 187–208. Athens: Hellenic Institute of Marine Archaeology.

1999b   Mycenaean pottery in the central Mediterranean: Imports and local production in their context. In *The complex past of pottery: Production, circulation and consumption of Mycenaean and Greek pottery (sixteenth to early fifth centuries BC). Proceedings of the ARCHON International Conference, held in Amsterdam, 8–9 November 1996*, edited by J.P. Crielaard, V. Stissi, and G. van Wijngaarden, 137161. Amsterdam: J. Geiben.

2000–2001   Preliminary remarks on Mycenaean pictorial pottery from the central Mediterranean. *Opuscula atheniensia* 25-26:107–115.

Vagnetti, L., and F. Lo Schiavo

1989   Late Bronze Age long distance trade in the Mediterranean: The role of the Cypriots. In *Early society in Cyprus*, edited by E.J. Peltenburg, 217–243. Edinburgh: Edinburgh University Press.

van Andel, T., and C.N. Runnels

1987   *Beyond the acropolis: A rural Greek past*. Stanford: Stanford University Press.

van Dyke, R.M., and S. Alcock, eds.

2003   *Archaeologies of memory*. Oxford: Blackwell Publishers.

van Effenterre, H., and M. van Effenterre

1969   L'Atelier des tailleurs d'obsidienne. In *Fouilles executees a Mallia: Le Centre politique, l'Agora (1960–1966)*, edited by H. van Effenterre and M. van Effenterre, 17–21. Études Cretoises 17. Paris: Geuther.

van Horn, D.M.

1976   *Bronze Age chipped stone tools from the Argolid of Greece and their relation to tools manufactured from other materials*. Ph.D. dissertation, University of Pennsylvania.

1980   Observations relating to Bronze Age blade core production in the Argolid of Greece. *Journal of Field Archaeology* 7: 487–492.

Vanschoonwinkel, J.

2002   Earthquakes and the end of the Mycenaean palaces. *Les Études Classiques* 70(1–2):123–137.

van Wees, H.

1992   *Status warriors: War, violence and society in Homer and history*. Amsterdam: J.C. Gieben.

1994   The Homeric way of war: The *Iliad* and the hoplite phalanx (I) and (II). *Greece & Rome*, 2nd ser., 41(1):1–18 and 131–155.

van Wijngaarden, G.J.

1999a   Production, circulation and consumption of Mycenaean pottery (sixteenth to twelfth centuries BC). *The complex past of pottery: Production, circulation and consumption of Mycenaean and Greek pottery (sixteenth to early fifth centuries BC). Proceedings of the ARCHON International Conference, held in Amsterdam, 8-9 November 1996*, edited by J.P. Crielaard, V. Stissi, and G. van Wijngaarden, 21–47. Amsterdam: J. Geiben.

1999b   An archaeological approach to the concept of value: Mycenaean pottery at Ugarit (Syria). *Archaeological Dialogues* 6:2–23.

2001   The cultural significance of Mycenaean pictorial kraters. *Pharos* 9:75–95.

2002   *The use and appreciation of Mycenaean pottery in the Levant, Cyprus and Italy (ca. 1600–1200 BC)*. Amsterdam: Amsterdam University Press.

Varias, C.

1998-1999   The personal names from the Knossos B-tablets and from the Mycenae tablets. In *A-NA-QO-TA: Studies presented to J.T. Killen*, edited by J. Bennet and J. Driessen, 349–370. *Minos* 33–34. Salamanca: Ediciones Universidad de Salamanca.

Ventris, M., and J. Chadwick

1953   1st edition.

1973   *Documents in Mycenaean Greek*. 2nd ed. Cambridge: Cambridge University Press.

Verdelis, N. M.

1952   Anaskaphikai Ereunai en Thessalia. *Praktika tes Archaeologikes Etaireias* 75:164–185.

1953   Anaskaphikai Ereunai en Thessalia. *Praktika tes Archaeologikes Etaireias* 76:120132.

1954   Anaskaphe Pharsalou. *Praktika tes Archaeologikes Etaireias* 77:140–146.

1955   Pharsala. *Bulletin de Correspondence Hellenique* 78:134–135.

Vichos, Y., and Y. Lolos

1997   The Cypro-Mycenaean wreck at Point Iria in the Argolic Gulf: First thoughts on the origin and nature of the vessel. In *Res Maritimae: Cyprus and the Eastern Mediterranean from Prehistory to Late Antiquity. Proceedings of the Second International Symposium Cities on the Sea, Nicosia, Cyprus, October 18–22, 1994*, edited by S. Swiny, R.L. Hohlfelder, and H. Wylde Swiny, 321–337. Cyprus American Archaeological Research Institute Monograph Series 1. Atlanta, GA: Scholars Press.

Vickery, K.D.

1983   The flint sources. In *Recent excavations at the Edwin Harness Mound, Liberty Works, Ross County, Ohio*, edited by N. Greber, 73–85. *Midcontinental Journal of Archaeology* Special Paper 5. Kent, OH: Kent State University Press.

Vitelli, K.D.

1984   Greek Neolithic pottery by experiment. In *Pots and potters: Current approaches in ceramic archaeology*, edited by P. Rice, 113–131. Los Angeles: UCLA Institute of Archaeology Monographs.

1993   Power to the potters: Comment on Perlès' "Systems of exchange and organization of production in

Neolithic Greece." *Journal of Mediterranean Archaeology* 6:247–257.

Voutsaki, S.

1995a Social and political processes in the Mycenaean Argolid: The evidence from the mortuary practices. In *POLITEIA: Society and state in the Aegean Bronze Age*, edited by W.-D. Niemeier and R. Laffineur, 55–66. Aegaeum 13. Liège: Université de Liège; Austin: University of Texas at Austin Program in Aegean Scripts and Prehistory.

1995b Value and exchange in premonetary societies: Anthropological debates and Aegean archaeology. In *Trade and production in premonetary Greece: Aspects of trade. Proceedings of the Third International Workshop, Athens, 1993*, edited by C. Gillis, C. Risberg, and B.L. Sjöberg, 7–18. Uppsala: Paul Åströms Förlag.

1998 Mortuary evidence, symbolic meanings and social change: A comparison between Messenia and the Argolid in the Mycenaean period. In *Cemetery and society in the Aegean Bronze Age*, edited by K. Branigan, K., 41–58. Sheffield Studies in Aegean Archaeology 1. Sheffield: Sheffield Academic Press.

2001 Economic control, power and prestige in the Mycenaean world: The archaeological evidence. In *Economy and politics in the Mycenaean palace states. Proceedings of a conference held on 1–3 July 1999 in the Faculty of Classics, Cambridge*, edited by S. Voutsaki and J. Killen, 195–213. Cambridge: The Cambridge Philological Society.

Voutsaki, S., and J. Killen

2001 Introduction. In *Economy and politics in the Mycenaean palace states: Proceedings of a conference held on 1–3 July 1999 in the Faculty of Classics, Cambridge*, edited by S. Voutsaki and J. Killen, 1–14. Cambridge: The Cambridge Philological Society.

Voutsaki, S., and J. Killen, eds.

2001 *Economy and politics in the Mycenaean palace states: Proceedings of a conference held on 1–3 July 1999 in the Faculty of Classics, Cambridge*. Cambridge: The Cambridge Philological Society.

Wace, A.J.B.

1949 *Mycenae, an archaeological history and guide*. Princeton, NJ: Princeton University Press.

Wace, A.J.B., and M.S. Thompson

1912 *Prehistoric Thessaly*. Cambridge: Cambridge University Press.

Waetzoldt, H.

1972 *Untersuchungen zur neusumerischen Textilindustrie*. Rome: Centro per le Antichite la Storia dell'Arte e dell'archeologia classica.

Walberg, G.

1998 *Excavations on the akropolis of Midea: Results of the Greek-Swedish excavations, Vol. I. 1–2, the excavation of the lower terraces 1985–1991*. Stockholm: Paul Åströms Förlag.

Walcot, P.

1967 The divinity of the Mycenaean king. *Studi Micenei ed Egeo-Anatolici* 2:53–62.

Walløe, L.

1999 Was the disruption of the Mycenaean world caused by repeated epidemics of bubonic plague? *Opuscula atheniensia* 24:121–126.

Wallerstein, I.

1974 *The modern world-system. I. Capitalist agriculture and the origins of the European world-economy in the sixteenth century*. New York: Academic Press.

Walz, C.A.

1997 Black Athena and the role of Cyprus in Near Eastern/Mycenaean contact. In *Greeks and barbarians: Essays on the interactions between Greeks and non-Greeks in antiquity and the consequences for eurocentrism*, edited by J.E. Coleman and C.A. Walz, 499–502. Bethesda, MD: CDL Press.

Warren, P.

1965 Two palatial stone vases from Crete. *Annual of the British School at Athens* 60:154–156.

1967 A stone vase maker's workshop in the palace at Knossos. *Annual of the British School at Athens* 62:195–201.

1969 *Minoan stone vases*. Cambridge: Cambridge University Press.

1972a *Myrtos: An Early Bronze Age settlement on Crete*. London: Thames and Hudson.

1972b Knossos and the Greek mainland in the third millennium BC. *Athens Annals of Archaeology* 3:392–398.

1975 *The Aegean civilizations*. London: Elsevier Phaidon.

1979 The stone vessels from the Bronze Age settlement at Akrotiri, Thera. *Archaiologike Ephemeris* 1979: 82–113.

1986 *Minoan religion as ritual action*. Goteburg: Gothenburg University.

1991 The destruction of the palace of Knossos. In *Proceedings of an International Symposium "The Civilizations of the Aegean and their Diffusion in Cyprus and the Eastern Mediterranean, 2000-600 B.C.,"* 18–24 September 1989, edited by V. Karageorghis, 33–37. Larnaca: Pierides Foundation.

1995 *Minoan Crete and Pharaonic Egypt*. In *Egypt, the Aegean and the Levant: Interconnections in the Second Millenium BC*, edited by W.V. Davies and L. Schofield, 1–18. London: British Museum Press.

Warren, P., and J. Tzedhakis
1974   Debla, an early Minoan settlement in western Crete. *Annual of the British School at Athens* 69:299–342.

Watson, A.
1983   Chipped-stone artifacts from Servia in Greek Macedonia. *Journal of Field Archaeology* 10: 120–123.

Watson, V.D.
1986   *Obsidian as tool and trade: A Papua New Guinea case.* Burke Museum Contributions in Anthropology and Natural History no. 4. Seattle: University of Washington, Burke Museum.

Weber, M.
1978   *Economy and society: An outline of interpretive sociology*, edited by G. Roth and C. Wittich. [Translation of Weber, M. (1956): *Wirtschaft und Gesellschaft: Grundriss der verstehenden Soziologie*.] Berkeley and Los Angeles: University of California Press.

Wedde, M.
2000   *Towards a hermeneutics of Aegean Bronze Age ship imagery* Peleus: Studien zur Archäologie und Geschichte Griechenlands und Zyperns 6. Mannheim and Möhnesee: Bibliopolis.

Weinberg, S.
1965   Ceramics and the supernatural: Cult and burial evidence in the Aegean world. In *Ceramics and man*, edited by F. Matson, 187–201. Chicago: Aldine.

Whitbread, I.
1995   *Greek transport amphorae: A petrological and archaeological study*. British School at Athens, Fitch Laboratory Occasional Paper 4.

Whitelaw, T.W.
2001   Reading between the tablets: Assessing Mycenaean palatial involvement in ceramic production and consumption. In *Economy and politics in the Mycenaean palace states: Proceedings of a conference held on 1–3 July 1999 in the Faculty of Classics, Cambridge*, edited by S. Voutsaki and J. Killen, 51–79. Cambridge: The Cambridge Philological Society.

Whitelaw, T.W., P.M. Day, E. Kiriatzi, V. Kilikoglou, and D.E. Wilson
1997   Ceramic traditions at EMIIB Myrtos Fournou Korifi. In *TEXNH: Craftsmen, craftswomen and craftsmanship in the Aegean Bronze Age*, edited by R. Laffineur and P. Betancourt, 265–274. Aegaeum 16. Liège: Université de Liège; Austin: University of Texas at Austin Program in Aegean Scripts and Prehistory.

Whitley, J.
2004   Cycles of collapse in Greek prehistory: The House of Tiles at Lerna and the "Heroon" at Lefkandi. In *Explaining social change: Studies in honour of Colin Renfrew*, edited by J. F. Cherry, C. Scarre, and S.

Shennan, 193–202. Cambridge: McDonald Institute for Archaeological Research.

Whittaker, H.
2005a   Response to Metaxia Tsipopoulou, "Mycenoans at the Isthmus of Ierapetra: Some preliminary thoughts on the foundation of the (Eteo)cretan cultural identity." In *Ariadne's Threads: Connections between Crete and the Greek Mainland in Late Minoan III (LM IIIA2 to LM IIIC). Proceedings of the International Workshop held at Athens, Scuola Archeologica Italiana, 5–6 April 2003*, edited by A.L. D'Agata and J. Moody, 335–343. Scuola Archeologica Italiana di Atene, Tripodes 3. Athens: Scuola Archeologica Italiana di Atene.

2005b   Social and symbolic aspects of Minoan writing. *European Journal of Archaeology* 8(1):29–41.

Wiener, M.H.
1984   Crete and the Cyclades in LM I: The tale of the conical cups. In *The Minoan thalassocracy: Myth and reality*, edited by R. Hägg and N.Marinatos, 17–26. Skrifter Utgivna Av Svenska Institutet I Athen, 4, XXXII, Stockholm.

1990   The isles of Crete? The Minoan thalassocracy revisited. In *Thera and the Aegean world III*, vol. 1, edited by D. Hardy, C. Doumas, J. Sakellarakis, and P. Warren, 128–161. London: The Thera Foundation.

Wilson, A.L.
1977   The place-names in the Linear B tablets from Knossos: Some preliminary considerations. *Minos* 16:67–125.

Winter, M.
1989   From the Classic to the post-Classic in pre-Hispanic Oaxaca. In *Mesoamerica after the decline of Teotihuacan A.D. 700–900*, edited by R. Diehl and J. Berlo, 123–130. Washington: Dumbarton Oaks.

Wiseman, J.
1998   Reforming academia. *Archaeology* 51(5):27–30.

Wobst, H.M.
1977   Stylistic behavior and information exchange. In *For the director: Research essays in honor of James B. Griffin*, edited by C. Cleland, 317–342. University of Michigan Museum of Anthropology Anthropological Paper 61.

Wolpert, A. D.
2004   Getting past consumption and competition: Legitimacy and consensus in the Shaft Graves. In *Emergence of civilisation revisited*, edited by J. Barrett and P. Halstead, 127–144. Sheffield Studies in Aegean Archaeology 6. Oxford: Oxbow Books.

Wolters, P.
1889   Mykenische Vasen aus dem Nördlichen Griechenland. *Athenische Mitteilungen* 14:262–320.

Wright, J.C.

1984   Changes in form and function of the palace at Pylos. In *Pylos comes alive: Industry and administration in a Mycenaean palace*, edited by C.W. Shelmerdine and T.J. Palaima, 19–30. New York: Archaeological Institute of America.

1990   An early Mycenaean hamlet on Tzoungiza at ancient Nemea. In *L'Habitat égéen préhistorique. Actes de la table ronde internationale organisée par le Centre National de la Recherche Scientifique, l'Université de Paris I et l'École française d'Athènes (Athènes, 23–25 juin 1987)*, edited by P. Darcque and R. Treuil, 345–357. *Bulletin de Correspondance Hellénique*, suppl. vol. 19. Paris: École Française d'Athènes.

1994   The spatial configuration of belief: The archaeology of Mycenaean religion. In *Placing the gods: Sanctuaries and sacred space in ancient Greece*, edited by S. Alcock and R. Osborne, 37–78. Oxford: Clarendon Press.

1995a   From chief to king in Mycenaean Greece. In *The role of the ruler in the prehistoric Aegean: Proceedings of a panel discussion presented at the annual meeting of the Archaeological Institute of America, New Orleans, Louisiana, 28 December 1992, with additions*, edited by P. Rehak, 63–80. Aegaeum 11. Liège: Université de l'État à Liège; Austin: University of Texas at Austin Program in Aegean Scripts and Prehistory.

1995b   Empty cups and empty jugs: The social role of wine in Minoan and Mycenaean societies. In *The origins and ancient history of wine*, edited by P. McGovern, S. Fleming, and S. Katz, 282–309. The University of Pennsylvania Museum of Archaeology and Anthropology, Philadelphia: Gordon and Breach Publishers.

1995c   The archaeological correlates of religion: Case studies in the Aegean. In *POLITEIA: Society and state in the Aegean Bronze Age*, edited by W.-D. Niemeier and R. Laffineur, R., 341–348. Aegaeum 13. Liège: Université de Liège; Austin: University of Texas at Austin Program in Aegean Scripts and Prehistory.

2004a   A survey of evidence for feasting in Mycenaean society. In *The Mycenaean feast*, edited by J. Wright, 13–58. Princeton, NJ: American School of Classical Studies at Athens.

2004b   The emergence of leadership and the rise of civilization in the Aegean. In *Emergence of civilisation revisited*, edited by J. Barrett and P. Halstead, 64–89. Sheffield Studies in Aegean Archaeology 6. Oxford: Oxbow Books.

2004c   Comparative settlement patterns during the Bronze Age in the northeastern Peloponnesos. In *Side-by-side survey: Comparative regional studies in the Mediterranean world*, edited by S.E. Alcock and J.F. Cherry, 114–131. Oxford: Oxbow Books.

2004d   Mycenaean drinking services and standards of etiquette. In *Food, cuisine and society in prehistoric Greece*, edited by P. Halstead and J.C. Barrett, 90–104. Sheffield Studies in Aegean Archaeology 5. Oxford: Oxbow Books.

Wright, J.C., ed.

2004   *The Mycenaean feast*. Princeton: American School of Classical Studies at Athens.

Wright, J.C., J.F. Cherry, J.L. Davis, E. Mantzourani, S.B. Sutton, and R.F. Sutton

1990   The Nemea Valley Archaeological Project: A preliminary report. *Hesperia* 59:579–659.

Wyatt, W.

1962   The Ma tablets from Pylos. *American Journal of Archaeology* 66:21–41.

Wylie, A.

1985   The reaction against analogy. In *Advances in archaeological method and theory*, vol. 8, edited by M.B. Schiffer, 63–111. New York: Academic Press.

Xenaki-Sakellapiou, A.

1985   *Oi thalamotoi taphoi tôn Mykenôn*. Athens: TAPA.

Yerkes, R.W.

1988   Woodland and Mississippian traditions in midwestern North America. *Journal of World Prehistory* 2:307–358.

Yoffee, N.

1993   Too many chiefs? (or, safe texts for the '90s). In *Archaeological theory: Who sets the agenda?* edited by N. Yoffee and A. Sherratt, 60–78. Cambridge: Cambridge University Press.

1995   Conclusion: A Mass in celebration of the conference. In *The archaeology of society in the Holy Land*, edited by T.E. Levy, 542–548. New York: Facts on File.

2005   *Myths of the archaic state: Evolution of the earliest cities, states, and civilizations*. Cambridge: Cambridge University Press.

Yoffee, N., and G.L. Cowgill

1991   *The collapse of ancient states and civilizations*. Tucson: University of Arizona Press.

Zaccagnini, C.

1987   Aspects of ceremonial exchange in the Near East during the late second millennium BC. In *Centre and periphery in the ancient world*, edited by M. Rowlands, T.M. Larsen, and K. Kristiansen, 57–65. Cambridge: Cambridge University Press.

Zangger, E.

1991   Prehistoric coastal environments in Greece: The vanished landscapes of Dimini Bay and Lake Lerna. *Journal of Field Archaeology* 18:1–15.

Zangger, E., M.E. Timpson, S.B. Yazvenko, F. Kuhnke, and J. Knauss

1997 The Pylos Regional Archaeological Project, part II: Landscape evolution and site preservation in the Pylos region. *Hesperia* 66:549–641.

Zerner, C.

1988 Ceramics and ceremony: Pottery and burials from Lerna in the Middle and early Late Bronze Ages. In *Celebrations of death and divinity in the Bronze Age Argolid: Proceedings of the Sixth International Symposium at the Swedish Institute in Athens, 11–13 June, 1988*, edited by R. Hägg and G. Nordquist, 23–34. Stockholm: Svenska Institutet i Athen.

1993 New perspectives on trade in the Middle and early Late Helladic Periods on the Mainland. In *Wace and Blegen: Pottery as evidence for trade in the Aegean Bronze Age 1939–1989 (Proceedings of the International Conference held at the American School of Classical Studies, Athens, Dec. 2–3, 1989)*, edited by C. Zerner, P. Zerner, and J. Winder, 39–56. Amsterdam: J.C. Gieben.

Zielinski, J., and A. Day.

1998 Traditional programs and future directions: Interdisciplinary insights into the future of classical archaeology. Paper presented at the 63rd Annual Meeting of the Society for American Archaeology, March 23–29, Seattle.

Zipf, G.

1941 *National unity and disunity: The nation as a bio-social organism*. Bloomington, IN: Principia Press.

1949 *Human behavior and the principle of least effort: An introduction to human ecology*. Cambridge: Cambridge University Press.

EDITOR BIOGRAPHIES

MICHAEL L. GALATY is associate professor of anthropology in the Department of Sociology and Anthropology at Millsaps College in Jackson, Mississippi. Since 1998 he has conducted fieldwork in Albania. From 1998 to 2003 he field directed the Mallakastra Regional Archaeological Project. Currently he directs the Shala Valley Project, an interdisciplinary program of archaeological, ethnohistoric, and ethnographic research based in the high mountains of northern Albania (www.millsaps.edu/svp). His most recent edited volume is *Archaeology Under Dictatorship* (2004, Kluwer Academic/Plenum Press).

WILLIAM A. PARKINSON is associate professor of anthropology in the Department of Anthropology at Florida State University in Tallahassee, Florida. Since 1996 he has conducted fieldwork in Hungary. He directs the Körös Regional Archaeological Project, a regional studies project aimed at understanding the later prehistory of the Great Hungarian Plain, including excavation of two Early Copper Age (4500–3900 BC) settlements, Vésztõ-Bikeri and Körösladány-Bikeri (www.anthro.fsu.edu/research/koros/). His most recent edited volume is *The Archaeology of Tribal Societies* (2002, International Monographs in Prehistory).

LIST OF CONTRIBUTORS

Vassiliki Adrimi-Sismani
Archaeological Institute of Thessalian Studies

John Bennet
University of Sheffield

Emmett L. Bennett, Jr.
University of Texas at Austin

John F. Cherry
Brown University

Eric H. Cline
George Washington University

Jack L. Davis
University of Cincinnati

Jan Driessen
Université Catholique de Louvain Collège

Michael L. Galaty
Millsaps College

Paul Halstead
University of Sheffield

P. Nick Kardulias
College of Wooster

John T. Killen
Jesus College, Cambridge University

Charlotte Langohr
Université Catholique de Louvain Collège

Susan Lupack
University College London

William A. Parkinson
Florida State University

Daniel Pullen
Florida State University

Robert Schon
Wellesley College

Cynthia Shelmerdine
University of Texas at Austin

David Small
Lehigh University

Thomas Tartaron
University of Pennsylvania

INDEX